Cultural Citizenship in India

Cultural Citizenship in India

Politics, Power, and Media

Lion König

OXFORD
UNIVERSITY PRESS

OXFORD
UNIVERSITY PRESS

Oxford University Press is a department of the University of Oxford.
It furthers the University's objective of excellence in research, scholarship,
and education by publishing worldwide. Oxford is a registered trademark of
Oxford University Press in the UK and in certain other countries

Published in India by
Oxford University Press
YMCA Library Building, 1 Jai Singh Road, New Delhi 110 001, India

ISBN-13: 978-0-19-946631-3
ISBN-10: 0-19-946631-9

Typeset in ScalaPro 10/13
by The Graphics Solution, New Delhi 110 092
Printed in India by Replika Press Pvt. Ltd

To the citizens of India—legal as well as moral

CONTENTS

TABLES AND FIGURES

TABLES

FIGURES

ABBREVIATIONS

ABVP	Akhil Bharatiya Vidyarthi Parishad
ACK	*Amar Chitra Katha*
AIADMK	All India Anna Dravida Munnetra Kazhagam
AIR	All India Radio
AIMPLB	All India Muslim Personal Law Board
BJP	Bharatiya Janata Party
CBFC	Central Board of Film Certification
CSDS	Centre for the Study of Developing Societies
DU	Delhi University
FD	Films Division
FIR	First Information Report
GoI	Government of India
GC	Grassroots Comics
IFI	Information Films of India
IIMC	Indian Institute of Mass Communication
INC	Indian National Congress
INP	Indian News Parade
ISAF	International Security Assistance Force
LPFM	Low Power Frequency Modulation
JNU	Jawaharlal Nehru University
LGBT	Lesbian, Gay, Bisexual, Transgender

MAS	Mizoram Artists' Society
MIB	Ministry of Information and Broadcasting
MSM	men who have sex with men
NAI	National Archives of India
NESC&H	North East Support Centre and Helpline
NGO	non-governmental organization
NRI	Non-Resident Indian
OED	*Oxford English Dictionary*
PIB	Press Information Bureau
PIO	Person of Indian Origin
PSA	Political Studies Association
RSS	Rashtriya Swayamsevak Sangh
STD	sexually transmitted disease
ToI	*Times of India*
UIDAI	Unique Identification Authority of India
UPA	United Progressive Alliance

PREFACE AND ACKNOWLEDGEMENTS*

Writing a monograph is a crucial element in a larger identity-constituting process for a researcher. Before the writing process can start, the prospective author is confronted with an array of questions which require careful consideration, for the kind of answer which is given determines the future course of life to a not insignificant extent. To which subject area does one wish to contribute? In what language is the book to be written? And to what end? Not all of these questions can or should be posed as yes or no questions, and even with regard to those that appear to be unambiguous, I have to admit that I am still undecided. While questions are certain, answers are not. There is no absolute truth, and the search for it is futile.

In lieu of a supreme truth, what we can do is to approach it as closely as possible by asking questions—to ourselves and to others. It is in this vein that I would like to thank the universities I studied at (Edinburgh and Heidelberg) in general, and the South Asia Institute, the Cluster of Excellence Asia and Europe in a Global Context, my Doktorvater, Professor Subrata Kumar Mitra, and my second supervisor, Professor Christiane Brosius in particular, for welcoming me, and for furthering my ability to raise questions and ask them in an informed manner. I am very grateful to the Institute for Defence Studies and Analyses in New Delhi for hosting me—the *seemingly* odd one out—as a Visiting Fellow, and the Internal Security Cluster for inviting me to join them and participate in their curriculum. It was during the period from September to December 2011 that I was able to collect important findings in Delhi which have enriched this work. I am indebted to Professor Hemant Joshi from the Indian Institute for Mass Communication for having facilitated my access to survey reports. Furthermore, I would like to thank Saif Eqbal from Jawaharlal Nehru University, New Delhi, for rendering invaluable help during the fieldwork phase, and Dr Bharat Wariavwalla and the India International Centre, New Delhi, for permitting me to use their library. If it were not for PD Dr Stefan Herbrechter, his excellent analytical insights, his dedication to theory, and the many long and fruitful discussions we have had, this work would not be what it is.

I am ever so grateful to my mother, Magda König, for always having supported me, and encouraged me to pursue my path. It is not least because of her that this book was written. Moreover, I would like to thank Manika Premsingh not only for crucial translations and for help with drawing some of the figures, but more importantly for always being there in the many hours of need, and for being the person that she is and that I love. It is thanks to the many informants in India who have taken precious time out to listen to my questions and give helpful answers, that this work has its empirical base. I dedicate this work to the citizens of India, hoping that they would find something in it that they recognize, appreciate, and can take further.

Lion König
New Delhi, October 2015

---

* Except where otherwise indicated, all the translations in this book are by the author.

INTRODUCTION: CULTURE AND CITIZENSHIP

MAPPING THE FIELD OF ENQUIRY

Spaces are real precisely because they are imagined.

(Radhakrishnan, 2003: 27)

Culture is one of the two or three most complicated words in the English language. This is partly so because ... it has now come to be used for important concepts in several distinct intellectual disciplines and in several distinct and incompatible systems of thought.

(Williams, 1983: 87).

CULTURE, CITIZENSHIP, AND CENSORSHIP: BUILDING A CONNECTIVE STRUCTURE

Ours is an age of multifold asymmetry. It is an era of asymmetric warfare, growing economic asymmetries within as well as between states and world regions, and asymmetric societal compositions, which have upset the structures that dominated the old nation-states of Europe for centuries. It is thus also a time when social science concepts are being rethought and, as a result, sometimes 'stretched', as it were, to correspond to quickly changing social realities. Increasing global movements of people push the idea of the old nation-state to its limits, and raise new questions about belonging that defy easy answers. The old idea of citizenship is now being rediscovered and is coming into analytical focus, with the concept being stretched so as to be able to respond to new challenges.

Asymmetry is both a cause and a consequence of a world that is in flux due to an unprecedented mass of people populating the earth, many of them moving temporarily or permanently to different parts of the globe, taking their ideas, opinions, views, and attitudes with them. Thus, the trope of 'cultural flow' forms one of the core concepts of this work. Both citizenship, with its derivate 'cultural citizenship', and censorship, which constitute the central analytical categories of this book, are considered to be the outcomes of processes of 'cultural flow'. In the analysis of the central concepts of citizenship, censorship, and the media, all linked by the analytic prism of 'flow', this work straddles the endogenous and the exogenous in search of a new trajectory. The book explores this general theme with reference to mediated discourses which underline the constructed character of the national narrative of which citizenship is a part, and the relativity of categories which are negotiated between different parts of the world in terms of flow and counterflow, as well as within a nation-state by setting up counter-discourses.

Connected to the ongoing relativization of categories is the stretching of citizenship beyond the legalistic understanding to take into account time, cultural memory, and space—that is, excluded classes and categories. Cultural and conceptual flow is the means through which this exclusion can be understood and—on a more interventionist level—can be overcome. By situating this research on citizenship in the context of postcolonial India, in the political framework of a state-nation rather than a nation-state (Stepan et al., 2011) where citizens have 'multiple but complementary identities' (Stepan, 2008: 4), the overall questions that emerge are: What can the book contribute to an understanding of citizenship and the role of culture in the making of the citizen? And what can India, in turn, bring to an understanding of larger theoretical questions; in other words, how can general political theory be enhanced by studying a specific context? The nation, which especially in the postcolonial context is marked by an inherent diversity in language, religion, ethnicity, and culture, is in Benedict Anderson's terms (1991) an 'imagined community' constructed through discourse. Hence, investigating citizenship in terms of the representation of citizens in that discourse is a way to understand the complexities of belonging and alienation within society. Drawing on Anderson's formula, the political scientist and subaltern studies scholar Partha Chatterjee (1993) rightly asks, 'whose imagined community?',[1] that is, who are the agents behind the discursive construction of the nation? Chatterjee situates his question in the colonial context, arguing that since nationalism (like the nation) was a European project exported to Asia, the colonial world was restricted to imagining itself within those limits. However, one could also pose the question in a more contemporary context, and ask who imagines the Indian nation today, more than sixty years after independence, and in what way? If, as Mitra (2008a, 2010a, 2010b, 2011a, 2012b) has argued, citizenship is a twofold concept which comprises a legal right to the soil and a moral affiliation to it, then the question arises whether that attachment is natural, or whether it is created, and if so, how, and by whom? It is assumed here that what plays a vital role in this respect is culture, which is negotiated in the media sphere.

The aim of this research is thus threefold: first, to investigate into citizenship in India from a media perspective and to link the conceptual novelty of 'cultural citizenship' with empirical data to test its validity against the diverse and multivocal background of India; second, to make the case for an interdisciplinary approach to studying citizenship in India, combining theoretical tools from political science with those of cultural studies; and third, to contribute to building a theory which goes beyond the cases under consideration and feeds into a thorough conceptualization of flow and interdisciplinarity. This will help to determine whether there is a correlation between media representation and citizenship as a form of belonging to a national community. This correlation will be established by means of a discussion on media use (passive and active), the perceived potential of various media for agenda setting, and the feeling of inclusion in the media and the national community as a whole. Like the nation which they imagine and help to build, media have boundaries. These are necessary to demarcate the discourse and secure a specific interpretation of the media message. However, such a media discourse is never uncontested, because the idea of the nation never is. In that way, the 'crossing' of these discursive boundaries as an interventionist strategy is a means of identity affirmation and a way of strengthening collective cultural consciousness. Intervention in the creative discourse is essentially contestation. 'Crossing', which will be discussed in greater detail in Chapter four, with its parameters of power, space, and asymmetry, can be seen as a practice with the potential for theory building across regions and disciplines. As mentioned earlier, India is the empirical anchor for this study, but the book does not constitute a study of India as such. It is predominantly a theoretical work which illustrates itself by referring to empirical case studies. Groups of citizens to be looked at through the lens of media representation include sexual minorities and citizens from India's north-eastern region.

If the nation, and, following from it, citizenship, is a discourse in the construction and (re)negotiation of which the media play a vital role, then censorship is a constituent variable in an analytical framework that brings together culture and citizenship. Censorship is an important tool of control over a discourse and its modification. It can be official and unofficial, and operates on various levels, which can be overlapping and mutually reinforcing.

Censorship, which exists in every state to varying extents, including democratic ones, is not necessarily an illiberal idea. If it is made fair, transparent, and accountable, it can act as a measure to safeguard liberalism. In order to be able to do that in a generally acceptable way, it needs to be institutionalized and built into the structure of the state along these parameters of fairness, transparency, and accountability. If this is done in a manner that allows the institutional structures to change over time and react to new inputs, censorship can be an important instrument of any democracy to protect weak and vulnerable elements of society, as well as the liberal nature of democracy itself, which the state tries to maintain in a diverse societal set-up (as is the case in India, but of course also increasingly in the old nation-states of Europe). This societal diversity is what is often referred to as 'the multiplicity of cultures', or 'multiculturalism'. 'Culture' is the best—and at the same time the worst—term there is to describe such heterogeneity and contrast, which cut across many different spheres of life. Thus, in a work on citizenship in a society like India's, so deeply divided along various fault lines, a discussion of culture is essential.

In line with the discursive reading of the core concepts of this work, culture is not understood only as a system of shared symbols through which social and political systems are expressed, but is conceptualized as a conflict of meaning which requires constant negotiation. It is a highly dynamic concept, which strictly speaking defies definition, as this would go against its very nature of an all-encompassing wholeness. What can be claimed though is that like citizenship and censorship, culture is always linked to power and closely related to institutions (Foucault, 1979), which is why linking 'culture' and 'citizenship' in an analytical framework is not only desirable but required. However, the lack of consensus on what the concept of 'cultural citizenship' entails calls for an advanced conceptualization in which media, representation, identity, and power form central elements.

The question which this book revolves around concerns the relation between media representation and citizenship. If citizenship is dual belonging, that is, both in a legal and a moral sense, then 'belonging' is the dependent variable here, variation in which is explained in terms of active media use, representation, and the place citizens occupy in the mediated national narrative. This complex relationship is explored here in terms of the following hypotheses:

1. If the nation is an imagined community created through discourse, (Anderson, 1990 [1983]) then an affiliation to the nation-state, the feeling of being part of the nation, can arise only when this mediated nation discourse is democratic, accessible, and susceptible to change.
2. The media discourse is not monolithic. There are various discourses which socio-political actors can try to access or even open up themselves. Those discourses can complement or challenge each other. If small- and larger-scale discourses converge, the chances of bringing about change in the narrative of the nation increase.
3. Censorship, which is an unavoidable analytical category in any media framework, is the instrument with which the media discourse is shaped and categories of inclusion and exclusion are determined. It has a direct impact on citizenship.
4. Censorship is exercised either by the state or by non-state actors. If there are overlaps between those two spheres, in the sense of

the state giving in to societal pressure, this causes a strengthening of the censorship regime, but also an increase in the reaction against it, and a decline of institutional legitimacy.

5. Cultural citizenship emerges out of the interplay of state, society, culture, and censorship. The democratic state occupies a central role in this framework. Cultural citizenship can best be achieved if the state balances rights of cultural expression with selective censorship to protect the weak, without establishing a tyranny of the minority.

6. None of the concepts discussed here is a monolithic unit. If one wants to explore their full analytical potential, they have to be regarded as themselves subject to a discursive process. Conceptual flow is the paradigm in terms of which the formation of these concepts, their development, and applicability to different socio-political and historical contexts can be understood.

7. If social science concepts are susceptible to change due to conceptual flow, then the generalizations of a concept beyond its context are called into question. The citizenship of Great Britain would thus not be the citizenship of India, but both can change and develop in the same or the opposite direction, which also holds potential for hybridization at any given point in time.

These are hypotheses which, due to their liminal character of combining questions of social cohesion, governance, and cultural expression, best explored in an interdisciplinary research set-up. As a work which takes interdisciplinarity seriously, this volume therefore critically engages with different subject areas, with the ultimate aim of overcoming boundaries which are perceived here as artificial and to a certain extent arbitrary. More often than not, the subject labels are unnatural dividers, splitting the corpus of knowledge. Rather than making knowledge accessible, such boundaries serve the objectives of self-protection and upholding of status, and in doing so, have a detrimental effect on research and the generation of new knowledge. The breaking up of labels thus serves two purposes: it enables the researcher to take a broader and more undisguised look at socio-political processes, and it ideally helps to open up a debate on the analytical value of interdisciplinarity and a transdisciplinary research framework.

In its empirical part, the book does not have one in-depth case study but employs a cluster of related narratives which illustrate the various strategies of citizen making and citizen breaking in the realm of representation in the visual media. The work thus takes into account what has been termed 'alternative modernities' (Gaonkar, 2001). On the level of the state, it reveals the cultural forms, social practices, and institutional arrangements in terms of which 'modernity has travelled from the West to the rest of the world' (Gaonkar, 2001: 14), with citizenship as one of its most prominent exports. But it also shows the discrepancies and the cacophony of voices in a pluralistic society and the manifold, context-dependent ways of the state to deal with them, underlining the dynamic character of culture and society. In-depth interviews with scholars, civil servants, civil society activists, and media practitioners (both lay and professional) provide the basis for an analytical narrative of the alternative strategies of communication, citizen identity formation, and belonging.

Rather than analysing one particular topic to produce an in-depth narrative, this book explores different areas of social action to suggest a new way of looking at political processes and understanding academic disciplines. The study remains grounded in political science, for that discipline, with its focus on power, process, and institutions, opens up the trajectory in which (cultural) citizenship and censorship can best be analysed. Yet it is a work of 'border crossing'. The book aims at crossing the borders of scholarly disciplines, geographical areas, theoretical concepts, and empirical data. Border crossing is a necessary act in a work that engages with culture, because the dynamism inherent in the concept renders it impossible to confine the concept to a single discipline, area, or theory. This book is written on the understanding that these categories—discipline, area, and theory—themselves are not monolithic entities either, but are the outcome of continuous exchange processes and border crossings. Chapter one will demonstrate this with regard to the theoretical camps of political science and cultural studies, while Chapter two employs the trope of conceptual flow (Mitra, 2011b) to investigate the dynamic undercurrents of the major analytical variables this work revolves around, namely citizenship, its derivate 'cultural citizenship', and censorship. On a conceptual level, the book engages with asymmetry, flow, and hybridity, takes them further and deepens their understanding by linking them. A significant part of the writing is also concerned with learning more about the theoretical concepts themselves as well as the mechanisms and structures behind their development through time and space by looking at them through the analytical lens of 'flow'.

While this approach makes it possible to show the diverse public spaces in which culture and citizenship are negotiated, it also reflects the oscillating nature of the boundaries between these spaces and various performative acts. Discursive borders are manifestations of power, and the crossing of borders, with the aim of the alteration of power structures, is a central trope in this respect. Borders, however, are also zones of cultural production, and spaces of meaning making and meaning breaking (Donnan and Wilson, 1999). Following Malcolm Anderson (1996), it may be argued that borders are both institutions and processes. In the context of citizenship, for example, borders are understood in terms of institutions which regulate who is a citizen and who an alien. In addition to these legal borders, there are discursive borders which simultaneously regulate inclusion in and exclusion from the national community. While this work puts the analytical focus on the discursive side of citizenship, it also shows that discursive and institutional spaces overlap,[2] thus empirically illustrating Figure I.1. Discourses and institutions are not separate, but constitute and shape each other. With reference to the 'Ramanujan issue', it will be shown in Chapter four that the discourse around a cultural product—in this case

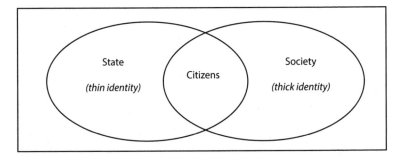

Figure I.1 The Modern 'Postcolonial' State, Traditional Society, and Citizenship: Overlapping Legal and Moral Categories
Source: Mitra (2012b: 96).

a scholarly text—and the way in which that text is presented can have a direct influence on the working of an educational institution.

With regard to the methodological approach, this work, as will be discussed in Chapter one, follows the method of the analytical narrative to explore mechanisms of citizen formation from 'above' (as exercised by either the state or powerful socio-cultural groups) vis-à-vis identity articulation from 'below'. A cluster of interrelated narratives forms the analytical body of the work. Drawing on archival sources, interviews, and secondary material, it will explore how far different media have acted as tools of nation-building, what strategies have been adopted to democratize the media (that is, to make them accessible, participatory, and transparent), and who the agents behind these processes are. The book analyses the alternative medium of 'grassroots comics' and discusses its relevance as a participatory and an impact medium. Do the grassroots comics run in parallel to the larger, established media, or do they constitute a case of 'discursive crossing'? With regard to the crossing between media spaces, the hypothesis is that if different public spaces exist without the interventionist phenomenon of 'crossing' to occur, that is, if they exist as parallel public spaces, this reduces the potential of the public space for systemic change.

As far as the balance between theory and empiricism in this work is concerned, the study is intended to be read as a work of theory that uses India, and specific cases from India, as an empirical anchor. It tests the applicability of theoretical concepts such as 'cultural citizenship' to the chosen socio-political context. The empirical background of the initiative of grassroots comics as a mode of citizens' self-expression provides the possibility of further work along quantitative empirical lines. Anchoring a theory such as 'cultural citizenship', first formulated and developed in a Western academic context, in the empirical context of India shows the possibility for a theory to travel, but also makes apparent the limits of universality and generalization.

CITIZENSHIP AND CULTURAL CITIZENSHIP: CONCEPTUAL APPROACHES

Citizenship, as it is understood here, is a liberal idea. It is not only a legal right to the soil and a moral affiliation to it (Mitra, 2008a); it is also closely connected to democracy. The idea of the 'citizen' was first holistically conceptualized in the philosophical tradition of the Enlightenment, and theorized in this light in the mid-twentieth century by the British sociologist T.H. Marshall (1965 [1949]). Following this intellectual tradition, the citizen is understood as a political category expressed in terms of the rights of free speech, active and passive suffrage, and a minimum of social welfare and egality among all classes. Based on this understanding, it would be difficult to position nationals of non-democratic states—be they fascist or communist—in this classification, for they lack significant elements of what constitutes the European Enlightenment's idea of the 'citizen'. Reading citizenship against the Western tradition, some analysts are even sceptical with regard to the existence of citizens in Islamic states: John Jandora argues that in non-Western, particularly Islamic, societies, while the 'symbol of freedom' has been adopted, some of the underlying values are lacking, making them 'states without citizens'. The 'Enlightenment belief that all humans are intrinsically equal' (Jandora, 2008: 3) is not always adhered to in non-Western societies, particularly not with regard to women's role in society.

Citizenship does not exist in a vacuum, and hence historical identification with a country plays a significant role. In the West, citizenship stands at the end of a long and painful process of state formation. In the course of that process, the many who died for the idea and their descendants have imbibed an attachment to a soil they have fought for, and which they consider to be theirs. This, however, is a process which does not have an equivalent in the non-West. Those sceptical of the existence of citizenship in the East argue that 'Western societies created their own states, whereas Islamic societies had their states created for them through occupation and pressure by the West' (Jandora, 2008: 5). As a consequence of the often arbitrary drawing of boundaries, many Islamic states lack the legitimacy which cultural factors like belonging to an ethnic group or a religious community bring. Using the example of Pakistan, Jandora notes that 'the ethnically diverse peoples of various regions became "Pakistanis" overnight, assigned an identity through a linguistic invention[3] that had no connection to any historic place-name' (Jandora, 2008: 5). Geopolitical borders were often drawn arbitrarily, cutting across (and separating) pre-modern communities of tribe and ethnicity. Those bonds, however, and the allegiances that came with them, were often much stronger than the allegiance to the new state, which has had a negative impact on state legitimacy. Staying with the example of Pakistan, then, the sentence 'I have been a Pakistani for 60 years, a Muslim for 800 years,[4] and a Pathan for 5,000 years' does not evoke surprise. Also, in the special case of Pakistan, a state with no historical antecedent, created from a territory carved out of British India, people relocated from different parts of the country to a new land that was completely unfamiliar to many of them. If citizenship is understood to be more than a legal concept, these are factors which do not seem to enhance it. However, while it is true that states which are founded on the basis of religion often put religious minorities in a disadvantaged position vis-à-vis the majority, citizenship, as we commonly understand it today, is no monopoly of the West. It has been argued that citizenship also exists in India, with adaptations specific to context. While these are changes which have been made to a general Western model, that model itself is not ahistorical, but is also changing in the light of a changing social structure, taking into account some of the features that have been developed elsewhere. Citizenship, as this book sets out to show, is thus a dynamic concept, subject to ongoing change.

In order to be able to explore the relationship between culture and citizenship, the conceptual framework in which both categories operate needs to be sketched. On a superficial level, culture and citizenship might appear to be mutually exclusive, and the term 'cultural citizenship' comes across as paradoxical. It obfuscates, since 'the cultural', which strictly speaking is immune to definition, is commonly held to be the primordial, the diverse, the chaotic, whereas 'citizenship' is the constructed, the man-made, the orderly, the restricted, and planned. Surely this paradox was chosen deliberately, since the category of 'citizenship' itself is not as orderly and static as might be thought at first, but is dynamic and constantly evolving, even more so since the debate has focused on the role of culture in the making of the citizen. A perspective which sees culture as primordial, as opposed to the constructed, artificial idea of 'citizenship', overlooks the conceptual development of both, in which they have moved closer to one another. Both culture and citizenship have moved from an exclusive to an inclusive and 'popular' understanding. Chapter three discusses in detail the evolutionary path that citizenship has taken, from a socially exclusive regime in the Greek polis, via the egalitarian ideas of Rousseau, to a group-specific theory developed in the West in the late twentieth century and its application in the form of a citizenship regime of positive discrimination in the Indian Republic. An understanding of cultural citizenship has to be preceded not only by a detailed outline of the development of citizenship, but also by the path that culture as a scholarly concept has taken.

Even more so than in the case of general citizenship, it makes sense to speak of cultural citizenship only in a democratic context. That is, as a liberal *product*, cultural citizenship can only come into existence in a politically democratic setting. As far as the *process* dimension is concerned, however, the struggle for cultural citizenship is visible in non-democratic contexts as well, and there probably much more consciously. In those settings, cultural citizenship, in its liberal sense of being an advancement of the Enlightenment citizenship regime, works in opposition to another *practice* which can also be conceptualized as cultural citizenship, namely the construction of a unified citizen by means of a monopolized, unified understanding and use of culture. In the way that citizenship stands in the Enlightenment tradition of rights vested in the individual and power in the majority, cultural citizenship is linked to the democratic set-up because the concept builds on Rousseau's participatory democracy, which, in turn, constitutes the core of later theories of political participation, for example, the theory of 'group-differentiated citizenship' as outlined by Iris Marion Young (1989). The idea of cultural citizenship combines existing liberal theories and develops them further. The interesting question to ask is what the discussion on cultural citizenship can add to the theorization and deeper understanding of citizenship.

Cultural citizenship is not an altogether new form of citizenship. Philosophical-historical analysis shows that what is understood by cultural citizenship has formed part of the modern—and to a lesser degree even the ancient—conceptualization of citizenship. The freedom of expression, which forms part of the civil sphere of T.H. Marshall's triadic model of citizenship, is a crucial constitutive element of cultural citizenship. More than earlier theories of citizenship, however, cultural citizenship puts its focus on the necessary plurality of voices from which the citizen springs. Plurality of voices in a democracy, however, does not mean choral singing, but rather cacophony. Bryan S. Turner describes cultural citizenship as 'cultural empowerment, namely the capacity to participate effectively, creatively and successfully within a national culture' (2001: 12). This is done in at least two ways: by inscribing cultural rights—and duties—into the Constitution, and by the ability of citizens to enter the media discourse, contribute to it, and alter it. Cultural citizenship thus relates to issues of representation of linguistic, religious, ethnic, and gender groups on two levels, the legal as well as the cultural, and is therefore closely connected with identity politics. It is a significant aspect of citizen making in diverse societies, as it illustrates the role that mass as well as non-mass media play in citizen-making.

As is the case with the general category of citizenship, its derivate, cultural citizenship, works on two levels. Just as citizenship is a bundle of rights and duties, cultural citizenship refers to cultural rights and entitlements, as well as duties in a multicultural society. In both cases, these can be quantified, and we can measure the form in which they are adhered to or violated and, following from that, the extent to which culture can be practised in a society, and the role of these regulations in determining the degree of inclusivity. The second aspect is the more complex one. As in more recent general citizenship theory, where the sphere of moral belonging has been introduced as a crucial addition to the legal sphere (Mitra, 2012b), the notion of participation in the media discourse which cultural citizenship implies is abstract. It cannot be measured, because it cannot be regulated by law, as this would necessarily entail exclusion. It is in this field of tension between legal and moral, abstract and concrete, that citizenship and cultural citizenship emerge, are negotiated, and take shape.

OVERLAPS BETWEEN CITIZENSHIP AND CULTURE IN INDIA

In the postcolonial context, citizenship acquires an additional edge, investigation into which requires a different analytical approach. Citizens in postcolonial states are the inhabitants of a liminal space which lies between what can be termed the cultural and the legal spheres. Especially in highly diverse societies, legal identification in the form of a passport cannot and does not capture the entirety of citizen identity, because prior to their legal membership people used to express their identity in terms of different—and often competing—ethnic, religious, and linguistic affiliations. As noted earlier, Mitra (2012b) suggests a model of citizenship which shows that in the modern postcolonial state, the citizen constitutes the crucial connective structure between the modern state and the traditional society (see Figure 1.1).

In the context of India, the citizen, as the brainchild of Western Enlightenment philosophy, is equipped to act as the hinge between old societal and new political culture. What many commentators have identified as the source of India's cohesion is the recognition of cultural diversity by the Constitution in terms of both rights and obligations,[5] and the creation of institutional structures which allow for the interplay between tradition and modernity, religion and secularism, the singular and the plural.

In India, in addition to Article 30(1), every religious community is free to regulate civil issues, such as matters of marriage and divorce, according to their respective sets of personal laws. Under these regulations, an Indian Muslim can have up to four wives, provided there is consent on the part of the women, while, according to the Hindu Marriage Act of 1955, an Indian Hindu can have only one. These personal laws coexist and are complemented by general law which applies to all citizens. In the case of language, Hindi, as the majority language,[6] is the national language, while English enjoys constitutional status as a language for official purposes. According to the three-language formula, laid down in Article 345,[7] all member States of the Indian Union have the right to decide on one or more languages spoken in the State as languages of official purpose. All these languages, presently numbering twenty-eight, also enjoy constitutional status and are listed in the Eighth Schedule of the Constitution, making India the country with the largest number of officially recognized languages in the world. Linguistic federalism, a policy framework under which the member States of the Indian Union were rearranged according to linguistic boundaries in 1956, ended the fierce language movement in the south, the home of the Dravidian languages, where it was feared that the numerically dominant speakers of the north

Indian, Indo-Aryan language of Hindi would linguistically disadvantage and therefore eventually politically marginalize non-Hindi speakers. Not least, it is this strategic political accommodation of cultural identity which has acted as a source of cohesion of the Indian union. The plurality of law, language, religion, and education is meant to balance out the disadvantages of cultural minorities, while at the same time integrating them into the realm of the nation and heightening their sense of belonging. These strong cultural rights are however not seen as determining but as complementing each other, leading to a composite culture, which to value and preserve is the duty of every citizen of India.[8] It is by means of those positive rights that a strong, direct connection between culture and citizenship is established. The Indian Constitution lists cultural rights as well as cultural duties of the citizens, thus making a case for what Turner (2001: 13–14) has described as a 'rather neglected' area of cultural citizenship: 'If one can in fact articulate a notion of cultural rights, is there a cultural obligation which corresponds to or matches this assertion of rights to cultural resources?' India thus offers a solution to Turner's conceptual problem 'to think of a clear and direct cultural obligation' (Turner, 2001: 14).

The Indian republic deviates from the model of the European nation-state where the formula of *one* people, *one* language, *one* religion was regarded at the time of state formation as the successful route to creating *one* nation. India's neighbours, Pakistan and Sri Lanka (then Ceylon), on the other hand, led in their formative years by the ardent modernizers Mohammad Ali Jinnah and S.W.R.D. Bandaranaike respectively, followed the European example of one language and one religion, irrespective of the deep plurality of their societies. Pakistan was rigorous about its language policy, insisting on Urdu as the only official language, with the effect that the Bangla-speaking East Pakistan broke away in December 1971 after a thirteen-day civil war. Similarly, in 1956, when India adopted the three-language formula, the Ceylonese parliament passed the Sinhala Only Language Act, making Sinhala the sole medium of interaction. This, along with Bandaranaike's declaration of Buddhism as the official religion, further alienated the Hindu, Tamil-speaking minority. The sad consequence, a civil war between the government and the Tamil rebels fighting for a homeland of Tamil Eelam, which has now ended in what can only be described as a fragile peace, is a sign of contemporary history for those trying to solve problems of diversity by the imposition of artificial unity.

Taking into account *context* thus appears to be a crucial precondition for the successful import of *concepts* such as citizenship. Emphasizing the comparatively successful management of cultural diversity here is not meant to suggest that India is free from cultural conflict; on the contrary. Communal conflict and violent clashes between members of different religious groups are a regular occurrence. Also the decision to adopt various sets of personal laws and various official languages is meant to be only a temporary measure. The Constitution states that 'the official language of the Union shall be Hindi in Devanagari script' (Article 343[1]), and it was only for a brief period of fifteen years after the commencement of the Constitution that the English language was to be used for official purposes (Article 343[2]). The brief yet important and much-discussed Article 44 emphasizes a uniform civil code for India, thus abolishing the different personal laws.[9] This is to show that tradition and modernity are in constant tension, even in the institutional sphere itself, the logic being that only once the state acknowledges diversity and tradition and gives them constitutional space can the state move beyond the specificities of culture and the mutual exclusions that they entail to a more singular national outfit.

CULTURE: THE CONTINUOUS TRANSFORMATION OF A CONCEPT

'Culture' has moved not only from an exclusive to an inclusive conceptualization, but also from a tangible to an increasingly intangible understanding. E.M. Forster's writings on culture constitute an interesting case in point for the shifts in the scholarly understanding and conceptualization of culture that took place around the middle of the twentieth century. In 1940, Forster still regarded culture as a commodity and used the term 'to describe the various beautiful and interesting *objects* which men have made in the *past*, and handed down to us' (Forster, 1965b [1940]: 108; emphases added). Then as much as now, on a conceptual level, culture was embedded in the social structure, and Forster was aware of (and grateful for) the conceptual and social broadening of the term to include the hitherto excluded social classes. 'Culture', he wrote, 'thank goodness, is no longer a social asset, it can no longer be employed either as a barrier against the mob or as a ladder into the aristocracy' (Forster, 1965b: 111). But Forster, the accurate observer of class consciousness and class differences, still regarded 'culture' and 'working class' as two different, monolithic, and largely incompatible spheres. The following line from Forster's essay 'Does Culture Matter?' (1940) reveals the discrepancy that the writer observed between the sacred sphere of 'culture' and the mundane world of the worker: 'I know a few working-class people who enjoy culture, but as a rule I am afraid to bore them with it lest I lose the pleasure of their acquaintance' (Forster, 1965b: 113).

After Forster wrote those lines, it would take another eighteen years until the publication of Raymond Williams's seminal text 'Culture Is Ordinary' (1989 [1958]). Williams, who from a working-class background moved on to become one of the founding fathers of the new intellectual branch of cultural studies, identified culture as an entire way of life. In his programmatic essay, he spoke against the understanding of culture as 'cultivated' (in the sense of higher taste) and abolished the distinction between 'high' and 'low' culture. To Williams, culture is ordinary, which is why no one is excluded from culture (Williams, 1989: 95). Williams, unlike Forster, would therefore not have thought that people giving up Dante was 'a sign that they are throwing culture overboard' (Forster, 1965b: 110). Williams stretched the concept of culture to subsume various forms of expression, which marked an important step towards a theory of inclusion that would later be developed further by cultural studies. It was in this context that the opposite of what E.M. Forster had assumed occurred. Forster, like many of his contemporaries, was convinced that 'crooners, best-sellers, electrical-organists, funny-faces, dream-girls and mickey-mices cannot do it.... They are all right when they don't take themselves seriously. But when they begin to talk big and claim the front row ... and even get to it, something is wrong' (Forster, 1965b: 111). Forster here anticipates the abuse that cultural studies as a discipline would have to face later. The dismissive label 'Mickey Mouse studies' was the price cultural studies had to pay for choosing popular culture as its area of analysis, with all the elements on Forster's sarcastic list as its subjects of study. The idea that 'culture' and 'rationality' are mutually exclusive categories, an idea handed down to us by the Enlightenment, is still often adhered to today, and not only among lay audiences. However, the view that culture is rational, and that rationality is also culture-specific and context-dependent, is increasingly gaining ground.

Even before cultural studies in general and postcolonial and sub-altern studies in particular emerged as the intellectual line of work for the consideration of those who are relatively unaccounted for by society and history, and to unearth their stories and make their voices heard—a scholarly as much as a political undertaking—it was the literature of the pre-Romantic and Romantic period, opposed as it was to the cold rationality of the Enlightenment, that shifted the subject of poetry from the courtly realm to the quotidian. This was one of the key spheres with which the Romantic movement engaged, and where it found what it was looking for—sentiment. In his most famous poem, 'Elegy Written in a Country Churchyard' (1751), Thomas Gray (1716–1771), a pre-Romantic, extended the domain of literature to the so-called 'common people' who had hitherto—with the exception of individual comic characters, or threatening masses in Shakespeare's plays—hardly been the subject of literary consideration.[10] When 'commoners' formed part of Shakespearean plays, they usually did so as an indistinguishable mass, and, differently from individual characters, they were presented as a 'thoughtless rabble, controllable only by aristocrats', as in *Henry VI* (Boyce, 1996: 126). In the Roman plays, in *Julius Caesar* as well as in *Coriolanus*, they are 'mostly mute', but in the former play 'common people' are depicted as an 'urban mob that ... flares into riot' in Act III and upsets the political order, suggesting that they needed to be controlled and closely monitored. In *Coriolanus*, they stress an important theme of the play, namely that 'the common people, as a group, are susceptible to inflammatory rhetoric and are therefore unreliable participants in political life' (Boyce, 1996: 126).

Along with the other 'graveyard poets',[11] of whom he is the best-known representative, Thomas Gray thus anticipated the Romantic tendency to focus on the quotidian, one of the distinctive notions of that literary movement. Situated roughly between 1770 and 1848, Romanticism has been described as 'a violent reaction to the Enlightenment. Politically it was inspired by the revolutions in

America and France.... Emotionally it expressed an extreme assertion of the self and the value of individual experience ... socially it
championed progressive causes' (Drabble, 1985: 842–3, cited in Day,
1996: 1).[12]

Robert Burns's 'To a Mouse: On Turning Her Up in Her Nest
with the Plough (1785)', which revolves around mourning a dead
mouse as 'a fellow mortal', and William Wordsworth's 'We Are
Seven' (1798/1800) on the issue of child mortality in a rural family,
directed the look of the literary audience towards the plight of 'common life' and socio-economically marginalized sections of society.
In the 'Elegy', the lyrical 'I' contemplates the humble graves in the
countryside, wondering what heroic deeds unaccounted for by history
the people buried there might have accomplished:

> Some village Hampden that with dauntless breast
> The little tyrant of his fields withstood,
> Some mute inglorious Milton here may rest,
> Some Cromwell guiltless of his country's blood.
> Th' applause of list'ning senates to command,
> The threats of pain and ruin to despise,
> To scatter plenty o'er a smiling land,
> And read their history in a nation's eyes.

In the poem, Gray focuses on the plight of the poor who live and die
unacknowledged by the ruling classes and therefore by history. The
poem's eighth stanza brings 'the poor', who constituted a vast seg-
ment of the population in mid-eighteenth-century England, into focus:

> Let not ambition mock their useful toil,
> Their homely joys, and destiny obscure;
> Nor Grandeur hear with a disdainful smile,
> The short and simple annals of the poor.
> The boast of heraldry, the pomp of power,
> And all that beauty, all that wealth e'er gave
> Awaits alike the inevitable hour.
> The paths of glory lead but to the grave.

Literary scholarship has described Gray's attitude towards the poor
as 'sympathetic to the plight of the beleaguered' (Sha, 1990: 338). In
alluding to 'the poor', Gray addresses 'one of the more vexing political
issues of his time', and by referring to the poor's 'short and simple

annals', he not only upsets class distinctions—'annals' only recorded the history of the gentry (Sha, 1990: 340)—but also gives the undocumented a form of identity, and makes them visible to others—to supporters as well as to opponents. Calling the annals 'short' and 'simple' has not only been read as an ironic reference to the brevity of peasants' lives, but as an 'unconsciously euphemized version of Thomas Hobbes's description of the state of nature as "nasty, brutish, and short"' (Sha, 1990: 340), thus emphasizing both the political awareness of the poet, as well as the social intention behind the poem.

Gray was indeed well aware of the political situation of his time and the philosophical innovations and debates that were then coming up. In 'Liber Quartus' (1742), the Latin poem on which he was working, he included a translation of John Locke's *Essay Concerning Human Understanding* (1689). Also, one finds in Gray much of his contemporary Jean-Jacques Rousseau (1712–1778), whose writings had a strong impact on the Romantics, and who has even been identified as 'the central man of Romantic tradition' (Bloom and Trilling, 1973: 5), because he rejected the idea of the supremacy of reason and instead chose sentiment as his central trope. In *Emile*, where he introduces his educational model, Rousseau's emphasis is on the education of feelings (Day, 1996: 70), making him a figure not representative of the Enlightenment, although in many ways 'he did the work of the Enlightenment' (Gay, 1973, II:552, cited in Day, 1996: 71). Rousseau's influence on the thought of his own as well as subsequent generation is shown in the work of artists and poets of the late eighteenth and early nineteenth centuries, who adopted Rousseau's idea of the state of nature as the ideal (to which, in their understanding, common people were much closer than members of the higher social orders). The state of nature, uncorrupted by civilization and its technological advancements, was where people, in Rousseau's understanding, were 'free'. Both Rousseau and Gray thus paved the way for the Romantic Movement, which was a political movement all through. Gray and Rousseau conceptualized the individual in thought and practice, both social and literary. What Gray added to this discourse was the voice of the commoner, who might have been as brave as Oliver Cromwell (1599–1658), the founder of the Commonwealth of England, and as lyrical as John Milton (1608–1674), the poet and civil servant in Cromwell's republic, but who is not known, because history is the history of the victors, in Walter Benjamin's formulation; until the twentieth century, this essentially meant court history.[13]

In response to such subjugation, throughout Gray's 'Elegy' reigns the spirit of revolution, from the ploughman in the first stanza, symbolic of the local farm labourers in the eighteenth century who had a history of revolt, like the 'Buckinghamshire diggers', a radical group that dug and cultivated common land (Sha, 1990: 346), to the explicit naming of English radicals like Cromwell and his combatant in the English Civil War, John Hampden (1595–1643). Thomas Gray's lifetime was marked by repeated nation-wide food riots (1709–10, 1727–9, 1739–40, and 1756–7), which were actually 'extremely common in the year 1740: just a few years before Gray would begin writing his elegy' (Sha, 1990: 349). Gray knew about the social situation of the peasantry, as did his readers: 'crowds', the literary scholar notes, 'would have been very much on the minds of those who read the poem' (Sha, 1990: 348–9).

In trying to break up the elitist character of history and narrative, social analysis in the nineteenth century paved the way for the emergence of subaltern studies and 'history from below' in the second half of the twentieth century.[14] As Mitra (1999a) notes in his discussion of the formative years of the Indian republic, it was the country's first prime minister Jawaharlal Nehru who inducted the 'little man in history' into India's political mainstream. Drawing on the social history of Europe, Mitra unambiguously states that it was 'the marginal peasant, women and children, the Jew, the Catholic, the Gypsy and the heretic, [who] were starved, moved around, separated from their families, hanged, shot, broken on the wheel or tortured in other ways'. It was 'the marginal men and women [who] paid for the building of Europe's nation, state and market with their bodies and those of their loved ones' (Mitra, 1999a: 30–1). As he rightly observes, 'they did not have CNN and the human rights activists to report on them' (Mitra, 1999a: 31), but we see in poets like Gray and Wordsworth and in thinkers like Rousseau an honest attempt to do exactly that. Without wanting to give Romanticism too much credit, a certain political advocacy in favour of the marginalized, socially stigmatized, and under-represented can certainly be detected in the movement. Does Romanticism then provide the earliest instance of an unfolding of cultural citizenship in the liberal sense of the term? As has been argued above, there is no clear-cut distinction (in time or ideology) between Enlightenment and Romanticism—Rousseau unites both strands in his thought. The Enlightenment's agenda points of secularism, humanity, cosmopolitanism, the right to free speech, freedom of trade, freedom of aesthetic response, and freedom of moral man to make his own way in the world (Gay, 1973, I:xii, 3, cited in Day, 1996: 66) are the philosophical foundations of modern, liberal citizenship. But it is in the combination of Enlightenment reason and free speech, with the power of imagination and the centrality of the quotidian which Romanticism brings, that one sees the blueprint for the cultural citizenship of today. Because Enlightenment and Romanticism were not oppositional but rather complementary movements, cultural citizenship is also not a counter-concept of citizenship, but its extension and complement.

Further evidence for this claim is provided by Gaonkar (2001), who argues that it was the Romantic Movement starting in the late eighteenth century which, through popular media, gave rise to 'cultural modernity' as an alternative imaginary space to the dominant 'societal modernity'. While the latter involved 'the growth of scientific consciousness, the development of a secular outlook, the primacy of instrumental rationality and individualistic understandings of the self', enforced with the help of 'bureaucratically administered states, mass media and urbanization', cultural modernity, with imagination as its ally, 'in its quest for the self' emphasized the importance of spontaneous expression and 'creative and carnal urges' (Gaonkar, 2001: 2). Romanticism then was also the starting point for the popularization of culture—a project which, as shown earlier, was properly theorized and in effect accelerated by cultural studies in the twentieth century, and which constitutes a conceptual precondition of cultural citizenship.

It is safe to assume that as an Englishman, T.H. Marshall knew about the 'Elegy', one of the most famous contributions to English literature. In his triadic model of citizenship, he explicitly links citizenship to social class (such is the title of his seminal essay), and he singles out the eighteenth century with its struggle for civil rights, which are individual rights such as the liberty of the person, the freedom of speech, thought, and faith, and the right to own property, as the first constitutive phase of modern citizenship. For Marshall, the eighteenth century then marks the beginning of the era of the individual and the struggle for the rights associated with it. Gray in his own poetic way also reflects this by pointing to the graves of those who might have died of starvation, or in an unsuccessful fight to end it, and remained unaccounted for both as a group and as individuals.

Besides the insights into conceptual history, what is the value added by this literary excursion? We know that political science is hesitant to look for politics outside the realm of institutions; the focus on government and the institutionalist paradigm often hinders the discipline from acknowledging non-institutionalized politics as politics, and thus narrows the focus.[15] Yet, the cultural and the political spheres are neither monolithic nor wide apart; they influence and determine each other in manifold ways. Beyond Gray, Rousseau, and Marshall, the objective therefore is to further understand the familiar (politics) in terms of the unfamiliar (literature and culture).[16]

CITIZENSHIP AND THE MEDIA: BELONGING THROUGH REPRESENTATION

Every work is marked by two crucial points: one, when the central idea is conceived of and articulated; and a second point at which it is affirmed that the idea is a valid one. In the social sciences, this is often the point when the researcher realizes that the theoretical construct with which s/he is operating has a real-life bearing; that one's research actually *matters* to society. I had that experience when I was a Visiting Fellow at the Institute for Defence Studies and Analyses in New Delhi in 2011. After a (Indian) speaker presented a paper on the Indian movement for independence and the formative years of the republic, one of the discussants, an Indian Muslim, made a remark which I recall very clearly. The discussant opened his statement with the following words:

> On hearing your paper one could think that all the people who have fought for India's independence are male. One could also say that all the people who have fought for India's independence are north Indian. One could even say that all the people who have fought for India's independence are Hindus. Where are we? We are not there, and it hurts.

The final words of the statement are particularly relevant as they testify to the fact that there is an actual feeling connected with the modes of national narrative and representation. To the Muslim, being absent from the narrative of that crucial phase which transformed Indians from subjects to citizens meant being excluded from the nation altogether. The episode illustrates that—to borrow Homi Bhabha's (1993) phrase—nation *is* indeed narration. Outer perception has an influence on self-perception, and not to figure in the national narrative means not to feel like a citizen.

One of the ways in which nation and narration, the remarks of the Muslim discussant and cultural citizenship, can be linked is by analysing a popular medium like the Indian *Amar Chitra Katha* (ACK) comics, which will be done in greater detail in Chapter five. Launched in 1967, the series has sold eighty million copies of its 400-plus titles, with 100,000 issues sold every fortnight in various languages[17] (Nayar, 2006: 116). It has been assigned a central role in the construction of a postcolonial Indian identity, with the series described as 'a powerful tool for the propagation of ideology, because stories are perhaps the best mechanism for delivering ideas and notions of identity, history and culture' (Nayar, 2006: 116–17). Content analyses of the ACK can illustrate this statement. In the 'Makers of Modern India' series, neither a single woman nor a single Muslim leader or thinker is listed. As Nayar emphasizes, on the cover of the ACK bumper issue *The Story of the Freedom Struggle*, 'there is no Muslim leader or south Indian.... The only Muslim leader shown is Jinnah, and that too as a dour, uncompromising man who propagated the "Islam in Danger" and "Two nations" slogans.... There is no mention of any other Muslim leader' (Nayar, 2006: 129). South Indians for their part are merely footnoted: Nayar shows that the Tamil writer, independence activist, and social reformer Subramania Bharati (1882–1921) is the only representative of the southern part of the country who is referred to in the issue, along with the Telugu leader Alluri Sitarama Raju (1897–1924), who finds mention only in the editor's note at the end (Nayar, 2006: 129).

As far as women are concerned, ACK comics certainly feature some of the historical female figures, but in a very particular way. It has been argued that in those stories that revolve around influential women like the Rani of Jhansi (1828–1858), Chand Bibi (1550–1599), and others—none of them a twentieth-century or even late-nineteenth-century figure—the heroine, who is also always projected as the 'Indian woman' prototype, is invariably 'a particular kind of woman who, even when she is ruler/soldier, remains a devoted mother/wife and [her] sense of duty always involves religious rituals, mother- or wifehood and fidelity to the family' (Nayar, 2006: 126).

In addition to the absence or, at best, one-sided portrayal of Muslims and women, what Nayar does not refer to is the lack of a political figure from the country's north-east on the covers of the magazine's 'Makers of Modern India' series. Chapter five will also discuss the sense of alienation that north-easterners have ascribed to this continuous silence on their role in India's struggle for independence. These omissions are 'serious', as Nayar observes, and make for a reading of India's independence (and, following from that, an interpretation of the values the republic is grounded on) which is biased in favour of Hinduism, with the oft-observed effect of 'India' and 'Hindu' becoming synonyms.[18] Such analysis which seeks to bring the popular and the political into closer dialogue matters because, as has been argued, 'the comic book is an integral component of public culture ... a vehicle for ideologies and cultural opinions' (Nayar, 2006: 129).

THE ROLE OF THE INDIAN MASS MEDIA IN NATION-BUILDING

In India as everywhere else, the media are, and always have been, closely linked to nation-building. Chapter five explores this particular issue to show that citizen identity is indeed formed in and through the media. Media messages are sent 'from above' as well as 'from below'. While media use 'from below', that is, from the non-institutionalized, non-mass, and often non-electronic sphere, has gained ground only after the privatization of radio frequencies, media 'from above'—electronic media monitored by state institutions—have a greater outreach and a much longer history. Until the liberalization of the Indian economy in 1991 and the advent of private satellite television, the government held the monopoly over the two electronic information mass media—Doordarshan, the public television broadcaster, and All India Radio (AIR). The main responsibility for running those media still lies with the Ministry of Information and Broadcasting (MIB).

The MIB, set up in 1947, has been ascribed a vital role in the nation-building process. The ministry predominantly comprised colonial parts with AIR, the Press Information Bureau (PIB), and the

Films Division (FD) as central institutions that were all of colonial origin and were then incorporated into the republican institutional set-up, largely without even a change in name. The young republic drew on the communication infrastructure set up by the British, who had effectively employed it for propaganda purposes. India realized the 'important role which broadcasting can play in cultural and national integration' (MIB, *Annual Report, 1948–1949*: 4) and made considerable efforts to expand in that direction. The first annual report of the MIB, published for the period from 1948 to 1949, states that while on 15 August 1947, due to the partition of the country, AIR, set up by the British in 1936, was left with only six stations, three more were added by the end of the financial year 1947–8, and there was already a total of fourteen stations by the time of the publication of the annual report. India was not only keen to cover 'all important linguistic areas' in its radio broadcasting, but also provide specialized broadcasting to different social and occupational sections of society. The MIB thus highlighted the production of special programmes for factory workers and highlighted its Calcutta programme, broadcast daily in Bengali and Hindustani in time slots arranged in consultation with the Labour Department of the Government of Bengal. Very much in line with the colonial precedent, there were also specific programmes for the armed forces: once a day, in the evening, 'Special Programmes in Hindustani' were broadcast to Indian troops, with a special programme in Gorkhali added for Gorkha soldiers on 16 January 1949 (MIB, *Annual Report, 1948–1949*: 6).

Established in 1919, and reorganized in 1938, the Press Information Bureau had—and has to date—the task 'to collect, coordinate and provide information, verbal, textual, and pictorial, on the activities of the Government to the Press, to keep the Government informed of the main trends of public opinion as reflected in the Press, and to effect liaison between the Press and Press correspondents, Indian and foreign and the Government' (MIB, *Annual Report, 1948–1949*: 9). The dramatic political changes on the subcontinent created an enormous increase in the demand for information from the press, and the MIB reported a 'continuous flow of information and background material on the Integration of States' (MIB, *Annual Report, 1948–1949*: 11).

The regional film censor boards, which were constituted by the British colonial authorities in 1920 (Bhowmik, 2003: 3148), were restructured and renamed as the Central Board of Film Censors in 1952, and as the Central Board of Film Certification (CBFC) in 1983. In 1948, it was proposed and then decided in January 1949 that the existing regional boards of film censors were to be replaced by a central institution, a 'single censoring Authority to be appointed by the Central Government with a view to remove various anomalies and to introduce uniformity in censorship which would help to raise the standard of films as a medium of education and healthy entertainment' (MIB, *Annual Report, 1949–1950*: 5).

From the political personnel that headed the MIB, one can deduce the significance attached to the ministry: there have been frequent overlaps in personnel and ideology between the MIB, the Home Ministry, and the Prime Minister's Office. Among the heads of the MIB have been important political figures such as Sardar Vallabhbhai Patel, Indira Gandhi, I.K. Gujral, and L.K. Advani. Patel, India's first Home Minister and Deputy Prime Minister from 1947 to 1950, was also the first Minister of Information and Broadcasting; Indira Gandhi held the office from 1964 to 1966 before becoming Prime Minister in the same year. I.K. Gujral, who served as Information and Broadcasting Minister from 1972 to 1977, became the Prime Minister in 1997, and L.K. Advani, 'India's most media-savvy politician' (Farmer, 2005) who was Home Minister from 1998 to 2004, succeeded Gujral as head of the MIB from 1977 to 1979. He would during that time acquire or enhance the expertise that would later enable him and his party, the Bharatiya Janata Party (BJP), to play the media keyboard in such masterly fashion.

Doordarshan and AIR

In her analysis of the relationship between mass media and nationalism and communalism, Victoria Farmer (2005) argues that before the advent of transnational satellite television and private channels, the Indian National Congress was free to televise its conception of the Indian nation. Using the Doordarshan screenings of the epics *Ramayana* (1987–8) and *Mahabharata* (1989–90) as focal points, she notes that 'increasingly through the 1980s, television was used as a tool for cultural engineering and electoral gains through creation of an "Indian" national character closely identified with the ruling party'

(Farmer, 2005: 106). The instrumental character of other serials such as *The Sword of Tipu Sultan* (1990) and *Chāṇakya* (1991–2) substantiate the argument. With regard to the televising of the life of the eighteenth-century Muslim ruler Tipu Sultan (1750–1799), Farmer argues that the story

> did not fit easily into Doordarshan's nationalist paradigm, because it depicted the Muslim, Tipu, as being modern and progressive, and it was broadcast on Doordarshan only after lengthy arbitration. The result ... was that a disclaimer was aired before each episode to say that the story was fiction, not history, thus marginalizing Tipu Sultan as a historical figure and contributing to a nationalist history in which Muslims somehow become non-Indian. (Farmer, 2005: 106)

A similar strategy of sidelining was followed with regard to the historical figure of Chāṇakya (or Kauṭilya) in the television serial by the same title. Farmer shows that the film series which focused on the Mauryan Empire did not centre on the ruler Ashoka, under whom the empire reached its greatest extent and whose symbol, the pillar carrying his name, is the official emblem of the Republic of India. Instead, the narrative revolved around Chāṇakya, the Brahmin adviser to the king and alleged author of the *Arthaśāstra*, an ancient manual on statecraft (see Chapter three). It even depicted him—rather than Ashoka—as the hero of the Mauryan Empire, since the emperor had converted to Buddhism (Farmer, 2005: 107). Referring back to the statement of the Muslim commentator who felt that he and his community did not figure in the national narrative, one can observe a congruence between state-owned and large private-owned media, like Doordarshan and ACK. It is this congruence which furthers a strongly Hinduized reading of India's past, thus purporting a certain exclusive character of the media message, and intensifying an already existing feeling of alienation among members of minority communities.

It is, however, not only the content but also the form of the media message which creates and furthers this sense of exclusion. With reference to the audio mass media, Farmer outlines the difference between commonly spoken Hindi, or Hindustani,[19] and what has come to be known as 'Doordarshan Hindi', a stylistically Sanskritized form of the language. She shows how under the first two ministers of information and broadcasting, Vallabhbhai Patel and B.V. Keskar,

AIR promoted a Sanskritized vocabulary over Urdu forms in spoken language (Lelyveld, 1990), and devalued Muslim musical contributions (Farmer, 2005: 100). In fact, Lelyveld (1994) has argued that B.V. Keskar, the Minister of Information and Broadcasting from 1950 to 1962, along with other Maharashtrian Brahmins was at the 'forefront of Indian nationalism, often defined as a reassertion of Hindu culture, as opposed not only to the British, but to Muslims" (Lelyveld, 1994: 117). The work of the MIB in the first decades of the Indian Republic is indeed a fitting example for the close connection between culture and nation-building. Lelyveld notes that Keskar, 'the major formulator of the musical ideologies and policies of All-India Radio' (Lelyveld, 1994: 116) was also responsible for introducing prerecorded programming, usually distributed from Delhi to the various stations across the country. This move was 'designed to free these stations from reliance on local talent and, more particularly, to familiarize audiences with musical styles from other parts of the country so that eventually a "national music" might emerge' (Lelyveld, 1994: 120). Thus, the importance of mass media, the radio of course much before the television, is not to be underestimated. More than entertainment, they were strategic tools in the process to build a nation and cultivate a citizen with acquired taste and a certain cultural outlook.

The Films Division

The Films Division (FD), a colonial creation, is yet another part of the MIB which has gained importance in independent India. As an institution, the Films Division constitutes a merger of Information Films of India (IFI) and the Indian News Parade (INP), both founded in 1943 as tools in an 'imaginative and careful approach to propaganda' (Garga, 2007: 97). Abolished in April 1946, the Films Division was revived towards the end of 1947 with the main task of producing documentaries, as the Government of India realized the importance of the motion picture film as a medium of publicity (MIB, *Annual Report, 1948–1949*: 20).

Works on the political and social effects of the mass media abound, both theoretical and empirical, including those with specific reference to India. Because of the sheer size of the body of writing on mass communication—which in the context of a young democracy with a developing economy and a quickly growing population like India's is certainly justified—the empirical focus of this book is not on electronic mass media and identity construction 'from above', as in most studies. Rather, it looks at non-electronic media and identity expression 'from below', as it were. The brief discussion of the work of the Films Division in Chapter four is illustrative of the various different but complementary mass media processes steered by the Indian government, pointing towards the deep entanglement of (audio-visual) media and processes of citizen making and citizen breaking. By sketching a discursive cultural space in which the citizen operates, the media more than anything else determine the modes of inclusion and exclusion in society. The FD is an interesting case in point, since, as opposed to commercial feature films, which have already been the subject of thorough academic research,[20] the message disseminated by documentaries has not yet been systematically decoded. Also, since the films are exclusively produced by the government, they can be clearly identified as strategic elements in the project of nation-building.

In exploring these visual building blocks in the construction of the ideal citizen, the book complements an earlier work by Srirupa Roy (2007) who, in her discussion of the power of audio-visual discourse in Indian postcolonial nationalism, similarly employs the films produced by the FD as an empirical background against which to discuss the image that the nascent democracy projected of itself. Similar to the table provided in Appendix I, which lists the films that have been produced on the general theme of citizenship, Roy supplies a table summarizing the representation of Muslims in Films Division documentaries produced between 1949 and 1972 (Roy, 2007: 52). As a matter of fact, this empirical narrowing down to the Muslim community, the largest and most visible religious minority in India, is a common phenomenon in the scholarly works that engage with the study of citizenship in India.[21] Abdelhalim (2016) engages in a theoretical quest for the imaginative space in which Indian Muslims situate themselves as citizens, and Asif (1998), Kidwai (2003), Farouqui (2009), and Mecklai (2010) set out to establish interrelations between media representation and the perception (both inner and outer) of the Muslim community. The common denominator in these works is the Indian Muslim community, but while Abdelhalim's work, as a contribution to political science, is restricted to the discussion of the ongoing negotiation between general theories of citizenship and Islamic thought, the works of Asif, Kidwai, and Farouqui are largely media studies. Although they make a connection between media representation and societal inclusion, they do not contribute to an enhanced understanding of the concept of citizenship in its connection with the media. This is one of the points that this book addresses: as a work of political science which takes culture and the media seriously, it overcomes the mental barrier between political science and cultural studies. It bridges an unnatural divide caused by the reluctance of political science to engage with anything that carries the label 'culture', and by cultural studies emphasizing its prerogative over the study of culture, which it defines as immeasurable and non-quantifiable, and thus situates outside the analytical reach of (conventional) political science. However, what is all too often overlooked by the cultural studies camp is the fact that political science is indispensable for the analysis of structures and processes of social and societal power: it is not possible to talk about society in a meaningful way without also talking about the state and its institutions which condition and shape that society.

MEDIA 'FROM BELOW': NEW VOICES IN THE DISCOURSE

Against the long dominance of state control over the electronic media, there has been a growing interest in small-scale private or community-run media, often referred to as 'grassroots' or 'citizens' media'. The expanding body of literature on the theme testifies to a conceptual shift in the relationship between media and society, complementing the approach of media *for* the people with the approach of media *by* the people. However, to date, authoritative studies of non-electronic community media are lacking, and the huge potential that they have for development and identity expression remains unacknowledged— a gap in research which this book tries to fill.

As in the case of the mass media, the focus of the discussion on non-mass media is on electronic media, and the corpus on community radio, as a very prominent representative, is constantly growing. Pavarala and Malik (2007) are among those who have presented a thorough account of the development of the medium in the Indian

context and the opportunities it offers, not only for development communication, but also for the expression of views, identity, and, following from that, for greater social visibility and de-marginalization of
formerly marginalized communities. Community media constitute
a subcategory of *participatory media*, on which the literature is also
growing continuously. Much of what Manyozo (2012) describes
against the background of the African school of development communication, which emerged around the 1960s with African scholars
beginning to rethink concepts of culture, communication, and development, is also applicable to the Indian context. The African school,
as Manyozo notes, comprised two faculties, rural radio and folk
media. Among the latter, a branch which developed was 'theatre for
development', aimed at 'sensitising and empowering communities to
improve their status quo' (Manyozo, 2012: 42). Similar developments
can be observed in postcolonial sub-Saharan Africa and postcolonial
India, where local modes of narration replaced those informed by the
colonial paradigm. Manyozo notes that 'university travelling theatres
have, since the 1980s, moved away from performing English plays
in the Shakespearean tradition and started developing indigenous
language plays which carry social educational messages on popular
issues of alcoholism, adultery, witchcraft or agriculture' (Manyozo,
2012: 42).

Similarly, some of India's civil society organizations have used
what they understand to be 'traditional' or 'folk' media to reach out
to people who can hardly or not at all be reached by electronic media.
The non-governmental organization (NGO) Calcutta Creative Arts
Performers, which uses theatre to promote social change, illustrates
the social action that can spring from a theatrical performance, thus
stressing its direct impact:

> So, in that area we go and hold a workshop. After the workshop, do you
> know, what the people did? The people went into different islands, gath-
> ered people and they showed the drama about addiction of drink—local
> liquor—and drug abuse. So, the students gathered and showed the drama.
> After that the villagers moved to the *bhati*—the *bhati* is the place where the
> local liquor is made. They broke the *bhatis* with the help of the local police.
> So, it has a big impact. First, we think that after this workshop the people
> became so much aware, after we came from this place, they moved the
> theatre and motivated other villagers and broke the *bhati*. So, it has a big

impact.... After this workshop, we believed that theatre has strength, can do anything, can change a society.[22]

The medium is brought into very close connection with power here, and the incident reveals the destructive potential of creativity and performance. Social change is a process marked not by harmony but by contestation, since any such change seeks to alter existing power structures. This contestation does not necessarily have to take the form of brute force, but can also be of a more intangible, ideological nature. Indian Mime Theatre, an NGO also based in Kolkata, uses a different theatrical form to generate social change. According to its director Niranjan Goswami, the group consciously chose mime as a media alternative, not only in the sense of traditional over modern, but also as a way to emphasize indigenous forms of expression over Western ones. In a personal interview, he explained the underlying motivation for his successful arts project in the following terms:

> When the TV came, the children are seeing the cartoons etc. and the serials—*Mahabharata, Ramayana* etc. Actually there is no good performance. They don't even have any good children's films. They are making very few films every year for children and now they have started organising festivals—children theatre festivals and there are many groups participating in it. Their subjects are child psychology, adolescent problems, relationship with the parents, changing socio-economic conditions. All these plays they produce, behind them there [are] positive thoughts behind every production. So, theatre that way helps in a society by doing and seeing as well.[23]

In its work and approach, the art project tries to dissociate itself from forms of representation commonly regarded as Western. The recourse to Sanskrit sources is emphasized as a way to resurrect 'Indian' theatre, strengthen indigenous culture, and overcome what is regarded as a Western cultural project. The NGO draws on the *Natyashastra*, an ancient Indian text on the art of theatrical performance.[24] On that specific source, Goswami notes:

> It was written in Sanskrit, later it was translated in English. Now it is available in the regional languages as well. But in our education system, all the theatre departments, all the theatre groups are working; only they are copying European theatrical forms, which were started by the British here. Seeing the British people they started. And now there is another trend here, of using folk elements. But nobody is giving a thought to what

is written in the *Natyashastra*. There is the preparations for the actors, how the actor prepares himself, all the physical exercises, mental exercises, aesthetics, *bhava rasa*....[25] That way, it's very good, but nobody is taking interest in it.

The NGO thus posits its medium of choice, mime theatre, as an alternative modernity, and its specific cultural form as a tool for societal integration and nation-building. In the mode of this strategic understanding and choice of media, this volume explores different readings, adaptations, and hybridizations of 'Western' media in Indian cultural contexts, and inquires into their position in the framework of nation building and citizen making. It thus asks whether there can be a general notion of citizenship despite the lack of a 'homogeneous modernity' (Nayar, 2006: 64), and explores the role culture plays in this project, whether it eases or obstructs.

1

TOWARDS A NEW PARADIGM

BRIDGING POLITICAL SCIENCE AND CULTURAL STUDIES

No conclusive disproof of a theory can ever be produced.

(Popper, 1959: 50).

For most researchers, the trick is how to choose theories, define frameworks, ask questions, and design methods that are most likely to produce research with a plausible shelf life.

(Appadurai, 2000: 12).

INTERDISCIPLINARY RESEARCH: OPPORTUNITIES AND CHALLENGES

At the theoretical–methodological heart of this book lies the attempt to bridge political science and cultural studies in order to arrive at a holistic understanding of the role of culture in politics. It is explored in how far social science can be stretched to explore new source material and based on that, offer new perspectives on pressing socio-political issues. The two disciplines—political science and cultural studies— show a significant overlap in terms of their subject of analysis, but are currently separated by a methodological gap which prevents them from harvesting what they otherwise could. Cultural studies researches[1] power—which the discipline regards as the underlying variable of most social relations. At the same time, political science, also deeply concerned with power relations, investigates concepts such as state, nation, and institutions, which are not fixed givens but the outcome of discursive processes that constitute and shape them. Grounded in political science, this work is aimed at demonstrating that in order for political science to effectively approach and understand the complex nature of citizenship—a category in which the power of discourse manifests itself—political science needs to become interdisciplinary, or at least activate the many disciplinary components that already make it an interdisciplinary subject.

This, however, is a challenging undertaking. Interdisciplinarity, a noun which was added to the *Oxford English Dictionary* (*OED*) as recently as 1993, supplementing the earlier adjective entries 'interdiscipline' (1930) and 'interdisciplinary' (1937), is not always a welcome guest at the academic table. Doubts persist that the additional knowledge which interdisciplinary research brings might be limited. The editors of *Victorian Studies*, which was launched in 1957 as an interdisciplinary academic journal, reflected that 'if ... pursuit of one's own discipline is severely limited by lack of understanding of other disciplines, how can any single scholar sufficiently master peripheral disciplines so as to increase his competence in his own?' (*Victorian Studies*, 1963: 205). Obstacles that are posed by interdisciplinary research include finding a common vocabulary or a metalanguage in which to communicate. The editors of *Victorian Studies* thus rightly wondered: 'if the methods of the various disciplines are as widely different as their various idioms, is there any possibility of evolving a mutually intelligible language?' (1963: 205). The question that was asked in the early 1960s is still relevant at the beginning of the twenty-first century: 'does the interdisciplinary idea, by insisting on the potential relevance of *every* discipline, reduce each discipline to a section in an intellectual supermarket, or does it suggest that the existing disciplines are a row of old curiosity shops which now merely subserve administrative convenience?' (*Victorian Studies*, 1963: 205). In other words, does doing something of everything essentially mean doing nothing of anything *really*? The 'discomfort' about the dangers to the integrity of their own subjects on the part of those involved in interdisciplinary research that the ambitious founders of the interdisciplinary journal detected (*Victorian Studies*, 1963: 204) is still acute today.

New, hybrid research initiatives, which are pushing the frontiers of knowledge and are deliberately bringing together representatives of diverse disciplines to engage with cutting-edge areas of research, often face an opposition which, in the name of disciplinary purity, sets the standards and determines the structures in which works are evaluated, thus preventing full interdisciplinary and creative potential from unfolding. The old university faculty structures, with their restrictions on who can write on what, and what is then examined by whom, while serving as a bastion upholding the integrity of a subject, do not correspond any longer to the scholarly realities of our times. On the other hand, proponents of interdisciplinarity are obliged to provide answers to the pressing questions of what, in fact, interdisciplinary studies are being interdisciplinary about (*Victorian Studies*, 1963: 205)—the theme, the theory, the method, or all three? If scholars reflect on these questions, they can effectively contribute to interdisciplinarity, and in doing so also 'find a better way to pursue [their] own discipline' (*Victorian Studies*, 1963: 205).

Knowledge of 'the other' is imperative to understanding 'the self', and since an interdisciplinary work is written for a heterogeneous, multidisciplinary audience, it leads to a rethinking of one's own (disciplinary) approaches, thus refining, enhancing, and advancing them. Many of what can be called 'hyphenated subjects'—disciplines which emerged from such dialectic considerations—have come into existence in recent years. One of the difficulties is how and where to draw the line between a compound and a discipline in its own right. Are 'economic history' or 'political economy' subfields of history and political science respectively, or can they be classed as stand-alone subjects? It is this fuzzy nature of interdisciplinarity which needs to come under closer scrutiny in order to disentangle the concept and determine its heuristic value.

INITIATING A DIALOGUE BETWEEN POLITICAL SCIENCE AND CULTURAL STUDIES

To begin with, it seems safe to assume that no scholarly discipline is mono-disciplinary. The chemist cannot do research without knowledge of biology, its theories, and methods. More recent additions to the canon of academic subjects, like biochemistry, a term first used at the end of the nineteenth century (Kleinkauf et al., 1988: 116), only emphasize the strong nexus between the disciplines. Just as the art historian is incapable of understanding the complexity of a Renaissance painting if she lacks sound knowledge of philosophy and theology, political scientists would not be able to explain the nature of conflict, its resolution, or prevention without the contributions of sociology, philosophy, history, psychology, economics, and—especially in the South Asian context—religious studies. In turn, those disciplines have employed methods, theories, and findings from political science in their own research frameworks, which makes for a dynamic interplay between the disciplines (see Table 1.1).

The diversity of topics that political scientists engage in, and the multiplicity of subfields intersecting with other disciplines, is probably what has led outside observers and inside actors alike to speak of the subject in the plural voice. 'Political sciences' is a term which exists in various languages (*Politikwissenschaften* in German, *sciences politiques*

Table 1.1   Disciplines Related to Political Science and Intersecting Research Fields

Neighbouring Discipline	Overlap with Political Science in the Research Areas of
Philosophy	Political theory; history of political thought; philosophy of science; epistemology
Sociology	Empirical social research; psephology; political socialization and communication; party and organizational sociology; social theory
Law	Constitutional law; administrative law; theory of institutions; international law
Economics	Political economy; economic and financial policy
Communication studies	Political communication; media impact studies
History	Contemporary history; intellectual history; all historical research that takes into account political conditions

Source: Adapted from Mayer (1995: 26–7).

in French, or *ciencias políticas* in Spanish), and is meant to underline the theoretical and methodological plurality within the subject, to the extent that one cannot speak of *one* unifying scholarly approach any more. Such plurality is then seen as an obstacle to offering a coherent message, which is the prerequisite of effective analysis. Before special-ized subfields emerged within political science as a consequence of the crossing of disciplinary boundaries, Charles Eisenmann observed that 'the political sciences are a very fair illustration of the following: as a whole they are sure neither of their methods nor even of their subject matter, but [are] hesitant and groping; and further, taking it all in all, can they really boast of a sufficiently abundant harvest of achievement to resolve doubts about their essential premises?' (1950: 91, cited in Amadae and Bueno de Mesquita, 1999: 272).

Political science is a relatively new discipline. It is true that Aristotle is sometimes referred to as 'the Father of Political Science', and is also known as the first comparativist due to his comparative study of differ-ent ancient Greek city states. Yet political science as a scholarly disci-pline and university subject came into existence only in the nineteenth century.[2] It is a field of study that, due to its composite character, has also faced identity crises and pressure for self-legitimation as a field of academic research. Hence, it is the one discipline among the social sciences which can least do without interdisciplinarity. Moreover, poli-tics, the overall subject of study, touches upon all spheres of life and is in turn influenced by those spheres (Mayer, 1995: 26).[3] Therefore, a segregation of political science from the economic, the societal, the legal, or the cultural spheres would be a futile exercise, which at best would leave us with an inanimate, truncated torso. In this vein, Mayer (1995) emphasizes a complementation of his list of disciplines directly related to political science (see Table 1.1) with additional subjects, such as cultural studies, social psychology, and anthropology. Connections in content do not stop at the borders of a subject, and few interesting topics can be limited to one discipline only (Mayer, 1995: 27).

POSITIVISM: STRIVING TOWARDS A SCIENTIFIC STUDY OF POLITICS

For many decades now, its excursions have taken political science even beyond the humanities to the cognitive sciences. Political psy-chology is a field that, in taking its methodology from psychology, aims at perfecting the study of perception, so crucial to the analysis of political action.[4] More than that, political scientists demand an increased dialogue with disciplines as wide-ranging as evolutionary psychology and biology, biological anthropology, behavioural economics, behavioural genetics, behavioural ecology, and cognitive neuroscience. In sketching a new political science research agenda, Rose McDermott (2009) argues for a clear theoretical convergence around evolutionary development models, and their successful application to the analysis of political decision-making. To this interdisciplinary research perspective, political science can then add critical input concerning human social and political behaviour, including bias against out-groups, the formation and maintenance of coalitions, and the origin of preferences in decision-making (McDermott, 2009). The cognitive sciences and neurosciences are close to political science in so far as they stress the significance of measurement and quantifiability in their methodology. The scholarly approach to the study of politics is not unjustifiably called 'science' in Anglo-American usage, with the scholar carrying out such work labelled as a 'scientist'—a terminology one otherwise encounters only in the natural *sciences*, not in the humanities.[5]

The idea that human motivation cannot be studied like physics or chemistry (cf. Osborne and Van Loon, 2004: 25) is the polemical argument against a theoretical and methodological strand in the social sciences, especially in sociology and political science, which has come to be known as 'positivism'. A positivist approach to the study of politics has for a long time been favoured especially in the United States. Positivism claims to build scientific theories of society through observation and experimentation, thus demonstrating the laws of social development. Positivists believe in the unity of the scientific method, and hence claim to be able to show objectively how social structures work on the basis of quantifiable results. In other words, it is believed that general laws can be derived from comparing evidence directly known to the observer. As is the case with most ideas, positivism is also a child of its time. the French thinker Auguste Comte (1798–1857), who is credited with having coined the term 'sociology', was influenced by the radicalism and turmoil that France experienced during his lifetime, notably the Second Restoration in 1815, the July Revolution of 1830, and the anti-monarchist June Rebellion of 1832.

Comte developed sociological positivism as a 'deeply conservative reaction to revolutionary politics' (Osborne and Van Loon, 2004: 24), and presented it in his work *Discours sur l'ensemble du positivisme* (*A General View of Positivism*) first published in 1844.

In political science, it was a school centred on William H. Riker at the University of Rochester in the 1960s which launched 'the positive political theory revolution'[6] (Amadae and Bueno de Mesquita, 1999: 269). What Riker called 'positive political theory' has two essential elements, described by his students as follows:

> [I]t upholds a methodological commitment to placing political science on the same foundation as other scientific disciplines, such as the physical sciences or economics..... The goal of positive political theorists is to make positive statements about political phenomena, or descriptive generaliza-tions[7] that can be subjected to empirical verification. This commitment to scientifically explaining political processes involves the use of formal language, including set theory, mathematical models, statistical analysis, game theory, and decision theory [borrowed from economics], as well as historical narrative and experiments (Amadae and Bueno de Mesquita, 1999: 270).

The second constitutive element of positive political theory is the understanding of individual decision-making as the source of collec-tive political outcomes. These decisions follow the logic of rational self-interest—interests, as opposed to attitudes, are thought to be the motor of action. It is therefore the motivation to maximize expected payoffs which provides the explanation for political action (Amadae and Bueno de Mesquita, 1999: 270–1). William Riker himself described his approach as 'formal, positive political theory', where by formal he meant the expression of the theory in algebraic rather than verbal symbols. The term 'positive' in this context implies the expression of descriptive rather than normative propositions (Amadae and Bueno de Mesquita, 1999: 276). Riker outlined this theoretical approach, which drew heavily on economics and the mathematical theory of games, in his *Theory of Political Coalitions* (1963), which has been referred to as the 'manifesto for positive political theory' (Amadae and Bueno de Mesquita, 1999: 276). He further developed his ideas into a method, together with Peter Ordeshook, in their *Introduction to Positive Political Theory* (1973). In his introductory chapter to the ear-lier volume, aptly titled 'The Prospect of a Science of Politics', Riker

(1963) placed himself in the tradition of sociological positivism, in an approach modelled on the rigidity of the natural sciences. He pursued a scientific approach to the study of politics, proposing to study it by analysing political agents whose actions could be modelled like those of particles in motion. 'Just as a particle's trajectory could be traced by knowing its momentum and the force on it', Riker argued, 'so an agent's actions can be predicted by knowing her preferences and the environment structuring her choices' (Amadae and Bueno de Mesquita, 1999: 277). Indeed, Riker's positive political theory, which drew heavily on quantification and formal analysis, resembled the successful programmes in the physical sciences (Amadae and Bueno de Mesquita, 1999: 279).

However, this focus on formality, replicability, and predictability did not remain unquestioned, even by representatives of Riker's positivist school. Subrata Mitra, who was a member of the graduate programme in political science set up by William Riker at Rochester University, and who later 'established a beachhead for rational choice models in the study of South Asian politics' (Amadae and Bueno de Mesquita, 1999: 282), has more recently moved beyond positive polit-ical theory to include variables like time, space, and memory (Mitra, 2011b, 2012c; Mitra and König, 2012, 2013) that equally influence rational actors and determine their behaviour. These variables might in effect be less easy to measure and more difficult to compare, because they necessitate a thorough research of the context(s) in which actors operate, in order to determine how far they are influenced by them.

This already hints at what is considered to be a main point of criticism of the approach of formal, positive political theory. Rigorous quantification and testing of formal hypotheses in order to arrive at general conclusions can certainly be undertaken in the laboratory conditions of the natural sciences. For political scientists, however, these are challenges that put their methodological abilities to the test. Experiments, which are a constitutive element in the methodology of the natural sciences, and are crucial for the verification or falsification of research results, are not feasible in political science. The Popperian idea of *replicability* is also central to the natural sciences, where it is a constitutive feature of an experiment and the *conditio sine qua non* for a legitimate claim to generality. Yet replicability is hardly realizable in political science.[8] Hence, the validity of the statement by Shome et al. (1996: PE-87) is undisputable: 'social sciences are not natural sciences and all branches of the former must recognize this funda- mental aspect. Otherwise, any approach to enquiry would fall short of finding meaningful answers to the questions that are set out to be addressed.'

BEYOND POSITIVISM: A 'SOFT' POLITICAL SCIENCE

Undeniably, Riker's Rochester school, like Comte's positivism ear- lier, was a child of its time, a product of the Cold War era where politics in a world conveniently divided into good and evil could (seemingly) be more easily quantified. In a bipolar world order, the next strategic move of either side could be, if not predicted, then at least analysed in terms of a preference ordering. In today's multipolar setting, where the firm structures of once all-powerful nation-states have given way to a global entanglement—which, even though it has existed all along, has only now broken through in all its complexity— the political scientist is well advised to consider the role of culture in determining the perception of the actor, account for the phenom- enological reality of the hybridity of categories, and engage with the fluid and dynamic nature of concepts which were earlier believed to be stable and hence measurable entities. What seems to be necessary in this changed trajectory is the opposite development of political science away from the natural sciences towards the humanities and cultural studies. This move I would like to call a 'soft political science' approach, where 'soft' is not coterminous with 'weak', or 'easy', but refers to the methodological nature of an approach which defies rig- orous quantifiability, and instead underlines the dynamism required of a scholarly discipline that aspires to study a world in flux.

What can potentially accelerate the formation of a 'soft political science' is the tendency not only of the social sciences to incorporate more humanistic elements, but also of the humanities to become more scientific. This tendency is evident, for example, in the use of statistical methods. The social sciences are now already paying increased attention to the historical dimension of social processes; they show a heightened interest in textual, discourse analytic, and ethnographic methodologies and are more appreciative of qualita- tive methods (Craig, 1993: 30). What has been witnessed since the end of the Cold War could be a 'blurring of boundaries [which] calls into question the metatheoretical vocabulary of explanatory scientific theory in social sciences, according to which the social sciences can advance only by becoming *harder*, more quantitative, more like the physical and natural sciences' (Craig, 1993: 30).

In line with the 'blurring of boundaries', I would like to suggest a more intense dialogue between political science and cultural studies and critical theory. If cultural studies is considered to be a pluralistic 'mode of inquiry committed to understanding the complex terrain of the cultural in connection with relations of power' (Dean, 2000: 2), then the interlinkages that cultural studies has with political science are strikingly obvious—to an extent where the interface between political theory and cultural studies has been labelled 'quite seamless' (Dean, 2000: 1). 'Power' is of course not only germane to cultural studies, but constitutes a central component of most definitions of politics. Researching into the various ways in which power manifests itself, is exercised, asserted, challenged, and reasserted is one of the main objectives of political science analysis.[9] Political science, which is far from being a clear, unified discipline with regard to theory, method, and subject of analysis, as outlined above, and which has in fact been referred to as a 'rainbow science' with respect to both its internal diversity and its cultural particularity, has 'consistently pursued a common object of analysis—power—which in some measure gave it a general sense of mission and identity'[10] (Andrews, 1982: 4–5, cited in Gunnell, 2002: 344). But, if both cultural studies and political science seek to reveal the mechanisms behind power, then what is the added value of combining elements of both disciplines in one work? Apparently, they complement rather than contradict one another.

Both political science and cultural studies are theory-driven, but they differ markedly in their methodological approaches. Cultural studies does not subscribe to the strong emphasis on quantification and measurement of positive political science. On the contrary, cultural studies possesses neither a well-defined methodology nor clearly demarcated fields of investigation (During, 1999: 1). The sources of the cultural theorist are different from those of the political scientist. The cultural theorist would object to what s/he perceives as an inflationary use of the word 'data', which the political scientist counts among the most frequently used words in their vocabulary. Cultural studies is, in short, 'not an academic discipline quite like others' (During, 1999: 1). The most remarkable feature distinguishing cultural studies from positive political science is that it concentrates on subjectivity and studies culture in relation to individual lives,[11] thus breaking with social scientific positivism (During, 1999: 1). Cultural studies research is also hardly 'replicable', thus calling into question one of the central elements of positive political science. Cultural studies research is of an interventionist nature, and therefore challenges the postulate of 'value-free research' in the social sciences as outlined by Max Weber. As Appadurai (2000: 11) observes, with the application of 'value-free research', which had thus far only be employed in the natural sciences, to the social and human sciences in the late nineteenth century came a divide between the forerunners in theory, such as Aristotle and Plato, and modern researchers. Also, 'value-free research' drew a line between researchers in the strictly academic sense of the term and modern thinkers like John Locke and Immanuel Kant. Against this background, Appadurai notes that 'the importance of value-free research in the modern research ethic assumes its full force with the subtraction of the idea of moral voice or vision and the addition of the idea of replicability' (Appadurai, 2000: 11). In the aphoristic comment of George Stocking, however, replicability is also one of the elements that makes *re-search* out of a mere *search* (cited in Appadurai, 2000: 11). If 'replicability' is understood broadly enough to also entail the checking of sources, the verification of citations, and the confirmation of calculations by one or many other researchers (Appadurai, 2000: 11), then cultural studies, or the 'soft political science' approach outlined here, could also indeed be classified as 'replicable'.

By moving closer together, both disciplines, political science and cultural studies, can benefit from each other. A skills transfer from the former to the latter, for example with regard to survey research techniques, would help cultural studies to place its findings on solid empirical ground, turning cultural studies into a *falsifiable* science, and therefore a 'true' science in Popper's sense.[12] Political science, on the other hand, can with the help of cultural studies explore new hunting grounds: cultural studies can help to pluralize the notion of the 'political', as it 'does not presume ... that politics is centred in the state or can be summed up with analyses of voting behaviour'

(Dean, 2000: 3). Indeed, while they are unmistakably political in character, the subjects that cultural studies sets out to explore differ from those that classical political science considers worthy of investigation.

This book opened with the observation that ours is an age of asymmetry, where political reality has in some cases moved beyond concepts as defined by political scientists. Politicians and analysts of parliamentary Germany have argued for a long time that the ISAF military intervention in Afghanistan, which lasted from 2001 to 2014 can not be called a 'war'; to them it was an armed conflict, because war, by definition, can occur only between two states.[13] This is to show that reality has moved past the confines of the scholarly concept, and it is here that cultural studies can come to the rescue of political science. With its less strictly defined research agenda and much more interventionist character, cultural studies may be able to draw scholarly attention to new areas which require proper social investigation, or direct the social scientist towards the need for rethinking and reformulating established concepts. The reactionary nature of their discipline might enable the cultural theorist to confront the political analyst who does not see—or refuses to see—a war which happens in front of their very eyes, when it does not correspond to the accepted definition.[14]

WHERE POLITICAL SCIENCE AND CULTURAL STUDIES MEET: SKETCHING THE INTERFACE

Political science and cultural studies are often opposed to one another in theory and method, but it is this opposition which is fruitful, and out of which a productive relationship can emerge. On the whole, cultural studies have been less rigid (or more innovative, depending on the point of view) with regard to the definition of and adherence to concepts, which has also given the discipline a reputation of being arbitrary. In an academically fruitful interdisciplinary relationship, however, all the disciplines involved have to act as the thorn in each other's flesh, drawing attention to flaws, shortcomings, and the inability to advance single-handedly with respect to the problem under consideration.

If one thinks of interdisciplinarity as a marriage not of love, but of reason, then a much-needed dowry that cultural studies can bring is *context sensitivity*. 'A state, is a state, is a state', where 'state' can be substituted by almost any other concept, is the oft-heard mantra of the rigorous political science generalist. But in cultural studies, the contexts of time and space matter. In the normative approaches of political theory, as well as in the grand theories of political science, like the theory of realism, one easily gets the feeling that politics is perceived as a 'black box' or, to put it more eloquently, that there are some political theories that 'claim to provide an Archimedean point of "view from nowhere", that can set out universal principles' (Dean, 2000: 4). Cultural studies, on the other hand, appreciate the fact that there will always be excesses that escape and subvert the concepts through which the political is formatted (Dean, 2000: 4). It would be wrong to assume though that political scientists have studied politics regardless of context. For example, Mitra (2008b) links positivist rational choice to cultural-historical context. Discussing the issue of liberal democracy in South Asia, more specifically India, Mitra concludes that while the regional case study offers evidence for liberalism's claim to universality, Indian specificities, the unique features of an Indian reading of democracy,[15] also make the case difficult to generalize from (Mitra, 2008b: 573–4).

The existence of intervening variables grounded in the culture of a specific region has led positive political scientists to dismiss regional studies as idiosyncratic, exotic, and therefore flawed. If, by means of an interdisciplinary dialogue, cultural studies can sensitize political science to new sources and contexts, it is political analysis which will benefit.[16] Also, if cultural studies aspires to be more or at least something other than literary studies with the additional capacity to deconstruct non-written and non-verbal texts, it needs political science and the skills and toolkit necessary to make policy recommendations. This would then enable the discipline to work towards putting its often 'interventionist' agenda into practice.

One of the areas in which political science and cultural studies need to arrive at a consensus is the question of the subject of analysis. While conventional political science has a clear understanding of what is considered political, cultural studies can potentially see the political wherever relations of power and dominance manifest themselves—that is, practically in every sphere of life. The assumption that everything is political, or for that matter cultural, creates the problem of abandoning the heuristic potential that the theoretical and methodological tools of political science and cultural studies provide. The analysis is then in danger of becoming overextended, with the result of the analyst losing sight of the wood for the trees, which, in the worst case, renders the own reasoning untenable. While Dean's remark that today, everything is political, and indeed 'our whole culture has become political and our politics cultural' (2000: 5) might not be entirely baseless, it should also be noted that such statements are themselves often politically motivated. They are evidence of cultural studies' attempt to increase its influence by assuming the broadest possible subject range. The same indiscriminate understanding of 'the political' has also been detected in the discipline of anthropology. In her introduction to *The Anthropology of Politics* (2002), Joan Vincent claims:

> Anthropology's definition of politics and its political content has almost invariably been so broad that politics may be found everywhere, underlying almost all the discipline's concerns. At one time, colleagues in political science criticized anthropologists for viewing politics simply as a matter of power and inequality (Easton, 1959). Today, political anthropologists consider sensitivity to the pervasiveness of power and the political a prime strength (Vincent, 2002: 1).

On the other hand, much like the traveller to distant shores, or the diasporic individual who turns much more nationalistic in their outlook than they would have in their place of origin, scholars who by choice or less fortunate circumstances find themselves in an interdisciplinary environment become protective of their own discipline, which is then increasingly regarded as *the* identity-constituting base. This is to say that even when strong interdisciplinary elements prevail in a scholarly work, they are not necessarily identified or acknowledged as such. Works by political scientists that actively engage with cultural studies, and label it as such, are not easy to find, which is not to say that they do not exist. Political scientists have formed categories like 'hybrid democracy',[17] or devised methods such as 'analytic narratives' (Bates et al., 1998) combining rational choice theory and historiography. The fact that this interdisciplinary relationship more often than not remains implicit rather than explicit shows that there is still significant hesitation towards interdisciplinary exchange, again more on the part of political science than cultural studies.[18]

Undeniably, political science is a highly pluralistic discipline, but 'it needs to make clear exactly what is involved' (Gunnell, 2002: 347). Because the methodological discrepancies have seemed too vast, political science has been especially reluctant to actively engage with cultural studies. Gunnell remarks that political science scholarship has 'hardly settled questions about the scientific universality of the field or about the relationship between culture and social science' (2002: 347). In addition to context-sensitivity (see above), what political science can bring to the table in a marriage of reason between political science and cultural studies is 'a more adequate account of leadership' (Dean, 2000: 14) and, as far as methodology is concerned, a degree of systematization and more or less consistent approaches, as well as firm grounding in concepts. In this vein, political scientist Paul Brass, in a discussion of Michel Foucault and methodology in cultural studies, asks:

> Where is the framework, the methodological guidelines? In fact, there is no framework, for that would be inconsistent with the very scholarly and political enterprise that Foucault set forth, to escape from existing frameworks and to keep moving in such a manner that one does not get entangled in a fixed set of concepts that would then congeal into another imprisoning discourse (Brass, 2000: 312).

But is the existence of concepts, on whose basic elements a disciplinary community agrees, not the prerequisite for a discussion out of which these concepts, and consequently the scholarly discipline itself, can develop? Does political science always have this conceptual clarity that puts it in a position to avoid ambiguity? On the whole, the logical conclusion of the preceding discussion seems to be that the term 'political science', which comes out of a positivistic understanding of the discipline, is a misleading one. Even in the positivist tradition itself, it is difficult to uphold the standards that a natural *science* sets. Generalization and replicability might be what political scientists strive towards, but because of the dynamic nature of their concepts, and of their objects of research, that is, the decisions and actions of human beings which are subjective and susceptible to manifold influences (intervening variables), the laboratory-like conditions of the sciences cannot be upheld. It has been shown that political science bears many overlaps with the humanities in general and with cultural studies in particular. In light of the conceptual difficulties that the term 'political science' implies, and as a statement in favour of a theoretical turn, the term 'political studies' is reaffirmed here as an alternative label for the discipline.[19] A reconsideration of labels might help to bring out the 'essence' of a subject,[20] it would attenuate the claims of positivism while at the same time underlining the leaning towards the humanities, which the discipline undeniably shows, much more so than towards the natural sciences. Naturally, a changed (self-) understanding of the discipline impacts on methodology, and the 'soft political science' or 'political studies' will have to rework and expand its methodological toolkit in order to be able to do justice to its changed research framework and new self-understanding.

METHODOLOGY: OVERCOMING THE QUANTITATIVE/QUALITATIVE DIVIDE

With regard to the state of method in the research set-up, Appadurai (2000: 12–13) makes some interesting observations:

> Though there are numerous debates and differences about research style among natural scientists, policy makers, social scientists and humanists, there is also a discernible area of consensus. This consensus is built around the view that the most serious problems are not those to be found at the level of theories or models but those involving method: data gathering, sampling bias, reliability of large numerical data sets, comparability of categories across national data archives, survey designs, problems of testimony and recall, and the like. To some extent, this emphasis on method is a reaction to widespread unease about the multiplication of theoretical paradigms and normative visions, especially in the social sciences. Furthermore, in this perspective, method, translated into research design, is taken to be a reliable machine for producing ideas with the appropriate shelf life. This implicit consensus and the differences it seeks to manage take on special importance for any effort to internationalize social science research.[21]

These points seem especially relevant against the background of interdisciplinary research. In the face of a hydra-like proliferation of new concepts, is method the anchor with which to hold fast the scholarship in the troubled sea of theory? The truth is that there is no 'pure' methodology just as there is no 'pure' theory.

According to Popper, methodology is a 'theory of the rules of scientific method' (1959: 49). Methodology, which differs from method in so far as the former delineates the study of the principles and theories which guide the choice of the latter (Burnham et al., 2008: 4), is conceptualized on the basis of an assessment of what is out there to know about, what one can (hope to) know about it, and how one can go about acquiring that knowledge (Hay, 2002: 64, cited in Burnham et al., 2008: 4). Particular research methods such as elite interviewing, content analysis, or opinion surveys are 'the medium and outcome of research practice' (Sayer, 1992: 3), which is determined by the theoretical and methodological framework. The theoretical approach to a problem determines the methodology; it suggests where the researcher should look for what kind of data. The fact that this is a work at the interface of political science and cultural studies, and that it seeks to make theoretical observations based on a case study of a specific non-Western region, modern India, requires an approach that looks at the vernacular and translates it into political science. What Shome et al. (1996) note with regard to ethnography is true for cultural studies at large: 'all knowledge and background are considered valuable and for this reason, there is no single point of view more important than another' (Shome et al., 1996: PE-89). A political science that takes culture and context seriously must sub-scribe to what has been called the 'democratization of knowledge', an interpretation 'that simultaneously deprivileges our academic inquiry while serving to help recover ideas and practices from other points of view—whether of marginal or oppressed peoples, whether close to home or geographically and culturally remote' (Rose, 1990: 11, cited in Shome et al., 1996: PE-89).

A 'soft political science' or 'political studies' approach should also take into consideration different languages, not in a strictly linguistic sense, but as modes of expression.[22] Social actors can use different media in order to communicate different messages, or the same medium to reach out to different audiences. As will be demonstrated in this study, there is great value in exploring differ-ent media sources such as comic strips and university curricula, data which are largely alien to the conventional political scientist. However, these sources will be substantiated by quantitative find-ings. That way, the analysis can claim to constitute a holistic account of the problem under consideration, and is in a position to counter the objections against a leaning towards either the quantitative or the qualitative approach. While a purely quantitative approach, in its effort to be able to draw general conclusions from the analysis, may result in an oversimplification, a purely qualitative approach might appear to be neither rigorous nor systematic, and at worst unscientific and subjective, not allowing for generalizations (cf. Shome et al., 1996: PE-91–PE-92).

The attempt made here is to acquaint political science with new questions and in-depth investigation of non-elite sources, and at the same time familiarize the cultural theorist with research tools like content analysis and opinion surveys. Also, historical methods play a certain role in this work. Political science has been described as 'a "junction subject" born out of history and philosophy' (Burnham et al., 2008: 36), and a work which seeks to contribute to a theorization of 'cultural flow'—a new term to describe an old phenomenon—cannot do so without considering history. More concretely: an understanding of modern citizenship in India is not possible without studying pre-modern developments, or without looking at the role that the British played in the colony as well as at home. Insight into what censorship means in the Republic of India would be all too limited without an informed excursion to the days of the Raj. The analysis of archival documents is one of the ways in which this book engages with the argument that historical research can add to a larger understanding of the issues at hand. Benedetto Croce claimed that 'all history is contemporary history' (Croce, 1941, cited in Allan, 1972), and the international relations theorist and historian E.H. Carr described his discipline as 'a dialogue between the past and the present' (Carr, 1961), and hence as a relevant contribution to the study of political processes. Especially in a study of citizenship such as this one, an analysis of historical records is indispensable, since the national narrative, which determines who is a member of the 'imagined community' that is the nation, is an ongoing construction which takes frequent recourse to the deep historical or even mythical past. Historical analysis is thus central to understanding citizenship because cultural memory, which constitutes the intellectual basis for any citizenship regime, is the sum of past experiences which are interpreted by political actors in the light of the present.

In connection with this research postulate, the 'analytic narrative' approach mentioned earlier will briefly be discussed here, since it takes history and positive political theory equally seriously and thus sets a well-known example of how to link quantitative and qualitative research. Robert Bates et al. (1998: 10) describe their approach as follows:

> [W]e call our approach analytic narrative because it combines analytic tools that are commonly employed in economics and political science with the narrative form which is more commonly employed in history. Our approach is narrative; it pays close attention to stories, accounts and context. It is analytic in that it extracts explicit and formal lines of reasoning, which facilitate both exposition and explanation.

The 'analytic narrative' is seen to stand in the idiographic tradition in the social sciences and thus contributes to the 'historical turn in the social sciences' as outlined by McDonald (1996a, 1996b, quoted in Bates et al., 1998: 10). The approach also constitutes a conscious move away from positive political theory and its aspiration towards generalization. Analytic narratives are 'problem driven, not theory driven', which can also be seen as a concession to the critics of Riker's positive political theory who think that the preoccupation with theory development makes research 'theory driven rather than problem driven' (Bates et al., 1998: 11). However, at the core of the approach still lie central elements of a Rikerian political science: it is the use of rational choice and game theory which transforms narratives into 'analytic narratives' (Bates et al., 1998: 12). Even though game theory as such does not figure here, what the present work takes from the idea of the 'analytic narrative' is its understanding of sources—reading documents, carrying out archival work, interviewing, and surveying the secondary literature—in order to understand 'the actors' preferences, their perceptions, their evaluation of alternatives, the information they possess, the expectations they form, the strategies they adopt, and the constraints that limit their actions' (Bates et al., 1998: 11). It is here that the link between citizenship, culture, and power becomes apparent. Qualitative sources are analysed in light of how political actors devise strategies and employ media to either demarcate discursive boundaries, or to challenge and overcome them. In line with a Gramscian understanding, culture is considered to be a contested site on which power struggles take place, and the rational choice understanding of actors as outcome-maximizing players with a clear preference ordering is certainly helpful in so far as it points towards the potential for clash and contestation that a researcher in the politics of culture has to consider.

What is pursued in this study is a multi-method approach: the two main sources from which data have been collected are elite interviews and the analysis of archival documents. Opinion surveys and media content analyses have not been carried out specifically for the purpose of this particular research; instead, the work draws on 'secondary analysis of survey data' (Ultee et al., 1993) in order to give as precise as possible an account of problems of quantification in the study of 'cultural citizenship'. Survey data on various issues that are of central relevance to this research, like audience reaction to films, opinions on different aspects of censorship, and citizenship have been acquired, and are put in relation to one another and interpreted qualitatively.

A central methodological distinction is to be made between a quantitative and a qualitative approach, not only with regard to this particular research. Like the disciplines of political science and cultural studies, no diametrically opposed schism exists between the two methodological strands; rather, they often overlap and enhance each other. The differences in the epistemological bases of the two research traditions are not as sharp as might at first appear (Schnapp et al., 2006: 14).[23] Qualitative research differs from quantitative research in its stronger emphasis on a constructive worldview, its exploration of causality in microstructure (causal process observation), and its detailed study of one or a limited number of cases in order to develop a theory or reveal causal mechanisms. The aim of quantitative research, on the other hand, is mainly theory testing; hypotheses are examined as to their validity (Schnapp et al., 2006: 12).[24] Schnapp et al. (2006: 14) argue that the epistemological bases of quantitative and qualitative methodologies are not all that different, with the exception that the qualitative tradition puts greater emphasis on a constructivist perspective: it disputes conceptualizations which are derived from an actor-independent truth. Also, qualitative methodology appreciates the role of context to a greater extent than does quantitative research.

With regard to the aim of this book, which deals with the theorization of cultural-political phenomena in a regional, non-Western context, an emphasis on qualitative methodology seems essential. This is not to imply that the contributions of quantitative research to a holistic understanding of analytical problems are neglected. Again, as in the closer interaction between political science and cultural studies advocated above, the overlaps between quantitative and qualitative methodologies and the mutual benefits that both traditions can gain from an interaction with one another are apparent. As is the case with most other social science research works, quantitative and qualitative methodologies are linked here, and commonalities rather than differences are emphasized. This is done in full knowledge of the fact that the combination of the two strands does not constitute a cure-all for the problems of empirical research (Schnapp et al., 2006: 18). However, the combination seems relevant, since this work sets out to research causal mechanisms and thereby contribute to theory building, while at the same time seeking to test the actual existence of these assumed, or hypothetical, mechanisms[25] (cf. Schnapp et al., 2006: 19). The potential which a combination of both quantitative and qualitative research offers includes the explanation of counter-intuitive statistical data with the help of qualitative methods. Unknown, intervening variables in a quantitative analysis can be identified with the help of qualitative methods, while quantitative studies can broaden the reach of qualitatively developed categories and typologies and prepare the ground for generalization from the research findings.

However, the methods followed in this work are mainly qualitative, since, as has been noted, quantitative data have not been generated but are analysed and brought into a dialogue with qualitative data from extensive interviews, historical records, and contemporary textual and visual sources, such as the public reactions to the withdrawal of A.K. Ramanujan's essay 'Three Hundred Rāmāyaṇas' from the history syllabus of the University of Delhi (DU) and what I, in analogy to 'citizen journalism', would like to term 'citizen art'—comic strips drawn by lay or 'citizen' artists with a political message related to their immediate environment, with the aim of directing attention to specific social issues and altering the status quo.

The interdisciplinary approach taken in this book calls for an interplay of qualitative and quantitative methodology. When linking the quantitative/qualitative dichotomy to the discussion on disciplinary approaches, one learns from During (1999: 18) that ethnography, on which cultural studies draws, has 'a long tradition in the positive social sciences'. Social scientists have undertaken quantitative research in the form of large-N opinion surveys, but they have also carried out qualitative research, for example by conducting focus group analyses and employing the method of participant observation. Cultural studies, however, especially cultural studies ethnography of media audiences, has 'mainly used qualitative research in order to avoid the pitfalls of sociological objectivity and functionalism[26] and to give room to voices other than the theorist's own' (During, 1999: 18). Indeed, the number of theoretical developments that the social sciences have witnessed since the structural functionalism of Talcott Parsons and others, such as conceptual stretching (Collier and Levitsky, 1997; Collier and Mahon, 1993), bounded rationality (Jones, 1999), 're-use' (Hegewald and Mitra, 2012), and conceptual flow (Mitra, 2012b), are windows that are increasingly being opened in order to gain a holistic view of social processes and strategies, particularly those underlying identity articulation, accommodation of citizen identity, and the overall processes of identity formation as an interplay of state and society. All these innovations, or paradigms (if not necessarily in a Kuhnian sense), share what Werner and Zimmermann (2006: 38) say of *histoire croisée*, entangled history, namely that it 'breaks with a one-dimensional perspective that simplifies and homogenizes, in favour of a multidimensional approach that acknowledges plurality and the complex configurations that result from it',[27] thus offering an advantage to positivist science.

The most recent developments in what could be labelled 'cross-disciplinary methodology', combining methods of different disciplines, include, for example, 'ethnographic political research', where, as an alternative to interviews and analysis of documents, participant observation is employed in order to explore the behaviour of political actors in their daily lives and to observe and analyse the dynamics and peculiarities of the political decision-making process (Pritzlaff, 2006: 125). This method differs from classical anthropological field research in so far as it is not centred on a group of people, and does not analyse social structures in a certain locality from a diachronic perspective, but focuses on a specific research puzzle with shorter phases of observation. The researcher prepares 'field protocols', which is a technique commonly used in works following the ethnographic method. In addition to voice and film recordings, data can include various types of non-verbal communication. It differs from political science in that, much like in anthropology, the aim here is a conclusive case study, rather than a generalization. It is a method that has not yet been widely established in political science, but that has nonetheless made it to manuals on political science research methodology.[28]

Against the background of these developments, I would like to conclude my theoretical and methodological considerations with Clifford Geertz, who already in 1980 argued that the formerly clear boundary between the social sciences and the humanities had become indistinct, and scholars 'have become free to shape their work in terms of its necessities rather than received ideas as to what they ought or ought not to be doing' (Geertz, 1980: 167). Depending on the subject under consideration, there is a need to more closely link political science and cultural studies in theoretical as well as in methodological terms, to allow them to enter into an interdisciplinary dialogue and to provide a holistic picture of social reality.

One has to keep track of the developments in both disciplines to explore and develop new interfaces. Cultural studies has witnessed a shift in emphasis in recent years, bringing into focus new areas, with one of the most profound topical changes being the focus on 'cultural flow'. During (1999: 23) observes that the field of cultural studies is now 'much less focused on discrete, filiative national or ethnic cultures, or components of such cultures, than it was in its earlier history'. What emerges in the course of this shift is 'transnational cultural studies', which takes further the postcolonial studies of Frantz Fanon (2001 [1961]), Edward Said (1978), and Gayatri Spivak (1988), and makes a case for a more general perspective beyond the regional case—an approach much along the lines of political science. Objects of study are now decreasingly restricted or delimited by distance and locality, but are considered across national borders (During, 1999: 23), an approach which often finds expression in terms such as 'diaspora studies'. In the following chapter, a special form of such transnational studies is presented, wherein the study of the formation and re-formation of social science concepts such as citizenship and censorship by means of cultural and conceptual flow are examined. It is here that political science and cultural studies, with their foci on power and discourse, can enhance one another to effectively study the power of discourse that commands life realities and the formation of academic concepts alike.

2

'CULTURAL FLOW'

A CONCEPTUAL EXPLORATION

Πάντα ῥεῖ[*Panta rhei*] [Everything flows]

ascribed to Heraclitus (c. 535–475 BCE)

History matters. It matters not just because we can learn from the past, but because the present and the future are connected to the past by the continuity of a society's institutions. Today's and tomorrow's choices are shaped by the past. And the past can only be made intelligible as a story of institutional evolution.

(North, 1990: vii)

OPERATIONALIZING 'FLOW'

Analysing the central concepts which this book revolves around—citizenship, cultural citizenship, and censorship—in the light of the idea of 'flow' will not only further an understanding of their evolution, but will at the same time contribute to the analytical sharpening of the concept of 'flow', which has emerged as one of the central tropes of cultural studies. It will be demonstrated here that the process of flow, which can result from an encounter between individuals, collectives, political bodies, and institutions, leads to change in mutual ways, which means that the process of change also has an impact on the actor involved in it. 'Flow' is not an analytical category which social scientists are necessarily familiar with, but which can prove to be all the more helpful for their research, since accounting for the dynamics of change—of which 'flow' is one precondition—is a generic problem of social science (cf. Katz, 1963: 1).

To begin with, the term 'cultural flow' itself deserves elaboration and critical analysis here. 'Flow' suggests a natural process, like the flow of liquids. However, in order for liquids to flow, also the conditions, like precipitous terrain and current, have to be given. Therefore, in the following discussion, 'flow' is detected in selected fields connected with this work; the concept is broken up into smaller units of analysis to make it more accessible and feasible to analyse.

There is, for example, a *conceptual flow* (Mitra, 2012b) to be observed in the theoretical formation of the concept of 'cultural citizenship', which was first explored by Western scholars. Although the concept is of particular relevance to the eastern part of this world, or to the global South, with its diverse and heterogeneous societies, it has only recently been analysed by scholars both in the West and the non-West. Second, a *policy flow* can be detected: archival research has shown that Indian policymakers have at crucial points in time looked towards the West, and especially towards Europe and European history, to optimize their policy formulations. Third, there is an *institutional flow*, which can be seen as the combination of the first two subcategories of 'flow', the conceptual and the policy flow. Following this approach, political institutions themselves are seen as the outcome of 'flow'. Moreover, 'flow', read against the background of political science, is not seen here as an even and smooth process, but as having an inherent *conflict dimension*.[1] However, there are many open questions which expound the problems of the scholarly analysis of 'flow'. Is flow manufactured or natural? Is 'flow' really flow, or merely a continuation of policies and institutional modelling, or even a misleading term to describe social, cultural, and political universals? Is flow omnipresent or does it occur only at particular points in time and, if so, at which points?

'FLOW': EARLIER EXPLORATIONS INTO THE IDEA

The term 'cultural flow' is an academic neologism, and it was not until fairly recently that scholarly works emerged in the humanities and social sciences which explicitly took up the term (Mitra, 2011b, 2012b; Saurma-Jeltsch and Eisenbeiß, 2010). This, however, does not mean that the basic idea underpinning it has not been dealt with earlier, even though it was less well-pronounced conceptually.

Looking back at the events of the transfer of power from the British to the independent Indian state, E.W.R. Lumby in 1954 described three phases of reaction of Asian peoples to Western expansion. In Lumby's first phase, the traditional order 'hits back blindly at the foreign influences which threaten it, and which are feared all the more because [they are] only vaguely understood' (Lumby, 1954: 9). This is a strong claim, which the author tries to substantiate by citing the examples of the Boxer Rebellion in China, the Indian Mutiny of 1857, and the anti-foreign movement that followed Commodore Perry's minatory opening up of Japan in 1853. The second phase sets in after foreign influences have infected the educated minority of an Asian country with 'western ideas of nationalism and liberal democracy' (Lumby, 1954: 9). This is when the 'new intelligentsia', which is presumably the outcome of this flow of ideas, 'comes into conflict with its overlords on the question of how far and how fast this exotic political philosophy should be applied to its own country'. The third phase which Lumby delineates is marked by the spread of socio-economic phenomena like industrialism and social democracy, and a growing belief among the population of the receiving country that 'if political democracy is to be genuine, it must be accompanied by radical economic changes', thus giving rise to the phenomena of socialism and communism (Lumby, 1954: 9).

The notion that Indian modernity is the result of an encounter with the West is a well-established one. P.C. Joshi (1989) starts his analysis of culture, communication, and social change in India with a discussion of D.P. Mukherji's *Modern Indian Culture* (1947). According to him, 'what is called modern Indian culture was shaped by historical forces and processes, the most important one being the economic, political and cultural impact of the West' (Joshi, 1989: 1). The idea of 'flow' is therefore not new, and has been used to refer to both the process and the outcome of a cultural encounter. Table 2.1 lists the frequently used terminology in this context, along with the thinkers who coined different terms to refer to similar phenomena.

As is apparent from Table 2.1, scholars from various geographical and disciplinary backgrounds have, through the centuries, occupied

Table 2.1 Varieties of Terminology Referring to Processes and Outcomes of Cultural Encounters

Term	Meaning	Thinkers	Time	Academic Discipline
cultural hybrid/ hybridization	heteroglossia (diversity of languages within a single text); polyphony (different voices adopted by novelists)	• Mikhail Bakhtin • Edward Said • Homi K. Bhabha	20th century	Literary Theory
imitation	a form of cultural interaction	• Cicero • Virgil	from classical antiquity onwards	Philosophy Literary Theory
appropriation 'despoiling' (*spolia*) *ré-emploi*	alternative to imitation (cf. the bee metaphor: bees 'take only what is suitable for their work and leave the rest untouched'/the spoils of the Egyptians)	• Seneca the younger • Basil of Cesarea • St. Augustine • Thomas Aquinas • Gregory IX. • Michel de Certeau • Paul Ricoeur	Roman antiquity Middle Ages 20th century	Philosophy Theology
cultural borrowing	'the history of all cultures is the history of cultural borrowing' (Edward Said)	• Henri Estienne • Admantios Korais • Euclides da Cunha • Fernand Braudel • Edward Said	16th century 18th century 20th century	Linguistics History Literary and Cultural Theory

(*Table 2.1 Cont'd*)

Table 2.1 (Cont'd)

Term	Meaning	Thinkers	Time	Academic Discipline
acculturation *assimilation*	a subordinate culture adopts traits from the dominant culture		c. 1880 early 20th century	US Anthropology
transculturation	the Americans in their turn discovered Columbus (Fernando Ortiz)	• Fernando Ortiz	20th century	Sociology
transfer	widely used to refer to different kinds of borrowing		20th century	Economic History History of Technology
cultural *exchange*	any cultural movement asymmetrically goes in two directions	• Aby Warburg	20th century	History
accommodation	started as a political strategy for conversion; now revived to include both partners in an encounter (hybridization); offers more insight on human agency and creativity than the term hybridity does	• Cicero • Gregory the Great • Christian missionaries (e.g., Matteo Ricci)	Roman antiquity Middle Ages 16th century	Theology History of Religion

Term	Description	Authors	Century	Discipline
dialogue/ negotiation	alternative to accommodation view from below as well as from above		20th century 21st century	Cultural Studies
fusion *melting pot*(US) *amalgamation*	fusion of races, traditions, and cultural manifestations	• Karl von Martius • Gilberto Freyre • Melville Herskovits	19th century 20th century	Botany Nuclear Physics Music Cuisine
syncretism	political alliance analysing cultural contact	• Plutarch • Georg Calixtus • G. Pico della Mirandola • Melville Herskovits	Greek antiquity 17th century 19th century	Political Philosophy Theology Anthropology
métissage *interpenetration* *mestizaje*	intermingling of cultures central to definitions of national identity	• Roger Bastide • Vicente Riva Palacio • Leopold Lugones • Ricardo Rojas	19th century 20th century	Sociology of Religion
oicotype *localization* *glocalization*	adaptation to cultural milieu	• Carl Wilhelm von Sydow	20th century	Botany Cultural Studies Architecture

(Table 2.1 Cont'd)

Table 2.1 (*Cont'd*)

Term	Meaning	Thinkers	Time	Academic Discipline
cultural translation	the mechanism by which cultural encounters produce new and hybrid forms	• Bronislaw Malinowski • Godfrey Lienhardt • Thomas Beidelman • Edward Evans-Pritchard • George Steiner	20th century	Anthropology Literary Theory
créolization	• two languages in contact change to become more like each other and so converge to create a third one • creation of a new culture out of the confluence of two or more cultural encounters	• Ulf Hannerz	20th century	Linguistics Anthropology History of Science
acriollarse	adaptation of indigenous products and customs by colonizers	• José Luis Romero	20th century	History
convergence rapprochement	emphasis on the idea of *process*	• Melville Herskovits • Roger Bastide	20th century	Linguistics Cultural/Religious Studies

Source: Adapted by the author from Burke (2009).

themselves with the idea of cultural flow and its implications. The fact that the term 'flow' does not appear in Peter Burke's writing on which this table draws (Burke, 2009) is indicative of the novelty of the concept. Burke's list is thus by no means extensive: other representatives of particularistic theories of change could be added, such as William Isaac Thomas (1863–1947), a sociologist and representative of the strand of thought pertaining to assimilation, who was engaged in the scientific analysis of the process by which immigrants to the US took on the customs, manners, and values of American society (cf. LaPiere, 1965: 29). Other particularistic theories of change can also be listed, for example, *diffusionism*,[2] as represented by the anatomist Grafton Elliot Smith (1871–1937) who, along with his followers, 'tried to trace everything cultural to some particular centre' (LaPiere, 1965: 24). Smith's opponents from the theoretical camp of *parallelism*, such as Leslie White and V. Gordon Childe, who were convinced that originality is a very common characteristic of humankind, and that thus each people had independently developed its own cultural devices (cf. LaPiere, 1965: 24), are worth mentioning here. Burke (2009) also overlooks *cultural acceleration*, a theory put forward by Hornell Hart, who in 1931 claimed that culture accumulates at an accelerative rate through the addition of new inventions towards increasing efficiency (cf. LaPiere, 1965: 32).

Many of these theories of cultural change have been criticized for their 'common hazard ... of applying the scientifically untenable concept of simple cause and effect' (LaPiere, 1965: 23), that is, assuming that change in a society can be traced to one particular source. These approaches have come under attack for being based on selective historical facts to substantiate them[3] (cf. LaPiere, 1965: 15). This might also be a reason why the debate on particular theories, such as diffusion, was abandoned rather early (cf. Katz, 1963: 1). Nevertheless, cultural theorists, social anthropologists, and sociologists are devoting attention to the study of changes that result from the contact of cultures (cf. Katz, 1963: 1). One such strand of research is the one on 'flow', a term which is given preference here over other terminologies because, as will be shown in the course of this chapter, it is a concept which avoids the fallacies of the ideas that predated it.

When considering the terminology, the question inevitably arises whether 'flow' is merely a synonym for 'exchange', with 'cultural flow' being nothing but the more profane-sounding 'cultural exchange'. I would like to argue against this and propose the idea that 'exchange' is but one aspect of 'flow'. Again, taking recourse to more mundane examples proves helpful in making abstract terms concrete. In an exchange process, A is exchanged for B. This exchange can be uneven: if A is considered to be more valuable than B, two or more Bs, depending on their relative value to A, might have to be exchanged for one A. This basic principle holds true for all material commodities. Cultural exchange, however, does not follow this principle, which is why the term itself is misleading. 'Cultural flow' would be more appropriate, because cultural achievements are not always exactly measurable, nor are they always transferable into revenue. 'Exchange' has an economic connotation which 'flow' avoids. Inherent in the concept of 'flow' is the idea of fluidity and mutuality, thus highlighting the fact that a cultural encounter is not a zero-sum game in which one side gains what the other loses—a view which, according to Edward Said, characterized modern thinking about cultural exchange (Said, 1994: 195). 'Flow', therefore, is the word preferred over exchange here, as 'exchange' would suggest a quid pro quo relation between two giving entities that are at the same time also receivers. This, however, is an understanding which the concept of flow, based on a deeper asymmetry, does not entail.

What gives the term 'flow' an additional advantage over other conceptualizations of cultural exchange processes is that, as opposed to 'borrowing', flow encourages the idea of a new cultural element not necessarily only being added to an existing cultural canon, but shaping this canon and getting transformed itself in the process.[4] Flow, however, is not a theoretical cure-all, but has its own difficulties. It does not lend itself to easy conceptualization in terms of a cause and effect structure. Rather, it emphasizes the non-linear, ruptured nature of change in which beginning and end are more difficult to determine. An additional strength of 'flow' is that it can encompass more processes than other concepts, which are really not as strictly separable as Burke's listing might suggest, but which occur in combination with each other. Atal (1977: 464–5) thus rightly argues that 'the arrival of foreign elements—people, ideas, technology—are first accommodated and then in due course of time get assimilated in the cultural fabric of the society ... also, ... some new structural elements may be deliberately created, epigenetically, and hence a new entity might come into being.' All these ideas can be conceptually pulled together under the umbrella concept of flow, which makes it more universally applicable but also fuzzy, which is why 'flow' needs to be divided into smaller units of analysis such as conceptual and policy flow, as mentioned earlier.

CITIZENSHIP AS CONCEPTUAL FLOW

Citizenship is a prime example of conceptual flow. Originating in the minds of the thinkers of ancient Greece, the concept travelled beyond the boundaries of the Greek polis to the Roman Republic, to which the linguistic roots of the present-day term can be traced: the modern 'citizen' etymologically—and partly also conceptually—evolved out of the ancient *civis*. However, the rights and duties paradigm entailed in the concept of citizenship in Athens and Rome degenerated after the days of the early European republics, and went dormant during the period of the autocratic rules that succeeded them, until philosophers of the Enlightenment paved the way for a revival of the idea, and that too in an improved form. As has been noted in the previous chapter, John Locke (1632–1704), Charles de Montesquieu (1689–1755), and also Immanuel Kant (1724–1804) all in their own ways contributed to a further development of citizenship theory—Locke and Montesquieu by means of their liberal thought and by stressing the importance of the division of powers, and Kant by envisioning a 'world citizenship', a notion that was much later taken up by Jürgen Habermas[5] against the background of the idea of the European nation-state.[6] As will be shown in detail in Chapter three, it was the Enlightenment philosophy of Locke, Kant, and especially Rousseau which paved the ground for the events of 1789 and gave birth to the *citoyen* (and the *citoyennne*, since for the first time citizenship rights were also fully extended to women), the citizen, in the streets of Paris.[7] However, despite the vigour with which thoughts translated into political action, it took another 250 years before citizenship was taken up as a subject worthy to be considered in more theoretical detail.

Discussions on citizenship again surfaced in the second half of the twentieth century, and when they came up, they did so mostly in the wake of drastic events. The first modern, twentieth-century scholarly analysis of citizenship was English sociologist T.H. Marshall's *Citizenship and Social Class*, published in 1949. His paradigm, which formed the basis of all citizenship theories thereafter, was developed after the end of World War II and at the beginning of the Cold War—a time when many states were either reshaped, such as Germany and India, or were newly emerging, such as Israel and Pakistan. In his seminal work, Marshall presents a triadic model of citizenship. Arguing that the evolution of citizenship has been in progress for about 250 years—ostensibly taking 1789 as the starting point—he proposes to divide the historical development of citizenship into three stages. Marshall distinguishes between civil, political, and social citizenship, constituting the 'modern drive towards social equality' as the latest phase (Marshall, 1965: 78). He ascribes the three different sets of rights to three different centuries—civil (freedom of speech, thought, and faith) to the eighteenth, political (active and passive suffrage) to the nineteenth, and social rights (like welfare and economic security) to the twentieth century. It is a sequential model, with the attainment of social rights completing the sequence. Marshall's modern citizen is thus the sum of three historical parts. In other words, the process of becoming a citizen covers three stages; the product, the citizen, is therefore a three-dimensional concept.

Twentieth-century citizenship theory came in three 'waves', in which Marshall's work marks the first wave, which set in when Europe's fascist regimes fell and the old nation-states reached a turning point. Marshall's contribution to a conceptual deepening of citizenship, however, received only limited attention at the time of its publication. In 1978, almost thirty years after Marshall's *Citizenship and Social Class*, Herman van Gunsteren unambiguously stated that 'the concept of citizenship has gone out of fashion' (1988: 352). The second 'wave' of citizenship theory came only after a long pause, in the early 1990s when the Cold War had ended and people again had to think about issues of belonging and citizenship rights in the new world order that had emerged after the collapse of the Soviet Union. Together with new trends, like increasing voter apathy and long-term welfare dependency in the US, the stresses created by an increasingly multicultural and multiracial population in Western Europe, the backlash against the welfare state in Margaret Thatcher's Britain, the failure of environmental policies which rely on voluntary citizen cooperation, and the resurgence of nationalist movements in Eastern Europe, came a renewed interest in citizenship studies (cf. Isin and Turner, 2002). Citizenship studies first emerged as an incipient field in the decade following the collapse of the USSR.

In the third phase of citizenship theory, which came with increasing globalization, a process set in that, unlike in the first two phases, did not bring a new arrangement of nation-states. Instead, boundaries between the states became more fuzzy, and with this also emerged new claims for inclusion and belonging; the classic form of the nation-state began to disintegrate. Citizens were increasingly beginning to look beyond the nation-state, becoming part of transnational corporations, non-governmental organizations, and worldwide social movements. In addition, people who migrated to other countries did not want to deny their cultural origins. Mitra gives a very precise account of these problems of citizenship at the beginning of the twenty-first century, a time when

> the world-wide mobility of ideas and people—both legal and clandestine—has emerged as a challenge to political order in stable, liberal democracies where immigrants, often with a different religious background than that of the mainstream, demand both the legal right to citizenship at par with the natives, *and* the recognition of their ethnic right to difference in the public sphere. In changing societies, many of which adopted the norm of territorial citizenship at independence, trans-national networks and cultural flows have emerged as challenges to the norm of territorial citizenship, sometimes with violent consequences (Mitra, 2008a: 363).

The academic debate has responded to these new challenges by transcending Marshall's original notion of citizenship and its connection with the territorial state, a process that resulted in the proliferation of 'new citizenships', such as sexual citizenship, ecological citizenship, cosmopolitan citizenship, economic citizenship, health citizenship, liberal citizenship, republican citizenship, and cultural and multicultural citizenship, to name only the most widely discussed types.[8] With this evolution of citizenship theory, former theoretical approaches have been called into question. In 1994, Nancy Fraser and Linda Gordon criticized Marshall's three-dimensional model for 'fitting the experience of white working men only; a minority of the population'[9] (Fraser and Gordon, 1994: 93). Increasingly, issues of identity and belonging have been seen as essential components of the concept of citizenship. This conceptual stretch has also resulted in policy recommendations informed by a flow of concepts. As Western societies grow more heterogeneous, cultural pluralists argue that citizenship must take into account the new differences, since common rights of citizenship cannot accommodate the special needs of minority groups. These groups can only be integrated into the common culture, the argument of the cultural pluralists goes, if a 'differentiated citizenship' regime is adopted (Young, 1989). This means that members of certain groups would be incorporated into the political community not only as individuals but also as members of a community, and their rights would depend, in part, on their group identity. This process of differentiated citizenship, which Kymlicka and Norman (1994: 370) refer to as 'a radical development in citizenship theory', could be witnessed in Great Britain in 2008, when the Archbishop of Canterbury suggested an implementation of sharia law alongside British common law for the country's Muslim population. The huge uproar this suggestion caused in the media as well as among leading politicians, and the debate that followed, show that citizenship has, at least in Western societies, reached a turning point.[10] The extent to which these new ideas might have been informed by societies where group-differentiated citizenship exists, such as India, is a matter of further investigation. What this case shows, however, is that due to new influences in an increasingly globalized world, the original concepts of citizenship are being developed further and are adapting to the requirements of the twenty-first century.

CULTURAL CITIZENSHIP AS THE PRODUCT OF CONCEPTUAL FLOW

One of the forms which this development has taken is the formation of the concept of 'cultural citizenship', which was developed in the West and has for a long time been used only in academic debates related to that part of the world. An attempt to trace the origin of the concept reveals that cultural citizenship has been heavily employed in the US academic discourse; it has played a role in debates on educational democracy (Rosaldo, 1994a), feminist audience studies (Hermes, 2000), cosmopolitan art (Chaney, 2002), and even on scrapbooking (Hof, 2006). In these discussions, cultural citizenship is used to theorize the increasing diversity in the Western nation-state due to immigration and changing societal structures. In this context, new questions are being raised about belonging and identity, more precisely the provision of ideological space for the minorities by the majority, thus emphasizing the discursive character of the nation.

In the discussion on cultural citizenship, identity is seen in relation to culture and institutions, as in Renato Rosaldo's study of the American campus 'culture wars'.[11] Defining 'cultural citizenship' as the 'right to be different and to belong in a participatory democratic sense' (Rosaldo, 1994a: 402), Rosaldo argues that the notion of belonging means full membership in a group and the ability to influence one's destiny by having a significant voice in basic decisions. Criticizing the alleged ethnocentricity of the humanities, he remarks that the required reading list for the 'Western culture course' at Stanford University included no books written by non-white authors, nor any by female authors. Against the background of the much-contested issue of educational policy, the question is raised whether the institution can change in ways which are responsive to its new members; how it should change; and how the negotiations for change would work. For Rosaldo, the answer to these difficult questions lies in 'cultural citizenship', which he sees as a basis for 'cultural decolonization by recognizing the value of cultural life' (Rosaldo, 1994a: 410).

This shows that the concept of cultural citizenship is both a product of cultural flow, in the sense that it takes into account changed conditions in the ethnic, religious, linguistic, and social composition of nation-states, and a conceptual tool for further debate on the alternate situation, as well as a trigger of institutional change. As the concept is linked with institutions, conceptual and institutional change can be seen as interconnected. Related to this observation is the idea that the flow of concepts is a prerequisite for the change of institutions, which will be discussed in greater detail in the following section of this chapter.

The extent to which cultural citizenship has been informed by an intellectual dialogue between Asia and Europe is debatable, but it is beyond doubt that Western scholars have looked at Asia and vice versa. Still, very few Asian scholars have dealt with cultural citizenship in detail, and when they have done so, their work has been informed by Western definitions.[12] Harindranath (2009), for example, draws on Murdock's (1999) examination of public discourse and cultural citizenship, without adding many conceptual-theoretical specificities of Asian societies and polities. The reasons for this lack of an Asian contribution, and even more so of a specifically Indian contribution, might be grounded in the experience India has had with linking culture and citizenship too closely. The past—both the more distant as well as the more recent—has shown that a nexus between culture and citizenship can be a potential trigger for communal violence. In both theory (V.D. Savarkar) and practice (Ayodhya 1992 and Godhra 2002), India has experienced the effects of a very particular understanding of cultural citizenship, leaning more towards political action than political theory, being more dangerous than fruitful.[13]

Connecting citizenship with culture makes for a contentious concept, since the political actors who draw such a connection are predominantly located on the right side of the political spectrum. Thus, 'cultural citizenship' tends to be regarded as the politically orchestrated dominance of one group over others. The Indian psychoanalyst Sudhir Kakar encapsulates this problematic in his observation that 'the Indian analyst [is] also always a child of his culture' (Kakar, 1990: 86). Just as there are some subjects which, as Kakar shows, are sacrosanct (see the discussion in Chapter four), other areas seem to be 'untouchable', leaving both equally ill-discussed and under-researched. 'Western' literature on the subject, however, does not provide a very different picture. What deserves attention though is that in the Western discourse, some passing references to the Asian scenario can be found. Toby Miller (2007), in his study which otherwise focuses on the connections between the media and citizenship in the US, uses the example of India's CBFC to explore the idea of 'citizen censorship' and the 'neoliberal project of empowerment' (Miller, 2007: 31).

Thus, citizenship, cultural citizenship, and censorship are closely connected, as all three are determining variables in the nation-building process, and all three are outcomes of conceptual flow. Like citizenship, the term 'censorship' has its etymological roots in Latin, in this case in the word *censere*, to assess, which refers to the activities of the censor in Roman antiquity. Established in 443 BCE, the censor's task was to administer the census as well as supervise and regulate the moral conduct of citizens, that is, classify them numerically, socially, and morally (Bhowmik, 2009: 4). Censorship is universal in the sense that it has existed across time and space. In fact, it appears to come close to what can be labelled a political universalism. State and non-state actors in polities across the historical and political spectrum have made use of censorship as a tool to guide and influence the masses and exert either dominance or render support, that is, to either suppress or protect. Sue Curry Jansen (1991), for example, maintains that 'in all societies the powerful invoke censorship to create, secure and maintain their control over the power to name. This constitutive or existential censorship is a feature of all enduring human communities—even those communities which offer legislative guarantees of press freedom' (Jansen, 1991: 8). 'Specific canons of censorship (*regulative censorships*)', she claims, 'vary in time, space and severity.... Rules and conventions of censorship do change. But censorship remains a rule-embedded phenomenon. No revolutionary compact in human history—not even the scientific revolution of the seventeenth and eighteenth centuries—has ever abolished constitutive censorship' (Jansen, 1991: 8). With regard to the South Asian context, there is indeed a continuation of censorship policies: Kaur and Mazzarella (2009: 4) rightly ask to what extent 'contemporary discourses, practices, and conditions of censorship echo or reconfigure those of the colonial period'. Using Jansen's assumption that censorship is universal, that it has a static core,[14] but takes various forms as a starting point, the following section looks more closely into the mechanisms at work in the formulation of censorship policies, and tries to determine the extent of flow in that context. An investigation of policies of censorship and media regulation in India serves to highlight processes of flow between geographical spaces as well as between historical periods.

FLOW OF POLICIES: THE ROLE OF STRUCTURE AND AGENCY

'"No kissing!" said the Argentinian , genuinely shocked. "Then how do you ... well, what I mean is, what do you do.... That is, does it mean...." He gave it up. "No kissing!" he said again. "Incredible!"' This quote from an article that was published in the Indian daily the *Statesman* on 2 November 1961 captures the surprised reaction of a certain Mr Jacobson, Argentinian delegate to India, on learning about decency regulations in Indian films. Interestingly, the reporting in the article, entitled 'Care of the Child at Adult's Cost: U.S. Delegate's view on Film Censorship in India', laid the foundation for a flow of policies. The article opens by quoting the vice-president of the Motion Films Export Association of America, Irving Maas: 'We think the censorship in India is rather extreme, ... and seems designed to protect the interests of the child at the expense of the adult'. It uses the quote as a trigger to investigate the policies of film censorship in the US, West Germany, Romania, and Argentina. The article finds that none of these countries, not even then socialist Romania, had explicit censorship laws, and that the film industry there was self-regulating.

A day after the article was published, on 3 November 1961, an official in the Film Section of the MIB issued a directive stating that 'I would suggest that we should obtain full particulars about censorship arrangements in some of the countries of which mention has been made in this report of the *Statesman*. Actually, the position may not be quite as unfavourable as the newspapers in India make out to be.'[15] The Research and Reference Division of the ministry was then ordered to collect information about censorship systems in general as well as detailed instructions to censors in the major film-producing countries,[16] and India's neighbouring countries.[17] Information on most of these countries' censorship policies had already been collected in 1957, with the exception of the Federal Republic of Germany on which information was collected in July 1959 by the chairman of the Central Board of Film Censors.

The flow of information from abroad to the MIB was, however, slow. On 7 February 1964, a note was inserted into the official file observing that the suggestion to obtain particulars about censorship arrangements in selected countries had been made in November 1961. The Ministry of External Affairs was requested to collect the information from the Indian missions in ten different countries on the basis of a questionnaire prepared in consultation with the CBFC and the Research and Reference Division. This questionnaire was then sent to missions in ten countries on 3 April 1963, but the MIB received information only from the High Commission in the United Kingdom on 17 April 1963, and from the Embassy in the US on 20 June 1963.[18]

This example illustrates three points which are crucial for an understanding of 'flow'. Firstly, flow needs a *trigger*, a source from which further developments can spring, like the newspaper article which induced Indian policymakers to look beyond the geographical boundaries of India in order to obtain a justification for their policies. Flow is thus not an automatism, it requires *agency*. Secondly, flow requires a *structure*. Here, the initial analogy with the natural flow of liquids again proves valid. If flow should not be an end in itself, but rather a means to an end, a structure which furthers flow in a productive way is needed. If a river is meant to be effectively used for shipping, it has to be straightened and its riverbed artificially deepened. Similarly, to effectively administer a flow of policies, instruments of measurement have to be designed. In the above example, this was done with the help of a detailed questionnaire sent to the Indian diplomatic representatives in the countries on whose censorship policies information was to be gained. While the questionnaire listed rather general questions relating to the governing principles applicable to the censorship of films, such as whether there was any censorship of films at all in the concerned country, whether it was voluntary or statutory, and whether the authorities ever encountered any difficulties in the effective application of their principles, it also contained the request to provide a 'brief history of film censorship in your country since its inception, with special reference to the working of the present organisation/authority'.[19] 'Flow' is thus not only *horizontal*, but also *vertical*, that is, it does not only move from one geographical point to the other, but it permeates various historical periods and layers of time. Historical considerations are present at every stage of the decision-making process, and detecting historical influence is necessary to conceptualize the degree to which geographical and time spaces are entangled (see Figure 2.1).

As Figure 2.1 illustrates, flows, like the development which they trigger, are not linear and additive, but uneven and asymmetrical. Secondly, flow is not mono-directional; whatever flows, flows in various—albeit not random—directions (because of it being monitored by agents). For reasons of simplicity, only two geographical entities are given in the model, but as the above example shows, Indian policymakers encouraged flow from various geographical locations, including North and South America. However, the circular arrows

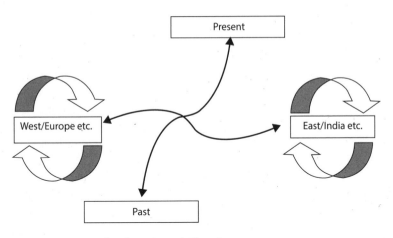

Figure 2.1   Vertical and Horizontal 'Flows'
Source: Prepared by the author.

indicate that flow can also occur within one geographical area—a fact which will be discussed in more detail later. The unevenness of flow also signifies the conflict dimension of the process alluded to earlier in this chapter. With regard to India, V.K.R.V. Rao (1977) emphasizes the multi-directionality of flow and the conflict underpinning it, in the sense that action creates reaction, and movement gives rise to counter-movement. Rao notes that

> [s]ocial change in India is not all in one direction. Against the growth of nationalism we also see the simultaneous growth of regionalism and linguism that seem to be drawing upon even deeper roots in the Indian soil and ethos.... Against the westernising influence of English we see the Indianising influence of Hindi. Against the move for industrialisation we see a conflicting trend of ruralisation and its idealisation. Against secularisation, we see renewed life emerging in Hindu and Muslim communal organizations (1977: 32).

As far as the dimension of time is concerned, Figure 2.1 takes up the point made by the Marxist historian Romila Thapar that not only does the past shape the present, the present also influences the past. 'Historical explanation', Thapar claims, 'creates an awareness of how the past impinges on the present, as well as the reverse' (2002: xix). Similarly, Edward Said, drawing on T.S. Eliot, argues that past and present inform each other and that 'how we formulate or represent the past shapes our understanding and views of the present'[20] (1994: 4). The importance of time in an analysis of change is also stressed by cultural anthropologists and social scientists in their research on one of the categories discussed earlier, namely cultural borrowing, with regard to which they state that 'most of the elements of many societies, and certainly many of the elements of all modern societies, have been derived in this fashion from the cultures of other times and places' (LaPiere, 1965: 105). Therefore, historical understanding and the knowledge of processes is one of the essential preconditions of policy flow, and hence historical analysis has to be given a prominent place in any work on cultural and conceptual flow. As Atal (1977: 464) points out, 'structural changes in particular, taking place over a period of time, can be understood only when the historical process is taken into account'. In order to provide historical evidence of flow, archival research has been undertaken and has proved to be a helpful method to research the workings of this particular phenomenon. It can, for example, help to determine the point in time when flow occurs. Very basically speaking, flow of policies occurs when there is a need for it.[21] Depending on the political system under consideration, the reasons for such a need differ. While in autocratic regimes, need is determined by the government, for example to substantiate its rule, in democratic settings, need for policy change is not exclusively but more frequently brought onto the political agenda in reaction to demands from within society.[22] To provide an example of the former, at the outbreak of the First World War, the colonial powers in India exchanged information about effective censorship measures. In a document of the Foreign and Political Department of the Government of India, dated 8 August 1914, the French military authorities inquired of the British about censorship restrictions in the areas under their administration. R.E. Holland noted that 'Colonel Malleson wishes us to ask the Local Governments concerned to arrange that censorship restrictions similar to those in British India may, if possible, be brought into force in French possession.' The answer from the secretary to the Government of India in the Foreign and Political Department came promptly by telegram to the Madras Government on the same day:

> [W]ill you kindly inform the French Governor-General at Pondicherry that, in order to prevent information regarding military movements from leaking out, strict censorship has been established in British India and that,

with a view to the suppression of any organizations that may be found to exist in French territory for dissemination of news, Government of India would be grateful for the assistance and co-operation of the French authorities in each settlement.[23]

A flow of policies and specific techniques has occurred in this case in order to improve governance. Theoretically speaking, this particular incident of 'flow', like the others which will be analysed below, can be explained by sociological theories of change. Equilibrium theory, stemming from functionalism,[24] claims that 'changes in social practices, ideas, and techniques are viewed as efforts to resolve antecedent disequilibriums and are presumed to lead inevitably and directly to greater functional equilibrium' (LaPiere, 1965: 73). Change, for which flow is an essential precondition, thus usually occurs when disequilibria have arisen. This theoretical consideration is crucial for understanding why flow takes place, and is further substantiated by the following findings.

In a meeting of the various media units of the MIB on 13 December 1961, publicity strategies to promote 'emotional unity and national integration' were discussed. A memorandum signed by P.C. Chatterji, the director of programmes, on behalf of the director general, was sent to the heads of all stations of AIR, the Indian public service broadcaster, with a copy to all programme branches. The memorandum shows that the ministry's publicity campaign was carefully designed, attributing importance to what can be labelled 'flow'. It issued instructions as to a number of themes, which 'may be kept particularly in mind in planning suitable programmes'.[25] The first on this list was labelled 'Lessons of History'. The authors of the memorandum explicitly draw on European history as a deterrent example to illustrate the consequences of fragmentation:

> European History shows, that the multiplicity of State[s] based on languages has made that part of the world a centre of instability from where most World Wars have emanated. There is a school of thought in Europe which still thinks in terms of a single federation. Fragmentation of the country, therefore, will make India unstable and may lead to chaos which prevailed here in the 18th Century.[26]

Indian policymakers here were looking selectively into the history of the European continent and emphasized a particular aspect thereof in order to justify their position, which again underlines the aforementioned importance of *agency* for cultural flow. Point four of the memorandum lists the methods chosen to present the topic of 'Unity and Integrity' of the country. While the authorities strongly rely on electronic audio media to spread their messages, for example through radio plays, slogans, and inserts in the midst of film songs as well as school broadcasting, older forms of communication are also considered for the dissemination of messages. One of the methods listed is the recourse to 'tales and stories', since, as stated in the policy document, 'story-telling has been an old method of propaganda in Indian tradition. It may be possible to put up some programmes of this kind on these subjects.'[27] This particular strategy is indicative of the vertical dimension of flow. Flow is not only exchange between representatives of different geographical areas, but also by residents of one given location; that is, flow is not only *inter-area*, but also *intra-area*[28] (see Figure 2.1).

LOCATING FLOW IN THE SOCIAL SYSTEM: MICRO- AND MACRO-LEVEL FLOWS

Another question that arises in the course of the discussion of flow is on which level it occurs. The examples given so far suggest that it is essentially a top-down mechanism in which decisions to enable flow are taken by political elites. This process is then translated into concrete policies which have an effect on the larger population of the political entity into which the new information 'flows'. This view is, for example, proposed by the political philosopher Charles Taylor, who, even though he is 'reluctant to speculate on the causal agencies of cultural change ... has to employ some sort of explanatory model' (Smith, 2002: 224), and thus regards cultural transitions as driven by the activities of elites. The picture he gives is one of 'conceptual, ideational and broadly speaking "poetic" innovations seeping through culture from top to bottom' (Smith, 2002: 224–5).

This, however, is only partly correct, and criticisms of Taylor's view have been voiced.[29] Flow can indeed be triggered on both the micro- and the macro-level. The term *micro-level flows* is used here to refer to the exchange between individuals. These could be, for example, colonizers, explorers, travellers, migrant workers, and artists entering a country from abroad, or moving within one geographical space.[30] *Macro-level flows* on the other hand are those that occur not on an individual level but on a state- or governmental level. These two levels are closely linked and subject to frequent mutual influence. Obviously, decisions taken at a high level translate into tasks which are assigned to individuals. Colonial troops are a case in point here: they are state-ordered, but might also encourage flow on a more individual basis, for example through personal relationships with colonial subjects. However, macro-level flow does not necessarily always have a trickle-down effect. E.W.R. Lumby, in describing the second phase of indigenous Asian reaction to Western expansion, discussed at the outset of this chapter, emphasizes that the educated minority that takes on new ideas originating in the West—although it may claim to speak for the nation as a whole—might concentrate on 'political objectives which may be expected to bring benefit mainly to its own class', thus leaving the masses unaffected (Lumby, 1954: 9). Flow on the macro level, in fact on both levels, can therefore be only partial: it can remain restricted to one level without having a further outreach. In most cases, however, examples show that the boundaries between the micro and the macro level are fuzzy, and hence permeable. Impact is not only a top-down process, and flows on the micro level also affect the macro level, as the following case reveals.

In 1970, the Film Censor Branch of the MIB published a report on censorship, the result of the aforementioned controversy. Chapter 3.1 of the report deals with the censorship regulations in 'some of the more important countries of the world'.[31] In stating that 'the committee have felt that they cannot be oblivious of what is happening around us, and the cultural trends and moral attitudes observable in countries with which we have constant communication and cultural exchanges, demand our particular attention',[32] the report testifies to the policymakers' attention to a changing cultural environment.

Their attention towards those changes was inspired by developments at the micro level: as noted in report, 'artists, musicians, actors, dancers, writers go abroad with cultural missions, and cultural groups of a similar nature from those countries visit us and tell us what is happening there.' Flow is accelerated by the movement of people and by direct communication. As the authors of the report are well aware, 'with the rapid increase in the speed of communications, the world is becoming smaller and cultural barriers are being notched and perforated.'[33] This means not only that flow of policies is encouraged and facilitated in an age of sophisticated means of communication and easily accessible media with immediate global outreach, but also that such flows might happen more frequently. Policy flows, it appears, are themselves the outcome of other flows. Like the newspaper article that triggered a flow of censorship policy, movements of international mass appeal can strongly impact the politics of a country.

The report on censorship is justified by the feeling that there is a 'pressing demand for greater freedom of thought and expression consequent upon the implementation of our democratic ideals, and the realization that we have a right to express ourselves and to think freely'.[34] The committee derives this feeling largely from the liberal tendencies prevalent among one particular section of Indian society, the country's youth. The student agitations, which India witnessed at the time when the report was compiled, were 'to a large extent inspired by what is happening in Europe and America'.[35] Therefore, the report of the Film Censor Branch focuses specifically on the extent of foreign influence and inquires into censorship policies and the closely related rights to freedom of expression in various countries, and recourse to history is taken again. Chapter 3.14 of the report deals with the freedom of expression in France under the declaration of 1789, which was confirmed by the Constitution of 1946. Other examples cited are the policies in the US, especially with regard to the Supreme Court's role in defending the freedom of speech and expression, the British Board of Film Censors, which was the role model for the Indian Central Board of Film Censors, and other European and South American countries. On the basis of these case study materials, the report arrives at the conclusion that

> norms and modes of film censorship vary a great deal. While in most countries of the world, censorship is exercised by an official body nominated by the Government, in the United States of America, the United Kingdom and Japan, the censors are non-officials appointed by the film industry. In Belgium and Uruguay there is no censorship of films at all.[36]

Taking into consideration the global developments and their effects on India, it is stated in the report that it is these liberal tendencies which have provoked a demand for a relaxation of the strict censorship rules in India, and the protection of children apart, a large section of intelligent and cultured persons in India are in favour of completely breaking away from the shackles of the present system of censorship and basing censorship on a much more liberal and balanced ideology.[37]

It would be wrong to assume, however, that flow is always sought after and welcomed enthusiastically as in the case of the Film Censor Branch of the MIB. As has been pointed out, flow of policies is a process which is set in motion consciously, and which is dependent on a number of factors. Based on this assumption, one can further distinguish between *conditional* and *unconditional* flow—two categories which do not function independently, but are closely linked to micro-level and macro-level flows.

Unconditional flow would mostly be witnessed on the micro level. As the term suggests, it implies an acceptance of new ideas and trends without conditions, the basis for which is a general openness on the part of the sender of the impulse or stimulus and its receiver. *Conditional flow*, on the other hand, is another way to characterize the macro-level flow. Allowing new policies into an institutional set-up is conditional on the need for policy modification, the willingness of those who govern, and, in democratic set-ups, of those who are governed. Conditional flow thus occurs only when those who trigger it see added value in it.

Another preliminary requisite for flow to occur on the macro level—in a democratic polity—is the need for change among the population. In the example at hand, the change in policy brought about by the resentment of members of the society to existing censorship regulations was dependent on flow. Whether there is a larger societal need for flow, that is, for the adaptation of policies following the examples of other states, was tested by the Indian government through survey research. Chapter five of the Film Censor Branch's report is devoted to the audience reaction to the existing films. The Indian Institute of Mass Communication (IIMC), a research and training body under the auspices of the MIB, was ordered to carry out a survey on 'changing film tastes and audience reaction to present-day films, both Indian and foreign'.[38] In the framework of this survey, research was carried out on: (*a*) film viewing habits; (*b*) purpose and motivation in seeing films; (*c*) opinion about Indian films; (*d*) reaction to romance and love in films; and (*e*) knowledge of and opinion about film censorship in India. The results obtained showed that many test subjects held the view that one of the objects of films should be to educate and promote social, cultural, and ethical values in society. With regard to the decency regulations addressed in the newspaper article cited earlier, the survey found that

> sixty percent of adults feel that since kissing and embracing are not per-
> mitted by Indian customs, these should not be permitted on the screen.
> Of the young people, the majority held the opposite view. Fifty-two per-
> cent of the girls questioned do not object to kissing and embracing being
> shown on the cinema screen, while only 35 percent of the boys hold this
> view.[39]

The result of this research process that revealed dissatisfaction among youth about the rigid moral codes that prevailed was not an entirely altered policy towards decency regulations in Indian feature films; but over time, standards became less rigid. The statistical research that the government had commissioned was meant to prevent what functionalist theory has labelled 'dysfunctional changes', that is, changes which are undesirable in the sense that they do not lead to a functional equilibrium. Since all change is 'experimental in the sense that ... its functional consequences are not predictable, ... it is only through empirical experience with the new that its functional effec-tiveness can be determined' (LaPiere, 1965: 75).

This shows that flow of information is encouraged by a stimulus,[40] which can, for example, be another incoming flow. The late 1960s student protests in Europe (particularly in France and Germany), and in the US against the war in Vietnam and the establishment in general, also mutually influenced one another, and finally brought about policy action. Macro-level flow, however, is not a smooth or spontaneous process; it is monitored, and therefore can be obstructed by political decision-makers and administrators.

Whereas Figure 2.1 illustrated flows in a general way as occurring between and within historical and geographical areas, Figure 2.2 provides a more detailed look at flow at the macro level of the nation-state. In combination, Figures 2.1 and 2.2 thus give a holistic picture

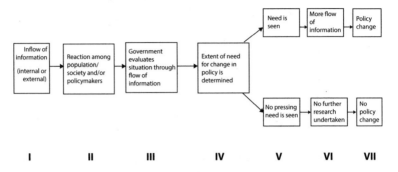

Figure 2.2 Policy Flow at the Macro Level
Source: Prepared by the author.

of flow, indicating the policy flow between as well as within states. Both models are also of trans-historical significance, and are applicable to different historical contexts. Figure 2.2 shows that 'flow' is present at every stage of the model. Flow, however, is not the end, but rather the means to change. The model calls into question LaPiere's point that social change is 'not directly produced by the society so changed' (1965: 39), as flow can be triggered from outside as well as from inside the social system; flow can be *internal* as well as *external*. It is therefore more in line with the idea that 'social change can be the result of the action of endogenous or exogenous factors,[41] or a combination of both' (V.K.R.V. Rao, 1977: 23).

What the model also shows is that flows are triggered or caused by other flows, but nonetheless every flow has a starting point. Figure 2.2 again emphasizes the relevance of *agency* and *advocacy*, thus stressing that flow is not an unconscious process. On the contrary, as LaPiere points out, perception of the advantage of a foreign element over a native one[42] is 'by no means automatic' and does not lead directly to this element flowing from one social system to another. Instead, 'the foreign element ... must be advocated, if converts to it are to be secured and it is to become incorporated into the social system' (LaPiere, 1965: 106). Similarly, V.K.R.V. Rao holds that 'change may be triggered off on the plane of ideas propagated by a charismatic personality' (1977: 23); Atal (1977), drawing on Marriott (1961), underlines the importance of cultural specialists acting as 'hinge groups' or 'cultural brokers' that communicate between different cultural levels, thus ensuring cultural stratification.[43] Also, the model emphasizes the fact that 'an innovation cannot be incorporated into the social system until it has been developed through *empirical experience* into a functionally effective part' (LaPiere, 1965: 142; emphasis added).

The other crucial point which one can harvest from Figure 2.2 concerns the relation between information gathering and flow. Information (as impulse) is received in stage I, and is evaluated by policymakers in stage II on the basis of the reaction that this new impulse has triggered among the population and/or the policymakers themselves. Depending on the policy area to which the new information stimulus relates, those responsible in the institutions then evaluate the need for a change in policy, possibly on the basis of additional information that is gathered (stages III and IV), as was the case in the opinion survey on film censorship that the MIB commissioned. Depending on whether this evaluation is positive or negative, further action will or will not be taken (stage V). This can involve yet more collection of information (stage VI), with the possibility of this also leading to further stimulus. A change in policy relating to the initial impulse received marks the end of this process (stage VII).[44]

Availability of information is also an element in a model representing different stages of the diffusion process in individual decision-making. This is an element that has been introduced in rural sociological research, the discipline that alongside anthropology has most accurately studied the ways in which social systems incorporate changes which originate 'outside' the system (Katz, 1963: 7–9). In this model, mass media bring the earliest information, thereby constituting the 'awareness stage'. At the 'interest' stage, a variety of sources are used to obtain further information. At the 'evaluation' stage—when the potential adopter is considering the applicability of an innovation for himself or herself—his/her fellows constitute the most important source of influence. Media and commercial sources thus bring first news of an innovation, but colleagues, friends, and trusted professional sources are required to legitimize decisions— a process which is described as a 'two-step flow of communication' (Katz, 1963: 9).[45]

Models in the social sciences are usually aimed at generalization. The question thus is to what extent this model is generalizable. With regard to the uprisings that occurred in the Middle East and North Africa in the first half of 2011, commonly referred to as the 'Arab Spring', one could ask how far the above model is applicable. The events had a clear starting point: the self-immolation of the Tunisian citizen Mohammed Bouazizi, news of which spread immediately (stage I) and triggered a revolution nurtured by long-suppressed anger and dissatisfaction with the political leadership, resulting in the resignation of Tunisian autocrat Ben Ali from the presidency (stage II). As information 'flowed' to the states of Egypt and Libya, similar processes took place: citizens took to the streets to express their deep-seated dissatisfaction and to bring about a policy change. The governments in the two states evaluated the situation based on the primary and secondary information they could obtain (stage III) and determined the extent to which a change in policies was needed (stage IV). They decided on either one of the options in stage V. While Egypt changed not only its policies but the entire regime, Libyan policymakers did not see the need for a flow of policies and stagnated, with the result of a civil war (stages IV and V). While this example elevates the model to a more general level, it also raises further questions about the terminology of 'flow' which lie beyond the scope of this chapter. Against the background of the example of the events in North Africa, one is tempted to ask whether 'flow' is coterminous with a 'chain reaction', or with what US policymakers in the 1960s and 1970s referred to as the 'domino theory', according to which ideology and state forms spread quickly from one country to another. Future research will have to shed more light on the question of whether flow is general or particular, that is, universal or context-dependent, and, following from that, whether a generally applicable model of flow is at all possible.

FLOW OF INSTITUTIONS AND CULTURE: A DEEP ENTANGLEMENT

Complementing conceptual and policy flow, the third broad category, the flow of institutions, can take two basic forms: either the institution itself transgresses its geographical or temporal boundaries, or the institution constitutes an outcome of flow. With regard to the former, examples such as India's CBFC can be mentioned, which was established in 1951 as the Central Board of Film Censorship. The body was a continuation of the provincial Boards of Film Censorship which were set up under British colonial rule, just like the Indian Cinematograph Act of 1952 that originated from its colonial predecessor of 1918, which remained in force until 1952. Even though it is claimed that pre-independence censorship belongs to an independent discourse that should be approached separately from the post-independence phenomenon (Bhowmik, 2009: ix), there are obvious continuities between the two periods as far as institutions are concerned. While this is an early example, there are also more recent cases of media institutions having travelled from the West to India. When asked in a personal interview about the role of community media in India, Hemant Joshi, a senior faculty member of the IIMC, stated that the idea of community media—newspapers, television, and radio stations with limited outreach catering to specific audiences and conceptualized as an alternative to the mass media—came from the United States.[46] While he emphasized the importance of a critical evaluation of new trends, since 'lots of evils come to us in the name of the West', he also points to the importance of a flow of information and the adjustment of it to the circumstances of the receiving society: 'as Gandhiji[47] used to say, we should keep our windows open so that the fresh air comes [in]. We are not scared, we are not afraid of ideas coming wherever they're coming [from] and we should always try to find how they will be useful for us.'[48]

There is, however, no one-to-one adaptation of institutions of different times and political regimes to other settings, even though some observers like Yogesh Atal claim that after having attained freedom, some Indian leaders, faced with the task of restructuring the system, took recourse to history to copy 'a blueprint from some earlier pattern' (Atal, 1977: 464). However, the most general point to be made here is that institutions are always subject to change; they are adapted to changed settings and altered circumstances. In this vein, the economic historian Douglass North theorizes institutional change based on economic models. He describes institutional change—as opposed to an institutional equilibrium[49]—as a change in relative prices leading one, or both parties to political or economic exchange, and to the perception that either or both could do better with an altered agreement or contract (North, 1990: 86). Cultural change is also discussed by North, but not with the same precision, which is also owed to his economic understanding of institutions and institutional change, not easily transferable to the realm of culture as it is understood here. On cultural change, for which he finds more empirical evidence on the micro than on the macro level, North notes, paraphrasing Boyd and Richerson (1985), that 'although we are not yet able to explain precisely the forces that shape cultural evolution, it is obvious that the cultural characteristics of a society change over time and that accidents, learning, and natural selection all play a part' (North, 1990: 87). 'Cultural evolutionary theory', as North calls it, is in its infancy, but he claims that 'the persistence of cultural traits in the face of changes in relative prices, formal rules, or political status makes informal constraints [a term under which he subsumes cultural evolution] change at a different rate than formal rules' (North, 1990: 87). North seems to distinguish here between 'culture' and 'institutions' (the expressions of formal rules), which is problematic, as the distinction fails to capture the continuous interplay between culture and institutions. North is a representative of the analytical separation between culture and politics which this book seeks to overcome. Following North's approach, it would be difficult to analyse the mutual impacts between culture and institutions, which are tremendous. The example of colonial educational institutions in India can illustrate this relationship of interdependence of culture and institutions, and the entanglement of what North treats as separate spheres.

The educational institutions which the British introduced in India largely ignored Indian history and culture in favour of education along the lines of the English system, leading young Indians 'to admire the ideas and institutions of Western parliamentary democracy' (Lumby, 1954: 11). However, political bodies which spread under colonial rule, despite the fact that they involved the new idea of elections and representation, 'seemed evidence of a desire not so much to import Western institutions as to build on the indigenous foundation of the *durbar*, or audience, whereat Indian rulers through the centuries had been accustomed to consult their notables and listen to grievances' (Lumby, 1954: 11).[50] Against this background, it would be more rewarding to see institutions themselves as the product of cultural flow, which calls into question North's dichotomy of the formal and the informal sphere. In this context, Daniel Lerner (1958) in his seminal study of modernization in the Middle East raises the important point that institutional flow is possible only in combination with conceptual flow—institutions cannot be transported to other contexts independently of the concepts underpinning them, precisely because they are the manifestations of those concepts, thus making institutions the political expressions of culture, context, and world view. Institutions which are new to a context thus have a greater chance of operating successfully when they are shaped by conceptual- and policy-flow. Lerner also points out that the growth of institutions is an outcome of the flow of people, which substantiates the point made earlier in this chapter that the micro level has an impact on the macro level. 'Physical mobility', Lerner observes, '... naturally entrained social mobility, and gradually there grew institutions appropriate to the process' (1958: 48).

In addition to being the outcome of cultural flows, institutions are also necessary measures to secure a flow of concepts and information. In British India, the new system of education in the English language medium created an elite educated along Western lines which shared 'new knowledge, new values, and new orientations' (Atal, 1977: 442). Setting up these institutions, however, was not an altruistic or 'developmental' endeavour on the part of the colonial rulers, but rather aimed at 'self-preservation and self-enhancement' (Atal, 1977: 442). As the 'political system rests heavily on the flow of information' (Atal, 1977: 452), institutions, educational and others such as postal and telegraphic facilities, were necessary to establish channels of communication—both for 'the downward flow of orders and upward flow of intelligence and complaints' (V.K.R.V. Rao, 1977: 442).

An example of the building of institutions informed by Western concepts in a colonial context is William Lee-Warner's 1898 book *The Citizen of India*,[51] which was approved as a schoolbook in various parts of India and was translated into vernacular languages.[52] According to its preface, the book was expected to 'lead some of the rising generation in India to value their heritage of British Citizenship, and to acknowledge the duties which they owe to themselves and their fellow countrymen'.[53] It is remarkable that the term 'citizen' is applied to British colonial subjects already in the late nineteenth century, not only in the title of the book, but also for example by the headmaster of the Municipal Board School of Karnal, who in 1903 wrote in his comment on the monograph that 'it is an excellent book, and should be read by every English-knowing citizen of India.'[54] Thus, a new concept, that of the modern citizen, was transported to India as part of an institutional curriculum. Again, this gives us reason to believe that flow is often elite-driven and serves the political purpose of invoking in its receivers, that is, in the pupils who are taught the book, an appreciation of the current political system. As J.A. Yates, the principal of Pachaiyappa's College in Madras, wrote on 23 September 1902, 'the apparent object of the book is to teach loyalty.'[55]

In discussions of the book, representatives of Indian schools and colleges devised the strategy of justifying new policies by contrasting them with old ones, which were shown in a negative light. E. Winckler, the principal of the Hindu College in Tinnevelly, for example, suggested to the Director of Public Instruction in Palamcottah that, for a possible revised edition of *The Citizen of India*, 'some account of the *old* systems, under the ancient Hindu Rajas, may be given, so that the readers may have something approaching a *complete* view of Indian methods of government from the earliest times and thus be better able to appreciate the benefits of British rule'.[56] Similar to Winckler, a further suggestion for improvement of the book that the headmaster gave was to stress 'how some old towns have decayed and now towns have sprung up under British rule'. However, he also recommended emphasizing 'the useful things and things worthy of note that existed in India during the Hindu and Muhammadan rule',[57] and encouraged the author to write on the 'lives of some of the Epoch-making men, both Indian and European'.[58]

As this case shows, colonial media tended to reinforce notions of asymmetry between Europe and India. Also, it stresses the fact that flow is hardly natural, but has to be 'manufactured' as it were, and is channelled through institutions. It is thus a combination of structure and agency that makes flow possible. Institutions, as has been shown here, are a necessary motor of flow. With regard to flow, they play a dual role: flow is both expressed and channelized through institutions, and institutions are also shaped by flow. It is this dual role which makes an investigation of flow through the institutional lens necessary, but which also complicates its assessment; analysis of the impact of flow on the institution, and how the institution determines the course of flow, becomes more difficult.

QUESTIONING EUROCENTRIC NARRATIVES: FLOW AND COUNTER-FLOW AS ANALYTICAL TOOLS

In the light of the theoretical and empirical considerations of this chapter, the question arises as to what the value added of a systematic study of processes of flow would be. Looking at the central concepts around which this book revolves—citizenship, cultural citizenship, and censorship—through the lens of flow helps to understand that they are not monolithic concepts, but are themselves products of conceptual- and policy-flow.

This chapter has operationalized flow by breaking it up into smaller units of analysis, making it more accessible and empirically verifiable. Flow, as has been shown, is a conscious and often highly regulated process. On the basis of the variables of time and space, and the central role of institutions in the process of flow, two models have been developed with the potential to generalize beyond the case study of India. However, further analytical broadening is required in order to explore the full potential of flow. Methodologically speaking, a cultural studies approach combined with the empirical rigour of the social sciences provides optimal conditions to research into cultural flow. Flow is an important theme which will increasingly occupy the minds of scholars from various disciplines. Many questions, particularly regarding the concept of 'counter-flow'—the idea of Asia 'exporting' knowledge to the West—remain to be discussed more fully, and will be addressed again in the concluding chapter. There is some empirical evidence for such processes taking place, such as the British attempt during the colonial period in India to utilize some of the traditional institutions and patterns of communication for their own purposes and as part of the communication structure they set up to strengthen the central authority. The colonial power's use of the institution of the village headman and the creation of new panchayats were measures adopted 'to ensure a proper flow of communication, enabling it to maintain its links with local levels of administration and strengthening its hold' (Atal, 1977: 446). Yet, research on 'counter-flow' is relatively scarce, and so the point is rightfully made that the histories and politics of various concepts, such as citizenship and censorship, and the ways in which different systems learnt from each other across time and space, are under-theorized: 'we do not know adequately', an Indian publication on censorship notes, '...

about how methods of identification experimented with and developed in India and other colonies were then perfected and deployed in Britain. This traffic in the knowledge of power ... requires detailed elaboration' (Sarai, 2007: viii). This is despite the fact that the idea of an Eastern 'counter-flow' was present fairly early in the writings of thinkers like Rabindranath Tagore, who urged Asian countries to carry on the 'experiments by which the East will change the aspects of modern civilization, infusing life in it where it is machine, substituting the human heart for cold expediency, not caring so much for power and success as for harmonious and living growth, for truth and beauty' (Tagore, cited in Joshi, 1989: 18). Tagore hoped that development would not be a one-way process dictated by the West, but rather a concert of ideas involving various worldviews, and therefore he encouraged Asians to 'apply [their] Eastern mind, [their] spiritual strength, [their] love of social obligation, in order to cut out a new path for this great unwieldy car of progress shrieking out its loud discords as it runs' (Tagore, cited in Joshi, 1989: 18). While Tagore both homogenized and stereotyped Asia, and created a fundamental opposition between 'Asia' and 'the West', the basic argument that he put forward is that conceptual counter-flows are needed if Asia wants to avoid subjugation by the West, thus again emphasizing the political nature and strategic deployment of flow and counter-flow.

It is precisely this idea that should inform scholarly research on 'flow'. An understanding of concepts, policies, and institutions as entangled, and as both triggers and outcomes of political processes of flow between different parts of the world, various political regimes, and historical periods, is one of the core concerns of this book, and must be explored further by political science. When looked at through the analytical lens of flow, one can see, for example, that as a concept, cultural citizenship goes beyond the conceptualization of T.H. Marshall. Marshall drew on a specific case—that of citizenship in England, considering solely the historical-conceptual evolution as it occurred in that context. Flow, which did not figure in his analysis, however shows that there are more factors to citizenship than Marshall took into consideration. His analysis was thus problematic in a double sense: while his model was restricted to the Western world only, he also treated that case as idiosyncratic, not specifically exploring influences that came from beyond Britain's national borders. Reading the concepts that this work deals with against the background of a theorization of 'flow' will thus not only help to see them as parts of a larger whole, and as dynamic outcomes of a conceptual *fluidum*, but will also enable other researchers to use them as heuristic devices for understanding processes of exchange between Asia and Europe, and between past and present. In this understanding, the following chapter goes beyond Marshall in showing that citizenship is non-linear and, drawing on the non-Western case of India, demonstrates that it is also non-universal.

3

FROM CITIZENSHIP TO 'CULTURAL CITIZENSHIP'

THE GENEALOGY OF A CONCEPT

Citizenship has to be understood as both signifier and signified of the cultural flow. It is both product and process, a window that provides a glimpse to the global flow of ideas, and is itself a product of the same conceptual flow.

(Mitra, 2012b: 95)

To be excluded from cultural citizenship is to be excluded from full membership of society.

(Stevenson, 2001: 3)

CONNECTING THE PAST TO THE PRESENT AND THE EAST TO THE WEST

It has been noted previously that culture and citizenship are linked conceptually across time and space, which is why one needs to talk about Athens if one wants to talk about Delhi in a meaningful way. The history of citizenship, as this chapter will show, is a history of conceptual shifts. Yet, the common thread running through the intellectual history of citizenship is the duality of rights and obligations, which has constituted the legal sphere of the citizen from antiquity to the present day, and which has only been differently evaluated in different citizenship regimes. As historical source material shows, seeing citizenship as performative and participatory is a practice which connects the past to the present, and Europe to India. Culture thus figures as a connective structure of citizenship, and this work sets out to show in how far different cultural industries have fed into nation-building, or been restricted in the process by means of different forms of censorship. Even though citizenship theory increasingly engages with the changing social, ethnic, and religious structure of the Western nation-state in terms of paradigms like 'cultural' or 'multicultural citizenship', few theorists look outside the West in search of cases to substantiate their claim. India remains largely unconsidered, which is surprising, given its record of successfully marrying democratic citizenship and cultural diversity. This would not have been possible, however, without drawing on the citizenship policies which sprang from the European philosophical tradition.

The core of citizenship—consisting of a bundle of rights and duties—has not changed since it was first conceptualized in ancient Greece in about 2000 BCE. Among the rights granted to Athenian citizens were passive and active franchise, the right to hold property, to attend, speak, and vote in the popular assembly, the *ekklēsia*, and, after having reached the age of thirty, to serve as a juror in law courts (Manville, 1990: 8–9). In that sense, citizenship is a Western concept that has travelled across the globe, and has been shaped and reshaped in the course of the centuries. Like most concepts in the social sciences, it is 'soft'; its outlook has been determined by the politically powerful throughout the course of history, and was adapted to the requirements of place and time. The present situation is marked by the emergence of citizenship studies as an incipient field,[1] and the scholarly engagement with what—in view of the disintegration of the old Western nation-states—is seen as an increasingly contentious issue. The following sections will investigate how citizenship, a seemingly obvious and simple concept, has been rejected, adapted, theorized, and problematized to present the observer with an ambiguous and puzzling outlook.

ANCIENT ATHENS: THE CRADLE OF CITIZENSHIP

The modern 'citizen', whose etymological roots can be traced to the Latin *civis*, shares more with the ancient predecessor than merely the name. In fact, our modern conceptual understanding of citizenship in both form and content dates back to the political practice of ancient Mediterranean peoples: 'what may be called the ideology of citizenship is essentially an early-modern (neoclassical) interpretation of Greek and Roman republicanism, and the current legal understanding of the concept has its sources in the later Rome of the empire and in early-modern reflections on Roman law' (Walzer, 1989: 211).

The ancient Athenian polis, the city-state, is commonly regarded as the world's first direct democracy, and as the cradle of the citizen.[2] But how was the citizen conceptualized, and what can we infer from this conceptualization for our modern understanding of citizenship? Citizenship is not primordial; it has not always been 'there', but is an idea which was slowly developed and given institutional shape. Its nonlinear evolution continues to the present day. Manville (1990) notes that while most scholarly treatments of Athenian citizenship describe the concept as 'static and timeless', it was in fact created by sixth-century political reformers working with a community of Athenians who increasingly defined themselves as 'a community of citizens'. By about the year 500 BCE, citizenship had become 'a fully formed institution and self-conscious ethos' (Manville, 1990: 210). Since the Athenian polis first emerged with the reforms of the statesman Solon (c. 638–558 BCE) in 594/593 BCE, citizenship as 'a formal institution and consciousness is first recognizable only then' (Manville, 1990: 211).[3]

The ancient Greek term for 'citizenship' is *politeia*, which can similarly have legal (passive) and social (active) meanings that are not clearly distinguishable. This is owed to the fact that 'the status of membership in the Athenian community could not really be separated from the role the citizen played in it; *politeia* appears in texts as "the condition and rights of a citizen", but also as "the daily life of a citizen" with both senses often implied at the same time' (Manville, 1990: 5).[4] The notion which is common today in Europe, especially among immigrants who have recently acquired citizenship, that being a citizen is equivalent to being a passport holder of a particular country—a passive perception of citizenship which is restricted to selected rights, but often leaves duties unaccounted for—is sharply contrasted with citizenship as understood in the polis. In the ancient Greek democracy, it is 'difficult to talk about a purely "passive" meaning of *politeia*, that is, an abstract legal status, because Greek citizenship was defined by the active participation of the citizen in public life' (Manville, 1990: 5), not by the mere inscription of the citizen's name on the *deme*[5] register, the *lexiarkhikon grammateion*—the ancient precursor of the passport (Frost, 2005: 27). Politeia, however, is also translated as 'state' (or 'commonwealth', 'republic', 'Constitution', and so on). Manville argues that along with these translations, 'citizen body' is another expression for the term, showing that 'citizenship and the polis were interdependent', while at the same time emphasizing that 'to be an Athenian citizen, as an Athenian himself might say, was to be *metechei tēs poleōs*: someone who *shares* in the polis' (1990: 7; emphasis added). With Solon's reforms, which included the right of every citizen to bring suit on behalf of another, Athenians could think of themselves 'as part of one organism, as the limbs that are all part of the same body'[6] (Frost, 2005: 36), while in pre-Solonian Athens full citizenship was probably limited to those who owned their own land (Hignett, 1952: 79).

Citizens and Non-citizens: Defining the Self against the Other

In the Greek polis, citizenship, Philip Manville notes, 'was simultaneously an institution, a concept, an ethic' (1990: 4). As the social historian observes, 'citizenship was membership in the Athenian *polis*, with all that it implied—a legal status, but also the more intangible aspects of life of the citizen that related to *his* status. It was simultaneously a complement of formal obligations and privileges, and the behavior, feelings, and communal attitudes attendant upon them' (Manville, 1990: 7; emphasis added).

As the personal pronoun in the quote suggests, citizens were native Athenian males who had reached the age of 18, and who had been duly registered in the same local Attic[7] village unit, or *deme*, to which their fathers belonged. They had to be freeborn and legitimate, that is, sons of lawfully married Athenian parents. Such categorization excluded not only women and slaves (*douloi*), but also foreigners (*xenoi*) and resident aliens (*metoikoi*).[8] As was the case in ancient Rome, where it was practised much more frequently, metoikoi could, in rare cases, be given citizenship if they had rendered special—often also pecuniary—service to the polis.

The categories juxtaposed against the Athenian citizen, in the literature often jointly referred to as 'non-citizens',[9] also emphasize the value attached to citizenship, and underline the special status that the citizen enjoyed. The other groups differed from the citizen in so far as 'unlike the citizen, the *xenos* could not hold public office, own Attic land, or marry an Athenian woman; if he wished to trade in the public marketplace, he had to pay a special tax (*xenika*); his rights and access to justice in the Athenian courts were severely limited' (Manville, 1990: 11). As mentioned earlier, women—with legal differences between Athenian and non-Athenian women—did not enjoy full citizen rights. Like slaves and children, they were thought to lack the rational capacities required for self-rule. In the first book of his *Politics*, Aristotle states very clearly that 'as regards male and female, the former is superior, the latter inferior; the former is ruler, the female is subject' (Bambrough, 1963: 388). Despite such denial of citizen equality, women, as will be shown here, created a culture of their own by asserting their opinions and participating in the social and political life of their community (Forsdyke, 2012: 32).[10]

Metoikoi—like douloi—were not entitled to be prosecutors, and even had to fear torture in interrogations. A look at the citizenship rights of Athens reveals striking differences with the modern scenario where universal human rights are inscribed into citizenship laws, and are also extended to non-citizens. In Greek antiquity, on the other hand, the murder of a non-citizen was a much lesser crime than the killing of an Athenian. While someone who slew a citizen (or his Athenian daughter or wife—in death, if not in life, women acquired a mediated citizen status at par with Athenian men) was tried before the court and could receive the death sentence, the man who ended the life of a *metoikos*, *xenos*, or *doulos* went before a lesser court and was liable only to exile (Manville, 1990: 12). What is noteworthy in this context, however, is that in Athens, as presumably in other city-states, 'the distinction to be made was not between the citizen and non-citizen but between substantial landowners and those who were either completely or partly dependent on them' (Frost, 2005: 31–2). Frost reports at least one incident where the term xenos, the stranger, does not denote a foreign person, but an inhabitant of rural areas, as opposed to a city dweller (2005: 36). The citizen is contrasted with the non-citizen here on grounds of different social and economic standing, which is also indicative of the economic inequalities that persisted in the polis. In fact, citizens were often distinguished in terms of their economic capacities, with lines drawn between *plousioi* (the rich) and *penetes* (the poor) (Fisher, 1976: 24). Wealth also determined the status and place of the citizen in the armed forces: while the wealthiest who could acquire their own horses served in the cavalry, those able to provide heavy armour were *hoplites* in the infantry, whereas those without the necessary financial means were assigned the unattractive position of rowers on battleships (Fisher, 1976: 22).

Belonging through War and Performance: Negotiating Citizenship in Terms of Culture

It was this duty to serve in the armed forces which was regarded as the 'primary obligation' of all citizens (Frost, 2005: 31), just like the duty to pay taxes. Above all, a citizen should be 'useful' (*chrēsimos*) to the republic (Manville, 1990: 22), and indeed military service was one of the crucial mechanisms of citizen making. Frost argues that only after the Athenians had successfully defeated three groups of invaders—the Peloponnesians, the Chalcidians, and the Boetians around 508 to 507 BCE—was the sense of a common citizenship consolidated.[11] Even though the political and economic inequalities in the polis persisted, these wars in which citizens fought side by side helped them overcome all psychological obstacles that had stood in the way of the notion of equal citizenship and 'put the seal of success on Athenian citizenship' (Frost, 2005: 39–40). Reflecting on these decisive military encounters and alluding to the writings of the ancient Roman historian Livy, the Renaissance philosopher Niccolò Machiavelli, and the principal author of the American Declaration of Independence Thomas Jefferson, Frost notes that 'to fight for one's country is one of the most meaningful acts of citizenship ... and this was the first time all Athenians had fought together as a national army' (Frost, 2005: 39). An early theorization of the close links between war and citizen formation can be found in Plato's *Republic*, where the philosopher writes that 'now, as though the land they are in were a mother and nurse, they must plan for and defend it, if anyone attacks, and they must think of the other citizens as brothers and born of this earth' (Plato, 1991: 94). It is military action in defence of a community, imagined here in the anthropomorphic shape of the nurturing

mother in need of protection, which unites the citizen body—an analogy which is found across the centuries and continents. The example
of Bharat Mata, Mother India, which is again referred to in Chapter
five, is a motive which is used in Hindu nationalist iconography to
invoke the idea of a nation that has to be defended against internal
and external enemies.[12]

One could therefore, in a variation on social historian Charles
Tilly's famous line that 'war makes states' (Tilly, 1985: 170), say that
war—be it real or merely projected—is a form of cultural production and a catalyst for citizenship, and it makes, or at least to a not
insignificant extent aids in making nations.[13] Rather than the idea of
a social contract that underpins the society as a voluntary union of
individuals with shared norms and expectations, as in the writings
of Hobbes, Rousseau, and Rawls, for Tilly, it is the actions of 'war
makers', which he—in line with rational choice thinking—sees as
'coercive and self-seeking entrepreneurs', that make the state (Tilly,
1985: 169). Disputing theories of the social contract, which will be
discussed in more detail later in this book, Tilly claims that it was
'war making, extraction, and capital accumulation [that] interacted
to shape European state making'[14] (Tilly, 1985: 172). This point is
subsequently taken up by Douglass North who argues that 'wars,
revolutions, conquest, and natural disasters are sources of discontinuous institutional change' (1990: 89). A 'discontinuous institutional
change' for North is a radical change in the formal rules of the game.
Political revolutions, for instance, lead to resolving a 'gridlock crisis'
by restructuring political institutions (North, 1990: 89). The ancient
example thus illustrates Tilly's and North's theory that war indeed
leads to institutional change, or rather gives meaning to institutions.
It is through war that citizens understand the meaning of a state,
and begin to see their co-combatants as fellow citizens, killing and
dying for the same cause. In the course of military action, citizenship changes from the abstract to the concrete, rendering this central
institution tangible and meaningful.[15]

What can now be deduced from this brief sketch of Athenian
citizenship for the modern understanding of the concept? It is justifiable to speak of a 'citizen' as a stakeholder in a democratic political
structure, a bearer of rights and duties. With the conceptual development of 'democracy', the notion of the citizen was also altered. The

ancient example nicely illustrates that citizenship was not limited to a legalistic discourse, but included 'important intangible qualities' (Manville, 1990: 210). Thus, the concept in a way already anticipated the current debate on the role of 'soft factors' like identity, memory, and emotional feeling that feed into the sense of 'belonging', which is now more than ever before considered crucial for the successful realization of the concept and is increasingly deemed worthy of scholarly consideration. Pfetsch (2012) refers to this as the 'psychological dimension' of citizenship: the affective aspect entailing the sense of belonging, and a citizen's identification with the community based on a shared sense of tradition, culture, religion, and ethnicity.[16] However, the notion of 'belonging', which is being discussed only now, has in various ways always been a central marker of citizenship. For Aristotle, a citizen was someone who 'belonged' to various units in multiple ways: first, to the *oikos*, the household or family; then to the association of *oikoi* that formed the village (*kome*); and finally to the association of *komai* that constituted the polis (Frost, 2005: 28). Belonging was thus moral on the most immediate level of the family, as well as legal and increasingly abstract on the superordinate levels. As has been pointed out, these different ways in which the citizen 'belonged' were also conflicting, and sometimes mutually exclusive. What has been identified as 'barriers to the notion of citizenship' were a strong loyalty to one's *oikos*, which might exclude loyalty to the larger regional community of the *kome* in the same way as inclusion in the *kome* with its economic and religious ties and identifications could stand in the way of a bond with the next administrative level, particularly in large territories like Attica (Frost, 2005: 28).

One can also see that the empirical realities which new analytical categories like 'economic', 'social', 'sexual', and 'cultural citizenship' seek to grasp have existed all along. Ancient historians have done some pioneering work before citizenship studies emerged as an incipient field. Frost's rural citizen, who is not addressed as *polites* but as *xenos*, underlines the multidimensionality of the citizenship concept where legal status does not seem to be sufficient to qualify as a citizen in the eyes of one's contemporaries. This bears strong resemblance to the outside- and self-perception of economically deprived and socially marginalized groups as 'second- or third-class citizens' in the national communities of today.

With regard to 'cultural citizenship', whose conceptual components will be discussed in greater detail in what follows, it can already
be said that the ancient example provides evidence for the close relation between participation in cultural activities, cultural expression,
and the status, definition, and basic principles of the citizen. Culture,
in its various expressions has been used as a platform on which
the form and content of citizenship have been negotiated. Manville
(1990) highlights the significance of the public sphere for citizenship,
and for the 'citizen values' which were instilled in the people through
public discourse and the media. Cultural assumptions and the morality of society were perceptible, for example in the Attic comedy and
the political discourse which 'lend credence to ... Perikles' vision of
politeia', the state, as well as the citizen (Manville, 1990: 20).[17]

Pursuing a functionalist approach, Manville's core assumption
is that 'human beings through history and around the world sometimes create similar institutions, sometimes find similar solutions
to similar problems, and sometimes adhere to similar problems'
(1990: 32–3). Citizenship is—like censorship, as will be shown in
the next chapter—a prime example for studying this conceptual flow
across times and continents. One can see that while the context and
particular attributes of the concept change, the essence remains the
same. Regarding the role attributed to culture, after its relevance had
been noted by the ancient Greeks, it went into oblivion for a long
time—probably more on the part of the observer than on that of the
actor—to re-emerge and re-enter the scholarly debate at the beginning of the twenty-first century under the label 'cultural citizenship'.

In an insightful and novel study, Sara Forsdyke reveals the strong
linkages between culture and citizenship in ancient Greece. Not only
in ancient Greece, but also much later in the Middle Ages, ordinary
citizens used ritualized forms of popular culture to express discontent—an observation from which Forsdyke infers that 'popular culture
is political', as popular discourses and practices reveal the negotiation
of relations between the powerful and the weak, the masters and the
slaves, and the rich and the poor (Forsdyke, 2012: 16). Popular culture
is not considered here as a monolithic entity, but as a dynamic and
ever-changing field of speech and action in which various groups
participate to varying degrees. The dynamic nature of the interplay
that opens up in the sphere of popular culture is shown by the cases

of convergence of interests of citizens and slaves (Forsdyke, 2012: 18), who, in reality, were not as sharply contrasted and segregated as the terminology might suggest.[18] Aristotle accepted slavery as a social institution, which he justified in terms of differences in the nature of the free and the unfree. He saw a natural physical contrast in the two groups 'from the time of birth', and argued that 'nature tries to make a difference between slave and free, even as to their bodies—making the former strong, with a view to their doing basic jobs, and making the free people upright, useless for servile jobs but suitable for political life' (Bambrough, 1963: 388). However, Aristotle also thought the two groups to be complementary, since

> there must be an association between that which naturally rules and that which is ruled, with a view to security. That which is able to plan and to take forethought is by nature ruler and master, whereas that which is able to supply physical labour is by nature ruled, a slave to the above. This is why master and slave have a common interest (Bambrough, 1963: 383).

Drawing on the work of Skocpol and Somers (1980), who have disproved traditional causal explanations of particular historical trajectories and constructed new historical generalizations by what they termed a comparative 'macro-causal analysis', Forsdyke (2012) argues that there are discursive patterns that transcend the historical specificities of time and place. She reveals patterns of the strong interlinkages between popular culture, political participation, and the shaping and articulation of citizen consciousness across a range of cases that are seemingly diverse and unrelated—classical Athens, sixteenth-century France, eighteenth-century England, and contemporary Southeast Asia. One of her central points is that 'ordinary farmers, craftsmen, and slaves made use of culture in ways that are similar to their counterparts in other time periods. Not only were folktales, fables, and festival ritual a medium for imagining a different social order, but they served as a crucial mechanism for the articulation of non-elite collective identity and opposition to those above them' (Forsdyke, 2012: 178).[19] What Forsdyke calls 'living forms of culture'—popular and actively pursued modes of participation in everyday life—were forgers of identity and effective tools of negotiation in the political process. The social ritual of hospitality, for example, was claimed by the powerless in ancient Megara[20] by breaking into the houses of the rich and abusing them verbally and physically (Forsdyke, 2012: 174–5). This, in turn, led to the passing of laws in favour of those whom social action gave a voice.

Taking cultural inclusion seriously, ancient Athens had welfare programmes to ensure that less well-off citizens could participate in cultural life, which was considered crucial for social cohesion; wide participation in public festivals was high on the agenda of the Athenian authorities. Traditionally, Greek cities had distributed 'unexpected surplus revenues' to all citizens equally, but the Athenians introduced a permanent and regular system that would provide some financial support for the poorer citizens. Economic support was a feature of the Athenian democracy, and a 'spectacle-fund' was established from which people were able to pay their entrance fee for important festivals, such as the Dionysia (Fisher, 1976: 26).[21] Also, earlier studies have shown the vital importance of culture and the media for citizenship in ancient Greece.[22] Nicholas Fisher (1976) argues that festivals were the 'the major occasions when the citizens gathered to ... feel most tangibly the value of the community'. Greek women participated in exclusively female festivals, such as the Thesmophoria, dedicated to the fertility goddess Demeter, thus securing socio-cultural niches for themselves. One can see a connection between theatrical performances and the challenging of social norms, or the negotiation of the role and status of groups in the larger citizen body. There were theatre plays with themes such as the relationship between unmarried people of citizen status, or women's claims to be heard on public matters. To date, research is not fully aware of the effects these modes of cultural articulation had on the polis (or to what extent legal rules and norms were 'deeply felt, or merely the subject of lip service' [Fisher, 1976: 15]). However, it is assumed that these specific forms of cultural participation may have been 'more than comic fantasy reversing the norms' (N. Fisher, 1976: 12).[23]

THE KAUṬILYAN STATE: A CASE OF ANCIENT NON-WESTERN CITIZENSHIP?

A cross-continental perspective further enhances the holistic understanding of citizenship. Even though the concept of the 'citizen' did not exist in ancient India the way it did in Greece, there are similar categorizations and different sets of rights and duties for different social groups. We find in the *Arthaśāstra*, or 'Science of Polity' (Auboyer, 1965: 38), a set of rules which regulate social interaction.[24] The *Arthaśāstra* is the central ancient Indian treatise on statecraft which dates to the fourth century BCE. It is said to have been written by Kauṭilya, who is believed to be identical with the historical Chāṇakya or Vishnugupta (c. 350–283 BCE), a minister under Emperor Chandragupta Maurya, the founder of the Gupta dynasty and the Maurya Empire (322–185 BCE).

Beginning with the campaign of Alexander the Great, who crossed the Hindu Kush in 327 BCE and reached the subcontinent via Kabul and what is today the north of Pakistan, relations between Greece and India increasingly developed. During his conquests, Alexander founded urban settlements populated with his former soldiers, and thus ensured an 'enduring [Greek] influence on the culture of the region', which manifests itself in the near-Greek look of Gandhāra art, in Greco-Roman architecture which had a strong influence in Kashmir, and in Greek astronomy impacting even modern Indian astrology (Witzel, 2003: 77). It was during the time of the Maurya Empire that Greece and the Indian subcontinent had increasing contact; but the Persian Empire which stretched from the borders of Greece to the Indus, and from Central Asia to the south of Egypt, also had an enormous cultural impact on India. Witzel (2003: 74) elaborates on the role of merchants who, among others, could have brought ideas of a 'modern' state form and administration to north India.[25] In turn, there was an early Indian cultural influence on the West in terms of trade (the Greek word for rice, *oryza*, stems from the Dravidian *arici*) and fashion: fifth-century Greece adored Persian fashion, which included Indian elements (Witzel, 2003: 75–6). Relations between Greece and India became more intense when, shortly before 305 BCE, the Greek ruler Seleucus Nicator, founder of the Seleucid Empire, reached the Punjab. He was confronted by Chandragupta Maurya, whose empire then stretched from the Indus to the Ganges, leaving Seleucus with no choice but to accept an alliance with Chandragupta, abandon all the territories of the Indus basin, and bestow upon him the hand of a Greek princess (Auboyer, 2002: 9–10). It was from this point onwards that 'India joined the ranks of the great powers of the age' (Auboyer, 2002: 10) and entered into diplomatic relations with Greece, with an ambassador based in the capital Pāṭaliputra (the modern Patna). Megasthenes (c. 350–290 BCE), in addition to being a diplomat, was also a keen observer of India, and produced a number of historical accounts which were later summarized in Arrian's *Indikā*,[26] and which affirm or differ from the records in the *Arthaśāstra*.

But was there more that came from Greece to India than ambassadors and young women who were sent there as slaves for the harem (Auboyer, 2002: 33)? Was there also a travel of ideas, a conceptual flow? Socrates, Plato, and Aristotle all died before the documented encounter of Seleucus and Chandragupta in 305 BCE. Aristotle, the youngest of the three, died in 322 BCE, and with the death of Alexander the Great, Aristotle's student, in 323 BCE, an era came to its end. In the ensuing Hellenistic period, Greek culture lost its influence, and the Roman Empire was on the rise. The loss of many of Aristotle's writings during that time might be a reason why one does not find much Greek citizenship philosophy in Kauṭilya. Besides, Kauṭilya, the 'Indian Machiavelli' (Witzel, 2003: 85) as he is frequently called, was a political strategist in an absolute monarchy. Chandragupta Maurya's empire was prosperous and expanding. With the Greek liaison and the establishment of diplomatic relations between the great powers, the emperor, as a rational actor, would not have seen the necessity of giving up power and establishing a republic—the state form which, as has been shown in the Introduction to this book, is the only one in which citizenship as it is understood here can be said to prevail.

Much like the ancient Greeks, the *Arthaśāstra* makes a distinction between locals and non-locals. The text mentions different terms for foreigners, for example, outsiders to a city who were not permitted to enter it (*bahirikas*), visitors (*agantuh*), or foreign or visiting artists (*agantukah*).[27] The text does not only differentiate between locals and foreigners, but also between Aryans, *mlecchas*, and slaves. Aryans, the ruling group, were Hindus of any of the four *varnas*. All slaves, on the other hand, were non-Aryans divided into four different categories: those born in the house, inherited slaves, bought slaves, or those obtained in some other way (Kauṭilya, 1987: 449). The status of slaves was judicially monitored, and forcibly changing the 'free or unfree status of a person [was] a serious offence punishable with a fine of 1000 panas' (Kautilya, 1987: 447). Mlecchas, literally 'jabberers', were a separate group who 'could have been of foreign or tribal origin'; in one word, they were 'barbarians' (Auboyer, 2002: 31). Mlecchas were generally non-Hindus who were considered ritually impure, and, because they were dispensable, they were used in the armed forces or as spies (Rangarajan, 1987: 52). Unlike in ancient Greece, in the Indian subcontinent a major criterion for the difference between resident and foreigner, between one who enjoyed rights and one who did not, was religion.

We learn from Jeannine Auboyer that foreigners were placed in the same category as those outside the caste system, the 'untouchables'. Even though they were 'not subjected to the same indignities', foreigners were 'untouchable by the very fact of not belonging to the *dharma* and not being initiated into the Veda' (Auboyer, 2002 [1965]: 31). Mlecchas, however, also enjoyed certain 'rights' which Aryans did not: in his chapter on labour law and employment, Kautilya writes that while an Arya minor shall never be sold or mortgaged into slavery, it is not a crime for a mleccha to sell or mortgage his child (Kautilya, 1987: 447). Mlecchas, however, in the expanding Maurya Empire, were not integrated into the state, unlike the peoples conquered later by the Romans and pacified under the system of Pax Romana. Rather, the ruler was advised in the *Arthaśāstra* to 'transfer and disperse' the mlecchas living in conquered territories (Rangarajan, 1987: 52).

Women formed a separate social category with very specific sets of rights and duties. On the question of whether women in the Kautilyan state enjoyed more rights than they do today, Rangarajan, who edited one of the modern translations of the *Arthaśāstra*, cannot provide a clear answer. He does note, however, that in certain respects like remarriage or right to property, they had a better position during the Maurya Empire than in subsequent periods of Indian history (Rangarajan, 1987: 65). Their main duty, as stated by Kautilya, was to give birth to sons. Although in earlier Vedic times gender divisions were less sharp and morality was of a much less conservative kind, in the third century BCE, females and their relationship with the opposite sex were subject to rigid control. Auboyer (2002) notes that 'although girls and boys in Vedic times had been subject to few constraints and were free to indulge in amorous intrigues without being necessarily disgraced as a result, the evolution of moral attitudes since those times had resulted in a total prohibition of such relationships' (Auboyer, 2002: 177).

The Kauṭilyan society was thoroughly patriarchal without the scope for deviance that prevailed in the cultural space of the polis. Unlike in Greece, there were no 'free' women in the Kauṭilyan state— a woman was a property, dependent on and subservient to her father, her husband, or her son. Without the permission of the male, a (married) woman could not drink, indulge in unseemly sports, or go on pleasure trips. She could not leave the house when her husband was asleep or drunk. She could not refuse to open the door to him and she was not allowed to attend cultural performances, with other men or even with women, either by day or by night (Rangarajan, 1987: 71). In his laws and regulations relating to martial life, Kauṭilya lists fines for wives who saw a show or went on a pleasure trip. Fines were higher if the show took place at night, and if women were accompanied by men (Kauṭilya, 1987: 408).

Even though the Kauṭilyan state was more restrictive than the polis, on the subcontinent also, cultural activities presented scope for deviance and offered various opportunities to second-class citizens or non-citizens to challenge social norms. Women, for example, were assigned an active and less restricted role during religious festivals, such as the festival of Kāma, the god of love, which took place two weeks after Holī, or on the occasion of the festival of the 'mother of the spirits' (bhūtamātṛ) (cf. Auboyer, 2002: 145–6). During this orgiastic two-week festival, which was celebrated in May and June, women dressed as men and vice versa, taking on each other's role in reverence to the androgynous goddess. During the festival, 'the whole population indulged in wild gesticulations, sang erotic songs and abandoned themselves to sensual debauchery' (Auboyer, 2002: 146). Similar to the case of ancient Greece, festivals were thus an opportunity to break out of gender and social divisions and enter into an egalitarian space in which traditional role patterns could be overcome. During the 'feast of lamps', modern Diwali, for example, the king mingled with the crowd (Auboyer, 2002: 148). While not enough is known about the character of those festivals and their social functions (in the case of India even less so than in the case of Greece), there is an interface between politics and culture. Analysing this interface is a contribution towards the formulation of a theory and a diachronic model of cultural citizenship.

With the exception of some religious festivals, sexuality was rigidly and directly controlled by the state. Brothels were state-owned, and the *bandhakiposhaka*, the keeper of prostitutes (a term which appears three times in the *Arthaśāstra*) was obliged to use the prostitutes to collect money in times of emergency, and subvert the enemy's army chiefs (Rangarajan, 1987: 65). Similarly, 'secret agents posing as rich widows were used to sow dissension among the chiefs of an oligarchy, or to draw the enemy from the safety of his sort' (Rangarajan, 1987: 67). Prostitutes, however, did not have only this tightly controlled, strategic role; they also performed a ritual function. On the third day of the Hindu 'feast of lamps', they went from house to house wishing people good luck (Auboyer, 2002: 148), a fact which alludes to their social role beyond the stigma associated with their profession. In the Maurya Empire, unlike in the Greek polis, homosexuality was a crime.[28]

In the Kauṭilyan state, with Brahminism as the state religion, and with Kauṭilya himself belonging to the highest varna, distinctions between Brahmins and non-Brahmins as well as between different social groups were sharp. The legal imbalances resulting from this social asymmetry provide another striking parallel with Athenian law. By analogy to the polis, where the murder of a citizen was a much more severe crime than the killing of a non-citizen (see the section on 'Citizens and Non-Citizens' earlier in this chapter), the legal code of the *Arthaśāstra* prescribes a fine of one hundred *panas* for raping a woman living by herself, and a mere twelve pana fine for the rape of a prostitute. A man raping a female slave due for redemption also had to pay twelve panas and was detained until the slave was freed. On the other hand, a woman found guilty of sexual relations with a slave was sentenced to death (Kauṭilya, 1987: 454). Equally, the punishments for city guards who 'misbehave with women' ranged from the lowest standard penalty if the woman was a slave, to death if the woman was a respectable person (Rangarajan, 1987: 68). Even though the *Arthaśāstra* says that 'judges shall discharge their duties objectively and impartially, so that they may earn the trust and affection of the people' (Kauṭilya, 1987: 377), different laws applied to different castes for the same offence. The *Arthaśāstra* has an entire subsection on 'Sexual Offences', from which one can infer that cross-caste relationships were prohibited, and legalistic double standards prevailed.

While an upper-caste Kshatriya man having a relationship with a Brahmin woman received the 'highest special penalty', the entire property was confiscated in the case of a Vaishya man entertaining a relationship with a Brahmin woman. A Shudra, as a member of the lowest varna, however, is burnt alive for having been found guilty of the same offence (Kauṭilya, 1987: 488). Comparing these legal regulations, one can see that in ancient times neither Greece nor India had the idea of a common law applicable to all in equal measure—this was only devised later in the Roman Republic.

In view of these asymmetries, can one speak of citizenship in the · Kauṭilyan state in the way it existed in ancient Greece? The answer is no. The most obvious reason for this would be that the Maurya Empire was a monarchy, not a republic. There was no constitution, no form of separation of powers, nor was there any opportunity for inhabitants of the state to influence the policy process. A lexical approach helps to shed further light on the issue of citizenship in the subcontinent in pre-modern times.

The Hindi word for 'citizen' is *nagarik* (नागरिक). 'Citizenship' would, by analogy, be *nagarikata* (नागरिकता). These are the terms that have been used in the large-scale opinion survey on citizenship in India (Mitra, 2010b), which is discussed in detail in chapter five. They are, however, mechanical translations: following a word formation pattern in the English language where the term 'citizen' is derived from the noun 'city' (or *cité* in French), or more precisely from the Latin *civitas* (state), which also meant a city-state, the Hindi term for citizen was constructed on the basis of the Hindi word for 'city', *nagar* (नगर).

In the *Arthaśāstra*, the word *nagarika* is used to denote the 'city governor-general', the officer in charge of administering a fortified city. Even though the term 'citizen' is used in the English translation of the text, the meaning is markedly different because the historical development which runs in parallel to the lexical development is a different one. The overview table of the conceptual development of citizenship, compiled by the historian Thomas Maissen (Mitra, 2012b: 88), shows that from the Greek polis to the early modern cities of Europe, citizenship was closely connected to the urban space—a relation which found its expression in the respective terminology. The citizen was 'civis' in Rome, *cittadino* in Italian medieval cities,

Table 3.1 Concepts of European Citizenship

	Greek polis	Rome	Italian Medieval Cities	Northern Early Modern Cities	Early Modern States	Liberal State	Modern Democratic State
Name	Polites (astus)	Civis	Cittadino	Bürger, bourgeois, burgher	Sujet	Citoyen	Citizen
Precondition	Descent, autarchy, virtue	Descent, residence, emancipation (slave), virtue	Descent, virtue	Privilege, *coniuratio* (oath)	Residence	Property, commerce, adherence	Birth, descent
Status	Landowner, oikia (rule in the oikios)	Legal person within tribus	Member of the popolo	Craftsman in guild	Subject	Sovereign member of the nation	Sovereign member of the nation
Residence	'suburban'	Cities (civitas)	Urban, villa in the countryside	Urban (within the walls)	Territory	Territory	Territory
Legal community	Polis and surrounding	Individual cities	City and contado	City	Territory	Territory	Territory

(Table 3.1 Cont'd)

Table 3.1 (*Cont'd*)

	Greek polis	Rome	Italian Medieval Cities	Northern Early Modern Cities	Early Modern States	Liberal State	Modern Democratic State
Quality	Participation (self-rule, offices, honour)	Soldier, participation, protection	Ruler, merchant	(Economically) privileged and free	Protected	Producer, equal in rights	Protected, equal in rights and participation, taxes, military service
Access to offices	Census, military service	Patrician status, cursus honorum	Patricians wealth (or foreigner: podestà)	Distinct families (Regimentsfähigkeit)	Nobility, bourgeois specialists	Meritocratic	Functional elites, university graduates
Distinction/ categories of non-citizens	vs. foreigners, metoikoi, women, adults, slaves	liber vs. slaves (and plebs), Romanus vs. foreigners	vs. rural nobility, peasants, signoria	vs. rural nobility peasants, princely rule	vs. foreign powers	non-productive and poor people (nobility, labourers)	vs. non-nationals (foreigners, immigrants)
Theory	Aristotle	Cicero	Machiavelli	(Calvin)	Hobbes	Sieyès	(Rousseau, Tocqueville)

Source: Table drawn by Thomas Maissen (cited in: Mitra, 2012b: 88).

and *Bürger, bourgeois*, or *burgher* in the early modern cities of north-ern Europe.[29] The German expression *Stadtluft macht frei* (urban air makes you free) dates back to medieval times when, with the aboli-tion of the *statutum in favorem principium* (Statute in Favour of the Princes)[30] in the Holy Roman Empire in 1231/32, under which cities were not allowed to protect subjects of worldly or spiritual rulers, the political status of the city was radically altered. After this change in legislation, cities and their inhabitants became free of external rule, and the inhabitants were not subject to a worldly or a spiritual author-ity anymore. The city thus constituted a liberal political space opposed to the otherwise feudal system. In line with this political tradition, the German city of Hamburg to date carries its title of the 'Free and Hanseatic City'. The territorial space was thus always that of the city, an urban environment, which was extended to the entire national ter-ritory only after the French Revolution. The events of 1789 and their political aftermath gave rise to the formation of the liberal state with the citoyen as its smallest political unit.

This historical scenario, however, is confined to Europe, and does not apply to Kautilya's India. Even though the word 'citizen' is used in the English translation of the *Arthaśāstra*, as in 'citizens shall take appropriate precautions against fire' (Kautilya, 1987: 370), the nagarik is not the same as the citizen, because 'nagar' is not equiva-lent to the European medieval city. Although the *Arthaśāstra* lists specific regulations for city dwellers (Kautilya, 1987: 369–69),[31] they did not enjoy a more liberal status than people living in the country-side. Reverting back to the ancient European example, Ronald Inden (1992) observes that there too, citizenship was 'defined in exclusiv-ist terms', and that the kin principle in the Greek polis was more exclusivist than it was in the Hindu caste system. Alluding to the uncompromising exclusion of slaves from citizen rights, he notes that in the context of early medieval India,[32] 'persons of other castes within the same village as the dominant caste were *not* reduced to the status of aliens and slaves (although the "untouchable" notion comes pretty close)' (Inden, 1992: 219; emphasis added). Drawing on Hocart (1970), who argued that caste can not only be seen as 'ritual' but also as a form of 'political organization', Inden argues that contrary to the general understanding, citizenship and subject-hood are not necessarily oppositional categories, but can coexist and have done so for a significant part of Indian history within the social framework of 'caste' (Inden, 1992: 218). Even though his work is reflective of the dangers inherent in regarding caste as an indigenous form of citizenship, Inden nevertheless cautions against the assumption that, because Indians in the 'early Middle Ages' were subjects, they could not have also been citizens (Inden, 1992: 220). He assigns this social phenomenon to a hyphenated 'third space' which he labels 'subject-citizenries'. Difficulties arising from this approach abound: Inden selects a specific time period, the eighth to thirteenth centuries CE, but where should historical research on citizenship in India start, and where does it end? What are the decisive turning points in the history of citizenship? And most importantly, what is specifically Indian about India's historical record of citizenship?[33]

This is particularly relevant, since Inden's discussion appears to be hardly more than an Eastern variation on a Western theme. The Greek polis remains the blueprint against which correspondences and deviations of the Indian case are sketched. Therefore, while projects like Inden's aim at overcoming the 'master narrative' of Western modernism, they often find themselves in the same trap as the discourses they have set out to counter. While the master narrative tries to construct a direct passage of concepts from the West to Asia, thus creating an Asian 'mimesis of the West', to borrow Raminder Kaur's term (2012), the countermove which suggests a reverse flow or a parallel development is often at best an addition to the growing canvas of 'politically correct' theory, because it is seldom substantiated by sufficient facts. At the same time, it consciously or unconsciously caters to the cultural-nationalist camp, which is trying to argue that 'India has had it all; and all along'. Proponents of this approach thus overlook Gaonkar's (2001) valid claim that we 'cannot escape the legacy of western discourse on modernity. Whoever elects to think in terms of alternative modernities (irrespective of one's location) must think with and also against the tradition of reflection that stretches from Marx and Weber through Baudelaire and Benjamin to Habermas, Foucault, and many other Western (born or trained) thinkers'. This is to say that 'one can provincialize Western modernity only by thinking through and against its self-understandings, which are frequently cast in universalist idioms' (Gaonkar, 2001: 14–15).

CITIZENSHIP IN ANCIENT ROME:
IN VARIETATE CONCORDIA

Shifting back to Europe, and moving forward in time, a consideration of citizenship in ancient Rome helps to see how the concept developed, and where the differences with the Greek understanding lie. The Roman Republic differed from the Greek polis quite markedly, even though Rome extensively learned and borrowed from Greece in all spheres of cultural and political life.

The relation between the two ancient civilizations is marked by the flow of objects, concepts, and ideas, with all the elements of adaptation, change, reconfiguration, and novelty that such a flow necessarily entails (see Chapter two). Interaction and the affinity to reception on the part of the Romans reached an extent that has led observers to remark that 'the cultural history of Rome became progressively the history of her transfiguration through contact with Greek ideas' (Wilkinson, 1975: 57). Greece became a model for Roman religion, literature, and visual culture. Greek gods were equated with Roman deities, and Greek epics, most importantly Homer's *Odyssey*, became the foundation for Roman literature. In philosophy, the impact of Greece on Rome was particularly visible, but not so much with regard to law. The Roman *ius civile*, the citizen law,[34] was quite different from the Greek model, even though the writings on citizenship by Plato were later taken up by Cicero in his *De Re Publica* (On the state). This was in part owed to the fact that while the political unit for citizenship in Athens was the more manageable polis, the ever-growing Roman Empire, in view of the heterogeneity of its population, had to conceive of a different citizenship regime to effectively administer an ethnic and cultural diversity which bore political dynamite.[35]

One of the commonalities between Athens and Rome was that the multitude of Roman citizens—the number of whom increased with the military successes of the empire—obviously took pride in their political status. As in the Greek polis, Roman citizenship was valuable, and was also used as a commodity: benefactors, or people who had rendered outstanding services to Rome, for example by building an aqueduct or donating a public building, were rewarded with citizenship (Wilkinson, 1975: 167–8). On the bearers of Roman citizenship, Wilkinson notes that 'their self-esteem was also fed by Triumphs; if they were insignificant individually as citizens of Rome, worth little more than a vote, they were collectively the lords of the earth' (1975: 87). One can see here a variation on the theme of the interdependency of military capacity and increasing self-identification as a citizen and as part of a 'nation', a theme which has already been observed in the case of Greece. The Latin *civis Romanus sum*, I am a Roman citizen, has become the phrase that epitomizes proud self-identification as part of a larger political body.

Long after the Roman Empire had perished, US president John F. Kennedy, on 26 June 1963, addressed the people of the divided German city of Berlin with the words: 'Two thousand years ago, the proudest boast was *civis Romanus sum*. Today, in the world of freedom, the proudest boast is *Ich bin ein Berliner*.' And, rhetorically turning the Cold War scene into a hotbed of political alliance, he closed his speech emphasizing that 'all free men, wherever they may live, are citizens of Berlin. And therefore, as a free man, I take pride in the words: *Ich bin ein Berliner*,' again illustrating the close links between war—be it hot or cold—and citizenship. However, the legacy ancient Rome left in terms of the conceptual development of citizenship extends far beyond this catchphrase. Roman citizenship was as valued as full membership in the Greek polis, so much so that 'even on his deathbed a man was glad to receive it' (Wilkinson, 1975: 134). Compared to the earlier Greek model, Roman citizenship was much more permeable in allowing former slaves to become citizens, albeit with some limitations. A former slave was unlikely to hold high office in Rome (though this was possible in the colonies), and his vote, although granted, was restricted. By 56 CE, however, some descendants of slaves had risen to be senators, which provides evidence of the permeability of the socio-political system.

Roman citizenship can be seen as an early success story. If we imagine ancient Rome, as historians do, as a precursor of a melting pot like New York City, a 'microcosm of the known world', with a heterogeneous population, 'a community made up of a coming together of the nations' (Wilkinson, 1975: 134), it seems only logical that the empire also introduced the model of dual citizenship. By the edict of Caracalla, passed in 212, practically all freeborn men in the empire, with the exception of the very lowest, chiefly rural classes, acquired Roman citizenship in addition to that of their home (Wilkinson, 1975: 139), thus producing an 'imperial inclusiveness' (Walzer, 1989: 214).

Citizenship, however, was not strong enough to bind the heterogeneous community together. Roman citizens were one of the first imagined communities, having no knowledge of one another and sharing neither history nor culture. They were highly heterogeneous, including 'people ethnically different from the original Romans, with different religions and different conceptions of political life. For these people, citizenship was an important but occasional identity—a legal status rather than a fact of everyday life' (Walzer, 1989: 215). Citizenship in the Roman Empire was different from that in the Greek polis in so far as the latter was marked by activity and inclusion in the legislative process, while the former was characterized by the passive receiving of rights and entitlements. In Rome, as Walzer notes, 'a citizen was more significantly someone protected by the law than someone who made and executed the law' (Walzer, 1989: 215).

As is the case with ancient Greece, the Roman example again underlines the relevance of 'soft' cultural factors for the instilling of citizen consciousness in the population and for the nation-building process. The Romans, who could rely on an excellent infrastructure, were able to disperse their literature throughout their sphere of control. Coins were among the most important visual media to bring the distant parts of the empire closer together and to transmit information, such as military victories, changes in leadership, or simply a knowledge and recognition of the fellow citizen, across immense distances.[36] Tourism, which was already one of the pleasures of the time, brought people mainly to Greece to admire its historical and artistic monuments, and thus contributed to the awareness and knowledge of the various cultures then amalgamated in the Roman Empire. To again take up Charles Tilly's phrase, it is, among other things, war that makes states, and the Pax Romana, the Roman peace,[37] contributed to that success story. The flow of objects (pots from the area of Arretium, the modern-day province of Arezzo in Italy, were found in what is today Pondicherry[38]) and ideas (the Elder Pliny in his writings idealized the Ceylonese for not having slaves) is evidence of the degree of cultural flow[39] within the then known world, and contributed to the cultural knowledge that circulated,[40] and, in turn, informed the conceptualization of the citizen.

The ancient period has been covered in some depth here, because elements that were constituted then were crucial to the evolution of citizenship. Participation in the legislative process and dual citizenship are elements which were devised in antiquity and continue to exist to the present day. More generally, Mitra, even though emphasizing the non-linear evolution in the conceptual content and quality of the idea of the citizen, speaks of the 'core concepts of the Greek city-state and the Roman Empire, representing, respectively, the salience of descent and law, [which] became the foundation stones of the European idea of citizenship' (2012b: 88). An analysis of the Greek and Roman traditions is indeed crucial, because, as Michael Walzer emphasizes, the inspiration for the various manifestations of citizenship in revolutionary France, the most decisive point for the conceptual evolution of citizenship in modern history, was classical—it derived from readings of Aristotle, Plutarch, Tacitus, and others. Walzer quotes the Jacobin tribune Saint-Just who said that 'Revolutionaries must be Romans', that is, 'citizens in the style of the classical republics' (1989: 212–13). Thus, it is correct to assert that 'the Greco-Roman tradition did not disappear with the onset of the European medieval period.... The original Republican tradition was revived by the early modern states, as the Jacobins of revolutionary France set off to liberate their own people and others in the name of restoring republican values' (Mitra, 2012b: 89).

CITIZENSHIP IN THE MODERN ERA: THEORIZING INCLUSIVITY AND CULTURAL PARTICIPATION

As one proceeds from antiquity onwards through the ages, it is apparent that culture and citizenship have at all times been closely linked. Russian philosopher Mikhail Bakhtin discussed the entanglement between citizenship and culture in his analysis of the carnival, during which hierarchies are upset and distinctions of class and politics are overcome,[41] while historian Simon Schama (1989) in his seminal account of the French Revolution details the role of culture in the making of the citizen. Schama devotes an entire chapter, titled 'The Cultural Construction of a Citizen', to the exploration of the linkages between culture and citizenship. He shows the immense impact of literary productions and debating societies on instilling citizen consciousness in their members. These historical accounts have served as an empirical base for theories of the public, and have fed into the concept of 'cultural citizenship', which was developed much later.

Jeremy Bentham's (1748–1832) essay *Of Publicity* (1791) is one of the first accounts of the relevance of the public for social life. Bentham, a defender of the liberty of the press, thought that the principle governing all social and political decisions should be the 'greatest happiness of the greatest number'. He was in this sense a precursor of Jürgen Habermas who, in *The Structural Transformation of the Public Sphere* (1989 [1962]), reconstructs the connection between communication and the liberal model of a 'citizen public' from a historical, sociological, and normative viewpoint. Until the end of the eighteenth century, European political culture was a culture of the court and the ruling feudal class. Then, on the eve of the French Revolution, public spaces beyond direct state control like literary salons and coffee houses emerged. The conversations and debates at those places were influential in the creation of the liberal image of the citizen. The public was thus a 'third space' between the private sphere and the sphere of state control. For Habermas, creating a public space is to create opportunity structures that enable people to see that they share interests with others; interests that are ignored by the feudal state. It is through this process that a civic public emerges. Public spaces serve to establish consensus, bring about socio-political change, and strengthen society. For Habermas and others (public) culture is a means to the end that is citizenship. Increasingly though, it has become more than that—a vital, constitutive part. As a student of Adorno and Horkheimer, and a representative of the critical theory of the Frankfurt School, Habermas emphasizes the role of the mass media which, used commercially, are seen as tools of subjugation rendering possible asymmetric power plays that infringe on the liberty of the individual in modern democratic states.

In addition, it was the political philosophy of the eighteenth and nineteenth centuries, notably the work of thinkers like Jean-Jacques Rousseau (1712–1778) and John Stuart Mill (1806–1873), that laid the ideological foundations for our modern liberal understanding of citizenship, and for the first time brought the individual to the centre of theoretical attention, making it the prime unit of citizenship analysis. Rousseau, as pointed out in Chapter one, has had considerable influence on the modern theory of the citizen. Walzer notes that it was

Rousseau who gave citizenship 'its modern philosophical grounding, connecting it to the theory of consent' (1989: 212). While Rousseau's writings were banned in absolutist France, they became manifestos of the Revolution, often abused for instance by Maximilien de Robespierre, the most influential figure of the Jacobin terror regime, who in response to Rousseau justified his educational dictatorship to mould the new citizen.

In *The Social Contract* (1973 [1762]), Rousseau deplored the loss of the state of nature which he—as opposed to Hobbes and Locke—did not see as 'poor, nasty, brutish and short', or as a fight of all against all, but as a state characterized by peace and harmony. People are virtuous by nature, but their morals are corrupted by society and civilization. By means of the law they are sentenced to a bonded existence.[42] Hence, Rousseau opened his work with the words, 'Man is born free; and everywhere he is in chains' (1973: 181)—a credo which twenty-seven years later would become the battle cry of the French revolutionaries.[43] Rousseau's strategy to overcome this state was the move 'back to nature' in order to regain lost liberty. To reach this aim, he developed an alternative model of society which is not hierarchical but egalitarian, with all citizens participating in the legislative process; a model which has later been termed 'participatory democracy', and brought Rousseau fame as 'the theorist *par excellence* of participation' (Pateman, 1970: 22). In Rousseau's model, as in the Kantian legislature, all are makers of the law and subject to it—a conceptualization of citizens which is already found in Aristotle, who described democratic citizens as 'men who rule and are in turn ruled'[44] (Walzer, 1989: 214). Citizen participation as outlined by Rousseau is one of the central elements of the concept of cultural citizenship. For Rousseau, participation not only ensures the well-being of the individual, but also has an integrative function. It 'increases the feeling among individual citizens that they "belong" in their community'—out of participation emerges a sense of commonality which prevents alienation in the way Rousseau expresses it in *Émile*, where a man, when asked what his country is, replies, 'I am one of the rich' (Pateman, 1970: 27).

Rousseau also, if more indirectly, linked the participatory element to culture and the arts, of which he was very sceptical. 'High culture', the *beaux arts*, to him was morally corrupting and an integral part of unequal society. In his *Préface à Narcisse*, he wrote that artists and poets merely weave 'garlands of flowers to cover the iron chains' that weigh down people (quoted in Shklar, 1969: 110). Because he saw culture and art not as participatory, but as exclusivist, he judged them 'not by the pleasures they give, but by the miseries they hide' (Shklar, 1969: 110). Much like the Frankfurt School nearly two hundred years later, Rousseau linked culture and the formation of public opinion. He was convinced that 'public opinion is easily shaped by the arts, and their message is always dangerous, since it always accelerates the progress of corruption and inequality' (quoted in Shklar, 1969: 110). The state of nature, the loss of which Rousseau deplored and to which he advocated a return, on the other hand, was a state of participation in culture and the arts. Taking recourse to the example of ancient Greece outlined above, where all sections of society shared in the cultural life of the polis, Rousseau wrote that his state of nature, the 'Golden Age', was 'one of song and dance': 'This is the art of communal participation, not of professional creation. Like the public festivals of antiquity, they unite men in shared joy and give simple people their rightful pleasures' (quoted in Shklar, 1969: 111). High culture, the learned art, on the other hand, was luxury for Rousseau, and hence exclusivist and anti-social. The evil of high culture for him, as Judith Shklar notes, was 'its destructive impact on society'—an effect which 'is willed by those who make it and by those for whom it is made, the intellectuals, the artists and their patrons, the rich and powerful' (Shklar, 1969: 111).

The fundamental problem for Rousseau was 'to find a form of association which will defend and protect with the whole common force the person and goods of each associate, and in which each, while uniting himself with all, may still obey himself alone, and remain as free as before'. The solution to this problem is provided by the *social contract*[45] (Rousseau, 1973: 191). Rousseau distinguishes between two forms of liberty that whoever enters into the social contract has to weigh against each other: 'what man loses by the social contract is his natural liberty and an unlimited right to everything he tries to get and succeeds in getting; what he gains is civil liberty and the proprietorship of all he possesses' (Rousseau, 1973: 196). The right to property constitutes an element of the contract theory of Locke, but Rousseau regarded the ancient Greek democracies as forerunners of the inclusive form of government, where laws were in line with the *volonté générale*, the general will, which represents the common good, and is more than the sum of individual wills (*volonté de tous*). In Rousseau's view, such a general will was possible, because as soon as the freedom to participate in the legislative process is present, all forms of inequality and injustice would disappear, and a feeling of a community of citizens would emerge; in other words, 'each man, giving himself to all, gives himself to nobody' (Rousseau, 1973: 192).

Central to Rousseau's thought is the individual, who for him, as opposed to Aristotle or Hobbes, is sacrosanct. For Aristotle, the polis was more important than the individual, and Hobbes regarded anarchy as the inevitable end to a society lacking in strong and powerful institutions. The theoretical considerations of Rousseau thus run like a connecting thread through the history of modern citizenship philosophy. A lot of it can be found in Henry David Thoreau (1817–1862), most prominently in his essay *Civil Disobedience*. Written in 1849, it makes explicit Thoreau's conviction that 'that government is best which governs not at all', because that would give citizens the opportunity to follow their conscience.[46] The individual is here the prime and ultimate social unit, because according to Thoreau, 'we should be men first, and subjects afterward' (Thoreau, 1989: 86). In Thoreau's writings, the supremacy of the individual that is already apparent in Rousseau culminates in the claim that

> there will never be a really free and enlightened State until the State comes to recognize the individual as a higher and independent power, from which its own power and authority are derived, and treats him accordingly. I please myself with imagining a State at last which can afford to be just to all men, and to treat the individual with respect as a neighbor (Thoreau, 1989: 104).

Thoreau's philosophy first found a mass audience not in the United States but abroad, and also had considerable influence on Mahatma Gandhi's concept of satyagraha. Originally distributed by the socialist Fabian Society, Gandhi—who is said to have always carried a copy of Thoreau's essay *On the Duty of Civil Disobedience* with him—was responsible for promoting it along with Thoreau's other works, in South Africa and later in India. The Mahatma saw this as a way to make his own idea of satyagraha clearer to the colonial rulers (Klumpjan and

Klumpjan, 1986: 135),[47] expressing it in terms of a familiar cultural context and vocabulary.

A contemporary of Thoreau, John Stuart Mill (whose father the Scottish philosopher and historian James Mill had founded the movement of the 'philosophic radicals' together with Jeremy Bentham) added another significant building block to the conceptualization of modern citizenship. A utilitarian like Bentham, Mill was inspired by the moral philosophy of Bentham and his principle of 'the greatest happiness for the greatest number', which Bentham had outlined in *An Introduction to the Principles of Morals and Legislation* (1996 [1789]). For Mill, however, not society as a whole, but the individual was at the centre of his philosophy. Society had to allow for individuals to pursue their happiness; any infringement of that freedom would be tyranny—regardless of whether it was the unjust rule of a single tyrant, or the collective tyranny of a democratically elected majority. A central instrument to prevent this tyranny is the unobstructed right of the individual to free speech. As a member of the British parliament, Mill condemned slavery, advocated the right to free speech, and—as the first parliamentarian—openly spoke in favour of women's suffrage.

We find in Mill's practical liberalism, which emerged from his utilitarian philosophy, significant building blocks of modern democratic citizenship in general and of cultural citizenship in particular. The acknowledgment of both the rights of individuals and the rights of social groups, in this case women, but also of other minorities—rights that are closely connected with free speech—are important determinants of the discursive understanding of the nation and the citizen which underlie this book. Free speech is necessary not only to ensure liberty and happiness, but also to secure one's status as a citizen and one's place in the nation, which is essentially a discursive community. One of the seminal texts by Mill is his essay *On Liberty*, where liberty means 'Civil, or Social Liberty: the nature and limits of the power which can be legitimately exercised by society over the individual' (Mill, 1975: 5). Like Rousseau, Mill is a philosopher not of the collective, but of the individual. The individual is his unit of analysis, and individuality is 'one of the elements of well-being' (Mill, 1975: 69). And like Rousseau, Mill saw the participation of citizens in civic affairs as being in the larger interest of state and society. Participation of the individual in public affairs is of mutual benefit: when the individual can participate in public affairs, he or she is 'forced to widen his or her horizon and take the public interest into account' (Pateman, 1970: 30).

In the twentieth century, the works of these earlier philosophers were taken up by social theorists such as T.H. Marshall (1893–1981) and John Rawls (1921–2002). Inherent in the liberal paradigm which they promoted and developed is the right to participation, visibility in the public sphere, and the acknowledgment of difference, all of which are central elements of 'cultural citizenship'. Even though culture is a necessary analytical category for understanding the processes of nation-building and citizen-making, it received little attention when citizenship first became a subject of scholarly consideration.

As outlined in Chapter two, it was the British sociologist T.H. Marshall who, after the end of the Second World War, when the world was reshaped and the populace had successfully entered politics, wrote *Citizenship and Social Class* (1965 [1949]). This work is commonly regarded as the starting point for a new scholarly discussion of citizenship. However, Marshall's triadic model consisting of the civil, the political, and the social spheres, which in combination constitute the modern citizen (see Chapter two), is constructed against the background of the experience of the English working class, and does not take into consideration other, non-European cases. Subrata Mitra, on examining the Indian case, observes that 'the Marshallian explanation fails to take into account the case of post-colonial states and societies, where political rights came *before* civil and social rights' (Mitra, 2012b: 98). Mitra thus comes to the aid of Reinhard Bendix who, unlike Marx and Marshall, does not see England and the English experience as an exemplary case of industrialization and citizenship. Bendix notes that 'no other country which has begun to industrialize since the 1760s can start where England did. England is, therefore, the exception rather than the model—in contrast to the view expressed by Marx in his preface to *Capital*, that "the country that is more developed industrially only shows, to the less developed, the image of its own future"' (1984: 102). Bendix works with Marshall's model in a comparative way, and finds that 'when I applied this model comparatively, it became apparent that each country had undergone its separate development, although all Western industrial societies had experienced a similar extension of citizenship' (1984: 105).

Another important critique in the context of this book is that Marshall fails to explicitly consider the role of popular culture in citizen-making. Some decades later, when the scholarly consideration of citizenship had gained momentum, this omission brought fierce criticisms to the fore. Marshall's model was perceived to be exclusive and static, a child of its time, unable to account for the changes in the social, ethnic, and religious set-up of Western nation-states at end of the twentieth century. Broadly speaking, two sets of criticism can be identified. The first set focuses on the need to supplement or replace the passive acceptance of citizenship rights with the active exercise of citizenship responsibilities, such as economic self-reliance, political participation, and civility (Kymlicka and Norman, 1994: 355). The second set focuses on the need to revise the current definition of citizenship to accommodate diversity. The increasing social and cultural pluralism of modern societies[48] is a pressing project that finds expression in the concept of 'cultural citizenship', which, in a normative sense, concerns the 'positive acknowledgement of difference in and by the mainstream' (Miller, 2002: 231). The academic debate has responded to the new challenges by transcending Marshall's original unified notion of citizenship and its connection with the territorial state. The mass of varieties of citizenships that emerged reflects the different political intentions of citizens, and their perceived need to emphasize certain policy fields which they feel are not high enough on the state's agenda and yet constitute vital parts of their self-understanding as individuals and as citizens (see Chapter two).

Like Marshall, other theorists of citizenship have more or less successfully tried to capture the intellectual evolution of the citizen. Referring back to the overview of concepts of European citizenship in tabular form developed by the historian Thomas Maissen (see the section on 'The Kauṭilyan State'), it should be noted that this table ends with the citizen of the modern democratic state, and with Rousseau and Tocqueville who provided the necessary theoretical underpinnings. Neither later theorists nor non-European examples are considered. For the case of India, which will be discussed in the following section of this chapter, a different conceptualization is required.

CITIZENSHIP IN THE REPUBLIC OF INDIA: THE ROAD TO THE NATION

India is an empirically rich case for the theorist of citizenship. It constitutes an interesting example of a young, ethnically, religiously, and linguistically diverse republic trying to become a nation and creating the first free citizens in the long history of the country. Despite the rich empirical data that it offers for the theorist of citizenship, a thorough discussion of the Indian scenario is almost entirely absent from the general literature on the subject; works of political sociologists like Reinhard Bendix (1964), Bhargava and Riefield (2005), and Niraja Gopal Jayal (2013) stand out as rare exceptions.[49] Other than that, India is still a blank spot on the map that charts out the academic reflection on citizenship. Scholars focusing on the regional context have not presented a full-fledged theoretical account of what makes citizenship in the Indian context special, whether it contributes to theory-building or to theory-testing, and what it can add to the general understanding of the concept. Even those theorists who explicitly focus on the relationship between culture and citizenship, like Kymlicka (1995) and Miller (2002), or those who sketch an agenda for multicultural citizenship like Joppke (2002), take the Western nation-state as their reference point, and either Europe or North America as their analytical unit.

The disregard of the Indian example is particularly unfortunate, not only because India provides an excellent case for the study of citizenship in culturally diverse societies, but because the conclusions derived from a sole consideration of the Western nation-state are inaccurate and misleading. Christian Joppke, for instance, in discussing multicultural citizenship, notes that 'no state, not even liberal states, can be culturally neutral; for example, in its selection of an official language a state inevitably promotes the majority culture, at the cost of the culture of minority groups that may reside in the same territory' (2002: 247). The Republic of India with its three-language formula contradicts this claim, which is why a scholarly focus on the Western states is dangerously narrow. The same is true for Will Kymlicka, one of the best-known proponents of pluralistic citizenship theory, who restricts his analysis of multicultural citizenship to the West, and that too mostly to the United

States. Considering the Indian example would have helped him put his hypotheses into perspective, and could have prevented him from postulating that 'societal culture'(Joppke, 2002: 247), the core concept without which for him 'there is no freedom'(Joppke, 2002: 247), builds on 'shared history, language and territory'(Joppke, 2002: 248). For Kymlicka, a 'nation' or a 'people' is thus 'an intergenerational community, more or less institutionally complete, occupying a given territory or homeland, sharing a distinct language and history' (Kymlicka, 1995: 18, cited in Joppke, 2002: 248). Such claims ignore Indian realities where a national consciousness prevails in spite of language divisions.

As a partial answer to the Eurocentric conceptualization of citizenship by Maissen outlined above, Mitra (2012a) provides a graphic representation of Indian positions on citizenship (Table 3.2). Arguing that 'Indian political theory is itself a source of the diversity of the discourse on citizenship' (Mitra, 2012a: 164), Mitra presents four ideal types to trace the understanding of citizenship in the Indian context, straddling between the traditional and the modern, change and conservation, and theorists and policymakers. There are two important points which have to be noted with regard to Table 3.2. While the table provides a collage of the influential figures that have shaped rival or complementary positions on citizenship, they all operate on the basis of Western thought on citizenship. From Nehru, the liberal modernist, to Savarkar, the traditional exclusivist, all those listed in the table have at best produced Indian variations on a Western theme. Also, the table is a still picture of citizenship thought taken around the time of independence. For a more comprehensive understanding, however, one would also have to take into account the policies of Rajiv Gandhi, Nehru's grandson, who succumbed to the pressure of the

Table 3.2 Values and Institutional Arrangements in the Making of Citizens: A Typology of Indian Thinkers

Salient values	Institutional Arrangement	
	Status quo	Radical Change of Institutions
Modern	Nehru	Subhas Bose (and Ambedkar)
Traditional	Tagore	Gandhi (and Savarkar)

Source: Mitra (2012a: 163).

All India Muslim Personal Law Board (AIMPLB) in the controversy around the divorce of the Muslim woman Shah Bano, discussed in more detail later in this chapter. Rajiv Gandhi's actions constituted a move away from the Supreme Court judgement of equality before the law, towards a community-differentiated citizenship.

The fact that apart from some recent reflections, the Indian case has received only marginal attention from theorists of citizenship can only be explained in terms of the larger global asymmetries that are reflected in, and are in turn enhanced by, the academia. More than anything else, this is to the detriment of theory-building, for India, as has been argued, provides the researcher with an intriguing scenario. The interest of the case stems from India's demonstration that citizen formation is a non-linear process marked by ruptures and incongruities. The eleven volumes of the *Constituent Assembly Debates* documenting the discussions of the body that met between December 1946 and December 1949 to write the longest Constitution in the world, which came into effect in January 1950, testify to the extensive exchange and competition of ideas and views of what the socio-political framework in which the Indian citizen operates should look like. The Constitution of India is a document of conceptual flow: it shows that the founders of the Republic—290 men and 9 women[50]—were in search of a conceptual basis upon which the citizen could be modelled.[51] While conservative Hindu groups like the All India Varnashrama Swarajya Sangh advocated that the Constitution 'be based on the principles laid down in ancient Hindu works' (Guha, 2007: 117), Jawaharlal Nehru, then chairman of the States Committee, the Union Powers Committee, and the Union Constitution Committee, tried to balance the claims of the traditionalists with a modern, secular outlook by invoking the spirit of the 'great past of India', and of modern precedents such as the French, American, and Russian Revolutions (Guha, 2007: 117). This view also found expression in the Constituent Assembly's solution to the question of what the basic unit of politics and governance of independent India should be. While some members advocated a constitution in the spirit of Gandhi with the village as the basic political unit, B.R. Ambedkar favoured the individual citizen as the core unit, a proposition which was ultimately accepted and institutionalized in the Constitution. In that, as in other respects, for instance in the question of the voting system where India, after the British example, adopted the majority, first-past-the-post system, the Constituent Assembly followed Euro-American rather than Indian precedents (Guha, 2007: 119).[52] Of all people, Karl Marx, who was convinced that Britain had a double role in India, a destructive and a creative one, destroying the old Asiatic order of society and building the material base for a Western order in Asia (Marx, 1960 [1853]: 221, cited in Wittfogel, 1962: 525), was sympathetic to the Western innovations that the British colonial power brought to India. Among those Marx counted 'the political unity of India, modern modes of transport, railways, steamboats and the telegraph, as well as an army, and a free press—the first to come into existence in an Asiatic society—as well as private land property and officialdom' (Marx, 1960, cited in Wittfogel, 1962: 525–6).

In his *Discovery of India*, first published in 1946, one year before the country gained independence, Jawaharlal Nehru contradicted Marx and was explicit about the lack of socio-political innovation that was to be expected from the British. Describing Indian society in the late 1930s and early 1940s, Nehru observes:

> There was vitality there, a bubbling life, a sense of tension, a desire to get things done, all of which contrasted strangely with the apathy and conservatism of the British ruling class and their supporters. India, the land of tradition, thus offered a strange reversal of roles. The British, who had come here as representatives of a dynamic society, now were the chief upholders of a static, unchanging tradition; among the Indians there were many who represented the new dynamic order and were eager for change, change not only political but also social and economic.... This reversal of roles was a demonstration of the fact that whatever creative or progressive role the British might have played in the past in India, they had long ceased to play it and were now a hindrance and an obstruction to all progress. The tempo of their official life was slow and incapable of solving any of the vital problems before India. Even their utterances which used to have some clarity and strength became turgid, inept, and lacking any real content (Nehru, 1985 [1946]: 378).

Political as the nature of the statement may be, it also illustrates that it was the interplay between the exogenous and the endogenous, the old and the new, the colonizer and the colonized, the Indian and the non-Indian—not homogeneous, clear-cut, antithetical pairs, but complex, overlapping categories—which has been so crucial for the development of the citizen and the Republic. Like the Constitution and other Indian political institutions, the citizen of India was born out of, and represents, the interplay between tradition and modernity, old and new, West and East, without necessarily leaning toward either side.[53] The Indian citizen can thus also be seen as a socio-political microcosm of the Indian Republic. He is a hybrid, a figure of the in-between, or a 'third space' in Homi Bhabha's sense.[54] As a conceptual tool to investigate the entanglement of cultures, ideas, and meanings, Bhabha refers to the 'third space' as having 'productive capacities'. With the idea of the 'third space' in mind, observers and actors alike may be in a position to conceptualize an

> *inter*national culture, based not on the exoticism of multiculturalism or the diversity of cultures, but on the inscription and articulation of culture's *hybridity*. To that end we should remember that it is the 'inter'—the cutting edge of translation and negotiation, the in-between space—that carries the burden of the meaning of culture. It makes it possible to begin envisaging national, anti-nationalist histories of the 'people'. And by exploring this Third Space, we may elude the politics of polarity and emerge as the others of our selves (Bhabha, 1994: 38–9).

Thus, the third space, 'though unrepresentable in itself, ... constitutes the discursive conditions of enunciation that ensure that the meaning and symbols of culture have no primordial unity or fixity; that even the same signs [in this case, citizenship] can be appropriated, translated, rehistoricized and read anew' (Bhabha, 1994: 37).

Much contested at the time of its framing, the Constitution has contributed significantly to the longevity of the Indian state and nation. The reasons for that enduring strength lie not least in the hybrid character of the document. Sixteen years after the coming into effect of the Constitution, Austin notes that

> although the constitution at some point defies nearly all the rules devised by constitutional lawyers for success, it has worked well. The credit for this lies—insofar as it can be assigned—in part with the British, who brought the vision and some of the reality of parliamentary democracy with them to India, in part with fortuitous circumstances, and in largest part with Indians themselves (1966: xiii).

Contrary to what the critics of the time remarked, the Indian Constitution is not a 'foreign document', but the sum of many international parts to which a distinct local edge has been added. Austin writes that 'many of the articles of the Constitution, either in wording or in content, have their origins in foreign constitutions. The members of the Assembly were not so chauvinistic as to reject the experience of other nations. Yet, although the Assembly borrowed freely, it fashioned from this mass of precedent a document to suit India's needs' (1966: xiii). Austin would not have been aware of the accuracy of his terminology: it was indeed a borrowing, since today the erstwhile homogeneous Western nation-states, on whose constitutional experience India drew, are looking eastwards in search of policy measures to respond to increasing ethnic, linguistic, and religious diversity. The debates that were opened up in Great Britain and Germany in 2008 and 2012 respectively, on the extent to which a sharia law can be introduced for the countries' Muslim populations, are a case in point. India inscribed in its Constitution the different sets of personal law for its many religious communities, in effect setting up a group-differentiated citizenship in Iris Marion Young's (1989) terms, rather than following Rousseau, the advocate of the individual, who thought 'that the ideal situation for decision-making was one where no organized groups were present, just individuals, because the former might be able to make their will prevail' (Pateman, 1970: 24). Changed social structures now seem to call for 'the West' borrowing from 'the East'. Austin thus rightly regards 'accommodation' as one of India's original contributions to democratic constitution making. Accommodation to him is

> the ability to reconcile, to harmonize, and to make work without changing their content, apparently incompatible concepts—at least concepts that appear conflicting to the non-Indian, and especially to the European or American observer. Indians can accommodate such apparently conflicting principles by seeing them at different levels of value, or, if you will, in compartments not watertight, but sufficiently separate so that a concept can operate freely within its own sphere and not conflict with another operating in a separate sphere (Austin, 1966: 317–18).

To Austin's list of examples for this strategy of accommodation, which contains the parallel federal and unitary systems of government, or the country's membership in the Commonwealth, could be added the 'differentiated citizenship regime' which India has adopted. A single, unitary citizenship is combined with different sets of personal laws for the country's diverse religious groups.

Today, in India as everywhere else, democracy and citizenship are two sides of the same coin. Undeniably, citizenship has developed very differently in East and West. The difference in the nature of citizenship in India and France, for example, has been called 'a story of fascinating contrasts, though not of necessarily welcome differences' (Alam, 2012: 77).

A striking difference between the citizenship regime in India and its Western counterparts is the constitutional emphasis on group rights. As B.R. Ambedkar very clearly said on introducing the draft Constitution, there is only one citizenship of India: 'the proposed Indian Constitution is a dual polity with a single citizenship. There is only one citizenship for the whole of India.... There is no State citizenship' (*Constituent Assembly Debates*, VII: 1, 34, cited in Austin, 1966: 189). However, citizenship as a bundle of rights and duties is finely nuanced and includes personal law, privileges for different religious groups, and ethnic and linguistic representation of minorities on all political and administrative levels.[55]

Drawing on Ambedkar, if cultural citizenship is understood as a normative concept, entailing the acknowledgement and accommodation of cultural difference, then India has it. However, cultural citizenship is not so apparent in the Indian context if it is defined in a more abstract sense as 'cultural participation', a share in the discourse out of which the nation is constructed. A 'cultural citizen' in that sense—and this is a crucial point—is a stakeholder in the overall cultural discourse which is not to be segregated from the national discourse. As will be shown in Chapter five, the media have been used by the Indian state after 1947 to instil citizen consciousness in the populace; bringing about 'national unity' in this manner has been one of the declared aims of the state and its political institutions.

CULTURAL CITIZENSHIP: CONCEPTUAL PROBLEMS AND PROSPECTS

As has been argued in the Introduction, understanding culture as 'ordinary', as does Raymond Williams (1989), is a necessary precondition for the unfolding of the concept of cultural citizenship.[56] It is only with the cognitive shift from culture located in the 'high', literary sphere, to a democratized understanding of the term where everyone has an equal share in culture, that cultural citizenship becomes possible. Citizenship over the course of the centuries saw a development from an exclusive, high-end notion in ancient Greece to the egalitarian conceptualization of the revolutionary *citoyen*, the grounds for which had been prepared by the liberal theory of Rousseau and others. Culture had first to be looked at in a different light so that the two concepts, 'citizenship' and 'culture', could merge and emerge as the new idea of 'cultural citizenship'.[57] In other words, something had to happen to the idea of 'culture' before one could proceed to conceive of 'cultural citizenship'. As a theoretical concept, cultural citizenship is of Western origin—Western in so far as it was first introduced into the debate by US scholars, and formulated against the empirical background of contemporary America (for example, Miller, 2007; Rosaldo, 1994a). From the beginning, it was directly connected with the media, but not exclusively tied to them. Rosaldo employs 'cultural citizenship' as an analytical category in his discussion of American educational policy vis-à-vis the Latino minority in the United States.

The crucial concern of cultural citizenship is the question of *identity*, more precisely the provision of space for the minorities by the majority. It has to be clear that cultural citizenship relates to issues of representation of specific groups, and is thus closely connected with identity politics. After defining cultural citizenship as the 'right to be different and to belong in a participatory democratic sense' (Rosaldo, 1994a: 402), Rosaldo goes on to argue that the notion of belonging means full membership in a group and the ability to influence one's destiny by having a significant voice in basic decisions. Against the background of the much-contested question of educational policy, Rosaldo raises the questions of whether the institution can change in ways which are responsive to its new members, how it should change, and how the negotiations for change would work— problems which, as will be shown, the analyst is also confronted with in the Indian context. For Rosaldo, the answer to these pressing questions lies in 'cultural citizenship' which he sees as a basis for 'cultural decolonization by recognizing the value of cultural life' (1994a: 410).

Therefore, as a second parameter of cultural citizenship, the role of the *institution* can be filtered. This point is repeatedly made in the literature, also by sociologist David Chaney who stresses the role of a 'sociology of the politics of cosmopolitanism—how cultural institutions have negotiated tensions between the indigenous and the global in the process of cultural change' (Chaney, 2002: 159). The link to minorities, which can also be found in Rosaldo, is once again emphasized by pointing out that art is 'not restricted to particular social worlds or formal traditions but becomes a general name for prestige, perceived creativity and minority appeal' (Chaney, 2002: 164). Drawing on Pierre Bourdieu and his notion of the unequal distribution of 'cultural capital', Chaney offers a very similar argument by saying that the consumption of cultural goods is dominated by socially privileged groups, in particular by the better educated, which is why the public subsidy of cultural institutions, 'far from delivering a general benefit to all, delivers a selective benefit of distinction to those who are equipped, by their social and educational formation, to make use of them' (Chaney, 2002: 162).

Thus, the policy concern has to be to bring 'culture to the masses' (Chaney, 2002: 168). Here, questions similar to those asked by Rosaldo emerge, namely: What is an appropriate cultural heritage? Who is to decide in multicultural environments? And what sorts of responsibility are appropriate for public authorities? Cultural institutions do play a significant role in this, which is why Chaney, in an effort to emphasize this point, takes up Nick Stevenson's definition of cultural citizenship, which focuses predominantly on the institutional side. Stevenson perceives cultural citizenship as 'a complex of policy issues around both the provision of cultural facilities, and the regulation of cultural industries, including "electronic and print media, music culture, heritage parks, museums and public libraries, to name just a few"' (Stevenson, 1999: 74). In the following, it will be shown how far different cultural industries have been put on India's national cultural agenda, and how cultural identities have become subject to restriction in the process of nation-building. In the context of contemporary India, this volume explores Chaney's liberal suggestion that 'rather than trying to decide what sort of culture [and policies for access] should be made available, policy-makers should be concentrating on ways in which they can facilitate citizens *deciding for themselves what is to count as culture and how it is to help them decide who they are'* (Chaney, 2002: 170; emphasis added).

While in theory, 'cultural citizenship' can facilitate a consensus between the agenda of civil society and classic nation-state actors, in practice, as Chapter four will show, this is not free from problems, because culture, especially in the field of the visual media, is determined by discourses of power. The social scientist and cultural theorist Toby Miller, an oft-cited author in the field of cultural citizenship, restricts himself to the role of televisual media in the creation of narrative modes of inclusion and exclusion in the United States. As is the case with general citizenship theory, to date, one looks in vain for a full-fledged adaptation of the concept to India, or a further theorization of cultural citizenship based on the Indian case. Apart from the work of Mankekar (1999) and Harindranath (2009)—where cultural citizenship is understood in terms of media representation—there is no significant conceptual consideration, and also those authors fail to give a substantial theoretical account.

What I would like to add to the theoretical construct of citizenship in general, and cultural citizenship in particular, is a dimension grounded in the central assumption of the Irish idealist philosopher George Berkeley (1685–1753): *esse est percipi aut percipere,* that is, to be is to be perceived, and to perceive. For Berkeley, there is no 'outer world' independent of the perception of the actor.[58] The world exists only in the ideas—which for Berkeley, following Locke, are associations of particular images (Renaut, 2000: 93)—and in the views that we have of it. In line with Lockean empiricism, insight can stem only from experience. While Berkeley rejected the notion of materiality and spoke of concrete objects as being nothing but 'objects of thought', ('the house itself, the church itself is an Idea, that is to say an object, an immediate object, of thought', cited in Renaut [2000: 98]), in the framework of this analysis, it helps to restrict the view to *intangible concepts.* Taking Berkeley's ideas into the more abstract level of citizenship, one could say that 'to be' is not only 'to be perceived', but to be acknowledged. It is perception that determines social action.

Employing Berkeley in this analysis raises the important question of whether citizenship can at all be an ontological category. Ontology asks the question of being, independent of the kind of our perception and experience. Citizenship, however, cannot be understood independently of perception. It is not a category of being which is fundamental, but one which is always dependent on context and perception. Mitra (2012b: 95–6) argues that citizenship is 'equal membership of moral and political communities', a 'liminal space with a political edge and a moral stretch'. It is a two-dimensional concept with a legal as well as a moral component. The citizen not only requires a legal right to the soil, but also has to have a moral affiliation to it in order to feel attachment to the national community. Certainly the legal dimension is not sufficient for a person to be a citizen, as suggested by Figure I.1 where it is the overlap between state and society that constitutes the citizen. To feel strong moral ties to the soil without having the legal right to it can turn people into rebels, whereas to be in possession of the legal right without any moral attachment means alienation and estrangement.

It is the moral component of this two-dimensional citizenship model which needs some further analysis. The citizen only exists if s/he is perceived by himself or herself *and* by the society and the state around him/her as such. This raises the question about the effects of one side not sharing this perception: if either the citizen herself or the state fails to acknowledge the individual as a citizen, does she then lack in citizenship? Self- and outside perception of the individual as citizen needs to reach a high level of congruence, even though the perceptions will never in all cases completely concur. In culturally heterogeneous societies, such congruence can be obtained only by entry into the national discourse. Reflection on one's own cultural and national standpoints, and change and adaptation where required, need to occur on the part of the majority as well as the minority community. Such adaptation serves to prevent the manifestation of parallel or counter-discourses which by envisioning and producing parallel societies hinder convergence.

One of the central elements of cultural citizenship is plurality—the plurality of cultures, views, and voices in the discourse. For Aristotle, plurality was more desirable for a state than unity: too much unity would actually mean the end of the state. To him,

> the state is naturally plural; if it grows in unity, it becomes a household instead of a state, and then an individual instead of a household. We would say that a household is more of a unit than a state, and similarly an individual more of a unit than a household. Therefore, even if one

could achieve this, one ought not to do so, since the state would then be destroyed (Bambrough, 1963: 393).

Apart from Rosaldo (1994a), one of the first definitions of the concept of cultural citizenship was proposed by Bryan S. Turner, who defined 'cultural citizenship' as 'a set of practices which constitute individuals as competent members of society' (1994: 159). Turner emphasizes that members of a society are constituted and constitute themselves by various social, legal, political, and cultural practices. For him, 'cultural citizenship consists of those social practices which enable a competent citizen to participate fully in the national culture' (Turner, 1994: 159). This is of course not a much differentiated definition, since it remains unclear what is meant by 'competence' here, and the casualness with which Turner uses the term 'national culture' is confusing. He also takes up Marshall's point of equal education opportunities for all members of society, which Marshall regarded as an element of the social part of citizenship. Turner lists it as a central building block of 'cultural citizenship', since education is seen as a significant symbolical resource without which citizenship cannot be realized. Anthropologist Aihwa Ong in her work *Flexible Citizenship: The Cultural Logics of Transnationality* (1999a) focuses on the coming-into-existence of citizenship under conditions of globalization and transnationality. Ong also mentions the active–passive dichotomy in her definition of 'cultural citizenship'. She sees cultural citizenship as 'the cultural practices and beliefs produced of our negotiating the often ambivalent and contested relations with the state and its hegemonic forms that establish the criteria of belonging within a national population and territory. *Cultural citizenship* is a dual process of self-making and being made within webs of power, linked to the nation-state and civil society' (Ong, 1999b: 264).

Similar to Turner, Ong argues that cultural citizenship is a process wherein a subject claims rights, but is also determined to a large extent by its environment. Most definitions of the concept remain vague and general. But since this book tries to narrow the concept down to the sphere of the media, which are used as an empirical anchor to ground the theoretical explorations in cultural citizenship, the following definition by the communication and media sociologists Elisabeth Klaus and Margreth Lünenborg shall be employed as a working definition. Klaus and Lünenborg perceive 'cultural citizenship' to be a 'significant dimension of citizenship in media society. It encompasses all those cultural practices that unfold on the background of uneven power structures and that make a competent share of the symbolical resources of society possible. Mass media are here motor and actor of self,—and at the same time heteronomous production of individual, group-specific and societal identities' (Klaus and Lünenborg, 2004: 200).

Cultural citizenship is deemed important because it opens up a space in which meanings circulate, that is, in which they are negotiated and then determined (Klaus and Lünenborg, 2004: 200). Claiming that differences can arise between media messages and readings by the audience, the sociologists state that cultural citizenship is in fact a cycle of the cultural production of meaning (see Figure 3.1). Since a media text is received differently by different audiences, the production side has to take this into account and bring elements of that reception back into the text. This is why Klaus and Lünenborg plead for understanding processes of identity formation on an individual, subcultural, or nation-state level within the context of media action. The media text itself does not materialize societal relations of power,

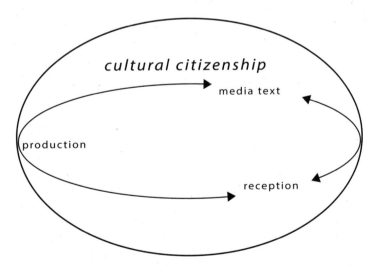

Figure 3.1 Cultural Citizenship as Context in the Circulation of the Production of Cultural Meaning
Source: Adapted from Klaus and Lünenborg (2004: 201).

but they are inscribed in the text by the producers and are allocated to the text during the process of reception by the audience.

Figure 3.1 suggests a highly dynamic, interactive process between media text, production, and reception. It is in this interplay that cultural citizenship (as an expression of the discursive side of citizenship) becomes apparent. The model is thus also a further take on the dynamic interface between state and society which shapes the citizen (Figure I.1). Similar to the interpretation of cultural citizenship as a concept grounded in participation (Figure 3.1), Pateman (1970) defines participatory democracy as a state form 'where maximum input (participation) is required and where output includes not just policies (decisions) but also the development of the social and political capacities of each individual, so that there is a "feedback" from output to input' (1970: 43).

Klaus and Lünenborg understand the processes of identity formation within the context of media action. Therefore, an affiliation to the nation-state can arise only if media choices exist for different social groups which make a discussion of already existing cultural practices possible and also allow for their development and modification. This process of cultural affiliation is a precondition for the creation of political and social rights (Klaus and Lünenborg, 2004: 201). According to Klaus and Lünenborg, 'cultural citizenship' requires the opportunity of cultural shares. Like Marshall, they speak of 'dimensions' of citizenship and suggest that citizenship be understood as a *four-dimensional process* in which the media play a crucial role. The present study differs from their understanding, however, in that the media, as has been argued in the Introduction, are not regarded as monolithic, but as comprising a sum of discourses which citizens can enter into or open up themselves. This complicates the model, as the discourses can complement and challenge one another, causing an increasing sense of belonging, or a decrease entailing alienation and conflict.

To their credit, Klaus and Lünenborg add a crucial dimension to the theory of participatory democracy. In line with other proponents of participation theory, Pateman claims that since participation has an integrative effect and aids the acceptance of collective decisions, the existence of a participatory society is a necessary prerequisite for a democratic polity. A participatory society is 'a society where all political systems have been democratised and socialisation can take place in all areas' (Pateman, 1970: 43). The most important area for Pateman in this sense is the industry. She regards it as a political system in its own right which offers areas of participation in addition to the national level. The media in all their complexity constitute yet another of those areas which are constantly gaining more scholarly attention.

GROUP VERSUS INDIVIDUAL: DIFFERENT THEORETICAL TRAJECTORIES IN EUROPE AND INDIA

In the context of this book, 'cultural participation' constitutes the most relevant dimension of participatory democracy. In the theory of citizenship, participation rights include labour market rights (for example, job security, discrimination protection), advisory or determinative rights (for example, collective bargaining, co-determination), and capital control rights (for example, wage earner funds) (Janoski and Gran, 2002: 15). Thus, one of the definitions of citizen participation is the right of individuals and groups 'to participate in private decision-making through some measure of control over markets, organizations and capital (Janoski and Gran, 2002: 16). In their discussion of 'political citizenship', Janoski and Gran show how the liberal paradigm of Locke, Marshall, and Rawls that sees the individual as supreme and political parties as aggregating categorical interests, with most political action taking place in representative legislatures, travels via the 'participatory Republicanism' of Habermas that regards individuals as under-represented in society and their participation in groups in need of encouragement through 'communicative procedures', which then leads to citizens' participation in community councils and other fora with the aim of establishing a 'just society', to the 'moderate postmodern pluralism' of Chantal Mouffe, Engin F. Isin, and Will Kymlicka.

This paradigm represents a move away from liberal theory and acknowledges the complex nature of citizen identities. In contrast to the liberal theory framework, where 'group rights do not exist for ascriptive categories, [and] groups have rights secondary to individuals', the postmodern pluralistic theory assigns cultural and procedural rights to cultural groups. Kymlicka, as opposed to Locke,

Marshall, and Rawls claims that 'social movements and the media are the motive force for institutional change' (Janoski and Gran, 2002: 18). In the understanding of the 'moderate postmodern pluralists', among which Kymlicka can be counted[59] "citizens pursue group identities through group or cultural rights, or resist and attain such rights in social movements' (Janoski and Gran, 2002: 18). Cultural citizenship, as it is understood here, is a combination of participatory republicanism and postmodern pluralism with a touch of liberal theory. Media are important tools of citizen formation and avenues for public participation and, following from this, of inclusion and the full attainment of citizenship. However, diverging from Kymlicka and other proponents of the moderate pluralist strand, the emphasis in this study is not so much on group rights. This is owed to the context: unlike in the West, where these theories aim at overcoming the individual as the sole reference point, in the Republic of India, group rights have been granted from the beginning. What we observe then is a counter-development in the West and in India: political theory is not independent of political practice, and as the homogeneous nation-states of the West changed their social structure with the end of colonialism and the ensuing unprecedented immigration waves, theorists like Kymlicka reacted by moving away from the individual as the main analytical unit, and developing a theoretical paradigm of cultural group rights. The underlying thought was that citizenship in the sense of belonging can only be obtained if the various individuals constituting a cultural minority group—be it ethnic, linguistic, or religious—are recognized collectively. Only then would they be able to have a strong political standing and visibility, which is the precondition for participation in socio-political processes, and for engendering a feeling of belonging to the larger national community.

In India, on the other hand, a reverse development has occurred. The country has always been culturally diverse, and this diversity has been acknowledged by granting special rights to minority groups. Everyone is free to speak their mother tongue, including in the official realm, and all religious groups have their separate sets of personal laws. Muslims, for their part, have the right to regulate matters of marriage and divorce according to sharia law. As the Shah Bano case illustrates,[60] in India, group rights are very pronounced, which can come at the cost of the liberty of the individual. Therefore, what is needed in Indian thinking on citizenship is a recourse to liberal theory, bringing into focus the individual.[61] In the Indian context, one can increasingly witness the emergence of the individual as a socio-political unit. Ever since the introduction of the quota system based on the recommendations of the Mandal Commission,[62] there have been protests by members of the upper castes who insist that personal qualification ought to count more than membership in a religious or ethnic group. They thus subordinate, in many cases even negate, their group identity in favour of their individual personality and achievements. The latest move relates to the Unique Identification Scheme or Aadhaar[63] scheme, a project launched by Nandan Nilekani as chairman under the auspices of the Unique Identification Authority of India (UIDAI), an agency of the Government of India and part of the Planning Commission. The scheme seeks to give every Indian citizen a unique legal identity by way of issuing a card which allows the cardholder to be unmistakeably identified on the basis of their fingerprints and their iris.[64] The idea behind this policy—which is criticized on the usual grounds of accumulation and storage of personal data—is to give a valid identity card to people who do not have any other document of identification, like a birth certificate, a passport, or a driving licence. This so-called 'Aadhaar card' makes these people eligible for food rations and voting cards and is meant to bring them from the margins into the sphere of legality. The document thus contributes to making them citizens, and is a significant policy measure to carving the individual out of larger social units like the family or the community.[65]

In Europe, the idea of the nation was built on the foundation of political, social, and economic liberalism identified with John Locke, Jean-Jacques Rousseau, and Adam Smith, and has been by and large preserved in that tradition. Here, the individual is not yet an endangered category. The different theoretical requirements in the West and in India thus illustrate the context-dependency of theory. Far from being universal, citizenship is a context-sensitive area, and its theorization and implementation operate along the fine lines of culture, history, and memory, all of which are constitutive parts of identity. In this vein, Anant (2011: 103) notes on the issue of a pluralistic theory of group rights that 'contemporary Indian thinking on the rights of groups, notably religious groups, has taken place in the language of secularism, individual versus group rights in liberal democracy, communitarianism and liberal multiculturalism, all of which have been given a nuanced interpretation in the Indian context'. Unlike the Western debate, in the Indian context, the struggle for group rights is not limited to cultural rights, and therefore the situation is 'far more complex'. Paraphrasing the work of Sheth and Mahajan (1999) who critique the Western take on cultural rights, Anant notes that 'the Western understanding of the issue of marginalisation and concerns of minorities is limited. One, the focus is mainly on cultural devaluation, two it ignores the construction of national hegemonies within the State and does not conceive of the nation-state as a plural entity and three, it believes that the preservation of minority cultures would solve all their problems' (Anant, 2011: 104).

Because the context is so strikingly different in Great Britain, a country with a long Christian tradition, a Christian majority, and a much more homogeneous society as compared to India's, policy suggestions like the one by Rowan Williams, former Archbishop of Canterbury, to introduce sharia law in the country to allow British Muslims to regulate civil matters, as is the case in India (see Chapter two), are not in a position to win a majority. For the realm of citizenship theory, these observations mean that citizenship and its derivatives, like cultural citizenship, are also always context-dependent. Quite different from Kymlicka's paradigm, when analysing cultural citizenship in India, the emphasis is not on group rights, because these are already granted, but on communicative action along the lines of Habermas's discourse model in order to supplement citizen rights—not to gain them in the first place—and to be able to shape the citizen discourse by having a voice in the media. While in the West the theoretical focus is presently on group rights, with the individual as a strong undercurrent, it might so happen that once cultural group rights have acquired the same political standing in Europe that they presently enjoy in India, there would again be a recourse to liberal theory with the rediscovery of the individual. Theory to a large extent always reflects the spirit—and fashion—of the times. This is why cross-continental explorations in theory need to be undertaken with caution, and the existence of such an entity as a 'universal theory' should be called into question.

On the question of the possibility of a 'universal theory', it should be noted that a theory is a kind of language (and, accordingly, a meta-theory is a metalanguage in the best sense of the term); people who know it can communicate with one another in abstract terms. As in the case of language, an increased level of complexity inevitably brings with it an increased number of exceptions. The more complex a language is, the denser is the set of rules and the higher the number of exceptions. The same is true for theory: the more advanced and complex it is, the more exceptions it has to carry and account for, and the less universally applicable it becomes. In consequence, if a theory has developed a high level of complexity, this might result in a Wittgensteinian silence—the death of language and of theory.[66] On the other hand, keeping theory basic ensures its applicability across a broad range of cases. Linking it to context (of time, or space, or both) can allow for its development and specification, but also means loss of its universal relevance. Cultural citizenship is a good example to underline this idea: when applied to the Indian context, the concept takes a form which is different from the one it has in the Western context.

What is chosen as a working definition here is one of many possible approaches to cultural citizenship. Theories applied to the Western setting reflect the 'cultural turn' in citizenship studies and proclaim what Janoski and Gran call 'categorical rights', that is, cultural or group rights often involving an 'exclusive entitlement to a particular activity or status, which others could use but cannot receive' (2002: 22), as is the case with Muslims in India, for example. This, however, is not how cultural citizenship is understood in the context of this book. It is not so strongly tied to rights of particular groups; it is not normative, but analytical. It is linked to a Weberian *Verstehen*[67] of why there is alienation in a society where all are equal citizens, and analyses the role which the media play in overcoming this alienation.

Like the plethora of definitions of censorship which stem from all possible disciplines (see Chapter four), the plurality of understandings of cultural citizenship obstructs the analysis. Therefore, what Joppke has said about multicultural citizenship, that the notion is 'too vague and multifaceted to be a useful tool of sociological analysis' (2002: 245), to a certain extent also holds true for cultural citizenship as discussed above. Much like E.M. Forster's questions to India that disappear only to come back as parts of larger questions,[68] it is left to the individual researcher to choose their own conceptual approach, bearing in mind context, disciplinary background, and desired outcome.

CULTURAL CITIZENSHIP AS A POLICY IN THE DEMOCRATIC CONTEXT

Set against the background of the experience of the Roman Empire, where heterogeneity prevailed, political theorist Michael Walzer's analysis of modern citizenship (1989) is marked by deep pessimism. Citizenship for Walzer 'is unlikely to be the primary identity or the consuming passion of men and women living in complex and highly differentiated societies, where politics competes for time and attention with class, ethnicity, religion, and family, and where these latter four do not draw people together but rather separate and divide them' (Walzer, 1989: 218). Is citizenship then merely a means to the individual socio-economic end of gaining benefits and being eligible for public services and office, which again, as Max Weber (1964) and Anthony Downs (1957) would say, serves to maximize the interest of the outcome-maximizing rational actor?[69]

Walzer's view, that 'democratic citizenship in its contemporary form does not seem to encourage high levels of involvement or devotion' (1989: 218), is debatable. His analytical frame is that of Western societies, where indeed not only a lower voter turnout but a decline in the overall participation in civic life has been noted. However, recent developments of civil rights movements in Russia, a debate on national versus supranational citizenship in the European Union member states, new heights of extra-parliamentary opposition, and the formation of new parties that emphasize direct citizen participation in various spheres of political life, speak against this assertion. India, deeply divided along cultural and social fault lines, has a voter turnout which has been relatively high over the past decades. It is precisely because of the many factors that divide the Indian society—which are increasingly also found in the West—that citizenship is valued and struggled for. Rather than taking away from citizenship, culture is a motor for the reconsideration and renegotiation of citizenship. Heterogeneity thus leads to a renewed interest in citizenship, not to an indifference towards it. The role of culture for a society increases as nations become larger and more diverse. It is at significant turning points in history, for example, when a country becomes independent or alters its social composition, that a reconsideration of and return to the narrative roots of the national construct takes place, again resurrecting and negotiating cultural signifiers in the process.

As noted earlier, cultural citizenship encompasses what Pfetsch (2012) has referred to as the 'psychological dimension of citizenship'. As in the conceptualization of Klaus and Lünenborg, Pfetsch's psychological dimension is identity-related. As stated previously, it refers to the sense of belonging, a person's identification with the community, and is 'closely linked to … culture' (Pfetsch, 2012: 112). However, Pfetsch's framework has some points that require elaboration. He writes that 'without the knowledge about others there can hardly develop a common-to-all feeling' (Pfetsch, 2012: 114), contradicting Benedict Anderson who perceived the nation as an imagined community of strangers, who develop a national feeling for a large multitude irrespective of the fact that they have only met and interacted with a small fraction of the total population. Pfetsch highlights the element of affection and emotion towards the community as a significant part of citizenship. In his understanding, it essentially means 'to feel comfortable with other citizens' (2012: 113). This, however, is not the main point of cultural citizenship. Rather than the subjective feeling of comfort, it is the opportunity to enter into the discourse on the nation that constitutes the main building block of cultural citizenship. Rightly then, Pfetsch also highlights the discourse model which Habermas developed in his *Theory of Communicative Action* (1987) and later applied to the case of a political Europe (1992b and 1996).

In Habermas's model, regions can be drawn closer together by intensifying transnational communication, which can, in addition, contribute to the formation of a European, supranational identity (cf. Pfetsch, 2012: 115). As Pfetsch (2003) shows, Habermas sees the reason for the democratic deficit of the European Union not only in its institutional structure, or in the claims to sovereignty by the national states, but in the lack of a 'European public', which again is the result of the lack of communication between the European Union and its citizens. Democratization on the supranational level is thus achieved by establishing a communication network, in which the national publics are included (Pfetsch, 2003: 653–4). Thus, what we get from Habermas is the idea that democratization and identity formation are

discursive processes which are produced in a public through communicative action.

The second aspect in which Habermas is relevant to this work on
citizenship is the theoretical space which he occupies, and the polit-
ico-philosophical gap that he bridges. Pfetsch argues that Habermas
constitutes the missing link between republicanism and liberalism,
and takes a 'mediating position' in the discussion which has been
ongoing since Locke and Rousseau (2003: 646). The dilemma is that
liberalism, which is based on the primacy of the freedom of equal
citizens, has to justify human rights, which, as Pfetsch shows, are not
liberal-democratic because they are pre-political. If then pre-political
elements set bounds to democratic decisions, the democratic nature
of the process can indeed be called into question. Republicanism, on
the other hand, situates human rights not in a fictitious state of nature,
but in the practice of democratic decision-making of equal and free
citizens. Human rights and sovereignty of the people are correlated.
For Kant, human rights are guaranteed by the rational character of
democratic decision-making. In the Kantian legislature, where everyone is a maker of the law, as well as subject to the law, it is impossible
that the democratic legislative violates human rights. Liberalism, in
turn, criticizes the republican model of democracy based on the claim
that the uniform will of the people is a mere construct.

As a way out of this dilemma, Habermas suggests a model of
democracy founded on the basis of discourse, which avoids the
liberal dilemma of the 'undemocratic constraint of the democratic
sovereign', as well as the danger of the tyranny of the majority connected to the republican model. For Habermas, the solution is what
he calls 'deliberative democracy'. He introduced the concept, which
he borrowed from US law theory, in his *Between Facts and Norms*
(1992a), where he substantiates his hypothesis of the shared origin
of sovereignty of the people and human rights, and further develops
his idea of democratic publics (Buchstein, 2003: 258). In this context,
deliberation basically refers to communication on political questions
in a media public. If properly institutionalized, Habermas sees potential in communicative interaction to contribute to the development
of the citizen competencies of those involved in the procedures, and,
as a consequence, expects a higher legitimacy for the larger political process. Deliberative democracy also acts as a 'moral filter', since

those involved in public discourse do not only argue for their personal interest, but also for the common good, which then replaces egoistic motivations—a process which has been referred to as the 'moralizing effect of public discussion' (Miller, 1992: 61, cited in Buchstein, 2003: 259).

There is thus a lot of Habermas in the model of cultural citizenship put forward by Klaus and Lünenborg (see Figure 3.1). Like that model, Habermas's idea of deliberative democracy builds on the equality of all participants, the transparency of the agenda, and the possibility of challenging the present discourse and the rules around which it is organized. What Habermas then calls for on the basis of his model is a less commercially organized media public to support deliberative processes (cf. Buchstein, 2003: 259). Chapter five applies this argument to an empirical reality, illustrating the relationship between active media ownership and media use, and deliberative democratic processes as understood by Habermas. While both Pfetsch (2012) and Habermas emphasize the central role of (transnational) communication in constituting a European identity, Pfetsch opposes one element of Habermas's deliberative democracy. In stating that 'the attachment towards abstract legal terms, such as freedom, equality, solidarity, etc. is ... a more rational than an emotional act' (Pfetsch, 2012: 113), Pfetsch argues against Habermas's concept of deliberative democracy, of which constitutional patriotism forms a central element (Pfetsch, 2003: 655).

To show that a Constitution and attachment to it are not sufficient for national integration and the development of citizenship is one of the core objectives of this book. Combining Habermas's emphasis on discursive processes as having an effect on citizen competence, and Pfetsch's scepticism regarding constitutional patriotism as one of the foremost identity-constituting devices, is the path chosen here to understand (cultural) citizenship in diverse societies.

INDIA AND EUROPE: CONNECTED IN THEORY AND PRACTICE

It has been shown in this chapter that culture has always been linked to participation, and hence to membership in a society. It is in the cultural arena that inclusion in or exclusion from a (national) community is determined. Older theorists have not spent precious ink and parchment elaborating on culture, because legal inclusion in the national community was the more pressing need that had to be accounted for. Cultural participation, however, has been linked to the status of the citizen implicitly, as in the writings of Rousseau and Mill. It was only in the second half of the twentieth century—once civil, political, social, and legal rights had been secured—that the focus shifted to more specific areas of social life where scope for improvement on the different levels of participation was seen. The 'citizenship with adjectives'[70] that was brought into the debate was expressive of the need for a holistic analysis of citizenship beyond the civil, political, and social triad. In view of the increasing heterogeneity of Western societies, the triadic conceptualization was regarded as insufficient, since it was unable to explain alienation in spite of political rights such as the freedom of speech and active and passive suffrage. 'Cultural citizenship' as understood in the context of this work—participation in the mediated discourse that constitutes the nation—connects the different stages of the evolutionary process of citizenship. It is a variable which has been present—overtly or covertly—throughout the conceptual history of the citizen.

This is also one of the reasons why cultural citizenship has not been the subject of deep theoretical consideration in India. Even though India has by and large formed the same citizenship regime as has the West, albeit with a necessary local edge, the issues of citizenship in India are different from those in Europe. Both India and Europe face immigration, India from the neighbouring states of Nepal, Bangladesh, and China (Tibet), and the European nation-states either from their former colonies, as in the case of Great Britain and France, or from the countries of origin of their former guest workers, as in the case of Germany. The scenarios, however, are not comparable: while in India we find the marginal citizen or the resident alien still often demanding civil, political, and social rights, the citizen of the Western welfare state, having already obtained those rights, turns to areas in which his cultural and citizen identity is at stake. While the marginal Indian citizen's (the *aam aadmi*'s) foremost desire is *roti, kapra, aur makan* (bread, cloth, shelter), more broadly speaking, social inclusion, the citizen of the West longs for more transcendental values.[71] That is not to say that culture comes last on the citizen's agenda, or that the pursuit of cultural inclusion is a pastime for those otherwise satisfied. But the observation challenges the one-to-one comparability between Europe and Asia, and the assumption of easy generalizations from the Indian case (see also Table 5.6). Citizenship, like culture, is not universal but context-dependent. This context-dependency of course defies a general theorization and a universal model of cultural citizenship across time and space.

And yet, there are citizens' movements in India that use different modes of cultural participation to gain visibility and access to tangible and intangible resources, but also to negotiate modes of belonging in the national discourse. The following chapter illustrates how valued cultural representation is, and what is done to modify and obstruct it. It will show where connections between India and Europe can be drawn to enhance the overall understanding of citizen-making and nation-building on a transcontinental scale.

4

CENSORSHIP IN INDIA

POWER IN AND THROUGH DISCOURSE

One must suppose ... that the manifold relationships of force that take
shape and come into play in the machinery of production, in families,
limited groups, and institutions, are the basis for wide-ranging effects of
cleavage that run through the social body as a whole.

(Foucault, 1994 [1981]: 164).

There is nothing self-evident about censorship, nor about the worlds it
makes. Censorship is not merely a constant forge of discourse nor is it
only a ruthless mechanism of silence. As a gamble on publicity, cultural
regulation is, for all its apparently routinized banality, an uncertain and
open-ended venture.

(Mazzarella and Kaur, 2009: 21).

DEFINING CENSORSHIP IN DIACHRONIC PERSPECTIVE

Censorship is the necessary analytical category to understand processes of citizen-making in the cultural sphere. If the nation is a
discursive project, then censorship is the instrument with which to
shape and monitor this discourse and set the standards for inclusion
and exclusion. As already stated in the Introduction, if exercised in

a transparent and accountable way, censorship is not necessarily an illiberal practice,[1] and the setting of standards by means of censorship might very well be the outcome of a democratic, majoritarian process. In any case, censorship is an act of power in the Foucaultian sense. If knowledge is power, then the regulation and structuring of what is to be known and disseminated are ways of both achieving and sustaining power. As has been shown in Chapter two, censorship requires both *structure*, which makes it possible for it to arise, and *agency* in order for it to be implemented. This chapter introduces different forms of censorship and discusses two contemporary cases of censorship in India, one of which predominantly involved state and the other non-state actors. Through these cases it seeks to illustrate the different political spaces in which the censorship regimes operate, and shows the effects that shifts in its location have on those spaces, and on the society as a whole.

As has been outlined in the second chapter, censorship, as a practice, is subject to flow. It has existed and continues to exist throughout time and geographical as well as political space. In Greece in 399 BCE, Socrates was forced to drink the hemlock cup, an iconic incidence of the author's execution as the ultimate form of censorship.[2] In this sense, Jansen rightly observes that 'censorship is an enduring feature of all human communities' (1991: 8). Thus, Reinhard Aulich, following the idea that censorship is exercised in any society, labels it a 'trans-epochal cultural phenomenon'[3] (Aulich, 1988: 183)—a phenomenon which is omnipresent and can be used to modify 'any form of discourse' (Müller, 2003: 3). Techniques and manuals of censorship are indeed found across time and space: it is established that censorship of written symbols was already present in the early Sumerian and Egyptian civilizations (Childe, 1951, cited in Jansen, 1991: 41). Rigid social controls were built into the structure of Chinese ideography from its inception (Weber, 1991),[4] and the Old Testament states that the Hebrews burned the prophecy of Jeremiah (36: 23) because the vision of the future it projected caused despair.[5]

Kauṭilya's *Arthashastra*, discussed in detail in Chapter three, states that 'kings shall never be insulted because divine punishment will be visited on whoever slights them. Thus the people shall be discouraged from having seditious thoughts. Spies shall also find out [and report] the rumours circulating among the people' (Kauṭilya, 1987: 510). The

Law of the Twelve Tables in the Roman Republic, which dates to 450 BCE, bans mock verses. The Roman censorial bureaucracy was established even earlier, with the first censors being commissioned in 443 BCE (Jansen, 1991: 41). Such official censorship regimes have persisted and developed throughout the ages. In the same vein, taking recourse to the practices of the Roman *censors*, in the seventeenth century Thomas Hobbes writes in his *Leviathan* that 'it is annexed to the sovereignty, to be judge of what opinions and doctrines are averse ... and who shall examine the doctrines of all books before they are published' (Hobbes, 1996 [1651], Chapter 18: 117).

These examples serve to show that close surveillance of people and cultural products is the necessary precondition for censorship, which, in turn, is a mechanism for identity construction. Censorship is a tool of subject-making, and it has from early on been linked to citizenship, with these links becoming stronger over time. In ancient Rome, as Jansen notes, in order to count citizens, the censors had to establish standards for citizenship, which included moral standards. In the event of failure to conform to these standards, that is, if the censors disapproved of a man's public or private behaviour, they could irreversibly deprive him of his citizenship (Jansen, 1991: 41).

The term 'censorship' is derived from the Latin *censere*, to evaluate, and from the noun *censura*, meaning 'assessment' or 'examination'. Originally used in ancient Roman tax policy, the word referred to the assessment of property by the responsible civil servant, the censor, thus also establishing a connection between censorship and ranking in the original sense of the term. Censorship is defined in various ways, for example, as 'any measure that is directed at controlling journalistic media and to prevent the dissemination of certain pieces of information or opinions' (Roether, 2008: 418). However, such exclusivist definitions that are solely focused on the media capture the phenomenon only insufficiently. Arguing in favour of a broad understanding of censorship, Judith Butler (2006) claims that it cannot be limited to the study of legalistic limitations of speech, but must be extended to a discussion on what can be considered the subject of an act of censorship in the first place. If certain forms of speech are not defined as speech to start with, and can hence not be subject to censorship, then an act of censorship has already been committed (Butler, 2006: 199–200). Much in line with this structural approach to censorship, Bodo Plachta (2006) defines it as the 'examination of a statement on a thing or person with regard to their congruence with existing rules as the precondition for any form of communication and its effect'. Plachta states that the understanding of censorship indeed varies according to the subject perspective (2006: 15). This can mean a narrow or broad understanding of censorship, which can include 'any form of discursive control' (Plachta, 2006: 15). In this vein, the sociologist Ulla Otto also understands censorship to be the 'authoritarian control of human statements' (1968: 3).

These broader conceptualizations, which point to censorship being locatable both within and beyond the realm of the media, are extremely valid, since they do not restrict censorship to a regulative instrument for a specific social site, but emphasize its character as an instrument of power pervading all forms of human interaction. Subscribing to this notion, Jan and Aleida Assmann (1987) regard censorship as 'the means of putting through a canon as an instrument to give meanings to texts and as a tool for the retention of power against subversive attacks'. Jansen (1991) provides an equally broad definition of censorship rooted in power and discourse. She conceptualizes censorship as 'a form of surveillance: a mechanism for gathering intelligence that the powerful can use to tighten control over people and ideas that threaten to disrupt established systems of order' (Jansen, 1991: 14). Due to her sociological approach to the study of censorship, Jansen's definition is 'much broader than definitions which have currency in Liberal free-speech theory' (Jansen, 1991: 221), and encompasses 'all socially structured proscriptions or prescriptions which inhibit or prohibit dissemination of ideas, information, images, and other messages through a society's channels of communication whether these obstructions are secured by political, economic, religious, or other systems of authority. It includes both overt and covert proscriptions and prescriptions' (Jansen, 1991: 221).

Broad definitions such as these are indeed needed to fully grasp the extent and significance of censorship. When one speaks of the censorship of texts, as Assmann and Assmann (1987) do, 'text' must be understood not in its narrow but rather in its semiotic sense, where any cultural artefact can be read as a text. The overall conception of what the realm of the media encompasses is conditioned by socio-cultural developments during the early modern and the modern age, which saw the steady rise of print media and the invention of optical and acoustic broadcast media. If 'media' are understood as broadly as the concept of the 'text', then the unit of analysis inevitably expands as well. Eisenkolb (2007), for instance, claims that the history of the media is as old as the history of mankind. She emphasizes the existence and relevance of media in proto- and early history, describing works of architecture and so-called 'storage media' like seals and coins as conveyors of information, meaning, and power (cf. Eisenkolb, 2007: 7). Following this conception, the act of destruction of the Babri Masjid in Ayodhya on 6 December 1992 by Hindu extremists would also constitute an act of media censorship, as it is an attempt to silence and *de-visualize* a particular religious community.

The 'conceptual stretching' of censorship beyond the literary sphere has been criticized for causing a decline in analytic precision, and censorship research has treated broad understandings of the concept with scepticism (Plachta, 2006: 18) on the grounds that these definitions have a 'tendency towards abstract generalization' (Müller, 2003: 18). Some scholars, however, go even further in their analysis of what constitutes censorship: informed by a Marxist understanding, Jansen (1991) introduces the category of the 'market censor' to refer to those who control the productive process and determine 'what is to be mass produced in the cultural arena and what will not be produced. These *market censors* decide what ideas will gain entry into the marketplace of ideas and what ideas will not' (Jansen, 1991: 16).[6] Beyond the liberal context, where Jansen situates this market censorship, censorship can be found in authoritarian political settings, such as in the People's Republic of China: there, a limited number of thirty-four foreign films per year are permitted to be screened in cinemas—for economic rather than political reasons. The Chinese leadership intends to promote and further national film productions, and therefore uses censorship as a tool of market foreclosure (Lee, 2013). Other examples of the close connection between market and (self-)censorship include the cutting of scenes that would make a film unfit for a certain audience, with the target audience being identified not by artistic criteria, but in terms of its buying power. For the United States, Claus (2013) gives the example of Marc Foster's *World War Z*, a horror film based on the bestselling novel by Max Brooks (2006), where many scenes were cut so that the film could be released with a PG-13 certificate[7] and attract a larger teenage consumer base. Films that are restricted to an older viewer group, it is argued, cannot make enough profit in the United States (Claus, 2013). Thus, the desire for family entertainment—and the revenue it generates—seals the fate of a film that is criticized for being lengthy and tiring. There are also more acute examples of 'market censorship'; for instance, in Turkey in 2013, the media did not report objectively on the Istanbul mass protests against the government, for the simple reason that the same companies that owned the private media also owned construction companies that thrived on government contracts.

In addition to the multitude of definitions, there are also various classifications of the different types of censorship. Karolides et al. (2005), for example, differentiate between censorship on political, social, religious, and sexual grounds. The first of these forms—political censorship—refers to activities by the government that lead to citizens being blocked from receiving information, ideas, and opinions that the government perceives to be critical, embarrassing, or threatening. The impression, however, that censorship for political reasons emanates only from national governments is misleading. As the authors point out, the second common source of such activity is the local community, where censorship is generated by citizens, individually or in groups. Social censorship is the label given to media that are suppressed for reasons of their subject matter and characters not conforming to the censors' social, racial, or sexual standards (Karolides et al., 2005: 395). Media are then banned on the grounds of language, racial characterization, the depiction of drug use, social class, the sexual orientation of characters, or other social differences that their challengers view as harmful to readers.

Suppression of media on explicitly religious grounds constitutes one of the oldest forms of censorship, and is the one that has been explored in most detail. Media censored on religious grounds are either branded with the charge of heresy, which is defined as an opinion or doctrine that is at variance with orthodox religious teaching, or with the charge of blasphemy, which is commonly defined as speaking in a profane or irreverent manner about the sacred (Karolides et al., 2005: 199). Probably the most widespread form of censorship in India is the suppression of media on sexual grounds. The opposition to late Muslim painter M.F. Husain's (1915–2011) nude portraits of the Hindu goddesses Saraswati and Draupadi on the part of Hindu nationalists points to the overlapping of the categories of censorship: groups exercising political censorship and thereby claiming cultural authority often present themselves as upholders of moral standards. In the case of Husain, his visualization marked a modern creative engagement with the traditional religious sphere. The ensuing de-visualization helps the censors retain a certain monopoly of interpretation, and thus constitutes a move against cultural citizenship as understood in this book.

Military censorship, which is mentioned here for reasons of completeness, is a specific form of censoring which occurs during times of war, inner conflict, and state emergency. Archival documents from the time of the two World Wars testify to the use of censorship of militarily and strategically sensitive issues in India. In his *Discovery of India*, written during his detention at Ahmadnagar Fort Prison Camp from 1942 to 1945, Jawaharlal Nehru uses the term 'double censorship' to refer to censorship in the colony during the Second World War. Censorship regulations were then exercised more strictly, with additional rules being applied. Nehru describes the regular censorship that the provincial governments were subjected to under the Imperial Criminal Investigation Department[8] as follows:

> Not only were our letters censored, but even the ministers' correspondence was sometimes subjected to this, though it was done quietly and not officially admitted. During the last quarter of a century or more I have not written a single letter, which has been posted in India, either to an Indian or a foreign address, without realizing that it would be seen, and possibly copied, by some secret service censor. Nor have I spoken on the telephone without remembering that my conversation was likely to be tapped. The letters that have reached me also have had to pass some censor. This does not mean that every single letter is always censored; sometimes this has been done, at other times selected ones are examined. This has nothing to do with the war, when there is a double censorship (Nehru, 1946: 378–9).

The year of the 'Quit India Movement',[9] 1942, was characterized by more intense censorship that went hand in hand with pro-British and anti-Indian propaganda. Writing about 1942, Nehru notes that

> a strict censorship cast a heavy veil over the happenings in India. Even newspapers in India were not permitted to give publicity to much that was daily taking place, and messages to foreign countries were subject

to an even stricter surveillance. At the same time official propaganda was let loose abroad, and false and tendentious accounts were circulated. The United States of America were especially flooded with this propaganda, for opinion there was held to count, and hundreds of lecturers and others, both English and Indian, were sent there to tour the country (Nehru, 1946: 491).

In this typology of forms of censorship, the 'Emergency Rule' needs to find mention as an Indian specificity. Fakhruddin Ali Ahmed, then president of India, declared a state of Emergency on 26 June 1975 under Article 352(1) of the Constitution.[10] It lasted for twenty-one months until 21 March 1977 and is often cited, also by some of the respondents interviewed in the course of research for this book, as the 'only time that there was censorship in India'. In a personal interview, Shivaji Sarkar, then Associate Professor of English journalism at the Indian Institute of Mass Communication (IIMC) in New Delhi and former president of the Delhi Journalist Association, described the period of the Emergency as follows:

> In Emergency we had censorship. Mrs Indira Gandhi had imposed censorship. And those days no media was free. Even in newspapers, you could not carry any news item unless it was passed by the censor. So, those were two years of very difficult days. Forget about those nineteen months, when of course, the Doordarshan and All India Radio were also under the direct thumb of the government. They could not have functioned in a different way. But apart from those nineteen months, censorship has never been successful. In fact, Mrs Gandhi also later realized, that because of the censorship, she could not get proper feedback. So, after that, no government freely wanted to clamp down directly or indirectly any kind of censorship the way it was done then. It was an experiment which failed.[11]

However, not all voices are that unambiguous. The journalist and writer Paranjoy Guha Thakurta holds that even though 'it was only during the Emergency in the mid-1970s that the subcontinent saw its press severely censored', today, at a time when the phenomenon of 'paid news'[12] is an issue, he perceives a different form of censorship, much in line with Jansen's economic approach to the matter. 'Most newspapers in India today', Guha Thakurta writes, 'deploy more subtle forms of censorship—those driven by the market, or by those in power who can bribe journalists with lavish international junkets' (2009: 140).

Lastly, self-censorship needs to find mention as a category in its own right. It is exercised by cultural producers themselves out of fear of external censorship and repression. One recent example is filmmaker Roland Emmerich, who directed and co-wrote the blockbuster *2012* (2009), an apocalyptic vision of the destruction of the earth by natural disaster. While the film shows the destruction of St Peter and the Vatican, Emmerich deliberately refrained from including the destruction of the Kaaba in Mecca for fear of putting his life in danger (Roll, 2010). Censorship thus is not only *product*, but also *process*. The anticipation of possible acts of censorship limits individuals, and sets narrow boundaries for creativity. Incidentally, since the 1960s it has been debated whether self-censorship is not actually the greatest threat to the freedom of opinion (Roether, 2008: 422). Under the constraints of self-censorship, journalists might not report on what they consider taboo, or topics which could potentially be unpopular with decision-makers in politics and the economy.[13]

Highlighting the processual dimension of censorship is crucial, because it allows the observer to analyse the position of the victims and the perpetrators in an ongoing power play. German national poet Goethe, whose work *Die Leiden des jungen Werther* (The sorrows of young Werther) was banned in several German states in 1774, the year of its first publication (Plachta, 2006: 8), knew that censorship is what the mighty claim and exercise, while freedom of the press is what the lesser people demand.[14] The existence of censorship thus is always a manifestation of an asymmetry of power prevailing in a given society.

When studying censorship in the Indian context—but not only there—a conceptual distinction needs to be made between official, institutionalized, or formal, and unofficial, un-institutionalized, or informal censorship.[15] These two forms can be contradictory and mutually exclusive, but, as will be shown below, they often overlap and reinforce each other, leading to a strengthening of the censorship regime, and a more pervasive and therefore more rigid application of its measures. Kalpana Sharma (2003) thus starts her account of the Gujarat riots of 2002 with the words, 'if the official censor does not get you, the unofficial one will.'

WHEN OFFICIAL AND UNOFFICIAL CENSORSHIP INTERSECT: A CASE STUDY OF THE 'RAMANUJAN ISSUE'

The case study chosen to illustrate and discuss this point of the over-lap between official and unofficial censorship is what has come to be known as the 'Ramanujan issue', the series of events that happened around the modification of the curriculum of the School of History of the University of Delhi in 2011.[16] This incident, which is not only topical but very crucial for an understanding of the processes that are at work with regard to censorship in India, is first narrated and then analysed in terms of a theory of crossing, belonging, and contestation.

In 1987, the South Indian historian and literary scholar A.K. Ramanujan (1929–1993) published his essay 'Three Hundred Rāmāyaṇas: Five Examples and Three Thoughts on Translation'.[17] In this text he laid out the multiplicity of narrative traditions of the *Rāmāyaṇa*[18] epic in India, South Asia, and Southeast Asia. Ramanujan's scholarly text describes the existence of many different versions of the *Rāmāyaṇa*, which in some cases also constitute counter-narratives contradicting each other, and in many ways diverge from the text as it is ascribed to the sage Vālmīki, which is often regarded as an *Ur-text*, to borrow Paula Richman's (1992) term. Drawing on the diversity of narratives, Ramanujan states that the *Rāmāyaṇa* is in fact not a set of texts, but constitutes a genre in its own right. In identifying some of the Rāmāyaṇas as 'counter-texts', Ramanujan observes the subversive character and, following from that, the political nature of the texts (1999: 157). In his essay, Ramanujan lists the many South-, East-, and Southeast Asian languages in which Rāmāyaṇas exist (note the use of the plural here),[19] and emphasizes the number of different narratives within each of the languages.[20] To the diversity of the narratives on the life of Rāma are added the many non-textual representations, for example in the form of sculptures, bas reliefs, mask-, puppet-, and shadow plays that are to be found in the various South- and Southeast Asian cultural traditions (Ramanujan, 1999: 134).

The 'five examples' for the narratological diversity of Rāmāyaṇas that Ramanujan discusses include a description of the Jain tellings of the epic. There, 'the Rāma story no longer carries Hindu values. Indeed the Jain texts express the feeling that the Hindus, especially the brahmans, have maligned Rāvaṇa, made him into a villain' (Ramanujan, 1999: 144). To substantiate his claim, Ramanujan quotes a Jain text that asks the following questions:

How can monkeys vanquish the powerful *rākṣasa*[21] warriors like Rāvaṇa? How can noble men and Jain worthies like Rāvaṇa eat flesh and drink blood? How can Kumbhakarṇa[22] sleep through six months of the year, and never wake up even though boiling oil was poured into his ears, elephants were made to trample over him, and war trumpets and conches blown around him? (Ramanujan, 1999: 144).

In effect, Ramanujan here cites a text that calls into question the *Rāmāyaṇa* as told by Vālmīki. It doubts divine power and, most importantly, labels Rāvaṇa, the epic's villain, a 'Jain worthy'. In the Southeast Asian example given by Ramanujan, the Thai *Ramakirti*, Rām is a subordinate of Śiva, as opposed to being one of the ten avatars of the god Viṣṇu as in the dominant Hindu mythological tradition. In the *Ramakirti*, Rām, of whom Thai audiences are less fond compared to Hanumān (Ramanujan, 1999: 149), is seen as a 'human hero, and the text is not regarded as a religious work or even as an exemplary work on which men and women may pattern themselves' (Ramanujan, 1999: 149). This is similar to the Jain texts, where Ram is portrayed not as a god, but 'only as an evolved Jain man who is in his last birth and so does not even kill Rāvaṇa' (Ramanujan, 1999: 155). Rāmāyaṇas, in Ramanujan's understanding, thus are 'indexical texts': the texts are embedded in a locale, a context, which they refer to and signify, and outside of which they would not make much sense (Ramanujan, 1999: 157).[23] Thus, the many Rāmāyaṇas also differ from one another in so far as they are always culture-specific statements. Ramanujan explains this by drawing on a folk legend which, contrary to the dominant narrative that singles out Vālmīki as the chronicler of the life of Rām, says that Hanumān wrote the original *Rāmāyaṇa* on a mountaintop after the war against Rāvaṇa and scattered the manuscript, which was many times larger than what exists today. Vālmīki is said to have captured only a fragment of it, which is why 'no text is original, yet no telling is a mere retelling—and the story has no closure' (Ramanujan, 1999: 158).

In 2006, Ramanujan's essay was put on the syllabus of the history course of the University of Delhi, which enjoys the reputation of being one of India's prime institutions of higher learning. Two years later, in 2008, Hindu right activists of the Akhil Bharatiya Vidyarthi Parishad (ABVP),[24] vandalized the office of the head of the Department of History, Professor S.Z.H. Jafri, in protest against the essay. The reason given by the political activists for their move was the 'indecent nature of the text' and its 'heretic character', which they saw manifested in sentences such as 'he [Indra, a sage] is cursed with a thousand vaginas which are later changed into eyes' (Ramanujan, 1999: 141), or in Ramanujan's description of the Thai *Ramakirti*, where he notes that 'neither celibate nor devout, as in the Hindu *Rāmāyaṇa*, here Hanumān is quite a ladies' man, who doesn't at all mind looking into the bedrooms of Lanka and doesn't consider seeing another man's sleeping wife anything immoral, as Vālmīki's or Kampan's Hanumān does'[25] (Ramanujan, 1999: 149–50).

It is illustrative of the larger significance of the issue that the Supreme Court of India, in reaction to the events, appointed a four-member committee to investigate the matter. On 9 October 2011, the Academic Council of the university, the body responsible for the arrangement of the teaching agenda, removed the essay from the syllabus of the B.A. Honours concurrent course entitled 'Cultures of India: Ancient'. This move was interpreted as a surrender to political pressure (Datta, 2011) and sparked large-scale protests among students, academic staff, intellectuals, and civil society organizations far beyond the DU campus. News of the removal of the essay has had large coverage in print, television, and electronic media. Students and teachers of the two most renowned comprehensive universities of the country, DU and Jawaharlal Nehru University (JNU), staged protest marches with banners demanding the reintroduction of the essay. To them, the decision to take the essay off the syllabus was a curtailment of academic freedom, and so they encouraged resistance against the 'saffronization' of higher education (see Figure 4.1).

The protest against the removal of the essay was supported by prominent academics, such as Mushirul Hasan, former vice-chancellor of Jamia Millia Islamia, like DU and JNU a central university in New Delhi, and former Director-General of the National Archives of India. Asked whether the ban on Ramanujan's essay on

Figure 4.1   Protests of Students and Academic Staff at DU against the Removal of A.K. Ramanujan's Essay 'Three Hundred Rāmāyaṇas'
Source: Vijetha, 2011. Available at: http://www.thehindu.com/news/national/history-dept-demands-reintroduction-of-ramanujans-essay-on-ramayana/article2568546.ece (last access: 20 October 2015).

the Rāmāyaṇas was an attempt to curtail academic freedom, Hasan replied:

> Of course it is. In fact it's a scandal that calls to question the collective wisdom of a university's supreme body for academic affairs—the academic council. How can an academic council approve such a decision in the presence of so many intellectuals? It's a worrying thought ... in such a scenario there can be no development, no intellectual inquiry and no freedom of expression (interview by Manash Pratim Gohain, *Sunday Times of India*, 30 October 2011).

The discourse around the removal of the essay is not a closed one, as will be shown in the discussion of the Indian media, and specifically 'grassroots comics', in the following chapter. One discourse feeds into other discourses and thereby opens up new spaces for discussion and engagement with the topic.

ANALYSING THE 'RAMANUJAN ISSUE' IN TERMS OF 'DISCURSIVE CROSSING'

The removal of the essay from the academic syllabus of DU's History Department is not at all an isolated incident. India's academic landscape has in the recent past been struck by policy decisions that were perceived as unjustified infringements on the freedom of the person and the freedom of expression. In 2010, Mumbai University dropped Rohinton Mistry's novel *Such a long Journey* (1991) from the English literature syllabus under pressure from the Hindu right party Shiv Sena, which held that the book shows Maharashtrians in a poor light.[26] The 2014 decision of the publishing house Penguin to discontinue the publication of Wendy Doniger's academic work *The Hindus: An Alternative History*, first published in 2009, is another recent issue which has attracted considerable attention and shows direct parallels with the Ramanujan case.

These incidents illustrate three significant points: first, they show that self-proclaimed cultural gatekeepers, in these cases the Hindu nationalist ABVP or the Shiv Sena, set borders to a discourse. Second, discursive plurality can challenge power structures which are manifested not least by means of censorship. Third, 'crossing' as an interventionist strategy and an oppositional move vis-à-vis those power structures is a means of identity affirmation, and an expression of belonging to the discursive sphere and therefore to the national community.

The Ramanujan incident is analysed here in the conceptual terms of the 'crossing' of discursive borders and its effects on the social system. Scholars of Group 4 of the Research Center for Social and Cultural Studies at the University of Mainz, Germany, have recently taken the term 'crossing' beyond its socio-linguistic context, where it is used to describe the phenomenon of speakers using languages or linguistic varieties other than their own. Instead, they propose to understand what they call 'discursive crossing' in three ways: as an intersection of various discourses, as a transgression of boundaries within discourses, and as the idea of exceeding the discourse itself.[27]

Borders are not necessarily geographical demarcations, but can be of a social, communicative, cultural, iconographic, and symbolic nature. When people cross such borders, be it visually or textually, they also cross spaces, which poses a challenge to the existing power (im)balance and can be a subversive act leading to an alteration of meaning (Donnan and Wilson, 1999). In the present case, these borders are patrolled by the self-proclaimed cultural guardians of the *Rāmāyaṇa*. Following the Gramscian idea of establishing cultural hegemony through control over the discourse, censorship is then a power mechanism directed at the modification of discourse and the establishment of structures of domination by the way of institutionalizing a specific reading of a text. Referring back to Benedict Anderson's (1983) assertion, noted in the Introduction, that the nation is imagined through discourse, a crossing of cultural and symbolic borders also constitutes a negotiation over belonging to a national community and a (re)positioning of the self in the discursive sphere.

In the words of Salman Rushdie, who was subjected to life-threatening censorship when a fatwa was issued against him by the leader of the Iranian revolution Ayatollah Khomeni: 'those who do not have power over the stories that dominate their lives, power to retell them, rethink them, deconstruct them, joke about them, and change them as times change, truly are powerless because they cannot think new thoughts' (quoted in Bery, 2003: 103). In other words, if citizens cannot cross discursive boundaries, let alone establish any, they are disempowered. In this context, power can be measured by one's share in the discourse.

It has been argued earlier that censorship is an instrument of nation-building. Looking again at the fate of A.K. Ramanujan's essay at the University of Delhi, it is by structuring and controlling an academic discourse that a particular reading of history, a particular understanding of religion, and hence a specific image of the nation, are constructed and inculcated in the minds of the future elites of the country. For instance, Heinrich Heine's (1797–1856) works were subject to censorship during his lifetime in nineteenth-century Germany, and again in the twentieth century when they were publicly burnt by the National Socialists. In his verse-epic *Germany, A Winter's Tale* (1844), a high point of political poetry, Heine satirically makes the point that censorship by institutions such as the Prussian Zollverein is regarded as a necessary precondition for (external and internal) national unity:

And many books also you'd see in my head,
If the top were only off it!

My head is a twittering bird's nest, full
Of books that they gladly would forfeit.

Believe me that matters are no worse off
In the library e'en of the devil;
E'en Hoffmann of Fallersleben[28] ne'er wrote
Any works that were half so evil.

A passenger who stood by my side
Remark'd that we now had before us
The famous Prussian Zollverein,
The customhouses' vast chorus.

'The Zollverein' thus he observed,
'Will found our nationality,
And join our scatter'd fatherland
In bonds of cordiality'.

'Twill give us external unity,
That kind that's material and real:
The censorship gives us the other kind,
That's ghostly and ideal'.

'It gives us internal unity,
In thought as well as in feelings;
A united Germany need we to rule
Our outward and inward dealings'.

Source of the English translation: Heine (2007: 7+9)

In this sense, the Ramanujan controversy is nothing new, but
stands in a long tradition of instrumentalization of literature in
general, and of the *Rāmāyaṇa* in particular. The Sanskritist Sheldon
Pollock (1993) asserts that

> there is a long history to the relationship between Rāmāyaṇa and politi-
> cal symbology. From an early period the story supplied, continuously and
> readily, if in a highly differentiated way, a repertory of imaginative instru-
> ments for articulating a range of political discourses. In fact, it may be
> doubted whether any other text in South Asia has ever supplied an idiom
> or vocabulary for political imagination remotely comparable in longevity,
> frequency of deployment, and effectivity. This is a history, however, that
> for premodern India, at least, remains largely unwritten (Pollock, 1993:
> 262).

The first broadcasting of the two great epics, the *Ramayan* (from 1986 to 1988) and the *Mahabharat* (from 1988 to 1990) on Doordarshan, the Indian public television channel, is often cited as a recent example of the phenomenon that Pollock (1993) describes: the proximity between readings of the epic and political symbolism. In the academic discourse, the serials have been used to illustrate how Doordarshan was employed in the ideological construction of nation, identity, and citizenship. Purnima Mankekar, for example, sees the state-run television as playing a leading role in the 'culture wars fought to define the Indian nation' (Mankekar, 1999: 5). She argues that with the introduction of entertainment serials in 1984, the state intensified its effort to deploy public television in the task of creating a pan-Indian national culture. The two great Hindu epics were phenomenally successful in creating mass audiences, which can be measured from the fact that the number of television sets purchased increased from five million in 1985 to thirty-five million in 1990. By 1992 then more than 80 per cent of the Indian population had access to television. In her chapter entitled 'Mediating Modernities: The *Ramayan* and the creation of Community and Nation', Mankekar situates the televisation of the *Rāmāyana* within a socio-historical context marked by the escalation of tensions between Hindus and Muslims and the ascendance of Hindu nationalism. Mankekar examines 'how the Ramayan shaped "commonsense" conceptions of Indian culture, belonging, and identity in an unfolding war of position' (Mankekar, 1999: 165).

Similarly, the political scientist Lloyd Rudolph elaborates on the relevance of the *Ramayan* serial in standardizing the epic and substituting a national version for a large variety of regional and local ones (1992: 1494). The screening of the epic, Rudolph argues, played a crucial role in creating a national Hindu identity and a form of group consciousness which had not existed up to then. While he is cautious in generalizing from this, Rudolph still notes that this 'nationalisation of culture' signifies that the diversity of local and regional imaginations, which has been the source of India's cultural richness, is likely to fall victim to national standardization (Rudolph, 1992: 1494). He cites the example of the village of Gatiali in the State of Rajasthan, where in 1993 the villagers decided not to perform their annual Rāmlila, a theatrical performance of the *Rāmāyana* which was an 'element of [the

village's] collective being, its consciousness of itself as a community'
(Rudolph, 1992: 1494). The reason was that a number of the leaders
of the village community had watched the Doordarshan version and
thought their version might diverge from what they considered to be
the 'true' *Rāmāyaṇa*—in other words, the villagers feared that they
'might get it wrong' (Rudolph, 1992: 1494). Rudolph thus concludes
that the series, in conjunction with the outlook and practice of Hindu
national organizations, opened the way to the communalization of
the epic. 'The intersecting of the megaseries with the revivalism and
fundamentalism of Hindu national movements and politics is not
only undermining and displacing the localism and diversity of religious identity', Rudolph writes, 'it has the potential for weakening the
pluralist toleration and inclusiveness of pre-TV religious identity and
esteem' (Rudolph, 1992: 1495). Likewise, Mankekar underlines the
fatal employment of the visual media for nationalist ends by stressing
that 'with its political, cultural and economic impact, Doordarshan ...
became centrally engaged in contemporary battles over the meaning
of nationhood, belonging and cultural citizenship'; as a consequence,
Indian culture would never be the same again (Mankekar, 1999: 6).

MONOPOLIZING DISCOURSE: JOSEPH LELYVELD'S 'GREAT SOUL' IN GUJARAT

In addition to the Ramanujan issue, a prime case of the intersection
and mutual reinforcement of social, political, and sexual censorship
is that of one of the latest, and certainly most controversial, biographies of Mahatma Gandhi. As much as the 'Ramanujan issue' is a
case of censorship from below, where a state institution succumbed
to non-institutional pressure, the fate of *Great Soul* in Gujarat is an
example of direct regulation by a State government.

Written by Joseph Lelyveld, the American Pulitzer Prize winning
journalist and former executive editor of the *New York Times* (1994–
2001), the biography of Gandhi, *Great Soul*, published in 2011, sparked
an ongoing debate in India and beyond, and was banned by Narendra
Modi's government in Gujarat, Gandhi's home State, which has its
capital named after him. A lot has been read into the text, the subtitle
of which—*Mahatma Gandhi and His Struggle with India*—can be
understood as a programmatic reassessment of the historical figure.

At the risk of over-interpretation, the unconventional choice of the preposition 'with' rather than 'for' can be seen as pointing towards the personal and emotional constraints that Gandhi faced in a social environment determined by tradition, conservatism, and, not least, sexual-moral hypocrisy. Lelyveld explicitly says in his initial author's note that he does not intend the book to be a 'retelling of the standard Gandhi narrative' (Lelyveld, 2011: xiii),[29] What he draws is thus a novel picture which more or less explicitly introduces new—and for some readers disquieting—ideas about the Mahatma. Gandhi himself in his autobiography, *The Story of my Experiments with Truth*, 'begins the account of his sexual preoccupations and struggles with his marriage at the age of thirteen' (Kakar, 1990: 86).

In his discussion of the autobiographical writings, the Indian psychoanalyst Sudhir Kakar also notes Gandhi's 'projection of his own turbulent sexual wishes and fantasies onto his wife' Kasturba, and the influence of Sheikh Mehtab, Gandhi's 'intimate friend', whom Gandhi is said to have portrayed as 'his evil genius', his 'tempter', who introduced the vegetarian to the 'guilt-ridden pleasures of eating meat', and with whom he is said to have visited a brothel (Kakar, 1990: 87–8). This is to say that Lelyveld is not the first to have written explicitly on Gandhi and sex, and that too in a very straightforward way. Why then is it that the new biography has created such huge controversy?

Lelyveld refutes what some have read into his book, namely that Gandhi was bisexual and had a relationship with the architect and bodybuilder Hermann Kallenbach. About Gandhi's relationship with Kallenbach, however, he writes that it was 'the most intimate, also ambiguous, relationship of his lifetime' (Lelyveld, 2011: 88). While it is true that the word 'bisexual' or 'homosexual' is not used in this context, or anywhere else in the book, the text, based on different personal accounts and scholarly opinions, argues that Gandhi and Kallenbach were a couple and lived together 'almost in the same bed' (Lelyveld, 2011: 88). Lelyveld cites an anonymous 'respected Gandhi scholar' who argues that the relationship was '"clearly homoerotic" rather than homosexual, intending through that choice of words to describe a strong mutual attraction, nothing more' (Lelyveld, 2011: 88). The author is thus careful to not say more than research can account for, but it is sentences such as 'it was no secret then, or later, that Gandhi ... had gone to live with a man' (Lelyveld, 2011: 88) which aroused negative sentiment in India. In fact, of the prologue to the book, one part is dedicated to Gandhi's vow of celibacy, including the line 'Gandhi ... pledged to be celibate for the rest of his days (as he had presumably been, after all, during all the years of separation from his wife in London and South Africa).' This quote from pages sixteen and seventeen of the book would suffice to free Lelyveld of the charges of ascribing homosexual tendencies to the leader of the independence movement, but are thoroughly overlooked by the opponents of *Great Soul*.

Their resentment is based on accounts by the biographer which are less ambiguous, for example, passages on Gandhi's relationship with his 17-year-old grandniece Manu. After his vow of celibacy or *brahmacharya*,[30] which he took in 1906, and which entailed that he would be celibate for the rest of his days, forty years later, in 1946, Gandhi deepened his personal *yajna*, his course of self-sacrifice. Manu, the daughter of his nephew Jaisukhlal Gandhi and a devoted penfriend of the Mahatma, had attended to Gandhi's wife Kasturba three years earlier, and had nursed her until the end. Manu was then invited to Gandhi's ashram, or in the biographer's words, was 'coaxed and cajoled ... to rejoin his entourage' (Lelyveld, 2011: 303).[31] Lelyveld's description of the grandniece's role in the ashram is ambiguous, for the sources on which it is based leave room for interpretation. That Lelyveld cites sources without taking a clear stance against or in support of them is part of the reason for the wave of criticism that the book faced. According to the biography, it was one of Manu's tasks to administer Gandhi's daily massage and bath, which sometimes exceeded one and a half hours and followed a clear course: 'first one part of the body, then another ... in invariable succession' (Lelyveld, 2011: 304). The author here draws on a memoir by Nirmal Kumar Bose, Gandhi's Bengali interpreter, but leaves the quotation without further comment, thus making his text prone to (over)interpretation and attack. What in this context can be considered a central passage, and has become a bone of contention, is quoted in full here:

> It turned out that Manu Gandhi would also be expected to play the female lead in the brahmacharya test the Mahatma now saw as essential to his self-purification. Starting in the late 1930s, he'd had female attendants sleep on bedrolls laid out to the side of his; if he experienced tremors or

shivers, as sometimes he did, they'd be expected to embrace him until the shaking stopped. Now he planned to have Manu share the same mattress. Perfection would be achieved if the old man and the young woman wore the fewest possible garments, preferably none, and neither one felt the slightest possible stirring. A perfect brahmachari, he later wrote in a letter, should be 'capable of lying naked with naked women, however beautiful they may be, without being in any manner whatsoever sexually aroused.' Such a man would be completely free from anger and malice. Sexlessness was the ideal for which he was striving. His relation to Manu, he told her, would be essentially that of a mother. None of this would go on in secret; other members of his entourage might share the same veranda or room (Lelyveld, 2011: 304).

The paragraph illustrates two significant points. For one, its intention is to prove that Mahatma Gandhi had a sex life, which paradoxically is characterized by 'sexlessness', and that this sex life was performed in the open rather than in secret; and secondly, in doing so, it humanizes Gandhi, shows that his brahmacharya was 'flawed', as Lelyveld writes on page 274. For the opponents of Lelyveld, this 'humanization' is in fact the desecration of a superhuman leader. As is the case with the controversy around Ramanujan's text, the crucial issue in tracing the path that a censorship of cultural artefacts can take, is that the debate over academic texts does not remain confined to academic or scholarly circles or follow academic conventions; rather, it is first distorted, then scandalized and politicized, and finally tabooed.

There are numerous other passages throughout the book where the author, partly with quotations from other sources, partly in his own words, emphasizes a certain centrality of sexuality in Gandhi's life. Quotations from Gandhi, such as 'I can suppress the enemy but have not been able to expel him altogether', which, for Lelyveld, testify to his 'sex urge' (Lelyveld, 2011: 272), and the line that the Mahatma 'experienced a sudden desire for intercourse', which, as Lelyveld notes, stemmed 'from encounters with a dentist who was extracting all his teeth', have apparently given readers a feeling of unease. One reason for this certainly is that the author in most cases fails to acknowledge the sources of the Gandhi quotes—which might even be excusable given the fact that he is a journalist rather than an academic, and in writing adheres to the conventions of his trade—or makes claims without providing references for them, as in the case of the statement: 'over the years [Gandhi] acknowledged wet dreams, but this was different: he was wide awake' (Lelyveld, 2011: 272). According to Lelyveld, Gandhi then goes on to talk to an unidentified 'female co-worker'. The biographer quotes Gandhi as saying that 'despite my best efforts, ... the organ remained aroused. It was an altogether strange and shameful experience' (Lelyveld, 2011: 272). It is this combination of unacknowledged sources, unclear references, imprecise causalities (as in the above-mentioned case of the dentist), and the use of worldly language and description of very worldly events in the near-sacred context of Gandhi that in some observers invokes the feeling of the author committing the despicable crime of character assassination.

The dubious nature of some allegations, along with the blunt language used, also implying value judgements on Gandhi, is identified here as the main source of antagonism to the book. Indeed, Lelyveld, as he outlines in the beginning, does not seek to rewrite the history of Gandhi, but rather uses the controversial passages to illustrate departures from the otherwise austere Gandhian norm. A statement like 'Gandhi sounds more like a discriminating pasha with a harem than the ascetic he genuinely was' (Lelyveld, 2011: 305), which refers to the replacement of Sushila Nayar, the sister of Gandhi's secretary Pyarelal, by Manu Gandhi as his attendant, testifies both to the journalistic background of the author as well as to the appreciation of Gandhi's self-disciplined nature. The light and matter-of-course manner in which Lelyveld, paraphrasing the personal secretary Bose, writes that 'Gandhi had allowed himself to use his bedmates as instruments in an experiment' (Lelyveld, 2011: 307), thus assuming a conscious 'commodification' of women by Gandhi, who bedded down next to Manu on a nightly basis,[32] can and in many cases has indeed come across as very disrespectful. The author's innuendo that Gandhi 'had a crush on Manu' is conveyed to the reader by means of a comment on the secretary Pyarelal, who 'had a crush on Manu himself' (Lelyveld, 2011: 306). As in the episode in which the biographer delineates a potentially violent incident between Gandhi and Manu, the truth is in many cases left to the reader to find. When Lelyveld describes how Gandhi, after the arrival of his grandniece, tells Sushila that Manu would be taking her place, he again quotes Bose, who testifies to having heard 'a deeply anguished cry proceeding from the main room [followed by] two large slaps given on someone's body. The cry then sank down into a heavy sob.' When the secretary caught sight of Gandhi and Sushila, they were both 'bathed in tears' (Lelyveld, 2011: 305). According to the ear-witness Bose, the cries were Gandhi's, and when his interpreter later asked him whether he had harmed Sushila, he denied, saying that 'no, I did not beat her, I beat my own forehead' (Lelyveld, 2011: 305).

The overall question that the biographer pursues is where the 'real motivation for Gandhi's actions and the *brahmacharya*[33] test is located'. Is it, Lelyveld asks,

> in his gnawing sense of failure for which a ratcheting up of his brahm-acharya might provide healing, or in his need for a human connection, if not the intimacy he'd long since forsworn? There is no obvious answer, except to say the struggle was at the core of his being and that it had never been more anguishing than it was in Srirampur (2011: 304).

It is here that the author comes full circle with the subtitle of his book. As was said at the outset of this section, the idea that imposes itself on the reader is that the struggle is that of a single person, Gandhi, with the rigid scene of his time—rigid not only in political but also in moral terms.

TRAPPED IN CULTURE? THE IMPLICATIONS OF CONTEXT FOR (SELF-)CENSORSHIP

Great Soul has not produced many new insights. Even earlier analyses have claimed that 'Gandhi's relationship with women and the passions they aroused are ... more complex than what he reveals in his own impassioned confession' (Kakar, 1990: 128). The Indian psychoanalyst Sudhir Kakar goes even further to attribute 'basic oral fantasy' and an Oedipus complex to Gandhi: 'His experiments with various kinds of food and a reduction in its intake ... appear as part of an involuted and intuitive effort to recover and maintain his merger with his mother' (1990: 128).

However, in a context where 'national heroes' do not tend to be viewed critically, and where '-ji', the suffix of reverence, is unanimously and unquestioningly attached to the great names of the politico-historical pantheon, it becomes difficult to engage with those figures in an objective and meaningful way. Is the leader cult a 'cultural reflex', as Lelyveld has called it (2011: xii), a cult that makes the observers blind or indifferent to the person behind the image?[34] Kakar, in his discussion of 'Gandhi and Women', notes that a deconstruction of Gandhi is beset with difficulties. Gandhi is, in Kakar's terms, the 'foremost culture-hero of modern India'. He is, like other intellectual or political founding fathers of India, a figure of reverence. 'For an Indian child', Kakar writes,

> the faces of Gandhi and other heroes like Nehru and Vivekananda are identical with the masks crafted by the culture in order to provide ideals for emulation and identification. Every child in India has been exposed to stock narratives that celebrate their genius and greatness, the portraits utterly devoid of any normal human blemish such as envy, anger, lust, ordinariness, pettiness, or stupidity (1990: 85–6).

Writing a biography of such a 'culture-hero' becomes difficult—the danger is that it quickly turns into hagiography. What has been said earlier in connection with the Indian reluctance to engage with the concept of cultural citizenship in an analytical and meaningful way is paraphrased by Sudhir Kakar:

> The Indian analyst, also a child of his culture, is thus bound to have a special kind of 'counter-transference' towards the culture-hero as a biographical subject. In other words, the analytic stance of respectful empathy combined with critical detachment, difficult enough to maintain in normal circumstances, becomes especially so in the case of a man like Gandhi. His image is apt to merge with other idealized figures from the biographer's own past, who were loved and admired yet secretly rebelled against. The analytic stance must then be charted out between contradictory hagiographic and pathographic impulses that seek constantly to buffet it (1990: 86).

To the globally conscious analyst, the question might arise why Western citizenries are less critical of the sexual escapades of their leaders. Why are national leaders like George Washington, John F. Kennedy, François Mitterrand, or for that matter even Bill Clinton, not discussed more controversially for having had extramarital relationships; why did it not override their historical significance? The answer is twofold: for one, Western societies are less hierarchical; according to the American narrative, anyone can make it—saint or sinner. Also, and probably more importantly, the majority of citizens in those Western countries do not believe in brahmacharya leading to *moksha*.[35] In this context, Kakar notes that Gandhi had a 'life-long conflict with the dark god of desire, the only opponent he did not engage non-violently nor could ever completely subdue'. While defeats in that conflict meant humiliation, victories were 'a matter of joy, "fresh beauty", and an increase in vigor and self-confidence that brought him nearer to the *moksha* he so longed for' (Kakar, 1990: 99).

In the discussion of Lelyveld's book, and the controversy around it that finally led to its ban in Gujarat, lies an important analytical point: as in the cases of A.K. Ramanujan's essay and M.F. Husain's paintings, the ostensible argument against the texts always was their sexual nature, degraded morals, and the disrespect with which they treated religion and culture. Beneath the surface, however, these are examples of an enterprise to achieve and sustain a monopoly of inter-pretation by essentializing discourses—religious, national, or cultural ones. All too often, the dividing lines between them are blurred.

CENSORSHIP AND CULTURAL CITIZENSHIP: THE CASE OF MINORITY PROTECTION

Censorship, however, is not only a necessary analytical category to illustrate processes of citizen-making, identity construction, and nation-building by securing the monopoly of interpretation; it also serves to illustrate the downside of cultural citizenship. It has been said in the Introduction that the state takes a central role in preventing a 'tyranny of the minority'. India has had this experience in connection with the banning of Salman Rushdie's *Satanic Verses* in 1988—the world's first democratic country to do so.[36] Muslims had felt offended by the book, and the Indian state imposed a ban on grounds of 'cultural relativism', as Thakur (1993: 652) notes. In this understanding, limits on the freedom of expression were imposed 'by probing attacks on beliefs that could lead to public disorder', amount-ing to 'penalizing the victim rather than the perpetrators of disorder' (Thakur, 1993: 652). Freedom of expression must, however, also include the freedom to offend, and while the text may have offended Muslims, no believer was prevented from practising their faith (Thakur, 1993: 652). The downside of cultural citizenship would thus be a situation where freedom of cultural expression is endangered without a regulating state that censors self-proclaimed censors who act in the name of minority protection.

In his novel *Fahrenheit 451*, Ray Bradbury (1991 [1953]) creates a future where reading publications other than trade journals, the confessions, or comics (!) is prohibited, and books are burned by state fire brigades. Captain Beatty, the superior officer, explains the situation to Guy Montag, one of his firemen and the protagonist of the story, in the following terms:

> Now let's take up the minorities in our civilization, shall we? Bigger the population, the more minorities. Don't step on the toes of the dog lovers, cat lovers, doctors, lawyers, merchants, chiefs, Mormons, Baptists, Unitarians, second-generation Chinese, Swedes, Italians, Germans, Texans, Brooklynites, Irishmen, people from Oregon or Mexico.... All the minor, minor minorities with their navels to be kept clean. Authors, full of evil thoughts, lock up your typewriters. They *did*. Magazines became a nice blend of vanilla tapioca.... It didn't come from the Government down. There was no dictum, no declaration, no censorship to start with, no! Technology, mass exploitation, and minority pressure carried the trick (Bradbury, 1991: 57–8).

In the world that Bradbury creates, censorship thus starts as a move to not upset minorities. Captain Beatty further informs Montag that:

> [O]ur civilization is so vast that we can't have our minorities upset and stirred. Ask yourself, What do we want in this country, above all? People want to be happy, isn't that right?... Colored people don't like *Little Black Sambo*? Burn it. White people don't feel good about *Uncle Tom's Cabin*? Burn it. Someone's written a book on tobacco and cancer of the lungs? The cigarette people are weeping? Burn the book (Bradbury, 1991: 59).

The fictional example of a society without books not only illustrates Swiss journalist Hans O. Staub's claim that 'the age of minorities has also become the age of intolerance' (1980: 161). *Fahrenheit 451* also emphasizes the point that 'no society can guarantee that all communicators will be able to express every possible content in every possible context' (O'Neill, 1990: 178). In the cases discussed here—those of A.K. Ramanujan and Joseph Lelyveld, as well as Salman Rushdie—the group overrides the individual. Because it is felt that the group will not approve of a cultural product, the individual—the author as well as the reader—is prevented from any further engagement with it.

The problem here is that the Indian state does not have a clear censorship policy. In some cases, as in that of *Great Soul* and *The Satanic Verses*, the state reacted harshly; in others, like Ramanujan's essay, it appeared lax, with state institutions giving in to political-cultural pressure without stating clear reasons for doing so. Similarly, Mazzarella and Kaur (2009: 10) contend that

> at times, the government clamped down and silenced dissent in the old, crude way. At others, however, the myriad voices emerging from inside and around the government seemed to be advocating the possibility of a more subtle co-optation, one in which consumer choice, religious assertion, and regional pride might perhaps still be harnessed to a collective national project. By the same token, of course, the legitimacy of the state as the final arbiter in public cultural matters, in matters of value, identity, and desire, was increasingly being called into question.

However, the discussion of censorship here is not as a phenomenon aloof from other policy areas. The unresolved debate between the proponents of a uniform civil code and the supporters of personal law, both of whom find support for their claims in the Constitution; the discrepancy between those who demand one national language and others who would like to retain the three-language formula, which the Constitution again equally offers; and the continuously undecided debate between secular and religious which appears in many policy decisions, puzzles both the observer of the law and those subject to it. Lloyd and Susanne Rudolph (1987) describe post-independence India in terms of a Hindu allegory, to allude to the various forms that the state can take:

> Like Hindu conceptions of the divine, the state in India is polymorphous, a creature of manifold forms and orientations. One is the third actor whose scale and power contribute to the marginality of class politics. Another is a liberal or citizens' state, a juridical body whose legislative reach is limited by a written constitution, judicial review, and fundamental rights. Still another is a capitalist state that guards the boundaries of the mixed economy by protecting the rights and promoting the interests of property in agriculture, commerce, and industry. Finally, a socialist state is concerned to use public power to eradicate poverty and privilege and tame private power. Which combination prevails in a particular historical setting is a matter for inquiry (Rudolph and Rudolph, 1987: 400–1).

Using the Indian example, Rudolph and Rudolph show here that governance is non-linear and context-dependent. While with regard to the area of political economy, promoting sometimes capitalist, and at other times socialist measures might be in the best interest of the country as it tries to reduce the huge economic inequalities in different ways, in an area like culture, which is easily claimed and even more easily used and exploited, this attitude might be of lesser strategic advantage.

The state's appearance in many different avatars also offers an opportunity: every observer can see it differently—some as fascist, some as socialist, some as Hindu nationalist, and others as weak and pushed around by 'pampered' minorities. The plethora of ways in which the Indian state can be read and understood sets free a huge creative potential. Because nothing is regulated, and there is no dominant cultural discourse of or by the state—at least not to an undemocratic extent—it is comparatively easy for citizens to open up other discourses. The interplay of discourse and counter-discourse about what constitutes the 'Indian' citizen is explored in the following chapter with primary reference to comics as cultural texts. The different modes of production—from above, with a clear organizational structure, where the private and the public sector cooperate, to production 'from below', where citizen-activists suggest a different narrative of the citizen *by* the citizen, often emphasizing what they find to be excluded from other popular media—illustrate the creative potential which can arise from the perception of a monopolized discourse of culture and citizenship.

5

THE INTERPLAY OF MASS AND NON-MASS MEDIA IN INDIA
RIVAL VISIONS AND COMPETING VOICES

[N]o medium has its meaning or existence alone, but only in constant interplay with other media.

(McLuhan, 1970: 35).

It is virtually impossible to prove causality in media studies.

(Farmer, 2005: 101).

MODERN MEDIA IN INDIA: FROM JESUITS TO GANDHIANS

This chapter explores the one area that this book engages with on which probably the most has been said and written. 'The media'—a misleading term suggesting coherence and commonality where only diversity and dissonance prevail—is yet another feather in India's cap of democratic achievements. After a phase of deep slumber from 1947 to 1991, the electronic audio-visual media *of* India and *in* India have been propelled to a vastness which is unparalleled in the world. India today has a dynamic and ever-growing media industry, which already is the largest in the world. But what *are* media, how can they be conceptualized in a political science framework, and to what extent does it make sense to speak of *Indian* media in a globally mediated world?

These questions are approached here in three steps. First, the (socio-political) history of the media in India is sketched, if only in brief, since other reference works and textbooks are much better placed to provide the broad picture that is required. Second, the role played by state-owned media in the process of nation-building will be looked at. The third section engages with the other big realm, the privately-owned media that came with liberalization and the open-ing up of the Indian economy in 1991. The chapter also analyses the media discourse 'from below', which, while having existed all along, intensified with the measures taken by the Rao administration. It investigates the media use of the Films Division which produces documentary films, and, especially in the first decades after indepen-dence, made films with strong links to national identity and citizen-ship. The work of the Films Division is contrasted with comics, both commercial, privately-owned media like the successful Amar Chitra Katha (ACK) series, and Grassroots Comics (GC), a non-governmen-tal, not-for-profit initiative which offers comics workshops for various social strata (mostly underprivileged groups) to enable them to enter the media discourse, setting up what Nancy Fraser (1990) has called a 'subaltern counterpublic'—a sphere which emerges in response to exclusion within dominant publics, expanding discursive space, and widening discursive contestation (Nayar, 2006: 68). The chapter thus offers an analysis of all three important media sectors in India— state, market, and civil society-dominated media. The latter two are explored and compared in terms of the same medium—comics— while the analysis of state media use is restricted to the documentary films as they best capture the nation-building agenda of the Indian government.

This threefold comparative set-up is justified on the understand-ing that also certain comics, in this case the 'Grassroots Comics', can be documentary media, not fictional texts. Hence, they can be analysed in line with the documentaries of the Films Division. While grassroots comics show the actual socio-political conditions of India as perceived by their authors—the actors on the ground—both the state-made documentaries and the commercial comics, notably ACK, show India as it ought to be according to the producers. This opens

up a highly intriguing area of tension in which to understand differences (and overlaps) between the conceptualization of the citizen by
the state, and by commercial and political art: the same concept is
expressed differently by 'ordinary citizens' and by civil society representatives. This juxtaposition lays open the inevitable clashes of ideas
and meanings resulting from such confrontation, but also illustrates
the processes of ongoing negotiation over the concept of the 'citizen'
carried out largely in the field of visual media, and the fruitful synthe-
ses that can emerge from this encounter.

The fact that media entail both clash and reconciliation becomes
apparent if one understands media as forms of communication which
enable the interaction of human beings, where voice, utterances, and
speech are the most primordial media. If, following from this, one
distinguishes between verbal and visual media—pictorial transmitters of information—then cave drawings are certainly among the
oldest media in the world. The history of pre-modern media in India
is long, with the Indus civilization as a creative hub and source of
media development.

With regard to modernity then, if it is conceptualized as the outcome of a process of accelerated globalization, the sixteenth century
has to be regarded as a cultural watershed: a new continent was,
if not discovered for the first time, then at least rediscovered and
subsequently settled; the Renaissance changed the cultural face of
Europe; and India was brought under Mughal rule. It was during
this time that modern media developed in India in the process of
cultural flow. A watershed in media development and ensuing global
communication was the invention of the printing press with moveable type by Johannes Gutenberg in 1457. From Germany, the technique spread to various places in Europe, and reached India on 6
September 1556. Jesuit missionaries first brought the printing press
to Goa, from where it was taken to various other parts of the country
as an important tool for accelerating the process of proselytization.[1]
Gutenberg, however, would not have been able to invent his world-
changing mechanism without paper, for which credit goes to ancient
China.[2] In the course of the centuries, this same medium has been
used in opposite ways: to rule and to rebel, to dominate, as well as
to liberate. The printing press has been instrumental in the spread
of literacy and the dissemination of information, and thus also laid

the foundation for later developments such as the 'digital revolution'. The example of the printing press in India thus provides insights into two very significant features of globalization.

First, it emphasizes the fact that globalization is circular rather than linear, and multi-dimensional rather than one-dimensional. Globalization is a cultural phenomenon, and hence comprises a mosaic of diverse and seemingly contradictory elements, which can encourage change or trigger conflict, thus contributing to an inherent dynamic. It can therefore only be conceptualized as an interaction which neither has a clearly locatable origin, nor a definite end point. Second, the example shows that globalization requires agency, and this agency can lead to significant twists, turns, and setbacks in the non-linear process of globalization. In 1780, the printing press enabled the Irishman James A. Hicky to publish India's first newspaper, the *Bengal Gazette*, which he used to criticize and personally attack the first Governor-General of India, Warren Hastings (1773–1785). Hicky was arrested in 1781 and again prosecuted and imprisoned for nineteen months in 1782; his printing press was confiscated and the *Bengal Gazette* ceased publication (Priolkar, 1958: 105).

One hundred and fifty years later, the Indian independence movement used the press very efficiently to express discontent with the status quo, propagate a vision for the future, and garner support for the ultimate aim of independence from Britain. Mahatma Gandhi and Jawaharlal Nehru, the leaders of the movement, who had both been educated in England and thus were products of a globalized education, were also gifted journalists and prolific writers who edited their own newspapers as effective instruments in their common cause.[3] It was the press which played a decisive role in India's independence movement, both on a regional level at the beginning of the twentieth century, for example in the Andhra movement from 1910 to 1914 (Subramanyam, 1989; Vaikuntham, 1989), or in the movement against the partition of Bengal in 1905 (De, 1989), as well as later on a countrywide scale (Sinha, 1994). The nation has emerged out of the interplay between democratic-pluralistic and exclusivist forces, both of which relied on their own media to put forward their issue: while Gandhi edited *Harijan*, his assassin Nathuram Vinayak Godse used his newspaper *Hindu Rashtra* to urge Hindus to actively defend their nation rather than passively abide while it was harmed by the British and the Muslims (McLain, 2007: 71). Even today, as the example of *Jaya TV*, the mouthpiece of the All India Anna Dravida Munnetra Kazhagam (AIADMK), the party led by Jayalalithaa Jayaram, a former film actress and frequent chief minister of the State of Tamil Nadu (1991–6, 2001, 2002–6, 2011–14, and 2015) exemplifies, politicians make use of their own media to advocate their causes. In this light, globalization with its flow of goods, people, and ideas can be seen as leading to rupture and change of world politics rather than to a continuation of dominance.

MEDIA AS TOOLS OF NATION-BUILDING: VARYING ROLES

Audio-visual media can indeed have different roles in times of peace and turmoil. They can be used to calm down as well as to agitate, to appease as well as to stir up sentiment, to invoke communal harmony as well as to encourage fierce disharmony and unrest. The founders of the Indian nation have been well-aware of the power of the instrument and the ways in which media can be deployed for purposes of nation-building.

Governments throughout the course of history have used the media as political tools, either to differentiate 'self' from 'other' and— mostly in authoritarian settings—mobilize against alleged external or internal threats, or—in democratic environments—to invoke unity and harmony in the populace. Either way, media have been inextricably linked to nation-building. The Republic of India was confronted with the challenge of forming a coherent nation against the background of a heterogeneous and deeply asymmetrical societal setting. Therefore, it has from its inception used the media, especially audio-visual media, to instil a spirit of 'Indianness' in the populace. Archival documents show that the Indian state has perceived media as direct promoters of national unity and citizenship.

The main instruments to bring about the desired national unity have been the Films Division and AIR. In view of high illiteracy rates, the MIB has focused heavily on non-print media, which can disseminate messages across wide distances, and can at the same time be received by a large audience, thus creating conditions for bonding and furthering the instilling of community feeling. The Films Division[4] as a body of the Government of India has been entrusted with the task of producing documentary films that familiarize Indians with the new political system, its democratic achievements and institutions, and their new role as bearers of citizen rights and duties. Set up in April 1948, the Films Division drew on colonial predecessors like Information Films of India (IFI) and Indian News Parade (INP), both founded in 1943 as units to propagate the British war effort and garner support among the colonized population.[5] The colonial institutions and the Films Division had similar aims: to serve 'public information, education and ... instructional and cultural purposes, [as well as] to focus attention on important aspects of the country's life and assist growth and development of documentary films as a medium of education and communication' (Garga, 2007: 130).

There was also continuity in personnel. With the former IFI man H.A. Kolhatkar at the helm, the Films Division started the regular distribution of newsreels and documentaries from mid-1949. In its first year, between 1949 and 1950, it produced an 'impressive record' of ninety-seven documentaries and newsreels (Garga, 2007: 133). The table reproduced in Appendix I, titled 'National Unity and Emotional Integration of the People—Selected Documentary Films of the Films Division (1949–1961)', provides evidence for the government's strong focus on issues related to citizenship in the formative years of the republic. The documentaries produced by the Films Division focus on the rights and responsibilities of citizenship, civic sense, and 'discipline'. The 1952 film aptly titled *The National Foundation*, for example, reveals the political strategy of using audio-visual mass media to promote images of the ideal citizen and using the cultural realm for the purposes of nation-building. Films were seen as effective media to familiarize the new citizens with the symbols of the Republic and its institutions, as is evident from the documentary *Our Flag* (1952), on the Tiranga (tricolour). *Our Constitution* (1950) and *Democracy in Action* (1951) introduce the foundations of the new Republic, while the film *It is Your Vote* (1956) was produced on the theme of elections. The 1957 film *Our Prime Minister* honours the popular Jawaharlal Nehru and depicts the daily life routine of the head of government.

The way in which the government approached the issue of national integration via the documentary film was, however, seen as having little effect and became subject to criticism. B.D. Garga, himself a documentary filmmaker and former member of the Film Advisory Board, notes that 'none of the spirit of a nascent nation coming into its own, or the new concept of citizenship, found its way into the films produced during this period' (Garga, 2007: 133). Garga sees the themes in terms of which citizenship was introduced as too abstract and remote to create effective means of popular identification: 'the concept of national pride was too often portrayed through images of parades against a skyline of flags flying, and seldom in meaningful analysis of India's people and their myriad problems' (Garga, 2007: 133). Indeed, the mode of representation of citizenship and its characteristics is often that of a top-down, hierarchical, and paternalistic teacher–pupil relationship.

In a normative way, some of the documentaries also engage with the habits and ideal behaviour expected of a citizen of India. The 1954 film *Case of Mr. Critic* deplores 'the habit of ridiculing everything that is done', thus trying to instil in the populace a sense of patience in view of the various challenges the republic was facing in its formative phase. Under the theme of 'National Unity and Emotional Integration', there is also a documentary on *Indian Minorities*, 'stressing the characteristics of India as a secular state and indicating the important part played by distinguished members of minority communities' in the national set-up. The 1956 picture *Children of God*, on the theme of Dalit welfare, is another move to bring the socially stigmatized former 'untouchables' into the cinematic limelight, and hence into the focus of social attention. While some films are devoted to the tangible cultural heritage of India, such as national festivals (*Festival Time*, 1950) and folk culture (*Folk Dances of India*, 1954), others deal with the technological achievements of the young republic in the field of research and industrial development (*Research Aid[e]s Industry*, 1950), as well as with its political successes, starting with independence from the British, and India's role on the international stage of the United Nations (*India and the United Nations*, 1955, and *In the Common Interest*, 1957). What these documentaries have in common is their aim of invoking patriotic pride in the spectator. The achievements are seen as being in need of protection and defence, and consequently the 1958 movie *Citizens Army* picks out 'military training for the people' as its central theme.

The early state-produced documentary film can thus be seen as a projection surface for official notions of citizenship, as a forum on which to start a dialogue between different cultural groups, and, following from this, as a method to link these two—citizenship and culture—in a pictorial discourse. The documentary films, however, seem to stigmatize some fellow citizens as exotic 'Others'. This is done not only by the focus on song and dance, but also by framing the adivasi population in separate film formats. The 1953 documentary *Our Original Inhabitants* covers the entire range of India's tribal populations, but restricts the report to dance performances, and that too with the women not bare-breasted, as is customary, but covered (Garga, 2007: 137). In this way, many of the documentary films achieved the opposite of what they intended: rather than bringing the citizens closer together, they deepened the divides by exoticizing the tribal population and invoking stereotypes.

In a 1961 communiqué on 'Emotional Integration' issued by the MIB, the production of further films, specifically films on the subject of unity, was highlighted as an objective that would continue to engage the Films Division. In this vein, one of the proposed films was entitled *Good Citizenship*, then scheduled to be produced in the years 1961–2 (GoI, 1961a: 5). Furthermore, as part of the publicity campaign for the integration and unity of India, the Publications Division of the MIB published a pamphlet entitled *Better Citizenship*, in which 'emphasis has been laid on the basic unity of the country and the dangers of casteism, linguism and other separatist tendencies'. The pamphlet was made available in English, Hindi, and the 'major regional languages'.[6]

As will be shown subsequently, one of the most pressing, yet still open questions researchers working at the interface of politics and media engage with, is that of causality and the degree of interrelation between the two. Up to now, there has not been a convincing system of measurement to explore this relationship in a quantitative way. As has already been argued in Chapter one, all the aspiring researcher is left with is to link qualitative and quantitative data, which, even though not directly related to each other, that is, not springing from the same sample or being collected against the same background, still explore the same analytical category. In his large-scale survey of citizenship in India alluded to in Chapter four, Subrata Mitra analyses citizen duties as well as the perception of who are 'un-citizens' of India, a category borrowed from Schama (1989). The findings provide striking parallels to the ideological mission of national unity that the MIB embarked on in the 1950s and 1960s.

Table 5.1 shows the positions of respondents with respect to citizen duties. The statements given are variations on the duties of the citizen as listed in Article 51A of the Constitution.[7] The question was asked of the respondents in the following way: 'Now I will read out a few statements. Please tell me whether you agree or disagree with each of them. (Probe further whether "fully" or "somewhat" agrees or disagrees).' The responses show 'a substantial amount of support for the Indian variations on the classic themes of citizen duties, such as regular voting and participation in public activities, respect for the national flag and other core symbols such as the National Anthem, and the territory of India' (Mitra, 2012a: 180). These are factors which again come into play in the characterization of the 'un-citizen' (see Table 5.2).

Table 5.1   Citizen Duties and Their Evaluation by Respondents (per cent)

Statements (citizens of India should ...)	Fully agree	Somewhat agree	Somewhat disagree	Fully disagree	No opinion
Vote regularly	80	10	2	1	7
Respect national symbols like the flag, the national anthem, and the integrity of the Indian territory	77	10	2	1	10
Send children to school	81	9	2	1	7
Promote a harmonious relationship between all religions	73	12	3	2	10
Safeguard public property like roads, trains, buses, government buildings	73	12	2	2	11

Source: Mitra (2012a: 179).

Table 5.2 The 'Un-citizens' as Perceived by the Respondents (per cent)

Category	Statements	%
1	Those who do not take part in elections and other affairs of the country	9
2	Those not born in India or to Indian parents, including illegal immigrants	29
3	Terrorists/separatists or those who help them	25
4	Those with loyalties other than towards India	11
5	Those who do not have respect for the flag, or unity of India	12
6	NRIs, PIO card holders*	4
7	Others	7
8	Don't know	3

Note: *NRI: Non-Resident Indian; PIO: Person of Indian Origin.
Source: Mitra, (2012a: 179).

On the understanding that the 'definition of the other sometimes help[s] define oneself more sharply', Table 5.2 shows the answers to the question, 'And who in your opinion are not citizens of India?', with the answer categories one to six being read out to the respondents (Mitra, 2012a: 178). With the aim of arriving at a social rank ordering of the given alternatives, the technique followed was to read out answers from top to bottom and bottom to top alternately, so as to ensure that no particular response was privileged in any way. What is immediately apparent here is that the legalistic understanding of citizenship predominates: 29 per cent of the respondents agree that those who are not born in India, or to Indian parents, including illegal immigrants, are not citizens. However, what Mitra refers to as 'entirely constructed categories', that is, those that do not have a basis in law (Mitra, 2012a: 178) but reflect the current state of affairs and sentiments in the country, also rank comparatively high in the responses. Thus, terrorists and separatists are perceived as 'un-citizens' by the second largest group of respondents (25 per cent). Interestingly, the third largest group, comprising 12 per cent of the respondents, felt that 'those who do not have respect for the flag, or unity of India' are non-citizens. It is not apparent whether in the survey multiple responses were possible, that is, whether those who were asked could affirm two or more categories. While from the results this does not seem to have been the case, taking this step would have been in line with the conceptual understanding of citizenship as two-dimensional, allowing respondents to name both legalistic and moral categories, without having to choose one over the other.

What the survey results show, however, is the shared connection between citizenship and respect for symbols and unity, among the researcher, the respondent, and the state and its organs such as the Films Division. Similar to the Films Division, the public service broadcaster AIR, as the other important state-owned mass medium, was used to pursue the strategy of 'emotionally integrating' the country and contributing to the building of the Indian nation. In the aforementioned communiqué by the MIB on *Emotional Integration*, radio is described as 'a powerful medium available to Government [which] has to be used to reach the widest possible circle of people' (GoI, 1961a: 4). This is not the intelligentsia, but 'that vast major-ity of people who are not prepared to think much on their own but who lend themselves easily to outside persuasion'. While the term 'propaganda' is repeatedly used in the documents to describe the broadcasting policy, it is also stated that 'open preaching or blatant propaganda on the subject of unity and emotional integration will prove ineffective' (GoI, 1961a: 5).

The Indian government not only relied on the electronic, and in McLuhan's sense (1970) 'hot' media of film and radio, but also made thought excursions into the use of 'cold' pictorial media. According to McLuhan, the latter allow for much greater participation by and involvement of the recipient in the decoding and mental completion of the message which the medium seeks to transmit. Less out of such theoretical reflections, and driven more by the wish to cater to various segments of society and also appeal to the (perceived) media needs of the younger generation, the MIB in their communiqué con-sidered the use of 'picture books' (in addition to exhibitions, posters and broadsheets, folders, and hoardings) as media of visual public-ity that specifically engaged younger people (GoI, 1961a: 6). Under the auspices of the Directorate of Advertising & Visual Publicity, a branch of the MIB, the visual material in combination with 'small pamphlets written in simple language' were aimed at the country's rural population. 'Picture books', or comics, are indeed an interesting medium to enhance nation-building efforts in a multilingual society struggling with high rates of illiteracy. However, the government is not the only actor to have made use of comics. For-profit publishers and not-for-profit civil society organizations are among those that have offered different perspectives on the medium, employing it for different ends. Thus, because of the multiplicity of views and voices inherent in the comic, because of their long history spanning across the ages, and not least because of their accessibility allowing for easy participation (as opposed to the electronic media), comics constitute an ideal case study for this work on cultural citizenship in a development context.

Comics are simultaneously old media, new media, and social media. They are old in so far as their origins can be found in the early woodcuts (McLuhan 1970) even though they actually date back to the earliest visual media, the cave paintings which narrate a story through a sequence of visuals.[8] In his *History of the Comic Strip*, Kunzle (1973) dates the earliest use of comic strips as a media form to around 1450. The essential idea behind the comic, namely to entertain while often also mocking, and hence calling into question established social norms and relations of power, is much older. As has been shown in Chapter three, popular culture in Greek antiquity was a forum on which various social issues, such as the modes of citizenship, could be discussed and negotiated. The Athenian comedy, which shares its etymological roots with the comic, was used to mock the powerful and create broad means of identification with the genre and the message amongst the audience.[9] The comedy, in speech and action, played a role similar to the pictorial caricature, cartoon, or the comic of later days. In discussing the so-called 'Old Comedy' of the period of the dramatist Aristophanes and his contemporaries, Dover (1974) notes that

> the comic characters of Aristophanes more often give us vicarious satisfaction by breaking moral and social rules as we too would like to break them if only we dared. Characters such as Dikaiopolis in *Acharnians*, Trygaios in *Peace* and Peisetairos in *Birds* speak and act for 'us' against 'them'—that is to say, against gods, politicians, generals, orators, intellectuals, poets, doctors, scientists, all those who in one way are superior to ourselves.[10]

The fact that comedy 'satirizes and caricatures many ingredients of actual morality and social usage' (Dover, 1974: 20) strongly appealed to the audience of the time. This aspect is an element of media that has not lost any of its attraction to this day. Even in the ancient period, towards the end of the fourth century BCE, the use of satire in connection with social issues increased in importance, as the element of literary parody diminished considerably (Dover, 1974: 22). The majority of Greek comedies written and performed at the time when Aristotle wrote his *Poetics* had characters that won the audience's sympathy 'essentially by the shrewd, coarse, roguish independence of thought and action'. Moreover, the comic heroes were characterized by sexual opportunism and a 'language uninhibited to a degree which was not tolerated in a serious setting' (Dover, 1974: 19). All these have remained as elements of the comedy to date, and from the stage, a lot of it was later transported to the visual sphere in the form of the caricature and later, the comic. The unhindered expression of thought diverging from social conventions is always subject to the interplay between liberalism and censorship: in the Greek comedies, often old-fashioned, censorious characters appeared as a counterweight to the comic elements, thus giving them a further boost.

While many elements stemming from the Greek comedy constitute features of the modern comic, comics in the narrower sense of the term are a much more recent medium: according to McLuhan, the first 'proper' ones were published in 1935.[11] Even though they 'lacked in a connective structure, literary content, [and] were as difficult to decipher as the *Book of Kells*', they still attracted the youth of the time (McLuhan, 1970: 167). In India, important contributions to the world of the comic, such as Anant Pai's *Amar Chitra Katha*, the 'Immortal Picture Stories', appeared even later, in 1967. While those comics attracted a large, mainly middle-class audience,[12] the comic as an art and literary form is still a novelty in India, and the market for it does not seem to be fully developed yet. 'Phantomville', India's first graphic novel publishing house, for example, does not rise beyond sales numbers of around 6,000 copies, even for bestselling titles (Smita Mitra, 2011: 78). As has been argued, the comic in general is both old *and* new, and the comic as an art form in India also serves to demonstrate the convergence of old and new by its content. *Amar Chitra Katha*, one of the most successful comics series, takes inspiration for its narratives from ancient Indian myths, history, classics, legends, and folk tales (Sreenivas, 2010: 1). Rather than the changing form and content of the comic, however, the focus of the present book is on its function as a socio-political tool. The comic thus is not understood here as 'art for art's sake', but as a low threshold entry into the media discourse, and, connected to this, the national discourse. Both the not-for-profit and the commercial comics analysed here are understood by their authors not as ends in themselves, but rather as the means to an end. Like the theoretical concept of cultural citizenship to which they add an empirical dimension, the comics serve the instrumental function of entering the discourse, with the ultimate objective of altering the socio-political status quo.

The comic, defined in the *OED* as a 'children's paper', has the aura of the infantile, which in the eyes of academics has, for a long time, not rendered it a subject fit for scholarly analysis. While cultural studies has been dealing with the form, comics are the poor cousin of the media family: comics—and that too not mass-produced ones, but those with small print runs and limited circulation—are a medium often overlooked by analysis in favour of electronic systems of information exchange which can reach out to a mass audience. Political science analysis which considers media, if at all, only as a marginal area of engagement better left to sociologists, anthropologists, and cultural theorists, has to date rarely analysed media in a significant way and has to the best of my knowledge left comics completely unconsidered.[13]

INDIA'S MAINSTREAM COMIC SCENE: DISCOURSE ON *AMAR CHITRA KATHA* AND *PARMANU*

Despite the overall academic hesitation to engage with comics in a coherent manner and treat them as empirical data, India's mainstream comics have been subject to scholarly analysis, although to a much lesser extent than their Western counterparts. Even though the Indian comic scene is much more diverse, the discussion has basically been restricted to the commercially successful ACK series, and the comic book series *Parmanu*, 'the atomic wonder man of India'. The number of (frequently cited) authors on the subject is equally limited, and does not include more than ten names.[14] The ACK as the leading Indian comic book series with its 440 mythological and historical titles and sales of over 86 million issues (McLain, 2007: 57) is mostly understood as a visual form which projects a national narrative and transmits a message of a Hinduized, masculinized citizenship ideal.

In her discussion on the videos produced by Jain studios in Mumbai, a company devoted to propagating the message of Hindutva, Brosius (2005) argues that the video *God Manifests Himself* 'fused visual and political representation into a Hindutva intervisuality by consciously banking on the success of a whole range of other media, such as ACK comic books or the tele-novella *Ramayan* by Ramanand Sagar' (2005: 102). Similarly, Chandra (2008: 15) shows how from the early 1980s onwards, ACK spread across other media, such as LP records, audio cassettes, and videos, 'to reduce the risk involved in selling a single product'. Amar Chitra Katha has provided fertile grounds for such fusion, as it 'reflects a desire within India's modern urban middle classes to "bring closer" to themselves manageable capsules of a commodified, "authentic" and predominantly elitist Hindu culture' (Brosius, 2005: 102). The video *God Manifests Himself* offers a historical chronology of the Ramjanmabhoomi movement for the construction of a temple on the alleged site of the birthplace of Lord Ram (see Chapter four), and includes footage of the 1989 Ram *shila puja*, the worship of sacred bricks for the building of the temple (Brosius, 2005: 99). It consciously employs the performative tools of storytelling through picture scrolls (*chitrakatha*) and folk theatre. In its narrative structure, the video points towards the utopian idea of participation in a casteless and classless society of devotees, and thus consciously blurs religious and political landscapes, contributing to the constitution of the 'new citizen' of Hindutva, the *deshbhakta*, along with *his* first and foremost duty—work for the nation (cf. Brosius, 2005: 103).

The example here underlines both the important phenomenon of intertextuality in a political media discourse, and the significance of ACK for the Hindu nationalist project, as well as the strong linkages between these forms of popular culture and the agenda for citizenship. This view is substantiated by the use of the ACK comics in Indian schools by a decree of the Indian Ministry of Education. In 1978, Union Minister of Education Pratap Chandra Chunder introduced the use of the series in the school syllabus, stating that '[t]here are biographies of great men from different parts of the country; there are tales from Sanskrit; classics and folktales of various regions—all of which could help in promoting national integration' (*The Role of*

Chitra Katha in School Education, 1978: 2, cited in McLain, 2007: 58).
The comics are thus perceived as an instrument to support the ongoing aim of national integration that the republic has been working
towards since its foundational years. The history and development
of the ACK series often overlapped with events in the national history of India. *The Story of the Freedom Struggle* (Bumper Issue No. 10,
1997) was officially released in 1997 by the then Prime Minister A.B.
Vajpayee on the fiftieth anniversary of India's independence (McLain,
2007: 67), despite the comics' biased canon of independence activists
as discussed in the Introduction.

The similarly political and social message inscribed in the
Parmanu comic series is analysed by the anthropologist Raminder
Kaur (2012). Kaur links the *Parmanu* series, which started out in 1991,
to the Indian nuclear tests of 1998 which sparked a proliferation of
nuclear imagery. With nuclear discourses entering into vernacular
culture, the comics are centred on the imagery of the 'nuclear man'
fighting against threats to India's integrity and security. In the comic
series, which is written in Hindi and—like ACK—draws on ancient
Indian phrases and symbols, she sees a case of neither mimesis nor
alterity, but of occupying a 'space in-between'. Kaur notes that the
atomic superhero comics 'occupy, in Homi Bhabha's (1994) terms,
an "enunciative space" that is neither an instance of mimicry nor of
its obverse, alterity, but one that negotiates the terrain between these
two poles in a dynamo of consonance and dissonance' (2012: 331).
Interestingly, the recourse to a mythical and glorified (Hindu) past is
a strategy that is employed in both ACK and the Atomic Comics, as
well as in the nation-building project of the MIB.

The internal Communiqué on the Integration and Unity of
the Country commissioned by the Minister of Information and
Broadcasting in 1961 strategically (and selectively) uses the past to
invoke the image of a country that has been unified for long parts
of its history. According to the MIB communiqué, unity equals
prosperity and achievement. What is noteworthy in this context is
that the republic refers to autocratic antecedents and Muslim rule
to emphasize the idea of political unity and stability: 'the history of
India shows that only when the country was united, whether in the
days of Ashoka or Akbar, was it prosperous and led to great heights
of achievements. Fissiparous tendencies of other days led to divisions

and subjugation of the country by invaders from outside.'[15] But the ministry also takes recourse to comparatively recent historical events, such as the Indian Mutiny of 1857.[16] In a proposal for the 'Utilisation of the Entertainment Media at present adopted by the Song & Drama Division for a Publicity Campaign for Unity and Emotional Integration', the mutiny is referred to as the 'War of Independence', a terminology also used by ardent Hindu nationalists like V.D. Savarkar. The Song and Drama Division of the MIB then set out to recover ballads, 'powerful songs', and other compositions which have dealt with the mutiny in different languages and 'render them to tune by expert Composers'.[17] The policy brief states that 'recitals of these songs and ballads by group [sic] of artists with suitable commentary are likely to be very effective to create the feeling of nationalism'. Likewise, songs that were sung during the Indian independence movement are regarded as a 'source of inspiration', 'bound to create that feeling of national unity'.[18] Obviously, a selective reading of the past as glorified content, together with the form of historical dissemination carefully adapted to the needs and technological means of the day, has been regarded as the policy recipe for national unity.

India's predisposition towards unity is, according to the MIB, grounded in culture. Contrary to what one might think, the government officials state an 'underlying unity of Indian culture' which has 'bound the country together, as otherwise with all the invasions that took place during history, the country would have been divided into completely separate units'. Within this framework of cultural unity, the ministry does not regard language as a crucial constituent factor, and sees the commonalities between the languages as outnumbering their differences. The communiqué claims that 'while language does not play an important part in culture, no one language can claim to be completely an entity by itself.... Our languages are linked together by a common origin. There is no impassable barrier between them.'[19]

Opposing this 'cultural unity' invoked by the state, the comics are seen as encouraging 'intervention' and 'transgression' of norms, not least by their use of swear words (Kaur, 2010). Moreover, structurally, comics per se have been read as transgression, authorized in and through their very form (Frahm, 2011: 156). On yet another level, Indian comics often transgress the form handed down to them by their Western predecessors. Raminder Kaur repeatedly makes the point that Indian comics are not copies of Western prototypes, but are 'indigenized' as it were, by weaving old local customs and traditions into new texts. The Indian 'Spiderman', for example, is not bitten by a mutated spider as in the original US comic, but is given a spider by a yogi to help him fight evil. The Hindi-language comics thus have 'evolved their own aesthetic, combining contemporary superheroes in modernized mythologies where a conflation of ideas from the scriptures (*shastra*) or "ancient spiritual science" (*paravigyan*) and developments in modern science and technology (*vigyan*) battle it out in dynamic graphics' (Kaur, 2012: 330).

In the comics, the villain is depicted as someone driven by the desire to overrun society. In Kaur's (2012: 338) words, villains represent an 'imminent future of chaos, lawlessness [and] a different social order'. The villain is designed as a 'non-citizen', and killing him is not considered murder. The status of un-citizen is further emphasized by its dehumanization: the villain is a *homo bestiae*, a human–beast hybrid. Throughout *Parmanu*, the connection between the narrative of the comic and citizen virtues and values is immanent. The comic's references to citizenship are made explicit by the appearance of Gandhi and Nehru as the fathers of the Indian nation. They stress what the atomic superhero stands for: an ideal state which is just, non-corrupt, and efficient. The people are shown as being in need of protection, and look up to the hero as a role model. The superhero comics, much like ACK, are seen as imparting a 'moral lesson about ideal conduct, citizenship represented as patriotic loyalty, and the nation-state' (Kaur, 2012: 332). They thus function as conveyors of a particular interpretation of the meaning and extent of citizenship. A major difference between ACK and the *Parmanu* series lies in the fact that while the former 'encourages convention and conservatism', the latter 'encourage invention and to some extent transgression', but firmly 'remain within the framework of a civic consciousness which exalts the benefits of science and ideas to do with "good citizenship" demonstrated in patriotic displays and the conduct of superheroes' (Kaur, 2012: 333).

COMICS AS SOCIO-POLITICAL MEDIA: A CASE STUDY OF *GRASSROOTS COMICS* (GC), INDIA

This section analyses the work of the NGO *Grassroots Comics* (GC), which is dedicated to exploring and furthering the potential of comic strips drawn by various societal groups in order to voice issues that are of concern to the individual, the group, or the larger society. At the same time, GC also provides its lay artists, who often write against an underprivileged social background, with a tool to gain a basic entry into the larger media discourse. Sharad Sharma, founder of GC India, refers to them as 'non-threatening media', which is not entirely correct. Depending on the content and the way the message is perceived by the recipient, any medium can be seen as a potential threat to law and order, or even to the political system at large.[20]

In a climate where cartoons are increasingly viewed with suspicion and where the Thorat Committee, set up by the United Progressive Alliance (UPA II) government recommended the removal of about forty cartoons from Indian schoolbooks which were believed to 'send a wrong message'[21] (Chopra, 2012), it is quite remarkable that, the GC initiative started a programme in 2015 which encourages teachers in public schools to use self-drawn comics (created by both teachers and pupils) to acquaint students with the teaching content, even in subjects like mathematics and the natural sciences. Supported by the United Nations Children's Fund and the Indian public school authorities, a pilot project was started in the States of Uttar Pradesh and Chhattisgarh in 2014. With input from both teachers and pupils, a manual has been created which introduces the curriculum in comic form.[22] While strengthening the role of comics in education, this also underlines GC's self-understanding as a participatory medium. The founders of the initiative describe comics as 'a participatory development communication method' and, more directly, as a 'tool for democracy'. Grassroots comics are defined as 'comics that are made by socially active people themselves, rather than by campaign and art professionals'. They are therefore seen as 'genuine voices which encourage local debate in the society' (Packalen and Sharma, 2007: 9). The motivation underlying GC is obvious from the short introduction, which is also given in the form of a comic strip and printed on small leaflets in both Hindi and English. Figure 5.1 illustrates GC's objective of encouraging different groups of people, often socio-economically marginalized sections of society, to narrate specific issues related to their personal life situations in the form of comics which can be publicly displayed as wall posters or leaflets, and can also be published in broader media formats such as newspapers or on the Internet. This is regarded by the inventors of this format as a strategy to gain entry into

Figure 5.1 A Visual Introduction to the Concept of Grassroots Comics
Source: Sharma (2010: 20). © Sharad Sharma.

the larger media discourse, draw policymakers' attention to specific conditions, and bring about change.

The GC initiative has attracted a lot of attention not only across Indian States, including the north-east, but also in Pakistan, Sri Lanka, and Nepal, where workshops have been held to 'train trainers' and ensure a skills and knowledge transfer. Beyond the borders of South Asia, other workshops were held in Tanzania, Benin, and Mozambique, as well as in Lebanon, the United Kingdom, and Finland. Mostly, these workshops have been targeted at specific and often socially marginalized audiences, such as Palestinian refugees in Lebanon, or ethnic minorities in the UK, with the objective of acquainting them with a tool that has the power to challenge an existing media discourse (see Figure 5.2). From these workshops then spring the communities' own initiatives to enlarge the network. This was the case in Nepal in 2005, where a GC workshop triggered a number of other workshops to train trainers, resulting in the formation of the World Comics Network Nepal, which brings together a number of activists from local organizations (Sharma, 2010: 2).

At the core of these comics workshops is the teaching of basic drawing skills using a four-panel format and A4-size paper. Drawings

Figure 5.2   Comics Power
Source: Grassroots Comics Brochure. © Sharad Sharma

are done only in black and white so as to ensure that no expensive resources are required and the drawings are easier to photocopy. Similarly, A4-size paper is used because it is easily available, even in remote locations, as often is a xerox machine. Putting two A4-size sheets together makes for an A3 format, which is seen as ideal for a wall poster, as it can be noticed from a distance and can be read without difficulty from a distance of about 1 metre (Packalen and Sharma, 2007: 17). The four-panel format of the comic (see Figures 5.3 and 5.4) is also attractive because of its clear arrangement and easy convertibility into other formats, like a comic strip (Packalen and Sharma, 2007: 157–8). In addition, four panels can convey only limited information, which therefore encourages the writer to express her message clearly and in a comprehensive way. Also, in a multilingual society with high illiteracy rates,[23] the comic in general and the short strip in particular (as opposed to the graphic novel, for instance) offers obvious advantages. While it has been suggested to the organization that it might be a good idea to focus on the creation of non-verbal comics so as not to let literacy become a threshold for participation, GC sees the

Figure 5.3 'Samaj ki Soch' (The Thinking of the Society): A Grassroots Comic on the Social Exclusion of Homosexuals
Source: *Ek Alag Chitra Katha*, The Humsafar Trust (2009: 19).

comic form, with the limited number of panels and words that are needed to depict an issue, as an aid in countering illiteracy. In their publication *Grassroots Comics: A Development Communication Tool*, which introduces the approach, Leif Packalen and Sharad Sharma (2007: 97) note that

> in India, illiterate activists have participated in some workshops. They had a lot of stories to tell and could often draw quite well. Other participants helped them with the texts in the comics. They wrote the text in pencil and the illiterate participants inked both their own drawing and the text.

In many workshops, towards the end, these participants started to identify words and letters and even managed to write some words themselves.[24]

Besides, one of the distinctive features of a comic is its combination of visual and textual elements. Paraphrasing Barry (1997: 107–40), Karline McLain notes that 'the power of the comic book medium lies in this very combination of verbal and visual languages, wherein words and images become superimposed on each other in the perceptual activity, and thereby stimulate both affective and cognitive responses' (2007: 60).

Starting in the seven north-eastern States, whose societal issues are still largely absent from the collective Indian consciousness, GC has gained wider visibility, and the discourse of the medium—both with regard to content and form—has travelled. In India, Sharad Sharma, founder and current Secretary-General of World Comics India, was awarded an Ashoka Fellowship[25] in 2005 for introducing Grassroots Comics as a socially innovative development communication method into the Indian civil society (Packalen and Sharma, 2007: 160). The concept of Grassroots Comics is gaining wider attention in exhibitions in India as well as abroad. Comics courses are now held at various educational institutions in India, for instance, at the Lady Irwin College at Delhi University, where Grassroots Comics have formed part of the curriculum of the Department of Development Communication since 2009. Here, students acquire not only the technique which they then teach to rural communities in fieldwork projects, but also study the impact of the comics on the community.

A conversation with faculty member Dr Aparna Khanna, Associate Professor at the Department of Development Communication who specializes in the design and appraisal of various media for rural communities, revealed the seriousness with which Grassroots Comics are regarded. Grassroots Comics are seen as a valuable tool in bringing about transparency and involving people in political processes, thus strengthening civil society and the accountability of institutions. In this particular department, which 'strives to train a cadre of professionals equipped to mobilize participation of women and youth for sustainable development through communication for social change',[26] the comics are seen as an important support structure for voicing issues and bringing about change, and hence form part of the course syllabus.[27] In the department, students are trained in behaviour change methodologies and acquire professional skills in developing radio programmes, documentary films, and print media. The comics supplement this media toolkit by adding the advantages of accessibility and simplicity. Grassroots comics are a personal medium that anybody can create and share easily with a larger audience. As noted above, comics lend themselves to group interaction since they are a medium that requires involvement; they are what McLuhan subsumes under his term 'cold media'—limited in detail and offering little visual information. Thus, they require a high amount of personal involvement and effort on the part of the receiver to assemble the fragments into a coherent picture.[28] The element of anonymity that they bring is seen as helpful to overcome the initial threshold of 'making media' and sharing mostly very personal issues with strangers. The validity of the approach of using self-drawn comics in development communication is thus summed up by Aparna Khanna:

> I feel definitely, it helps people to express themselves. Because so far, whatever media has been designed, has been designed by people outside, journalists, or for that matter, media contents from outside. This is a medium that I am creating for myself, by myself, to share my own issue. And, as a tool, I have to ensure that I use it to create that dialogue or debate. So once I put up a comic anywhere, let's say outside the wall of the local school that is running in my local community, just putting that up is not enough. You ... walk around the community, ask people to comment, visit the exhibition, or see the comics, and say let's sit and talk about it. That sitting, that talking, that discussion, that formulation of courses of action is what we are looking for; the comics are triggering that process. And [there is] the fact that they are authentic stories from the people themselves, so they are an authentic medium. And there is local ownership, because it [is] my comic, my issue. My neighbour's daughter's, my niece's, my nephew's, and so on. So to that extent there is a collective ownership of that issue and that medium. And it is accepted by the people, because it is telling the truth of their own.... So people will give it a lot more credibility as compared to any outside poster or banner which is being displayed there. Because it's their children who've made it; it is they themselves who made it. To that extent it is definitely very powerful.[29]

Grassroots comics do not necessarily always have development-related content, in the sense of drawing attention to shortcomings in public service supplies or lacks in infrastructure. They are also used as a forum to direct attention to social or ethnic stigmatization. For example, with support from the United Nations Development Programme, a workshop was organized by GC and the Humsafar Trust[30] in Mumbai in 2009 on the issue of homosexuality and its place in Indian society. It was also through the comics that homosexuals could interact, share experiences with homo- and heterosexual participants, and thus come to terms with daily rejection and exclusion. Figure 5.3 provides visual evidence of the social ostracism of homosexuals in India articulated in the form of a comic. Until 2009, homosexuality was a punishable offence under Section 377 of the Indian Penal Code, a colonial law against same-sex relationships passed in 1861. Even though homosexuality was decriminalized in a landmark judgement by the Delhi High Court in the case *Naz Foundation v. Govt. of NCT of Delhi* in 2009, it was set aside by the Supreme Court of India in December 2013, an act which, in the words of journalist Anand Grover (2013), has 'branded citizens as criminals'.

The Supreme Court judgement has been heavily criticized by civil rights groups, the LGBT community, and the media, but homophobia remains a widespread issue, also among political democratic elites. The ongoing controversy over homosexuals in India was fuelled in July 2011 by remarks by India's then Union Minister of Health and Family Welfare Ghulam Nabi Azad (INC), that homosexuality was an 'unnatural disease brought to India from the West',[31] which he is said to have made during a conference on HIV/AIDS, but later denied having made. These remarks give an empirical reality to the narrative that unfolds in the Grassroots Comics, thus indeed making them an indicator of the social state of play in India.

Asked about the relevance of the Mumbai workshop in a personal interview, Sharad Sharma stressed the liberating power—and the term 'power' was used repeatedly and consciously during the conversation in question—of the comics, which works in at least two ways: the very form of a workshop has the immediate effect of bringing members of the same sexual community together, and thus enables them to form ties and build a social network. Figure 5.2 is a leaflet published by GC to raise awareness about its workshops and clearly shows this understanding of self-drawn comics as 'powerful' tools in a media society.

The longer-term effect of the workshop was to reach out to a wider audience through the comics, which according to Sharma has worked successfully. First, residents of Mumbai took note of the comics in the form of wall posters. Then, some of the comics, including the ones in Figures 5.3 and 5.4, were displayed in an exhibition at the India International Centre Annexe, New Delhi, in June 2011. Thus, the comics attract different audiences in very different fora, changing form while staying true to the medium and its content.

Parts of the introduction to *Ek Alag Chitra Katha*,[32] the publication that resulted from the Mumbai workshop, are quoted here to underline the attitudes towards the event. In his preface to *Alag Chitra Katha*, the 'Community Comic Book on issues of MSM and Transgender',[33] Sharad Sharma under the headline 'Sexuality in Black and White' notes:

Figure 5.4 A Grassroots Comic on Religio-ethnic Discrimination
Source: Sharma (2011).

I asked one of my acquaintances in media in Mumbai to accompany me to a 'Comics workshop' with Humsafar Trust but he was quite apprehensive and expressed his preconceived notion about 'these' people. He had a fear that they forcefully convert people, he added. Then [when] I asked Mass Communication students to participate in the workshop their response[s] were also similar putting forth their prejudice. The views of those belonging to our media fraternity are enough to give us an idea of what common man's view would be on the issue of homosexuality and transgender. The three-day workshop with Humsafar at Santacruz[34] office was an amazing experience; it was altogether different from the other three hundred workshops I have conducted in different part[s] of the globe with ... varied organisations.

I realise[d] the participants were honest and frank to share their stories, which have been a cause for stigma to them for years. Each story had a personal touch and had plenty of information to clear all our misconceptions, which we carry in our mind. They not only talked of societal attitude towards them and discussed the legal provision on homosexuality. Each one grabs the grassroots comics' idea quickly [and] could see the direct use of the medium in their work. 'We will paste them inside toilets, trains and even to all notice boards', participants were quick to suggest soon after they completed the comics poster.

The comics drawn by the participants are powerful in a way that none of them claim[s] to be an artist but still the message [is] conveyed without any encumbrances (Sharma, 2009: 6).

The *Alag Chitra Katha* contains fifteen individual comics, drawn by different authors, all of which have been translated from Hindi to English for the purpose of this book. The translations in Appendix II provide an insight into the topics dealt with in the publication, which range from HIV/AIDS to social stigmatization.[35] Table 5.3 contrasts *Alag Chitra Katha* with the commercial comic series ACK, discussed earlier. While both share the same context—that of India—and both are political media, there are marked differences between them. While the former literally paints a picture of a strong India, masculine, heroic, and essentially Hindu, the latter, free of religious undertones, directs the spectator's gaze away from the national heroes to the unheroic and the marginalized. *Alag Chitra Katha* brings into focus those who are otherwise under-represented in the media discourse—MSM communities, transsexuals, and HIV/AIDS-infected people.

As noted above, the similarity in the titles is no coincidence, and in light of the differences pointed towards in Table 5.3, *Alag Chitra Katha* can be read as a supplement to ACK. Both narrate the nation, though in very different terms, and using very different imagery. *Alag Chitra Katha* fills a gap which ACK creates by focusing solely on 'national heroes', and even more so by constructing national heroes out of selected historical figures and deliberately excluding others. *Alag Chitra Katha* gives room to those whom ACK chooses not to put on the national stage.

In addition to its role as a medium in the sexual discourse, another example of Grassroots Comics used as a forum for social expression is provided in Figure 5.4, which considers the ethnic and religious

Table 5.3 *Amar Chitra Katha* and *Alag Chitra Katha* in Comparative Perspective

	Amar Chitra Katha	Alag Chitra Katha
Meaning	'Immortal Picture Stories'	'Different Picture Stories'
Founding Date	1967	2009
Content	Indian national history, Hindu mythology	Social issues, everyday incidents that the LGBT community faces
Mode of Production	Professional; vast number of professional authors and artists	Lay; limited number of volunteers
Outreach	Mass	Non-mass
Sequence	Serial; continuous	One-time
Interest	Commercial	Non-profit
Artistic Freedom	Limited; direct influence of the scriptwriters on the artists	Broad; artists choose the theme, setting, and message of the story
Goal	Identity creation along the lines of India as a Hindu country	Uplift of marginalized sections; making the invisible visible
Direction of Message	From above; elite to broader audience	From below; non-elite to broader audience

Source: Prepared by the author.

alienation of certain segments of the Indian citizenry as its central theme. It tells the story of two students at a university college hostel in the capital, who bond with each other but are discriminated against by their peers on the basis of religion and ethnicity. They report an incident of verbal abuse to their warden, who consoles them by saying that prejudices are based on misconceptions, and are not shared by everybody.

In a very subtle and visual rather than textual way, the comic makes an interesting point about the extent of discrimination that the students are facing. It is a double discrimination in the case of Apam from Nagaland, who is identified as both the ethnic and the religious 'Other'. According to the 2001 census, Nagaland, where adivasis constitute the majority of the population, and where 90 per cent of the population are Christian, is the Indian State with the largest Christian majority, followed by Mizoram with about 87 per cent, and Meghalaya with 70 per cent Christians. His ethnic features are visible in the drawings, and a Christian background of the student is highly likely from the 'Bible Study' volume on the desk in panel three. The cultural gap in terms of custom and habit is highlighted by the abuse 'dog eater' in panel two. People from a region where pork and beef constitute elementary parts of the cuisine can easily be subjected to cultural stigmatization in a country with a Hindu majority and a fairly large Muslim minority. However, the presence of the *Bhagavad Gita*[36] at the top of the pile of books in the third panel suggests an interpretation on two levels. First, Indian religious minorities such as Muslims and Christians identify with the cultural-spiritual tradition of Hinduism, rather than creating separate cultural spaces segregated from the majority practice. On a second, more indirect level, it points to the hypocrisy of the college bullies who exclude others, which goes against the inclusive broadness of Hinduism. In fact, the story of the exchange between Krishna and Arjuna on the battlefield has been interpreted as an allegory of the ethical and moral struggles of human life. A crucial point to mention in this context is that the *Bhagavad Gita* is also understood as a tale of dualism. Unlike the Upanishads, which stand in the tradition of monism, the *Gita* is a tale of mind and matter as two ontologically separate categories. Quite possibly, the mention of the text in the comic is meant to indicate that one can be a Christian, an adivasi, a north-easterner, and an Indian, all at the same time.

The third book on the desk is entitled 'Indian History', which is an obvious reference to the lack of adequate representation of the history of the north-east in Indian schoolbooks. To give but one example, in 2011, the regional newspaper *Nagaland Post* reported on Shiela Sengupta, Subhas Chandra Bose's niece's lament, that 'the government at the centre was not paying due attention to Nagaland in spite of the contribution made by the people of the state to Netaji and his army', which, as she put it, was 'simple devotion to make India free'.[37] This perceived lack of acknowledgement can give rise to, or intensify already existing, feelings of alienation.

More recent statistical data on the mass media perceived to have an exclusive character can be added: according to a report published in March 2011 by the North East Support Centre and Helpline (NESC&H), an NGO based in New Delhi, migrants from India's north-eastern States not only face discrimination, harassment, and assault in the capital, but also complain about 'media bias' (see Table 5.4).[38] The fact that a case of 'media bias' is listed alongside serious crimes such as homicide and rape is a statement in itself on the significance attributed to fair media representation.

The NESC&H, which compiled the statistics, however provides a balanced picture of the state of the Indian media. While the report appreciates the role of the media in giving a forum to the north-east and its communities, it also mentions scope for improvement as far as highlighting the poor socio-political and economic conditions in the north-east is concerned. In fact, both claims can be substantiated by evidence from commercial print media. While the *Indian Express*, a daily newspaper, published a four-column report on the research results of the NESC&H, in which the media bias complaints were also mentioned (Jamatia, 2011: 2), the weekly news magazine *Outlook* received a letter from one of its readers saying that after Arunachal Pradesh Chief Minister Dorjee Khandu died in an air crash, and 'after so much drama happened in this part of the country, ... all we got was a lousy two lines (with a spelling mistake) in your magazine' (Paman, 2011: 6). This is not at all an isolated incident, but finds recurring mention by readers, viewers, and students from the north-east who perceive the media bias just described to range from the under- and misrepresentation of north-easterners in daily news, to the unacknowledged role of members of the community in the Indian freedom

Table 5.4 Racial Discrimination Cases Recorded by NESC&H (in total and in per cent)

Cases	Total	Percentage	2005–8	2009	2010	2011	FIR4°	No FIR
Violence against Women								
Molestation	35	36.46	17	9	7	2	15	20
Rape	4	4.17	2	1	1	1	4	0
Beating girls	7	7.29	2	3	1	1	5	2
Girls' trafficking	8	8.33	5		2	1		8
Attempt rape	2	2.08	1		1		1	1
Total crime against women	56	58.33						
Beating boys	25	26.04		20	2	3	5	20
Murder	5	5.21	1	3			4	1
Non-payment salary	6	6.25	4	2			0	6
Rent non-refund	2	2.08	1	1			0	2
Media Bias	1	1.04	1				0	1
Missing person	1	1.04			1		1	1
Total	96	100.00	34	39	16	7	35	61
Percentage			35.42	40.63	16.67	7.29	36.46	63.54

Source: 'North East Migration and Challenges in National Capital Cities: A Research Report', NESC&H, March 2011: 22.

struggle. Scholarly research backs this subjective view: Daisy Hasan notes that 'reporting on violence and "terrorism" in the north-east is one of the few times that the region and its people are mentioned in the mainstream media' (Hasan, 2004, cited in McDuie-Ra, 2013: 1634). And based on fieldwork on the north-eastern community in New Delhi, McDuie-Ra (2013: 1637) argues that while they are economically included and find work in shopping malls, restaurants, and call centres, beyond these economic spaces, many north-easterners 'continue to live as outsiders', and are subject to 'racism, discrimination, harassment, and violence'. It is such lack of acknowledgement and a marginal place in the collective memory of a nation that can lead to or reinforce feelings of alienation. However, it is not only the resentment against the ethnic majority community, but also the traditionally strong ethno-nationalism and the separatist tendencies in the north-east, that have 'historically created hostility and ambivalence towards Indian citizenship' (McDuie-Ra, 2013: 1637).

These facts, together with the assaults upon north-easterners in major south Indian cities in 2012, and the ensuing widespread fear that caused an exodus of residents of Bengaluru and Chennai back to Assam and other north-eastern States,[39] serve to highlight the topicality of the message expressed in the comic in Figure 5.4. It is revealing that the two students are depicted trying to think of ways to overcome the discrimination they are facing, while in the background a map of the country, which carries the headline 'Mother India' is visible. Both Kashmir and the north-east are clearly visible on the geographical map, representing geopolitical coherence; the title of the map invokes the supposed emotional unity of the country. The terminological choice of 'Mother India' suggests familial ties between the citizens of the vast country who are all children to one mother. Interestingly, in the anthropomorphic depictions of Mother India, or 'Bharat Mata', the human shape of the 'mother' covers the entire subcontinent, with her feet resting in Kanyakumari, on the southern tip of India, and her head up in the Kashmir region. This led an anonymous interviewee to say that 'India's giving away of Kashmir [to Pakistan or to self-rule], would be equal to beheading Bharat Mata.'[41] Therefore, like the *Bhagavad Gita* on the desk, the map and the use of the Mother India trope are yet more strategic devices to reveal the hypocrisy of those who discriminate against the students. The map in the picture, as much as the image of the 'bodyscape'[42] of Bharat Mata which it evokes, represents Kashmir and the north-east as vital parts of the Indian union. Yet, the natives of those regions are stigmatized as a cultural 'Other' by representatives of the majority community. The Grassroots Comic is thus employed as a tool to counter this bias. Much in line with the overall objective of the GC network (see Figure 5.1), it provides an entry point into a media discourse, which is thought to yield more immediate results than a mass media coverage. The comics can thus be seen as part of a larger discursive project to let the people of the north-east speak in their own voices and tell their own stories beyond the dominant stereotypical representation as exotic 'Others' inhabiting a land caught in ongoing insurgency.

In accordance with this de-stereotyping strategy, the 2013 book *Che in Paona Bazaar: Tales of Exile and Belonging from India's North-East* by Kishalay Bhattacharjee, a senior news journalist and former resident editor of the north-east for the Indian news channel NDTV, is an attempt 'to represent the people as they are, their cuisine, their music, or even their biases.... It is a personal rendering of a people who are perceived as a single entity, wrongfully identified as a single entity and have been trapped in images that mark them as xenophobic, militant, aggressive, and different from the rest of "us"' (Bhattacharjee, 2013: 6). The idea for this book stems from the author's perception that in mass media reporting from the region, the people themselves remain unheard: 'in my long years of interaction with the people of the north-east, I've felt that they could neither speak the truth of their experience nor even make it heard through the mainstream Indian media.' The book thus constitutes 'an attempt to make the readers interact with real people and not "imagined communities"' (Bhattacharjee, 2013: 7).[43]

SITUATING GRASSROOTS COMICS IN A THEORETICAL AND EMPIRICAL FRAMEWORK

Through these narratives, grassroots comics appear to fill a void that mainstream media reporting has created. What is required therefore from an analytical point of view is a serious consideration of basic media tools such as grassroots comics by media practitioners, political decision-makers, and scholars alike. Building on the assumption that a nation is an imagined community constructed through discourse, and that citizenship is a 'two-dimensional concept entailing both a legal right to the soil as well as a moral affiliation to it' (Mitra, 2012b: 95–6), active participation in the media and the possibility of sharing in the discourse and modifying it is considered a central requirement to be a full member of the society, to 'belong', and thus be a citizen in the best sense of the term.

Thus, a detailed analysis of the effects of grassroots comics, and, following from that, a consideration of the extent to which those comics can be labelled 'impact media', is essential. Students and researchers in the aforementioned Department of Development Communication at DU's Lady Irwin College are engaged in systematizing comics and preparing them for content analysis to obtain concrete proof of the socio-political issues that are addressed, and the ways in which a group of respondents visualizes a certain theme, such as conflict in the north-eastern State of Manipur.[44] This would also have to include a concrete research framework for the assessment of socio-political change brought about by the use of the medium, and the effects of that change on the actor and his sense of inclusion into the community. As far as those larger issues are concerned, grassroots comics can only be effective if the discourse is elevated to a higher level with greater outreach. Both Sharad Sharma and Aparna Khanna, as informants of this study, confirmed the use of the comics in local newspapers (as envisioned in the visual introduction to the concept; see Figure 5.1) as a way to help mainstream the issues raised and introduce them to an audience beyond the immediate social network of their authors. In the interviews, Aparna Khanna has outlined a way 'from grassroots communities to facebook communities', where Internet users can upload a particular comic which they themselves or a friend has drawn, or which they saw in an exhibition or on the wall of the *panchayati bhavan*[45] to spread the message of the comic and raise awareness. This is certainly a long way in a context where the Internet is still mostly restricted to urban centres, and where not even electrification is always a given, but it is this hybridisation of media discourses which is essential for one's visibility in a multimedia society. The channel that 'Grassroots Comics' has launched on the Internet video platform *YouTube*, which will be discussed below, is a step in that direction.

In this context, some of the points that Reichert (2011) makes in his discussion of 'web-comics', a comic format primarily published on the Internet, seem relevant. Reichert distinguishes between four different types: *traditional, interactive, collaborative,* and *media-reflexive* web-comics. While traditional web-comics are nothing but print media published on the internet, interactive ones change the outlook of the comics, and show features of 'aesthetic independence', transgressing the dominant comic format. As the name suggests, collaborative web-comics are a thoroughly hybrid media form emerging from joint participation, and make use of the structures of digitally networked media, also critiquing (and seeking to overcome) traditional concepts of authorship and the commercial mode of comic production. In the style of 'software art', media-reflexive web-comics, as a fourth category, provide their users and creators with room for reflection on software, rather than treating it as a peripheral matter that should be moved to the background in favour of the comic narrative. Understanding software as more than only a means to an end, media-reflexive web-comics consciously foreground software and programming codes. The last three categories, for Reichert, constitute a theoretical paradigm shift in the comic as a medium, challenging its sequential aesthetics and its linear visual communication (Reichert, 2011: 122), and thus upsetting what Eisner (1992) singles out as the defining characteristics of that medium.

A further difference in form between conventional comics and web-comics is that the latter offer new interactive opportunity structures of production and reception, turning 'readers into narrators' (Reichert, 2011: 125–7). The interactive character of the Internet enables the authors of the comics to enter into a dialogue with other users, via blogs, community fora, comments, or newsfeeds (Reichert, 2011: 125). Interestingly, what Reichert describes here as a value added by the web-comic is a regular and essential feature of the Grassroots Comic. The Grassroots Comic is a low-threshold medium—a characteristic which Reichert (2011: 125) lists for the web-comic—that only exists and thrives on audience reception and participation. It thus also constitutes a practical application of the theoretical model of cultural citizenship offered by Klaus and Lünenborg (2004), where the reception side in a direct feedback loop enhances and alters the production of the media text (see

Chapter three). Anyone who reads a wall poster comic can reply and state their supporting view or their counterview in terms of the same medium, which is hardly always possible with other, especially audio-visual media. Noteworthy in this context is the discussion of *agency*. The web-comics are said to increase the sense of agency of readers, because they themselves can shape the course of the action; this is not the case with conventional printed comics, which are therefore said to lack agency (Reichert, 2011: 128).

Following this conceptual understanding, Grassroots Comics may be said to have agency in a double sense of the term: the content of these comics can be designed completely by the readers, and the final product can be used to enhance the agency of the author. One cannot fail to notice the overlaps between web-comics and Grassroots Comics: the latter show many features which are highlighted as conceptual novelties in the discussion of web-comics. What Murray (2000) refers to as 'procedural authorship', the 'process of writing the rules by which the text appears as well as writing the texts themselves',[46] not only holds true for online comics, but also for the self-drawn Grassroots Comics medium. Media-reflexive web-comics, where users can access the entire narrative structure of the comic and enter it at any point to develop the storyline in every possible direction, is another new conceptual addition to the expanding repertoire of the comic. In the particular form of Internet comics, 'interactivity is paired with grassroots democracy', because every new picture panel that is added requires the majority consent of the other users who vote on its inclusion in the joint project. The comics thus are a game of association as well as a test of new forms of cooperation (Heckmann, 2001, cited in Reichert, 2011: 137). The theoretical discussion of the potential of online comics thus reveals striking parallels with the offline grassroots comics. However, there are regional specifications. The dominant discourse has asserted that the internet is overtaking printed matter, including comics, with the veteran Marvel[47] comics artist and former editor Stan Lee proclaiming that 'the printed comic has no future' (cited in Patalong, 1999), and that the web-comic will take its place. Yet this discourse is the offspring of a purely Western perspective, failing to acknowledge developments in other parts of the world. While in the West, interaction and interactive media only seem to be possible with the use of technology and the Internet, India in a double way reveals a contrasting case: here, interactive media can still do with pen and paper, rather than with screen and keyboard, and a specific form of printed comics is only just experiencing its rise, rather than its decline.

However, in terms of bringing 'Grassroots Comics' into the digital sphere, a start has already been made with a homepage for the organization which records events in India, South Asia, and other world regions to where the technique has spread.[48] The creation of a *facebook* account and a *YouTube* channel for the organization, mentioned above, adds yet another dimension to the (self-) characterization of GC as a 'social media platform'. There, videos describing the work of GC in and beyond India,[49] documenting exhibitions,[50] and discussing its potential as a communication tool in the politically sensitive areas of Kashmir and the north-east,[51] are available. These videos showcase a range of areas where GC is thought to be able to make an impact citizenship, national cohesion, and even conflict resolution. Besides these short documentaries, Sharad Sharma has to date also posted additional documentaries and about forty different comic strips, in both Hindi and English, as videos on *YouTube*.[52] The comics are read out, often with different speakers, both male and female, standing in for the characters, and the comic strip is animated with the panel that is being presented moving to the fore.

This kind of inter-mediality underlines the point made earlier, that comics are not exclusively 'old' media because they are non-electronic, but rather that they are at the same time old and new, and blur the boundaries between the digital and the analogous world. This further substantiates McLuhan's claim that 'no medium has a sense or being by itself, but only gains it through constant interaction with other media' (1970: 35). Also, Grassroots Comics are a case in point that illustrates McLuhan's observation that 'a new medium is never an addition to an old one, nor does it leave the old one in peace; it never ceases to oppress the older media until it finds new shapes and positions for them' (1970: 172).

With regard to the content, literary and cultural value, as well as the socio-political impact of comics in general, scholarly analysis is still lagging behind social reality. Marshall McLuhan's words are thus as relevant today as in 1964 when they were first written. He notes that 'what we now need is an understanding of the formal character of print, of comics, and caricatures, which challenge and change the consumer civilization of film, photography, and the press' (McLuhan, 1970: 168). Even though many more electronic media have been added to the audio-visual arsenal since McLuhan wrote these words, his observation that comics constitute a challenge to other forms of representation remains valid.

For now, however, GC, which targets a rural rather than an urban audience, relies more on conventional non-electronic than on electronic modes of display to attract viewers' attention. Figures 5.5, 5.6, and 5.7 show different ways of bringing grassroots comics into the public domain. Depending on the resources available, there are different levels of campaigning with the medium of Grassroots Comics, from peer group distribution within a local community, to using comics in mass distribution (Packalen and Sharma, 2007: 14). As has been shown above, this specific comic format has formed part of various awareness-raising campaigns throughout India. In some cases, it has had lasting effects, as in the north-eastern State of Mizoram, where a Grassroots Comic has a fixed place on a school notice board (see Figure 5.5).

Even though, according to the 2011 census, Mizoram has the second highest literacy rate in India (91.58 per cent),[53] second only to

Figure 5.5   Display of a Grassroots Comic on a School Notice Board in Mizoram
Source: Packalen and Sharma (2007: 30). © Sharad Sharma.

Kerala (93.91),[54] the comics technique has found broad approval. In 2002, the Mizoram Artists' Society (MAS) entered into a partnership with GC and held a first workshop in the State capital of Aizawl. In the following months and years, workshops were organized regularly, and MAS set up a 'comics division', which has also resulted in the regular printing of the comic newspaper *Kawhhmuhtu* (The pointer) (see Figure 5.5). The first issue of that monthly 'toonpaper', as it is called by its makers, published in February 2003 in a print run of two hundred copies, dealt with the issue of slash and burn cultivation, locally known as *jhoom*. Gradually, these 'toonpapers' were displayed in various public places, such as schools, colleges, government and NGO offices, and press clubs, with permanent wooden frames being installed as notice boards (Packalen and Sharma, 2007: 29–30).

Examples from other Indian States underline the versatility of the medium of Grassroots Comics. Figure 5.6 shows a number of comics in different public settings in Goa: a bus stand in Mapusa, the Kala Academy in Panjim, and the direct presentation to tourists by the beach. Highly frequented and accessible places like the bus stand, with its additional advantage of people having to wait, thus allowing a closer look at the comics exhibited, make for an ideal platform to showcase the medium and its message. Some grassroots comic displays form parts of larger awareness-raising campaigns. The campaign in Goa, for example, was directed against the 'ills of tourism', among which the activist group 'Goenkar Changemakers', which was

Figure 5.6   Display of Grassroots Comics in Goa
Source: Packalen and Sharma (2007: 40). © Sharad Sharma.

behind the campaign, counted the exploitation of migrant workers and the issues of displacement, prostitution, and child abuse in various forms, including child labour and paedophilia. These problems were first discussed in workshops and then translated into comics: two hundred wall poster comics and fifty comic booklets were the outcome of five workshops stretching over three days. The comic material was then distributed in different ways in order to reach different audiences. In addition to the places shown in Figure 5.6, the comics were displayed in hotels, at roadside food stalls, bus stops, beauty parlours, and barber shops (Packalen and Sharma, 2007: 40).

Subsequently, the campaign grew into a State–society partnership, as the Child and Women Welfare Department of the State of Goa realized the potential of Grassroots Comics and sponsored the activist group (which by that time had expanded and was already offering courses to educate trainers) to exhibit the comics and introduce the technique in sixty remote villages in the State. For GC, the key to the success of the campaign lies in the question of ownership: as mentioned by Aparna Khanna of the Department of Development Communication of Lady Irwin College, owning and, more importantly, *authoring* the medium, being able to enter into the media discourse, be received, and ideally enter into a dialogue with peers, journalists, and political actors on different levels, creates important means of identification and agency. Packalen and Sharma (2007: 40) note that 'the success of the campaign was largely due to ownership. The students who pasted wallposter comics in the streets had a strong sense of involvement since they were themselves the creators of the campaign material.'

Lastly, Figure 5.7 shows yet another kind of display, in the open on bare walls, where passersby can easily spot the comics. As was the case in Goa, the comics depicted in Figure 5.7 formed part of a larger campaign in Rajasthan in 2005. The underlying theme of the campaign was what in India is subsumed under the umbrella term 'girl child issue', which includes the often restricted access of girls to education and the illegal abortion of the female foetus.

In the course of the campaign 'Rights for Our Daughters', more than 2,500 comics were drawn and distributed in the area of Barmer in western Rajasthan in 2005 alone (Packalen and Sharma, 2007: 15). Some comics were even printed on stickers as yet another mode

Figure 5.7 Grassroots Campaign 'Rights for Our Daughters' in Rajasthan, 2005
Source: Packalen and Sharma (2007: 15). © Sharad Sharma.

of display. As in other rural areas of India, also in Barmer, female infanticide has been practised. The organizers of the comics workshop report that it was at first difficult to involve female participants in the project, since people, in the words of a local activist, 'did not want to send their daughters'. At last, however, the activists were successful in inviting women to the workshops, who then centred their comics on themes such as the discrimination against girls, sexual harassment, female foeticide, and widow marriage (Packalen and Sharma, 2007: 33). Overall, 'Rights for Our Daughters' centred on the theme of women being treated as 'second-class citizens',[55] thus suggesting a direct connection between comics, the moral or, in the words of Pfetsch (2012: 112), 'psychological' dimension of citizenship, and the potential of the medium to alter the status quo. The organizers report that the recipients 'identified with the problems raised in the comics' a finding which is substantiated by an incident narrated by the organizers of the GC campaign: 'when we were distributing the comics in the villages, we saw some boys raising the slogan "Long Live Comics Power". They had not participated in any of our workshops but had learned how to make wallposter comics by watching others drawing' (Packalen and Sharma, 2007: 34). Again, this stresses the perceived potential for power inherent in the specific medium of Grassroots Comics (see Figure 5.2) and the sense of agency that it gives the author. There appears to be a perception that with this tool in hand, the boundaries of a media discourse can be crossed.

The comics campaign in Rajasthan received additional emphasis by means of a three-day motorbike rally held in 2006. Under the motto 'Rights for Our Daughters', about thirty motorcyclists rode from Barmer to Jodhpur, the State's second largest city, with the comics being distributed and displayed in every town and village on their route. The support which the campaign garnered was broad, and after the end of the bike rally, the campaign 'Rights for Our Daughters' continued with more comics being created.[56] Six months after the event, a respondent from one of the villages that the rally passed through was cited as saying, 'a wind of change is blowing in the area, and this year many more girls are enrolled in the schools' (Packalen and Sharma, 2007: 37).

It is difficult, if not impossible as Farmer (2005) holds, to assess the impact of media on political action and social change, and a full-fledged attempt to do so is not the main objective of this work. However, in a political science framework, this is an important question, and undoubtedly some of the persisting theoretical and methodological challenges connected to the informed assessment of media impact will have to be addressed.

MEASURING THE IMPACT OF THE MESSAGE: PERSISTING CHALLENGES TO QUANTIFICATION

While the strategic aim of the comics is apparent, namely to highlight and negotiate the current position of those on the fringes of society, the actual effects of the self-drawn and publicized comic strips on national cohesion and social inclusion are more difficult to determine. The relevance of imagination in the field of cultural production is 'an aspect that has been widely pushed to the periphery of cultural studies and anthropology, partly because of the difficulties faced by a scholar when trying to tackle the question of "measurability" of the imagined and the imaginary' (Brosius, 2005: 5). This, however, is crucial, since 'imagination plays a vital role in the process of nation-building' (Brosius, 2005: 7). Following Anderson, Bhabha, and McLuhan,[57] it is only through the narrative and the mediated form invoking a specific image of the nation that it comes into being.

Imagination and reason are not necessarily mutually exclusive categories. Recalling the quote from Rajagopalan Radhakrishnan with which this book opened, that spaces are real precisely because they are imagined (2003: 27), we are now coming full circle. In his discussion on postmodernism and 'the politics of spatiality', Radhakrishnan argues that there are 'discursive homes; homes that are not as yet real in history', and that each of the different 'lived realities, such as the ethnic, the diasporic, the gay, the migrant, the subaltern etc., needs to imagine its own discursive-epistemic space as a form of openness to one another's persuasion' (Radhakrishnan, 2003: 27). Grassroots Comics and their modes of presentation discussed in this chapter provide an excellent example to illustrate the openness of the discursive-epistemic space, which is 'neither totalized oppression (where, for example, "nationalist time/history" presumes to speak for all other times/histories), nor relativist isolation whereby each history remains an island unto itself' (Radhakrishnan, 2003: 27). The various forms that have been conceptualized to disseminate the messages in the comics to larger audiences illustrate what Radhakrishnan calls the 'emancipatory possibilities of postmodernism', namely to make localism and specificity 'available to the metropolitan gaze so that the remotest spot from the most underdeveloped sector of the third world may begin to satisfy the "epistemological thirst" of the metropolitan center' (Radhakrishnan, 2003: 30). The imagined thus also becomes real by and through 'unreal' media. This postmodern reading makes it possible to concretize the imaginary and give it an outcome-oriented shape. However, the problem of how to quantify and measure that imaginary remains. Regarding the issue of measurement, Farmer claims that from both a positivist as well as a non-positivist research perspective, it would be 'virtually impossible to prove causality in media studies. From a positivist social science perspective, adequate data simply do not exist. From more nuanced theoretical perspectives that are sceptical about empiricism, no amount of data would be conclusive' (2005: 101).

Among the scholars who have approached this problem of quantification and measurement of phenomena in the cultural arena, and their actual implications for politics and society, is Arjun Appadurai.

Appadurai stresses the social relevance of the imaginary, noting that 'the imagination has become an organized field of social practices, a form of work ... and a form of negotiation between sites of agency (individuals) and globally defined fields of possibility' (1997: 31). Within the domain of ACK, research has been done on the agency of the artist and the role of Anant Pai as the founder and mastermind behind the series. This helps to put the comics on more solid ground, and to render possible a political science analysis of the field of tension between artist, medium, and impact. McLain shows how Pai conceived of his comic series 'as a means of teaching Indian themes and values to middle-class Indian children enrolled in English-medium schools',[58] children who he feared 'were learning Western mythology and history at the expense of their own' (2007: 57–8). In order to use the comics most effectively to convey the desired message, the scriptwriters give the artists detailed written instructions about what to draw in each panel. In a 2002 interview, Anant Pai explained the text–image production process as follows: 'the directions we gave for *ACK* were very detailed: we even gave the composition to the artist—who is on the left, who is on the right.... We were very careful, because these *ACK* are authentic'[59] (cited in McLain, 2007: 61). Apart from this close monitoring that leaves nothing to fortune and keeps artistic creativity within close bounds, another point that is emphasized in the literature is that a majority of comic book producers are 'Hindu Brahmans based in Maharashtra' (McLain, 2007: 74). Together with the thematic orientation of the comics, this feeds into the Hinduization of the narrative and enhances an upper-caste reading of history.[60]

In order to explore the relation between the form of media production and the content of the media message in an interdisciplinary work like this, one needs to establish the link between the conceptual and the empirical. Survey research by Mitra (2013) explores the constitutive factors of democracy in South Asia (Table 5.5). It has been shown in this context that basic necessities like *roti, kapra, aur makan* (bread, clothes, and shelter)—the slogan promoted by various South Asian politicians from Indira Gandhi to Zulfikar Ali Bhutto and his daughter Benazir,[61] ranged highest on the citizens' agenda in a cross–South Asia perspective, with Indian respondents at 37 per cent. The 'freedom to criticize' on the other hand scores very low with only

Table 5.5 Most Essential Elements of Democracy in Cross-national
Comparison in South Asia (per cent)

South Asia/ Countries	Opportunity to change government	Freedom to criticize	Equal rights	Basic necessities	No opinion
South Asia	14	5	28	30	23
Bangladesh	11	3	27	**44**	15
India	20	4	20	**37**	19
Nepal	9	4	21	**35**	31
Pakistan	11	6	**33**	19	31
Sri Lanka	19	6	**40**	17	18

Note: The categories most salient in a given country have been bold faced for
quick detection.
Source: Mitra (2013: 239).

4 percent of the respondents naming it as the 'most essential element
to democracy'. From the South Asian perspective it is noteworthy that
in Pakistan and Sri Lanka, two states where in the past democracy has
been consistently weakened in favour of autocratic rule, equal rights
are regarded as the most essential element of a democracy at 33 and
40 per cent respectively. The three other South Asian states which
formed part of the study however, all ranked basic necessities highest
(see Table 5.5).

The important distinction to which Mitra (2013) draws attention is
that between behavioural and ontological categories. The former are
those which one associates with everyday life, the latter those that are
considered desirable. When asked about the most liked attributes of
democracy, respondents assigned supreme status to the right to free
speech and free action (see Table 5.6).

A juxtaposition of the two survey results suggests that both basic
necessities as well as freedom of speech are essential features of
democracy. Both 'behavioural' and 'ontological' categories matter to
the citizen, without one overriding the other. The issue that becomes
apparent in this context is the choice of categories. When behavioural
and ontological are considered within the same format, the respondent tends to go for the more immediate need. Another insight which
springs from this survey research is that measuring the need for

Table 5.6 Most Liked Attributes of Democracy in Cross-national Comparison in South Asia (per cent)

Answers to the following question: *'Different people give different answers about what they like about democracy. I will read out a few of these. Tell me which one of these do you like most about democracy. 1. Everyone is free to speak and act, 2. People have control over the rules, 3. The weak are treated with dignity, 4. The interest of minorities are protected 5. Any other.'*

Attributes of Democracy	South Asia	Bangladesh	India	Nepal	Pakistan	Sri Lanka
Everyone is free to speak and act	**38**	26	**39**	**41**	**31**	**54**
People have control over the rulers	8	6	12	4	7	13
The weak are treated with dignity	25	**54**	27	11	26	7
The interests of minorities are concerned	6	3	7	4	5	12
No opinion	16	0	2	39	20	13

Note: The categories most salient in a given country have been bold-faced.
Source: Mitra (2013: 239).

cultural participation, that is, quantifying cultural citizenship, is difficult for both the researcher and the respondent. For the researcher it is a challenge to put cultural citizenship into quantifiable categories, also because it is nealy impossible for the respondent to identify whether and in what way they are 'cultural citizens'. Even more than in the case of the political, social, and civil citizenship dimensions of T.H. Marshall, cultural citizenship is a sphere one can only be aware of and value when one is actively barred from it.

Therefore, focusing on a specific medium such as Grassroots Comics, which offer a forum for socio-cultural expression, seems to be an empirically valuable way to trace cultural citizenship. The impact of Grassroots Comics as a medium from below might be easier to assess than the changes in perceptions, attitudes, and behaviour triggered by media that are imposed on the citizen-audience[62] from above as it were, rather than evolving from among their own ranks. Most of those who have attempted to study the impact of media on audiences have focused on mass media, which is where the root of the analytical problem lies. What is disseminated via those mass media channels is, if at all internalized by the consumer, often internalized very subconsciously. In other words, a person watching the famous Doordarshan televised versions of the *Ramayan* and the *Mahabharat*, referred to in the Introduction and Chapter four, would probably not be able to clearly point out whether this experience made them feel more Hindu, or more Indian, or whether it led to a cognitive congruence of 'India' and 'Hindu' in their minds. This is why political science is reluctant to engage with the media, as its tools of quantification, such as survey research, would yield hardly any satisfactory results if applied. Political science thus leaves this issue to be tackled by the qualitative and interpretive toolkit of cultural and media studies, accepting the risk of losing out on vital aspects of deeper sociopolitical understanding. Rather than trying to determine the effect of a message sent 'from above' to the receiving levels 'below', assessing the impact of media from below on the political environment would be a much more promising approach, and would also create grounds on which political science and cultural and media studies can meet and mutually enhance one another.[63]

As of now, qualitative research is the best way to explore media impact, and can indeed produce relevant results: on reading the comics in *Alag Chitra Katha*, drawn by members of the MSM community, a female Indian informant and holder of a postgraduate degree from the University of Delhi remarked that 'a lot of their conflict is internal, but we might not know about it or be sensitized, and knowingly or unknowingly we might judge people around us'.[64] She regards the comics as important media, since they 'give outlets to people to express themselves. They are repressed minorities, so for them to express themselves is very important.'[65] On asking the informant to note down the impressions she had on reading the comic book in its entirety, she wrote the following:

> The comic book is an eye-opening account of the issues concerning the homosexuals in India today. Since it comes straight from the horses' mouth, it acquires a great deal of authenticity, as opposed to the hearing of a tale from a third person. *Ek Alag Chitra Katha* is an innovative

concept not just in terms of its content but also the very name itself. The title is a take on the very popular comic book series in India called the *Amar Chitra Katha*, which revolves around stories from Indian mythology. In that sense it is an interesting, even if unintended play on the title,[66] since *Amar Chitra Katha* is about stories that have entered into mainstream convention and consciousness, while the *Alag Chitra Katha* is the exact opposite: the latter aims to open our minds to the challenges faced by a tiny sliver of the Indian community, which is far removed from the average path that an individual takes. The stories themselves are at times quite moving, since gay people feel quite ostracized and it is important for others to sensitise themselves to their plight. There are also related issues that get highlighted, and not just with respect to the gay community. For instance, there is the issue of getting people to use condoms during sex. The overwhelming experience in this comic seems to point towards a disregard for practicing safe sex. This is somewhat shocking, since it reflects a recklessness about both yours and your partner's health. In other places, the comic highlights the orthodoxy and interference by community. While it is almost always a negative interference, the approach to dealing with it is often quite gentle. Sometimes one would wonder if rather than gentleness, exposing societal lack of boundaries is a better way to deal with this situation. This is especially to do with a comic where an individual is using the toilet multiple times and a stray individual decides to haul him up. In a free thinking environment, where everyone has the freedom to do as they choose, such behaviour came across as surprisingly meddlesome. In other cases, dealing with issues looks a lot like wishful thinking. For instance, the strip about a boy in a football field who is being teased by fellow boys, and he decides to win them over. My guess is, in the real world that would not be so easy. All in all, the comic book is a unique and novel way of dealing with issues around homosexuality, and providing an important creative outlet to individuals struggling to gain acceptance in society.[67]

Most definitely, the comics trigger a snowball effect: people who participated in initial workshops are now training others as comic tutors, thus spreading the idea about the concept. Grassroots comics further state–society interaction, and have been proven to make an impact at the level of both the civil society as well as the state. In Mizoram, volunteers of MAS who have been involved in conducting the comics workshops from the start have reported 'extensive viewing of the wallposters by the people [who] could relate to the stories because they were in their own language and they featured local characters' (Packalen and Sharma, 2007: 30). Similarly, in Sri Lanka, comics workshops have been conducted since 2005 when Oxfam launched a South Asia campaign to counter violence against women, inviting World Comics India to contribute to enhancing communication skills. Workshop participants here interviewed villagers on their perception of the comics. Many of them are reported to have asked for 'more comics that reflected the life and realities in the villages' (Packalen and Sharma, 2007: 56). On the governmental level, the potential of the medium of comics may be considered in so far as the Government of Goa has sponsored comic workshops in Goan villages, as discussed earlier, and the Government of Mizoram's Forest and Environment Department, noting the popularity of the *Kawhhmuhtu* posters that chose the fire clearances as their topic, has decided to sponsor them and make them part of their own awareness campaigns (Packalen and Sharma, 2007: 30). Most recently, of course, the use of comics as a tool to familiarize pupils with the school curriculum in three selected districts in Chhattisgarh counts among the obvious proofs of state institutions appreciating the (self-drawn) comic as a pedagogical method of information dissemination.

Connecting back to the debate alluded to in Chapter three on 'popular culture', an important point to make is that when the popular becomes the object of scholarly interest, it ceases to be popular, and moves on into a realm of exclusivity. What was once conceptualized as mass entertainment is now the literary and culturally refined refuge of a chosen few. Thus, in her discussion on ACK, Nandini Chandra notes that in 1995, she was the first researcher to interview Ram Waeerkar, the illustrator of ACK comics. Ten years later, the situation had changed radically, and 'the popular has taken on a new avatar as popular chic. In the light of its new respectability there is burgeoning interest in the category' (Chandra, 2008: 25). With regard to comics in general, this shift in perspective would also entail challenges for a 'comic science', which, if ever established, would in the words of Frahm (2011) have to be a 'weird science', dealing with 'weird signs'. This, however, is laden with difficulty, since these days, 'the peculiarity of the comic increasingly sinks into oblivion as established scholarship systematizes comics with its methods' (Frahm, 2011: 157). This is a variation on the Heisenberg principle, according to which the very act of measuring impacts that which is being measured. It constitutes a difficult situation rather caused than solved by the collaboration between political science and cultural theory. Finding a way to measure and categorize without destroying the form, or altering it beyond recognition, will be one of the foremost tasks of an ongoing intellectual exchange between the disciplines, and one of the central characteristics of a 'soft political science'.

CONCLUSION: COUNTER-FLOW AND TRANSCULTURALITY

BROADENING THE PARADIGM

The political scientist needs to explain the unfamiliar in terms of the familiar, but not shy away from the challenge of unfamiliar questions. What they cannot explain using general political science, they should use to stretch the conceptual boundaries of general political science.

(Mitra, 1999a: 33)

Social science is interdisciplinary because social problems are transcultural.

(Horowitz, 1964: 37)

WHAT REMAINS TO BE DONE? AGENDA POINTS FOR FUTURE RESEARCH

Theory-testing goes hand in hand with theory-building. In order to accomplish both, cultural citizenship has to be taken out of the Western context in which the theory was first formulated, and tested against the empirical realities of India. This is what has been attempted here, thus revealing the context-dependency of citizenship and its derivate, cultural citizenship, whose philosophical groundings have taken opposite routes, moving from individual to collective in the West, and increasingly from collective to individual in India. In analysing cultural citizenship, it has been shown that political science must be interdisciplinary, because politics is multifold. In exploring new concepts, the theoretical and methodological terms in which this exploration is undertaken also have to be put under scrutiny, in the best sense of a conceptual stretching.

Cultural citizenship is key to the understanding of a range of social processes. The concept developed out of the idea that the nation is an imagined community created through discourse, and draws on media representation as a condition for an inclusive society. On a theoretical level, cultural citizenship links politics and culture by showing their mutual dependency, while on an empirical level it can be used to demonstrate the different variables like culture and media that feed into the process of citizen-making (both autonomous and heteronomous). Overall, it helps to conceptualize the discursive space in which the processes of negotiation of inclusion and exclusion take place. Cultural citizenship (like citizenship itself) has been identified as both *practice* and *process* (Blanchetti-Revelli, 2003). It is dynamic, because culture is dynamic and subject to changing influences. However, cultural citizenship, in the normative sense of the term, is also *product*. In the normative reading, it is a state which is achieved when the monopoly of interpretation over the nation is replaced by a multiplicity of views, ideas, people, and opinions, which, though conflicting, share a basic common understanding of the nation. This increases the overall level of governance, and if the state—and only the state—carefully and selectively employs the instrument of censorship, it can lead to the building of a nation which does not rest either on a monolithic narrative, or a top-down narrated diversity, but constitutes a truly discursive project which allows for consensus and cacophony alike.

Another new concept explored in this book is conceptual flow, which has been identified as a central trope for concept formation in the history of ideas. The emphasis here has been placed on agency and the role of institutions through which conceptual flow is channelled. Freedom—particular freedoms like the freedom of expression, as well as the more holistic notion of individual freedom of which the former is part—is dependent on functioning, democratic institutions.

This becomes apparent in the hybrid character of India's institutions, balancing cultural diversity and unified citizenship, universal and particular law, and freedom of expression and censorship to protect minorities. As such, the general idea that the fathers of the Indian nation had in mind was a hybrid one. Nehru and the Indian National Congress (INC) wanted that, unlike in neighbouring Pakistan and Sri Lanka, in India one could be a Hindu, Muslim, Jain, Parsi, Jew, Christian, or atheist, a man, woman, or *hijra*, speaking Hindi, Telugu, Tamil, or Assamese, and still be an Indian citizen. From very early on, India made strategic policy moves, including the reorganization of federal States, the three-language formula, the arrangement of separate sets of personal laws, as well as the proclamation of abstract, idealistic notions, like inscribing the society's 'composite culture' into the Constitution. Ironically, it is this socio-cultural fragmentation which has created national cohesion. Unlike Pakistan, India did not break apart but managed to stay together as a union of States, and while it has seen insurgency and communal violence, India has, unlike Sri Lanka, never experienced a civil war. However, India has not managed to create a complete fusion of tradition and modernity in the sense of an identification of the entire population with the state as citizens. The state has used the mass media to bridge gaps, prevent violence, and instil a certain national consciousness in the population, and that too in a dynamic rather than a static way, always trying to keep up with changing times.[1] But different media have also been used by political groups that are opposed to the idea of a composite culture. Hindutva proponents have fought for a monocultural reading of India where the majority (Hindu, Hindi-speaking, heterosexual males) should define the parameters of citizenship. Striving towards a monopoly of interpretation, they have either produced their own media, from pamphlets and leaflets during the anti-colonial struggle to websites like hinduunity.org,[2] or have strategically played on mass sentiment sparked by popular media, such as the televisation of the Hindu epics *Ramayan* and *Mahabharat* or the *Amar Chitra Katha* series. While Hindu nationalists have not necessarily actively promoted these uses of media, they have often cleverly acted in the popular wake of these media events, adding to the discourse of other media and mediated forms of representation. The infamous *rath yatra* (chariot ride) which L.K. Advani carried out in 1990 after the broadcasting of the two

Hindu epics on Doordarshan is a case in point. However, media have also been used by those countering the Hindutva narrative, and/or those who do not find themselves appropriately represented in the picture which the state paints of the nation. Those groups—often vulnerable, socio-economically marginalized people—increasingly discover the power of the media, and often use small-scale media, like the grassroots comics discussed in the previous chapter, to communicate within the microcosm of the larger social unit of which they are part, like the village. As a consequence, they also reach out to a larger and more diverse audience.

What the three broad groups discussed here—the state and its institutions, powerful cultural-political groups, and the marginalized—have in common is that they regard the media as a means to an end. They all share a deeply political understanding of the media as a tool with which to create something: a more cohesive society, and a more inclusive (or exclusive) citizenship regime. They see the media as a motor to bring about concrete improvements like access to infrastructure, basic necessities, and, following from that, the abstract feeling of being part of the nation, of being a citizen.

The advantage of the approach adopted here—engaging in methodological stretching to render conceptual stretching possible—is also its major difficulty. In bringing together the quantitative and the qualitative, political science and cultural theory, the book bears the risk of not being able to do justice to either. A critical remark which cultural theorists might make on reading this work is that in its analytical trajectory it understands and treats culture, art, and the media merely as means to an end. By adding the 'cultural' to citizenship, the scholar pursues a specific political project: culture becomes a path to achieve political inclusion; art is not an end in itself, but an instrument to create that path. This book could thus also be read as the perfect product of this technocratic age of ours, an age which E.M. Forster had anticipated would replace the era of the World Wars, with fundamental effects on state–society relations. In his 1942 essay, Forster (1965c) essentially projected a merger of state and society, shifting the relation between art and society by asking not what art can do for society—which is the dominant pattern also in this book— but what the duty of society is to the artist. Following the ancient Greek philosophers' structure of writing, Forster engages a fictitious painter as a voice of society, and a bureaucrat as the representative of the state in a dialogue. The artist, who is interested in painting the new police station, denies the assumptions of the civil servant that art should be 'instructive', that it 'exist[s] to make men into better citizens'. Instead he states that his intention is to experiment and 'paint something which will be understood when this society of ours is forgotten and the police station a ruin', only to be told by the voice of bureaucracy that he did not 'fit in' the state's agenda, 'and if you won't fit into the State, how can you expect to be employed by the State?' (Forster, 1965c: 106). Forster constructs this dialogue

> in order to emphasize the fundamental difficulty which confronts the modern centralized State when it tries to encourage art. The State believes in education. But does art educate? 'Sometimes but not always' is the answer; an unsatisfactory one. The state believes in recreation. But does art amuse? 'Sometimes, but not always' is the answer again. The state does *not* believe in experiments, in the development of human sensitiveness in directions away from the average citizen (Forster, 1965c: 106).

Forster's dialogue, however, is not merely reflective of the difficult relationship between state and art, but has an uneasy topicality at a time of drastic budget cuts for the humanities, which are now increasingly dependent on third-party funding to be able to carry out substantial research. On a more abstract level, the dialogue is also reflective of the potential disharmony created by interdisciplinarity, of the uneasy relationship between political science and cultural studies, where a metalanguage has to be found to avoid a cacophony of voices. Forster ends his essay with an excursion to Plato, who 'all through his life was interested in the relation between the artist and the State, and was worried because the artist never quite fits in' (Forster, 1965c: 106). The cynic could now claim that since Plato nothing has changed, and since the artist fits uneasily into the agenda of the state, art is not a subject for consideration by political science because, after all, the discipline is concerned with the study of the state.

In a further embrace of the misleading dichotomy between 'culture' and 'rationality' as discussed at the outset of this book, we learn from Forster that Plato in his later years became much more enthusiastic about the state, at the expense of changing his attitude towards poetry and art, finally 'banishing poets from the ideal community, on the ground that they upset people and that you never know what they will say next' (Forster, 1965c: 107). Chapter one of this book was devoted to the differences in form, subject, and self-understanding of political science and cultural studies. It suggested a development towards 'political studies' as the outcome of a critical self-reflection and to bridge political science and cultural studies, thus overcoming the incompatibility outlined by Forster. However, Forster's point—which would also be that of a philosophy of art—stands as valid: art, like scholarly research, should not only be looked at in terms of its employability for political or economic ends, but should be appreciated for its own sake. For the social sciences, the next big step would thus be to engage with art (understood here as encompassing various forms and media of cultural expression) not only for politics' sake, but to let art 'experiment' as Forster's painter would like to, and see how society reacts to and is shaped by art, rather than the other way round. In other words, the task of political science would also be to discover a 'politics of the intangible', to see what happens to society and politics if artists 'experiment' rather than perform according to a detailed political agenda that has been set beforehand.

Putting this item on the agenda would be as challenging as pursuing the other major theme explored here, the systematic study of cultural and conceptual flow. And yet, the contributions of political science to this research agenda are essential. One of the findings of this book thus is that cultural studies, which would traditionally engage with questions of flow and the interpenetration of art and society, needs political science more than political science needs cultural studies, precisely because of the political nature of cultural studies' objects of research. Political science for its part is content with studying elections, international relations, and institutions, where culture can but does not necessarily play a role. However, in making the findings of cultural studies comparable on a concrete level, the methodological contributions of political science are not to be underestimated. Regarding the study of media's impact on consumers, a further step that could be taken would be to supplement the largely qualitative approaches of media and cultural studies with a quantitative survey format. Appendix III lists a range of sample questions specifically designed for this purpose. The survey questions have been phrased in a way that provides an empirical base to enhance qualitative research. The survey would then be an instrument to cater to the need to understand the vernacular of Indian politics in terms of concrete, quantifiable information derived from political opinions, attitudes, statistics, and rhetoric (Mitra, 1999a: 33). The opinion survey that can be undertaken is a quantitative supplement, not only crucial to established political science, but also instrumental in testing the findings derived from an otherwise qualitative approach.[3]

COUNTER-FLOW: IN SEARCH OF 'LOCAL' KNOWLEDGE

While this book has discussed the crucial role of *agency* as a condition for flow to occur, the question of 'counterflow' is one that remains largely open. A long-term perspective based on historical research would be necessary to reveal broader trajectories. Counterflow as a category has largely been left out of the analytical focus of this research, because the very terminology in the context of a work on Asia suggests that flow is mono-directional, with objects, ideas, and people moving predominantly from 'West' to 'East'. Counterflow then would be the translation into theory of a late-twentieth-century political awakening to a changed trajectory, much in the style of the postcolonial studies metaphor of the 'Empire writing back' (Ashcroft et al., 1989). Indeed, contributions such as that by Fisher (2004) on Indian immigrants to Britain, or the volumes by Thussu (2008) and Boyd-Barrett and Thussu (1992) which use the trope of the 'contra-flow' of media from a regional to a global level, and which stress the oppositional aspect by the choice of lexicon and by hyphenating the term itself, hint in that direction. The analysis, however, has shown that the study of 'cultural flow' (or its more accessible analytical compartment of 'conceptual flow') is not an extension of a postcolonial paradigm—if it were, it would be superfluous. Instead, Chapter two has shown that flow is not only geographically locatable, but also is a historical phenomenon which can manifest itself within one time period, or one state or society as 'internal flow'. Yet, a careful consideration of what counterflow could mean and imply beyond the politically correct jargon of the 'West learning from the East' is urgently required. Connected to that is the excavation of indigenous knowledge and endogenous conceptual history, linked, however, with a thorough discussion of the extent to which that conceptual knowledge can be labelled 'endogenous'.

In the past, attempts have been made to find and reveal such knowledge, invoking at best mixed feelings in the academic audience. Nevertheless, the question remains what contribution the non-West can make to enhance, substantiate, or contradict established Western systems of socio-political thought. Intellectual projects like Clifford Geertz's 'local knowledge' (1983), or McKim Marriott's 'Indian ethnosociology' (1990) that seek to overcome the dominance of the Western paradigm in the social sciences certainly deserve attention. Assuming that 'Western sciences often do not recognize and there-fore cannot deal with the questions to which many Indian institutions are answers', the anthropologist McKim Marriott set out to explore 'social science ideas that can be developed from the realities known to Indian people' (Marriott, 1990: 1). Marriott's ethnosocial science seeks to avoid the imposition of an 'alien ontology and epistemology' on India and aims at constructing a 'theoretical social science for a culture ... building from the culture's natural categories a general sys-tem of concepts that can be formally defined in relation to each other' (Marriott, 1990: 4), thus rendering 'ethnosociology' a discipline both *for* a culture and *of* a culture.

While the linking of disciplines—as in this case the social sciences and anthropology—and a serious consideration of context and its categories is much in line with the contribution this book has set out to make, it would have to be clarified whether ethnosociology is theory or method, or both, whether the approach is grounded in textual evidence (including the visual realm), or in oral history, which is what Henry Odera Oruka (1994) bases his *Sage Philosophy* on.[4] It would have to be determined whether ethnosociology is elitist or egalitarian, and how far the 'indigenous science', as Marriott calls it, is generalizable or at least transferable into a general system of thought. How can the vernacular be translated into the general, and then again into political science, without succumbing to the Western idiomatic-conceptual structure? While this larger issue abides, cer-tain building blocks of the approach are definitely relevant for future work, and together with the contributions by Ronald Inden discussed in Chapter three, can serve to give another dimension to the crucial aspect of concept formation and the larger field of intellectual his-tory. Thus, the analysis of the sources and courses of cultural flow provided in Chapter two can be enhanced by Marriott's discussion of a possible Hindu contribution to the concept of 'flow'. Attaching importance to the idea of flow, and arguing that Hindus generally refer to the world they live in as 'that which is moving (*jagat*) and as a flowing together (*saṃsāra*)', as 'a people who are etymologically "riverine"', Marriott notes that 'it is serendipitous that Hindus should have a set of sciences that respond so well to hydraulic metaphors' (Marriott, 1990: 18).

In trying not to subscribe to either the 'Western' or the increasingly emerging 'Eastern master narrative', this work has revealed the limits to political science's supreme aim of generalization. By elaborating on the particularity of citizenship—particular to historical era, geographical area, and political regime—and by emphasizing the impossibility of a universal application of citizenship theory, because that is in turn shaped by these trajectories, it has been argued that a serious consideration of context helps to test theory more thoroughly than does superficial generalization based on a selective range of parameters. A similar case can be made for censorship, the other major concept dealt with here. Regarding censorship, it would be justifiable to ask if an approach grounded in the significance of unofficial censorship, and emphasizing the overlap between official and unofficial modes of censoring, can be upheld in socio-political contexts which lack strong and relatively easily identifiable cultural pressure groups, or in the context of an all-encompassing state apparatus that prevents social groups from taking decisive censoring action.

At the outset of this book, it was said that the aim of this research is to cross borders of various kinds—of scholarly disciplines, geographical areas, theoretical concepts, and empirical data. This has been done with the result of suggesting an enhanced dialogue between political science and cultural theory, between Asia and Europe, and between citizenship and comics. In doing so, the book has advocated taking a third path, or creating a 'third space', a much-used trope throughout this writing. Because this book set out to be a work of 'border crossing', it has, in more ways than one, turned out also to be a work of *translation*. The content of the *Alag Chitra Katha*, written in Hindi, has been translated into English in Appendix II to fulfil two purposes. First, it makes the comics accessible—for the first time in English and in an academic context—and second, and more importantly, it translates the *vernacular* into the *political*.

Together with the discussion of A.K. Ramanujan's 'Three Hundred Rāmāyanas' and the political controversy around the pluralization of culture, making citizen-comics part of the political science research agenda is not merely a move towards the broadening of the political subject matter, but is considered crucial to understanding non-Western politics. The case studies chosen for this work thus also seek to answer the question of where politics and culture meet (Mitra, 1999a: 34) and provide insights into the issue of how societies come to terms with historical discontinuities, while also tackling the issue of how far the roots of the modern Indian state would have to reach into culture and history in order to generate and sustain legitimacy (Mitra, 1999a: 33).

The research was certainly informed by an understanding of the concepts of citizenship and censorship as not being clearly locatable within a certain cultural or historical trajectory, and an understanding of Indian comics as not being mimetic of Western models but of hybridizing Western and Indian forms and contents. Based on Ronald Inden (1992), such an approach does not trace the development of citizenship from West to East, but uses India as a vantage point to be able to make a contribution of a different kind. This is not to say that Inden's work does not suffer from an 'observer's paradox'. He is, like most researchers, independently of their country of origin, shaped by the dominance of conceptual categories and labels which are the product of a long-standing Western intellectual hegemony. The question of how this hegemony might be overcome—or if not overcome, at least encountered in a promising way—leads to the exploration of larger paradigms.

Drawing on the discussion of citizenship and its more recent derivate cultural citizenship, the researcher is faced with the question of what comes after cultural citizenship. Does it mark the end of a conceptual evolution, or does it only constitute an intermediary step? Some researchers, not only in cultural studies, do not regard the term 'culture' as sufficient to explain the complexity of social relations today. 'Culture' to them is not the conceptual be all and end all of social analysis. Hence, in academic discourse, alternative terms like 'transculture' or 'transculturality' have been suggested to denote 'the complex form cultures take today' (Welsch, 1999).

TRANSCULTURALITY: PROCESS, PRODUCT, OR PLEONASM?

Even though it has not constituted the focus of analysis, the idea of 'transculturality' certainly underpins this book. The reason that this work has not engaged with this interesting concept to a significant extent is that transculturality is seen here as constituting a third step, which follows from interculturality. Among the inevitable questions that arise from an engagement with the concept is whether it is product or process, whether it is to be used as a noun or an adjective, whether the grammatical form changes the meaning, whether it marks the beginning or the end of the research process, and most importantly, whether it is innovative or tautological. Unlike interdisciplinarity—discussed at length in Chapter one—transculturality has not yet made it to the *OED*, the supreme reference guide to all words in the English language. However, the concept is listed in its adjectival form—'transcultural'—and its meaning is explained as 'transcending the limitations or crossing the boundaries of cultures; applicable to more than one culture; cross-cultural'.[5] The entry was first added to the *OED* in 1986, citing the year 1958 as the first occurrence of the term. It was then used in the context of psychiatry to refer to 'disorders due to migration from one cultural context to another'. It appears from the *OED* records that in 1964, the term was first employed in the context of the social sciences by the sociologist Irving Horowitz, who linked the interdisciplinary and the transcultural: 'because social problems are transcultural', Horowitz argues, research on those problems necessarily is (or has to be) interdisciplinary (Horowitz, 1964: 37). Unfortunately, Horowitz's hypothesis stands in utter isolation with no further explicit reference to it, or any elaboration on how the concept of the transcultural is to be understood. It appears that the term then disappeared as quickly from the debate as it had entered it, and largely went into oblivion with the exception of a few sporadic occurrences in the academic literature. These are also listed in the OED, but the context in which they are used is to be ascribed to the realm of cultural studies.[6]

The philosopher Wolfgang Welsch is among those who have resurrected the concept, as both adjective and noun, at the turn of the millennium. Arguing against 'traditional' understandings of culture as single, closed entities, and dismissing the concepts of 'intercultur-ality' and 'multiculturality' as inappropriate, he advocates transcultur-ality as the way forward with the potential to transcend monocultural standpoints (Welsch, 1999: 201). His analysis, however, is based on a sketchy and one-sided understanding of inter- and multiculturality, regarding the former primarily as a tool to prevent intercultural con-flict, and the latter as a strategy to facilitate the cohabitation of different cultural groups within a given society. In situating the discussion on multiculturalism exclusively in the Western context—Welsch hints at conceptual differences in US and European understandings—he falls into the same analytical trap as does Will Kymlicka (1995) in his elaboration of the concept of (multicultural) citizenship, outlined in Chapter three.

It was shown in Chapter one that in the case of the term 'interdis-ciplinary', the adjective preceded the noun with regard to the time of entry into the *OED*.[7] A noun is a word of a different quality than an adjective. While the adjective denotes the quality of something, as in a *fast* car, or an *old* man, the noun denotes an entity, or a concept. In the case of 'transculturality', the evolution from adjective to noun shows that the lexical item has by now acquired a standing of its own, that it has a *quality* of its own rather than being a mere *qualifier*. The connection between 'interdisciplinary' and 'transcultural' is indeed a crucial one to make, for it also shows that the prefix 'inter-' has to precede the 'trans-'. While 'trans-' designates a metalanguage in which to communicate is the ultimate aim, as in 'translingual', 'trans-disciplinary', or for that matter 'transcultural', the prefix 'inter-' refers to the necessary dialogue in search of that metalanguage.

Future research needs to investigate the value added by a concept like 'transculturality'. Cultural anthropologists are likely to regard the term as a pleonasm, doubting its legitimacy. To cultural anthropology, all culture is transculture, since no culture is essential, monolithic, or self-contained; culture only exists and is meaningful in relation to other cultures, and thrives on ongoing exchange processes.[8] The *OED* definition of 'transcultural' then also stands as valid for the defi-nition of culture, since every culture actively crosses cultural bound-aries, and is passively shaped by such crossing. Like 'counterflow', the term 'transcultural' can thus be read as a lexical move to stress the dynamic nature underlying the idea, and to emphasize a certain

research agenda. Chapter two showed that an all-encompassing category like 'flow' can be broken up into smaller analytical categories,
specific kinds of flow, such as conceptual, policy, and institutional
flows, that bear greater heuristic value. In analogy, one might also
conceive of a similar strategy in the case of 'transculturality'. If 'culture' is operationalized in terms of broad subcategories such as are
commonly used in political science to approach the concept, like language, religion, and ethnicity, 'transculturality' could be approached
in terms of categories like 'trans-lingualism',[9] 'trans-religiosity', and
'trans-ethnicity'. While at first sight, this compartmentalization[10]
might appear to be a more promising way forward so as to engage
critically with the concept, the same problem that has been detected
in connection with transculturality remains with regard to those analytical units: they would assume pure forms, ideal types, where only
diversity exists.

Among the persisting questions is also why the transcultural—
unlike the transnational or the multicultural—is not an '-ism'. Why
can the word 'cultural', when it starts with the prefix 'trans-', not
end with the suffix '-ism'? Certainly, the concept is far from being a
coherent ideology or school of thought, but neither are many of the
other '-isms' that populate the scholarly register. It might have to do
with trying to avoid the danger of essentialization, which the suffix
'-ism' entails. However, the reason might very well also be the lack
of engagement with the idea that precludes a discourse. Trying to
come to terms with the phenomenon, possibly by means of exploring
relevant subcategories, is a necessary first step towards a discursive
expansion. Whoever takes the dialogue between political science and
cultural studies seriously, must not exclude the idea of a 'transcultural
citizenship' as the possible added value that could emerge from this
dialogue. Would the addition of the prefix 'trans-' enhance or diminish the heuristic value of the concept of cultural citizenship? Might
this cause a shift in the unit of analysis? Does it make more sense to
speak of cultural citizenship in the context of the nation-state, and is
then 'transcultural citizenship' the adequate term for the discussion
in a transnational setting? Which is to ask, is 'transcultural citizenship' complementary to 'transnational citizenship', as some writers,
like Jonathan Fox (2005) have conceptualized it, or does it occupy a
different end of the citizenship spectrum altogether?

Definite answers to these pressing issues are beyond the scope and intent of this book. However, it has raised a number of issues which scholars devoted to interdisciplinary, avant-garde research must and certainly will put under much closer scrutiny in the future. The further engagement with what can be labelled the 'transcultural phenomenon'—the exploration of transculturality, hybridity, flow, and other related concepts—is not only a requirement, but a necessity. It is a necessity precisely because it is those concepts that constitute the keys to understanding life realities in this age of asymmetry. Thus, they will continue to engage scholars in the years to come.

APPENDIX I

National Unity and Emotional Integration of the People: Selected Documentary Films of the Films Division (1949–61)

Year of Production	Name of the Film	Subject	Language in Which Produced
1949	India Independent	Documentary on India's struggle for independence culminating in the celebrations on 15th August 1947.	Hindi and English
1950	Our Constitution	Documentary picturing the salient features of the Constitution, e.g., fundamental rights, the federating units, the executive, legislature, judiciary, franchise, etc.	-do-
	Indian Minorities	Documentary stressing the characteristics of India as a secular state and indicating the important part played by distinguished members of minority communities	English
	Festival Time	Documentary on the popular national festivals of India covering Holi, Gokulashtmi, Ganesh Chaturthi, Dussehra, and Diwali	Hindi, Bengali, Tamil, Telugu, and English
	Research Aids Industry	Documentary on National Research Laboratories covering National Physical Laboratory and Road Research Institute at Delhi, National Fuel Research Institute at Dhanbad, National Metallurgical Laboratory at Jamshedpur, National Chemical Laboratory at Poona, Central Food Technological Institute at Mysore, the Central Leather Research Institute at Madras, and Central Electro-Chemical Institute at Kharaikudi	-do-

(Cont'd)

(*Cont'd*)

Year of Production	Name of the Film	Subject	Language in Which Produced
	Cave Temples of India (Series-I-Buddhist)	Documentary on Buddhist viharas and chaityas covering Bhaja, Karala Kangri, Ajanta and its frescoes, and Ellora	-do-
1951	*Rights and Responsibilities*	Documentary on rights and responsibilities of citizenship	-do-
	Green Glory	Documentary on the forest wealth of India	-do-
	Case of Mr. X	Documentary on civic sense	-do-
	Democracy in Action	Documentary on 'elections'	-do-
1952	*The National Foundation*	Documentary on discipline	Hindi, Bengali, Tamil, Telugu, and English
	Our Flag	Documentary on national flag	-do-
1954	*Folk Dances of India*	Documentary on folk dances of India organized during the Republic Day 1953 celebrations	-do-
	Case of Mr. Critic	Documentary on the habit of ridiculing everything that is done	-do-
1955	*Republic Day 1955*	Documentary on the Republic Day celebrations 1955 in Delhi	-do-
	Muslims in India		-do-
	India and the United Nations	Film on India's ten years at the United Nations	-do-

Year	Title	Description	Languages
1956	*Children of God*	Harijan welfare	-do-
	It Is Your Vote	Documentary on elections	-do-
1957	*Our Prime Minister*	Documentary depicting prime minister's day-to-day life	-do-
	Pilgrimage to Freedom	Documentary showing places and persons connected with freedom struggle	-do-
	In the Common Interest	Documentary on India and the UNO	-do-
1958	*Citizens Army*	Military training for the people	Assamese, Bengali, English, Gujerati [sic], Hindi, Kannada, Marathi, Malayalam, Oriya, Punjabi, Tamil, Kashmiri, and Telugu
1959	*His Memory We Cherish*	Documentary on Mahatma Gandhi	-do-
1960	*Sinews of Defence*	Documentary on defence production showing the activities and out of turm ordnance factories	-do-

Note: 'JSM'/10th.

Source: Government of India, Directorate of Field Publicity, *Proposal for National Unity and Integration*, 1961.

APPENDIX II

EK ALAG CHITRA KATHA (2009): TEXT TRANSLATION[1]

COVER PAGE

[Speech bubble] Don't know when the society's thinking about gay people like us will change?

PAGE 3

Title: Each one is thinking to him/herself

Panel 1 LHS[2]

Sonu [man with moustache]: Raju, no one goes near that broken-down house. We will go there and have a good time.
Raju [man in polka dots]: Okay, Sonuji.

Panel 1 RHS

Sonu: Monu, I saw you with Raju yesterday. Don't meet him, he does dirty things. He is 'Guud.'[3]
Monu: Okay, Sonu *bhaiya.*[4]

Panel 2 LHS

Sonu to Raju: Raju, wasn't it fun? We will meet here tomorrow again. Now go.

Raju: Okay, Sonuji.

Monu [thinks to himself]: Sonu bhaiya is here with Raju, oh, this is the matter!

Panel 2 RHS

Monu [thinks to himself]: Sonu bhaiya was keeping me from meeting Raju. So why is he meeting Raju there himself?

PAGE 4

Title: Fidelity

Panel 1, LHS

[Introductory text] Chintu has been married to Pinky for the past two years. However, even after two years, they have not had a child.

Pinky: Whenever you come home, why are you always in a temper?

Chintu: What to do, these days work is very stressful.

Panel 1, RHS

[Text] Next day

Pinky: You come back home late every day and you have also started to consume much alcohol.

Chintu: Since there is a lot of stress at work, I hang out with a few friends when I get out of office.

Panel 2, LHS

Chintu's friend: Chintu, you have HIV. Why do you not tell your wife that this is the reason you cannot give her a child?

Chintu: Because I do not want to lose Pinky.

Panel 2, RHS

Chintu [thinks to himself]: I cannot betray my wife. Today I will tell her everything.

PAGE 5

Title: Caution

Panel 1, LHS

Person 1: While having sex, always use protection [*nirodh*5] and keep away from HIV/AIDS.
Person 2: Yes, I will always use protection.

Panel 1, RHS

Person 1: Always use protection.
Person in the crowd [thought bubble]: What is my need? I will not use any protection.

Panel 2, LHS

One partner of a couple in the act [thought bubble]: Nothing has happened to me, I will not use any protection.

Panel 2, RHS

Person lying on hospital bed [thought bubble]: I wish I had had *safe sex*.6

PAGE 6

Title: Positive thinking

Panel 1, LHS

[Introductory text] A village named Rampur
Person 1: Raju is ill, do you know?
Person 2: Yes, I know.

Panel 1, RHS

Raju [lying on bed] [thought bubble]: Will I get well or not, what will become of me? What will become of my family members? Oh! This sexually transmitted disease.[7]

Panel 2, LHS

[Introductory text] A counsellor visits Raju.
Counsellor: Raju, you will be completely fine. Don't worry. Keep up your courage.
Unidentified person: Yes, he is saying the absolutely right thing.

Panel 2, RHS

[Introductory text] A few days later.
Raju: My illness was serious; however, I did not give up. Negative thinking leads a man to worry and fear.

PAGE 7

Title: Identity of the self/recognizing oneself[8]

Panel 1, LHS

[Introductory text] When I turned 15 years old, a strange emotion was created in me. Instead of girls, I used to like boys. I was in quite some thought.

Panel 1, RHS

Narrator/protagonist [thought bubble]: Like other boys, why don't I like girls as well?

Panel 2, LHS

Narrator/protagonist [thought bubble]: Maybe there is something lacking in me, I feel. What should I do? How should I live, I don't understand?

Panel 2, RHS

[Introductory text] A few months later.

Narrator/protagonist [thought bubble]: But today I am very happy, since I feel very good since I have visited Hamsafar Trust; I have found my own identity and I am very happy.

—*Mashuq Khan*[9]

PAGE 8

Title: Words of a friend

Panel 1, LHS

Person 1: Hi, Sonu, how are you?
Sonu: I work with an organization that works on HIV.

Panel 1, RHS

Person 1: Yes, I am a sex worker but don't believe in the condom.
Sonu: No friend, you should take precautions.

Panel 2, LHS

[Introductory text] A few days later.
Sonu: Oh! Sonu you?[10]
Person 1: Yes Monu,[11] the doctor told me I have HIV.

Panel 2, RHS

Person 1 [thought bubble]: I wish I had listened to your words.

—*Vrushal Nikum*

PAGE 9

Title: Here comes the change

Panel 1, LHS

[Introductory text] MSM worker was on his site one day, when suddenly ...
Person 1: Oh! Just go away from here!

Panel 1, RHS

Person 2 [to *Person 1*]: If the worker does not conduct their work here, where should they go?

Panel 2, LHS

Person 2: They come here only to give information about sex and condom usage and protect people from HIV.

Panel 2, RHS

Person 1 [thought bubble]: Oh! Is that how it is? In the future I will never behave poorly with the MSM workers.

—*Josh Sheikh Jabbar*

PAGE 10

Title: Responsibility of self

Panel 1, LHS

Person 1: Tomorrow I am going for an HIV check. Would you like to come along?
Person 2: Sure. Why not.

Panel 1, RHS

Medical practitioner [presumably at dispensary/hospital, to *Person 2*]: Always use protection.
Person 2: Oh! The report is normal, right?
[Signboard in the background] Now, protection is in your hands.

Panel 2, LHS

[Text] Three months later.
Medical practitioner: Don't have sex without protection again.
Person 2: My report is normal.

Panel 2, RHS

[Text] One year later.
Medical practitioner: See, you have turned HIV-positive.
Person 2 [breaks into a sweat]

—*Mr Satish R. Khedekar,*
Hivos Project, Kalyan

PAGE 11

Title: Take care of the limits (that is, Stay in check)

Panel 1, LHS

[Introductory text[12]] On one day, an individual was going in and coming out of the toilet again and again. Now further ...
Person 1 [thought bubble]: This boy must be going inside to have sex,[13] I am sure.

Panel 1, RHS

[Introductory text] Again next day
Person 1 [thought bubble]: Oh! It's the same boy again. Let me call him to me.
Person 1 [speech bubble]: Ae you, come here!

Panel 2, LHS

Person 1: Pray, what is this nonsense, why do you keep going in and coming out of the toilet every day? Don't come around here again!
Person 2: Oh my god! I am so sorry!

Panel 2, RHS

Person 2: That person was saying the correct thing. I will have to do everything in my life within a limit.

—*Shaikh Firoz Afzal*

PAGE 12

Title: Not foolish

Panel 1, LHS

[Introductory text] There are 74 people who stay in a house, who perform sex work at night.
Person 1: Ok sisters, do take care to use the condom.
Persons 2 and 3: Yes, yes.

Panel 1, RHS

[Text] Then they meet a truck driver.
Truck driver: Hey, come with me …

Panel 2, LHS

Truck driver [presumably]: Hey, I will give you more money today.
Sex worker: What is this? Why have you not worn the condom?

Panel 2, RHS

Sex worker: I can't have sex without a condom. I am young, not foolish.

PAGE 13

Title: Permission

Panel 1, LHS

[Introductory text] A boy from a social work organization goes to the Police Commissioner to get permission to put up a stall on HIV [awareness]

Panel 1, RHS

Police Commissioner [to the boy]: However, our police force is already informed about HIV/AIDS[14] and condoms.

Panel 2, LHS

Boy: So, can you properly put a condom on this penis made of wood?[15]
Police commissioner: Umm ... uhh! How? I don't know how to do this!

Panel 2, RHS

Police Commissioner [to the boy]: You were saying the right thing. Instead of feeling shy of talking about HIV, getting proper information about it, that is the right thing to do.

PAGE 14

Title: Societal mindset[16]

Panel 1, LHS

[Introductory text] Raju and Sanju loved each other.
Raju: ILU[17]
Sanju: ILU 2[18]
Unidentified lady [probably a mother]: This will never happen. You will have to marry girls.

Panel 1, RHS

Person at the civil court marriage department [to *Raju* and *Sanju*]: As per the law, you cannot have a same-gender marriage.[19]

Panel 2, LHS

[Introductory text] However, Raju and Sanju get married to each other.

Unidentified lady [possibly mother figure]: Shameless people, drown to death.[20]

Two unidentified people [in unison]: Yes, yes, homo![21]

Panel 2, RHS

Raju: I don't know when the society's thinking [mindset] about homosexual people like us will change.

Sanju: Yes, and laws too.

—*Santosh Bhoiyar, Hamsafar Josh Kalyan*[22]

PAGE 15

Title: Trust

Panel 1, LHS

Two men [in unison]: We are exclusive partners.[23] We don't use the condom.[24]

[Sign on building in background] TOILET

Panel 1, RHS

[Text] One day a social worker tells them ...

Social worker: If you don't use a condom, you can get a disease like HIV.[25]

One partner: No, but I have complete trust/faith in my partner.

Panel 2, LHS

Social worker: If your steady partner, by mistake has relations with a person infected with HIV/AIDS and then has relations with you without a condom, then even you can contract HIV.
One partner: Oh! I never thought of this.

Panel 2, RHS

One partner: Yes, from now on I will always use a condom and also get myself tested for HIV regularly.

—*Vinod Chauhan, Hamsafar KYN*

PAGE 16

Title: Riddle[26]

Panel 1, LHS

[Introductory text] A homosexual boy named Rahul used to think ...
Rahul: Why am I like this? Should I commit suicide?

Panel 1, RHS

[Introductory text] Right at that time he met Raju.
Raju: Hi.[27] I work as a social worker in an organization for homosexuals.

Panel 2, LHS

Raju: So what if you are a homosexual? Don't think of committing suicide, live your life well.

Panel 2, RHS

Rahul: There are many other people like me and they are happy. I came here and discovered this.

—*Ravindra Tikte, Yaarana*

PAGE 17

Title: Keep your habit good

Panel 1, LHS

Boy 1: I am a boy, but why am I not like other boys? Why do I feel that I am like a girl? And everyone teases me, what should I do?

Boy 2 [to a third friend]: Oh, this is the same boy. Let's go and tease him. It will be fun, let us go.

Panel 1, RHS

Boy 1: No, I will have to improve my habit[28] because what I am is right and I do not care what anyone has to say.

Panel 2, LHS

[Introductory text] A few days later.

Boy 1: Yes, why not? [handing a flower to the other two boys]

Boy 2: Hello friend, how are you? We were coming to you, if you do not mind, will you become our friend?

Panel 2, RHS

Boy 1: Now my life is fulfilled. With my good behaviour I won over people and I am right the way I am. This is what everyone around me says.

—*Shazad Khan*

BACKPAGE

There are many other people like me, and are happy, I came here and got to know.

APPENDIX III

SURVEY QUESTIONS: THE MEDIA, CENSORSHIP, AND CITIZENSHIP IN INDIA

1) Some people claim that free speech and free media are essential features of democracy. Do you agree?

   - YES
   - NO
   - WITHIN MEASURES (WHICH ONES?)
   - DON'T KNOW

2) Which media do you use on a regular basis (i.e. at least five times a week)?

   - NEWSPAPERS/MAGAZINES
   - BOOKS
   - TELEVISION
   - CINEMA
   - RADIO
   - INTERNET
   - OTHER (PLEASE SPECIFY)

3) Do you also actively contribute to any of these media? If so, which ones?

- NO
- YES (PLEASE NAME THREE)

4) Do you feel that you can express your opinion on matters that concern you freely at all times?

- YES
- NO (WHY NOT? PLEASE GIVE AN EXAMPLE)

5) Have you encountered a censorship of any kind, i.e. were you ever hindered from expressing your opinion?

- NO
- YES (PLEASE GIVE AN EXAMPLE)

6) Does this have any effect on your personal quality of citizenship, i.e. of belonging to the Indian nation? If so, in what way?

- I FEEL MARGINALIZED
- I FEEL CONTROLLED
- I FEEL PATRONIZED
- I DO NOT FEEL EQUAL WITH OTHERS

7) What should *not* be depicted in the media?

- NUDITY
- VIOLENCE
- OBSCENITY
- CRITIQUE OF THE GOVERNMENT
- DEITIES REPRESENTED IN AN UNDIGNIFIED WAY
- ANY OTHER. WHICH?
- I DON'T KNOW

8) Who in your opinion should *not* be given a voice in the media?

- PEOPLE WHO ARE NOT LOYAL TOWARDS INDIA
- TERRORISTS

- SEPARATISTS
- PEOPLE WHO CRITICIZE THE GOVERNMENT
- RELIGIOUS/ETHNIC MINORITIES
- HOMOSEXUALS
- PEOPLE WHO DO NOT RESPECT NATIONAL SYMBOLS LIKE THE FLAG, THE NATIONAL ANTHEM, AND THE INTEGRITY OF THE INDIAN TERRITORY
- ANY OTHER
- DON'T KNOW

9) Do you feel people like you/your community are adequately represented in the media?

10) Have you ever complained about something present in or absent from the media? To whom?

11) Were your complaints taken into account? If so, was there any visible change?

12) I would like to draw your attention to the informal censorship of the paintings of M.F. Hussain depicting Bharat Mata and the Hindu goddess Saraswati in the nude. What do you think about this issue? Should such paintings be displayed?

- ART SHOULD BE EXPRESSED FREELY AT ALL TIMES
- DEITIES MAY NOT BE REPRESENTED IN SUCH A MANNER
- THE DEPICTION IS OBJECTIONABLE BUT THE REACTIONS AGAINST THEM WERE INAPPROPRIATE AND UNJUSTIFIED

13) In your opinion, which cultural values of India ought to be protected?

- THE FOLLOWING ONES (NAME THREE CULTURAL VALUES IN ORDER OF THEIR IMPORTANCE TO YOU)
- NONE
- I DON'T KNOW

NOTES

INTRODUCTION

1. This is the title of the first chapter of Chatterjee's book *The Nation and Its Fragments* (1993). In the book he goes beyond Anderson in saying that the (formerly) colonized nation can only imagine itself in the terms passed on to it by the colonizers, which is why their imaginations 'must remain forever colonized' (Chatterjee, 1993: 5). Postcolonial nations are thus seen as perpetual consumers of modular modernity made available to them by Europe and the Americas, the 'only true subjects of history' (Chatterjee, 1993: 5).

2. It should be noted that, for analytical reasons, a distinction is made between discursive and institutional spaces. However, these are not understood as opposites. An institution is not static, as one might be tempted into thinking by this contrast. The institutional sphere is also discursive as institutions rethink and reinvent themselves. The police in Western immigrant societies increasingly drawing in members of minority communities is a case in point.

3. The term 'Pakistan' is a compound constructed out of the names of the five provinces. The 'P' in Pakistan stands for Punjab, 'A' for Afghania (later known as the North-West Frontier Province, and now as Khyber Pakhtunkhwa), 'K', for Kashmir, 'S' for Sindh, and the suffix '-tan' is taken from Baluchistan. The name of the state was coined by the nationalist Choudhry Rahmat Ali and introduced in his pamphlet *Now or Never*, published in 1933.

4. Founded around 600 CE, Islam is about 1,400 years old. However, it reached the area that is now Pakistan only with the Mughal conquests in the thirteenth century.

5. 'Culture', and what is referred to as 'composite culture', have a fixed place in the institutional discourse. Article 29(1) of the Constitution makes explicit that there are various cultures that exist in India, and grants them the right to peaceful coexistence, while Article 30(1) states that all minority communities in the country, 'whether based on religion or language, shall have the right to establish and administer educational institutions of their choice'.

6. According to the 2001 census, India has a total population of 1,028,610,328 people. Out of these, 422,048,642 are native Hindi speakers, which makes for a ratio of 41.03 per cent. Available at: http://www.censusindia.gov.in/Census_Data_2001/Census_Data_Online/Language/Statement1.aspx (last accessed 21 October 2015).

7. According to Article 345, the federal States may adopt 'any one or more languages in use in that State or Hindi as the language or languages to be used for all or any of the official purposes of that State'. This is meant to prevent the dominance of one language over others and ensure a greater legitimacy of political institutions.

8. Article 51A, which lists the 'fundamental duties' of the citizens of India, states: 'It shall be the duty of every citizen of India ... to value and preserve the rich heritage of our *composite culture*' (emphasis added).

9. Article 44 reads as follows: 'The State shall endeavour to secure for the citizens a Uniform Civil Code throughout the territory of India.'

10. I would like to thank John Mus for drawing my attention to this crucial point.

11. Along with Thomas Gray, his contemporaries Thomas Parnell, Robert Blair, Edward Young, and James Hervey are classified as the 'graveyard poets', a 'common term for those eighteenth century writers, never a formal school, who found inspiration in graveyards and the contemplation of mortality. They were especially fashionable in the 1740s and 1750s, but can be seen to feed the therapeutically melancholic side of Romanticism' (Ousby, 1994: 382).

12. Despite contrary perspectives, however, Enlightenment and Romanticism were not oppositional movements. Romanticism was inspired by the French Revolution, which was in part a direct expression of the French Enlightenment (Day, 1996: 6).

13. Note that the opposite reading of Gray is also possible. Sha (1990) argues that the lyrical 'I' in the poem 'subtly aligns himself with those who would keep the poor ignorant in order to preserve the social hegemony'. He argues that illiteracy is actually seen as a virtue here, since 'a silent and

unknown Milton would neither have written a defence of the regicide of King Charles nor have published praise of Cromwell.... The poet's conviction that the masses must remain illiterate leads him to reflect upon what might have happened in terms of the English Revolution had the poor had greater access to knowledge' (Sha, 1990: 344).

14. In the 1840s, the journalist Henry Mayhew documented the social situation of London's poor—among them members of the working class, prostitutes, and immigrants—in a series of newspaper articles which were later compiled into the book *London Labour and the London Poor* (Mayhew, 2008). Mayhew is thus credited for having developed a kind of 'social journalism', and bringing the issues of underprivileged sections of society into focus.

15. There is no rule without an exception: Mitra (1991) explores the 'room to manoeuvre in the middle', bringing together the general and the specific as well as the institutional and the non-institutionalized sides of politics.

16. See Mitra (1999a) quoted in Chapter six.

17. This data is based on ACK catalogue information. Pramod K. Nayar cites a 1992 catalogue, claiming that the comics have been translated into '38 languages of the world' (Nayar, 2006: 116).

18. Besides, as Nayar points out, the close connection between the chosen terminology for the ACK freedom struggle issue as 'epic' puts the event in close proximity with the Hindu 'epics' *Ramayana* and *Mahabharata*, making both the freedom struggle and the Hindu epics 'Indian': 'By sliding the freedom struggle under the same rubric, there is a subtle imbrication of the freedom struggle with the *Hindu* epics, which is then called *Indian*. The shift from freedom struggle to epic to Hinduism to "Indian" is a problematic ideological move' (Nayar, 2006: 127).

19. 'Hindustani' denotes a linguistic variant of a mix of Hindi and Urdu words, that is, words with Sanskrit or Persian roots respectively. The variant has been given a place in the Constitution as a manifestation of the 'composite culture of India' laid down in Article 351. The article reads: 'It shall be the duty of the Union to promote the spread of the Hindi language, to develop it so that it may serve as a medium of expression for all the elements of the composite culture of India and to secure its enrichment by assimilating without interfering with its genius, the forms, style and expressions used in Hindustani and in the other languages of India specified in the Eighth Schedule, and by drawing, wherever necessary or desirable, for its vocabulary, primarily on Sanskrit and secondarily on other languages.'

20. See, for example, Pfleiderer and Lutze (1985) for an early account of commercial Hindi cinema as an agent of socio-cultural change.

21. Though Muslims are the most widely discussed community in the context of media representation and national imagination, they are certainly

not the only one. Sikand (2010) is one of the various examples of an analysis of reporting on Dalits (which he discusses alongside Indian Muslims), while Sawhney (2010) provides an insightful account of the cinematic representation of Chharas, a nomadic tribe.

22. Interview with Calcutta Creative Arts Performers, Kolkata, 26 August 2010.

23. Interview with Niranjan Goswami, Indian Mime Theatre, Kolkata, October 2010.

24. The *Natyashastra*, written presumably between 200 BCE and 200 CE, covers different theoretical and practical aspects of the performing arts, including theatre, dance, and music. The authorship of the text is attributed to the sage Bharata Muni.

25. *Bhava* is Sanskrit for 'mood'. The term *rasa*, meaning 'essence', denotes the emotion invoked in the receiver of a work of art.

1. TOWARDS A NEW PARADIGM

1. Note that 'cultural studies', even though the term appears in the plural form, is used in its singular inflexion here. This is in line with the convention adopted in the English-language literature, which seems to emphasize the idea that despite the abundant diversity in the fields of investigation and possible approaches, this diversity has a common core which justifies the treatment of 'cultural studies' as a discipline.

2. Gabriel Almond argues that the history of political science 'properly begins with Plato' (429–347 BCE), even though his student Aristotle (384–322 BCE) was 'more of a hands-on empiricist' (Almond, 1996: 50, cited in Gunnell, 2002: 351).

3. A broad definition of 'the political' such as this certainly complicates matters, and one can argue about its heuristic value. This, as will be shown in more detail, is also true for the definition of censorship used in this work.

4. See Cottam et al. (2004), Elster (1993), Knutson (1973), and Sears et al. (2003) for the growing scholarly interest in political psychology. *Political Psychology*, the journal of the International Society of Political Psychology, which has been in existence since 1979, marks the establishment of the subject as an institutionalized field of inquiry.

5. German terminology does not make this distinction. Humanities are *Geisteswissenschaften*, like natural sciences are *Naturwissenschaften*, and social sciences are *Sozialwissenschaften*. This has to do with the fact that political science as we know it today has evolved in the United States, where researchers have established a tradition of a scholarly approach to the study of politics that largely builds on methods of quantification, measurement,

and generalization of the findings. The precision with which units of analysis are carved out, quantified, and compared, together with the strong emphasis on data, which was (and still is) considered as numbers rather than texts, has brought (American) political science much closer to the equally numbers- and generalization-oriented natural sciences than to the image-or text-centric humanities. For details see Gunnell (2002: 339) who regards the discipline of political science as an 'American invention'.

6.   Almond identifies the entry of deductive and mathematical methods, and economic models in the rational choice approach furthered by the works of Riker, as the third 'rising blip' in the history of political science, the other two being the emergence of the Chicago school of political science with its focus on empirical studies, and the spread of behavioural political science (Almond, 1996: 50, cited in Gunnell, 2002: 351). Needless to say, all of these were developments that originated in the US, which gives rise to the perception that political science has an 'American nature'.

7.   Like the natural sciences, positive political science longs for generalization, which is what differentiates it from the humanities. In meta-theoretical terms, the two research strands are labelled 'nomothetic' and 'idiographic'. Introduced by Immanuel Kant, the term nomothetic research describes the effort to derive, from generalization, laws that explain objective phenomena— a method which is predominant in the natural sciences. Idiographic research, on the other hand, has the tendency to specify, which is typical for the humanities. Often, though not exclusively, nomothetic approaches draw on quantitative methodology, while idiographic research is qualitative. This distinction and its relevance for the present work is discussed in more detail below.

8.   Popper says that a theory is falsifiable—and thus is a legitimate theory—only if a reproducible effect is discovered which refutes the theory (1959: 86). This claim is somewhat modified by Carl Gustav Hempel, a philosopher of science and a contemporary of Popper, who sees 'testability-in-principle and explanatory import' as only the 'minimal necessary conditions that a scientific theory must satisfy; a system that meets these requirements may yet afford little illumination and may lack scientific interest' (Hempel, 1966: 75).

9.   The leading American political scientist and former president of the American Political Science Association (APSA) Harold D. Lasswell (1902– 1978) famously gave what many see as the quintessential definition of politics in the title of his 1950 book *Politics: Who Gets What, When, How*. Burnham et al. (2008: 1) open their recent volume with the four-word sentence 'Politics is about power.'

10.   Gabriel Almond, another important figure in American political science, saw the concern with the institutional norms of a polity and with

standards for evaluating them as the 'two great themes of political theory' which have been considered ever since Plato—with whom political science properly begins, according to Almond—and Aristotle.

11. Even though the individual rather than the group is the unit of analysis in rational choice, which is a methodological expression of positive social science, it is assumed that the behaviour of those individual actors is informed by quantifiable preferences, rather than by a subjectivity grounded in cultural context.

12. See Popper (1959), chapter four, on the issue of falsifiability. In his work, Popper explores the 'empirical method', in which scientific statements need to be 'testable', that is, falsifiable (Popper, 1959: 49). Popper notes that 'a theory is to be called "empirical" or "falsifiable", if it divides the class of all possible basic statements unambiguously into the following two non-empty sub-classes. First, the class of all those basic statements with which it is consistent (or which it rules out, or prohibits): we call this the class of the *potential falsifiers* of the theory; and secondly, the class of those basic statements which it does not contradict (or which it "permits"). We can put this more briefly by saying: a theory is falsifiable if the class of its potential falsifiers is not empty' (Popper, 1959: 86). The two parts essential to fulfil the requirement of falsifiability are thus the 'methodological postulate' and the 'logical criterion' (Popper, 1959: 88).

13. The definition of war—the military confrontation between two states which has to last at least three days and has to involve a certain number of casualties—is challenged by the postmodernist Jean Baudrillard in three essays which were later collectively published under the title *The Gulf War Did Not Take Place* (1995). In his writings, Baudrillard questions the label of 'war' for the events in Iraq in 1990 and 1991 on the basis of numbers: of the 500,000 Western soldiers involved in the events, he argues, more would have died in traffic accidents had they stayed at home. The estimated 100,000 casualties were all on the Iraqi side, which renders the encounter an 'entirely asymmetrical operation' (Baudrillard, 1995: 281). As a cultural theorist, Baudrillard also elaborates on the role of the media in this 'televised war'. To him, the Gulf War became a media event which showed no human casualties, and was typified by 'clean' technological images of 'surgical strikes', thus rendering it a 'simulacrum', a mere image of the war. Cultural studies here draws attention to the role of representation and perception in understanding social phenomena.

14. This 'blindness' to reality outside the definition is, of course, also a protection mechanism which policymakers responsible for unpopular wars might conveniently, and knowingly, hide behind.

15. In a 2013 contribution, Subrata Mitra explores the question of the exceptional character of India's democracy. In analysing the conceptual differences between 'India's democracy' and 'Indian democracy', the comparativist notes that since the term *Indian* democracy suggests a cultural essence, rendering the case idiosyncratic and self-contained, in the light of the influence of general variables, such as 'path dependency, adroit institutional arrangements, strategic policy reform and political capital' it is much more appropriate to speak of 'India's democracy' as 'a special case of a general model' (Mitra, 2013: 227).

16. See also Mitra (1999b) for a further discussion on the applicability of Western political science models and theorems to non-Western politics.

17. See, for example, Collier and Levitsky (1997), Diamond (2002), and Karl (1995) for a discussion of 'hybrid regimes'. In political science research, the term is normally used to refer to regimes that defy easy typology. Often these are post-authoritarian states in Asia, Latin America, or Eastern Europe that combine democratic and authoritarian elements.

18. While the sheer increase in the use of terminology which is popular in cultural studies does not account for an active engagement with cultural studies approaches, the coining of terms such as 'hybrid democracy' is still remarkable, as most conventional political scientists would dismiss the idea of hybridity altogether.

19. The term 'political studies' has been in use for a number of decades now. The Political Studies Association (PSA) was founded in 1950, and the terminology is used in the titles of various academic journals across the world, such as *Political Studies*, the journal of the Political Studies Association, *Comparative Political Studies*, launched in 1968, and the *Journal of Political Studies* published by the Department of Political Science of the University of the Punjab in Lahore. For a terminological discussion of 'political studies' and 'political science', see Burnham et al. (2008: 30–7).

20. As early as 1975, at the height of the positivistic understanding of the subject, the political scientist Dwight Waldo claimed that although there might be a sense in which political science could be construed as a natural science, it was surely a 'cultural science' in that it was shaped by its historical and social environment (cited in Gunnell, 2002: 343).

21. Social scientists concur with Appadurai that 'the crisis of representation in the social sciences in the last decades has shifted from theoretical—based on 'grand theory'—to the level of method, epistemology and interpretation' (Shome et al., 1996: PE-89).

22. See, for example, Wierzbicka (1992), who draws on the traditional Western dichotomy between body and mind to investigate the problem of translation through the lexicons of different languages. Wierzbicka says

that not everything that can be said in one language can be said in another (Shome et al., 1996: PE-91).

23. As Hertz and Imber (1995) put it: 'Rather than assuming that qualitative and quantitative research methods are always at odds, the multi-method approach casts constructive doubts on relying on the use of any single source of data or method' (1995: ix).

24. As Schnapp et al. (2006) state, it would be a misperception to assume that quantitative research, since it is aimed at proving a theory, is by definition deductive, and qualitative research, which aims at the postulation of a theory is per se inductive. In fact, there have been researchers in the quantitative tradition, from Francis Bacon to Rudolf Carnap and Hans Reichenbach, advocates of logical positivism, who have worked inductively. On the other hand, a systematic inductive approach does not necessitate empirical testing (Schnapp et al., 2006: 15–16).

25. As Schnapp et al. (2006: 19) rightly note, there are strict limits to the qualitative analysis of standardized data, as the plurality of information which is required for such analysis but has been reduced in the process of standardization cannot be re-established. On the other hand, greater and more complex information can be reduced by standardization, which makes a quantitative analysis of qualitative data possible.

26. Functionalist theories, however, still have their relevance: we learn from Talcott Parsons (1951, 1969) that social changes, including language-based ones, alter the social equilibrium and thereby, along with conflict theories based on the writings of Marx, explain the desire to accept a dominant language of wider communication. This is done because one's own language (in the wider sense of discourse) is ghettoizing. Thus, the aim is to create a new order by rejecting the dominant language, or discourse (cf. Rahman, 2003: 12).

27. Werner and Zimmermann (2006: 38–9) present the manifesto of the new paradigm in the following words: 'To investigate relational configurations that are active and asymmetrical, as well as the liable and evolving nature of things and situations, to scrutinize not only novelty, but also change, is one of the aims of histoire croisée. Instead of an analytical model—which would result in a statist view of things—our aim is on the contrary to articulate various dimensions and place them into a movement; this requires a toolbox that, while integrating the well-tested methodological contributions of the comparative approach and transfer studies, makes it possible to apprehend in a more satisfactory way the complexity of a composite and plural world in motion, and thereby the fundamental question of change. The failure to achieve this is a weak, if not blind spot within comparative- and to some extent transfer approaches.'

28. See, for example, Burnham et al. (2008: 264–81).

2. 'CULTURAL FLOW'

1. As V.K.R.V. Rao (1977: 23) points out, 'components of the social structure may receive a shock from contact with external cultures or social systems that intrude upon them ... then there is confrontation, conflict, cooperation and compromise, with a revised social fabric emerging as a result of the interplay of the contending factors.'

2. As in the theories discussed by Burke (2009), the research on diffusion is also not restricted to one discipline, but is organized within a variety of different research traditions each of which has its own characteristic approach, emphasizing certain concepts and methods rather than others (cf. Katz, 1963: 11).

3. Hart, for example, used selected quantitative criteria as indicators of rates of change in the structure of society to prove his hypothesis of 'cultural acceleration', thereby making his sample unrepresentative (LaPiere, 1965: 33).

4. LaPiere (1965: 107) actually emphasizes this idea with regard to cultural borrowing, claiming that a borrowed element may be combined with native ones in an innovative way to produce something entirely new.

5. In 1992, Habermas devoted an article to the problematic relationship of citizenship and national identity in Europe, wherein he asked the question so hotly debated today, namely whether there can ever be such a thing as 'European citizenship', since the role of the citizen has hitherto only been institutionalized at the level of nation-states (Habermas, 1992b: 12). Referring to Kant, who in the context of the French Revolution speculated on the role of the participating public, and already identified a 'world public sphere', Habermas looks at global communication which facilitates worldwide protest. Thus, he sees the arrival of 'world citizenship' no longer as merely a phantom, although he believes that the world is still far from achieving it. State citizenship and world citizenship are increasingly perceived by Habermas as forming a 'continuum which already shows itself' (Habermas, 1992b: 18), with the cultural elites and the mass media playing an important part in this regard (Habermas, 1992b: 12).

6. For a detailed discussion of these philosophers' contributions to citizenship theory, see Schweidler (2004).

7. Schama (1989) provides a thorough historical analysis of the French Revolution and its relation to modern citizenship.

8. For a good overview of these recent conceptualizations, see Isin and Turner (2002).

9. By focusing on men rather than on women in his conceptualization of citizenship, Marshall puts himself in the tradition of Rousseau, who centred his theoretical reflections on citizens primarily on men. Critics argue that in *Emile*, where he outlines his educational model, Rousseau remains

'masculinist and anti-feminist' (Day, 1996: 69–70), and that 'his idea of the *Social Contract* turns out to be a space defined by gender inequality and lack of empathy towards others' (Marso, 1998: 446).

10. Similar suggestions were made by Jochen Hartloff, the then Minister of Justice of the German State of Rhineland-Palatinate, in 2012 and were equally heavily criticized by the opposition.

11. *Culture Wars* is the title of a book by James D. Hunter (1991). There, the sociologist describes what he sees as a dramatic realignment and polarization which had transformed American politics and culture. He argues that on an increasing number of 'hot-button' issues—abortion, gun politics, separation of church and state, privacy, homosexuality, and censorship—there have arisen two definable polarities. Furthermore, it is not just that there are a number of divisive issues, but that society has divided along essentially the same lines on each of these issues, so as to constitute two warring groups, defined primarily not by religion, ethnicity, social class, or even political affiliation, but rather by ideological world views (see Hunter, 1991).

12. There is a third category of scholars: they can be classed as 'transnationals', which complicates the detection of conceptual flow. With regard to the Asian-born Berkeley anthropologist Aihwa Ong, for example, who focuses on the coming into existence of citizenship under the conditions of globalization and transnationality (Ong, 1999b), the question arises as to whether she should be regarded as Western or Eastern, American or Asian. This is relevant for the question of whether the concept of 'cultural citizenship' has already shifted to the Asian academic discourse—a question which is as difficult to answer as it is to draw the boundaries of one such regionally defined discourse. Thus, the concept of 'cultural citizenship', flexible and prone as it is to change, serves well to investigate flow on various levels, and, in terms of its intellectual development, holds much potential for future research.

13. My experience in India has confirmed this: in the public lectures which I gave on my research, reactions from the (scholarly) audience have included the apprehensive question of whether this research does not feed into the Hindutva framework, with one discussant of a paper which I presented in Delhi in 2011 even labelling cultural citizenship a 'dangerous concept'.

14. Some scholars, however, resist the idea of universalism. Steward (1963: 8) states that particular cultural patterns are to be distinguished from universals, which constitute 'inherent human biological and psychological characteristics'. While the former are determined by history and by special local adaptations, that is, are 'superorganic', the latter are reducible to biochemical and psychological processes (Steward, 1963: 8). Steward cites the example of all human beings consuming food, but defines this not as a cultural but as an organic fact, universally explainable in terms of biological and

chemical processes. Another example is that of dance, the universal feature of which is bodily rhythm—a human rather than a cultural trait. From this, Steward concludes that 'no cultural phenomena are universal' (1963: 8). He sees the most rewarding course of investigation into processes of cultural change in the 'search for laws which formulate the interrelationships of particular phenomena which may recur cross-culturally but are not necessarily universal' (Steward, 1963: 29).

15. Government of India, Ministry of Information and Broadcasting, Film (C) Section, 1961, *Censorship Arrangements Obtaining in Foreign Countries—Collection of Information*, NAI File no. 19/29/61-FC.

16. The major film-producing countries are defined here as 'those countries not producing less than one hundred films per year, that is, Japan, USA, Hong Kong, UK, France, Italy, the Federal Republic of Germany, the USSR and Mexico.'

17. In this context, India's neighbouring countries are listed as: Pakistan, Ceylon, Burma, Malaya, Singapore, and Indonesia.

18. In the light of this slow gathering of information, the authorities actually considered whether it was worth pursuing the project further, as it was suspected that by the time the required information was received from other countries, the country studies available might have become outdated.

19. Government of India, Ministry of Information and Broadcasting, Film (C) Section, 1961, *Censorship Arrangements Obtaining in Foreign Countries—Collection of Information*, NAI File no. 19/29/61-FC.

20. Said finds evidence for his claim by drawing on the examples of the rediscovery of Greece during the humanistic period of the European Renaissance, and the 'Oriental Renaissance' from the late eighteenth century until the middle of the nineteenth century which discovered the cultural riches of India, China, Japan, Persia, and Islam and deposited them 'at the heart of European culture' (Said, 1994: 194–5).

21. In this context, Richard LaPiere directs attention to the importance of *structure*, and qualifies the view that necessity is a crucial precondition of 'flow'. Even though 'necessity is the mother of invention', he argues that 'what constitutes necessity is a matter of social definition, and hence a variable ... an individual who can transcend the definitions of his society and perceive as a necessity something that is not socially designated as such is a rarity' (1965: 113).

22. However, need and demands from within a society are not always perceived as an important trigger for policy change. Lerner (1958: 68), for example, argues that 'democracy has become a world fad, spread across national lines by symbolic *diffusion*, rather than an institutional outgrowth of needs internal to an increasingly participant society'.

23. Government of India, Foreign and Political Department, 1914, Secret (W) Proceedings, October 1914, Nos. 1–29, *Arrangements Connected with Censorship in British India during the Present Crisis*, NAI file no. 1/29/1914.

24. For a detailed discussion of equilibrium theory, see, for example, the works of Talcott Parsons (1951) and Robert K. Merton (1957).

25. Government of India, Ministry of Information and Broadcasting, 1961, *Publicity Campaign in Support of Unity and Emotional Integration of India—Role of All India Radio*, NAI File no. 8 (6)/61-B (P).

26. NAI file no. 8 (6)/61-B (P).

27. Government of India, Ministry of Information and Broadcasting, 1961, *Publicity Campaign in Support of Unity and Emotional Integration of India—Role of All India Radio*, NAI File no. 8 (6)/61-B (P).

28. This idea constitutes a departure from earlier approaches, such as the anthropological tradition of research on diffusion, which focuses on inter-group relations rather than intra-group relations (Katz, 1963: 9).

29. Among the critics of this view is Martha Nussbaum (1990), who argues that Taylor's portrait of the modern identity 'pays little attention to the many art forms of non-Western origin that help shape the sense of self in contemporary Western societies. For instance, there is no place in Taylor's account for the contributions made by African culture—via jazz and blues ... despite their enormous impact and power' (Smith, 2002: 225)

30. Ong (1999) argues that previous studies of globalization and trans-nationalism have ignored individual agency in the large-scale flow of people, images, and cultural forces across borders, which is why in her work she emphasizes the individual actor as an agent in the process of cultural transformation.

31. Government of India, Ministry of Information and Broadcasting, Film Censor Branch, 1970, *A Resume of the Report—Chapter-wise as well as Subject-wise*, NAI File no.: 19/7/70-FC.

32. Government of India, Ministry of Information and Broadcasting, Film Censor Branch, 1970, *A Resume of the Report—Chapter-wise as well as Subject-wise*, NAI File no.: 19/7/70-FC.

33. Government of India, Ministry of Information and Broadcasting, Film Censor Branch, 1970, *A Resume of the Report—Chapter-wise as well as Subject-wise*, NAI File no.: 19/7/70-FC.

34. Government of India, Ministry of Information and Broadcasting, Film Censor Branch, 1970, *A Resume of the Report—Chapter-wise as well as Subject-wise*, NAI File no.: 19/7/70-FC.

35. Government of India, Ministry of Information and Broadcasting, Film Censor Branch, 1970, *A Resume of the Report—Chapter-wise as well as Subject-wise*, NAI File no.: 19/7/70-FC.

36. Government of India, Ministry of Information and Broadcasting, Film Censor Branch, 1970, *A Resume of the Report—Chapter-wise as well as Subject-wise*, NAI File no.: 19/7/70-FC.

37. Government of India, Ministry of Information and Broadcasting, Film Censor Branch, 1970, *A Resume of the Report—Chapter-wise as well as Subject-wise*, NAI File no.: 19/7/70-FC.

38. Government of India, Ministry of Information and Broadcasting, Film Censor Branch, 1970, *A Resume of the Report—Chapter-wise as well as Subject-wise*, NAI File no.: 19/7/70-FC.

39. Government of India, Ministry of Information and Broadcasting, Film Censor Branch, 1970, *A Resume of the Report—Chapter-wise as well as Subject-wise*, NAI File no.: 19/7/70-FC.

40. The study of 'flow' can actually draw on earlier insights from mass communications research, in the context of which it was assumed that there is a stimulus–response process such that people immediately reacted, or not, to an influence attempt. The model informed by this assumption showed that an innovation spreads gradually through society via various combinations of mass media and interpersonal networks. The model also introduced the variable of time in order to trace the spread of influence (cf. Katz, 1963: 5).

41. V.K.R.V. Rao illustrates these factors with reference to the Indian subcontinent, where 'changes were brought about in the social structure by the endogenous forces released by Buddha and Sankara, and the exogenous forces released by Muslim invasions and Muslim political hegemony over the country' (1977: 22).

42. In a discussion of flow, 'foreign' and 'native' are of course not unproblematic categories. They are used here, however, to aid the operationalization of the model.

43. The ongoing structure–agency debate in the social sciences can also be applied to the study of flow. While this chapter highlights the vital importance of agency to enable cultural flow and implement its effects in the adaptation of concepts and policies, some see structure as overriding agency. Steward, for instance, claims that 'personality is shaped by culture, but it has never been shown that culture is affected by personality. It is of course true that in a normative sense a previously molded personality may by resisting innovations retard culture change and by modifying new patterns give change a special direction. But these are short-range changes.... In the course of time, culture develops qualitatively new patterns which cause and are not caused by new personality types' (1963: 7).

44. It should also be noted that while Figure 2.2 attributes great significance to governmental forces in flow and the ensuing policy change, not all observers share this view. Some claim that 'the force of government has ...

limited ability to induce its citizens to develop or adopt new cultural devices' (LaPiere, 1965: 459).

45. Different studies, for example on the diffusion of hybrid seeds in two Iowa farming communities (Ryan and Gross, 1943), revealed that earlier adopters of new techniques influenced later adopters, and that the earlier adopters were influenced by salesmen, farm bulletins, and more frequent trips to the city (Katz, 1963: 7–8).

46. A new technology developed in 1980 made it possible for local communities and other non-business organizations to set up LPFM stations to disseminate news and other information within a community at a very low cost. The technology was first used in the US and embraced by consumers because it brought more choice, fewer commercials, and increased local content (cf. Sinha, 2006: 129–30). The idea of the community media was then applied to India and adoapted to the regional needs, often by non-governmental organizations that saw in it a liberating device that would enable socio-economically marginalized communities to participate and make their voice heard in a media discourse. This is crucial for agenda-setting because the advocates of the concept of community media regard the media as exclusionary.

47. M.K. Gandhi made this point in a conversation with Rabindranath Tagore: stating that he wanted 'the windows of India to be kept open for receiving the cultural winds from all parts of the world including the West', he also stressed that "I want the culture of all lands to be blown about my house as freely as possible. But I refuse to be blown off my feet by any"' (cited in Joshi, 1989: 287). Culture, for Gandhi, was also a dynamic process susceptible to constant change through the incorporation of new elements. He wrote that 'the Indian culture of our times is in the making. Many of us are trying to produce a blend of all the cultures which seem today to be in clash with one another. No culture can live if it attempts to be exclusive' (cited in Joshi, 1989: 11). Similarly, he stated that he was 'humble enough to admit that there is much that we can profitably assimilate from the West. Wisdom is no monopoly of one continent or one race. My resistance to Western civilisation is really a resistance to its indiscriminate and thoughtless imitation based on the assumption that Asiatics are fit only to copy everything that comes from the West' (M.K. Gandhi, cited in Joshi, 1989: 287).

48. Interview with Professor Hemant Joshi at IIMC, New Delhi, 18 May 2011.

49. North describes the institutional equilibrium as 'a situation where given the bargaining strength of the players and the set of contractual bargains that made up total economic exchange, none of the players would find it advantageous to devote resources into restructuring the agreements' (1990: 86). This, as North points out, is not to say that every player is

content with the situation, but that on the basis of a cost–benefit analysis which the players undertake, 'the relative costs and benefits of altering the game among the contracting parties does not make it worthwhile to do so' (1990: 86).

50. In this context, Lumby argues that the Morley-Minto reforms of 1909 were 'in effect an attempt to meet the Indian politicians' demand for Parliamentary institutions by a system of enlarged *durbars* with somewhat wider powers than before' (Lumby, 1954: 11).

51. The book is divided into twelve chapters: (I) The Village, (II) The City, (III) The District, (IV) The Provinces, (V) The Native States, (VI) The Supreme Government, (VII) The Population of India, (VIII) The Trades and Occupations of India, (IX) The Public Peace, (X) The Public Health, (XI) Public Income and Expenditure, and (XII) The Forces of Education, emphasizing the terms of rule—the institutions—as well as the most salient feature of successful rule—education.

52. In a letter dated 11 March 1898, Lee-Warner informed the secretary to the Government of India, Home Department, that his publisher Macmillan was, after inquiries were made from India, 'prepared to publish translations in Urdu, Marathi, Gujerathi [*sic*] and Hindi, as well as any other languages which may be considered by them necessary, provided that they are assured of the patronage of the Departments of Public Instruction, and of their giving authority for the use of the book in the vernacular schools (NAI File no.: Progs. nos. 33–38, June 1898; Part A).

53. Government of India, Home Department, Education-Deposit, Proceedings, February 1903, no. 8, *Views of Local Governments as to the Suitability of Sir W. Lee-Warner's 'The Citizen of India' as a Text-book for Indian Schools*, NAI File no.: Progs. nos. 8, February 1903, Deposit.

54. NAI File no.: Progs. nos. 8, February 1903, Deposit: 11.

55. Yet, Yates found the book to be counterproductive, since it increased disloyalty among the students because of its 'argumentative nature' (NAI File February 1903, no. 8: 15).

56. NAI File no.: Progs. nos. 8, February 1903, Deposit: 26. Emphasis in original.

57. NAI File no.: Progs. nos. 8, February 1903, Deposit: 15.

58. NAI File no.: Progs. nos. 8, February 1903, Deposit: 15.

3. FROM CITIZENSHIP TO 'CULTURAL CITIZENSHIP'

1. The launch of the scholarly journal *Citizenship Studies* in 1997 is a case in point. The use of the plural is reflective of the multidisciplinary background of its contributions.

2. Ancient Athens is the epitome of classical democracy. According to Forsdyke (2012), when classical historians speak of 'ancient Greece', what they really mean is 'classical Athens'. The Athenian polis was exceptional among other Greek city-states (a number of which also were democracies) and contemporaneous civilizations due to its stable institutions and material prosperity. Also, the Athenian polis is the one most thoroughly documented ancient democracy.

3. A later milestone in the legal development of citizenship was the citizenship law of the year 451/450 BCE, whose main objective was the preservation of the 'racial purity' of the Athenian citizens by prohibiting the marriage of an Athenian man with a non-Athenian woman. For details see Hignett (1952: 343–7).

4. The terminology is contested: while some sources say that the word for 'citizen' in Greek antiquity is *polités* (Pfetsch, 2012: 111), others note that the term merely designates an inhabitant of a polis, with no universal benefits conveyed and with no 'content of citizenship' (Frost, 2005: 28).

5. *Demos* is the Greek word for people, but with the reforms of Cleisthenes in 508/7 BCE, it came to denote the village community as the local administrative unit.

6. Compare this metaphor to the cover illustration of the first edition of Thomas Hobbes' *Leviathan* where the subjects form the upper body and the arms of the sovereign.

7. 'Attica' is the region around the city of Athens, centred on the Attic peninsula. Today, Attica is also an administrative region of Greece which is more extensive than the historical unit.

8. In his classification, Frost adds the *atimoi*, the 'despised' or 'those without honour', as a fourth category to the list of those who were not citizens in the ancient Athenian polis (2005: 28).

9. Categorizing the 'non-citizen' is a proven strategy to determine who a citizen is. Such definition of the citizen ex negative is also used by Schama (1989) in his discussion of the French revolutionary citoyen and later by Mitra (2010b) in his survey of citizenship in India.

10. Loraux (1993) shows how the female, and the Athenian woman, was represented in the popular myth and on the stage of the time, thereby illustrating the discursive structures and negotiations of the woman and citizenship. This again substantiates Forsdyke's (2012: 145) claim that in the polis, 'the boundary between civic institutions and popular culture was much more fuzzy than currently recognized', leading to a reconsideration of our categories of the 'official' and the 'popular', the 'formal' and the 'informal', against the historical background.

11. This corresponds to Manville (1990), who cites 500 BCE as the year by which citizenship had become a full-fledged institution.

12. For a comparative analysis of the Indian national icon Bharat Mata and her French counterpart Marianne, see Mitra and König (2012, 2013).

13. The ancient Greek philosopher Heraclitus (c. 535–475 BCE) thought of war as the 'father of all, king of all'. While this claim might only partially be true, war is definitely related to nation-building, and therefore also closely linked to citizenship. We do find parallels with the Greek experience described above in the Indian case. For the inclusive role that the Indian armed forces played after independence, see for example Cohen (1969, 2002) and Gautam (2008). Both authors show that in the diverse setting of India, the military has brought people from nearly all backgrounds together and formed them into one group, thus evoking a common identity. Aided by the image of a common enemy, the military in all countries lends itself to this particular strategy of identity formation and nation-building. In France, the "Marseillaise", the national anthem written in 1792 against the background of the Revolution three years earlier, calls the citizens to arms: the chorus, 'Aux armes, citoyens, Formez vos bataillons, Marchons, marchons, Qu'un sang impur abreuve nos sillons' (To arms, citizens, Form your battalions, Let us march, let us march, So that impure blood will water our furrows) in martial terms emphasizes the formation of the republic through armed conflict, and the duty of the citizen to defend and purify it if necessary.

14. Tilly, however, sees this as an unconscious process: 'Power holders did not undertake those three momentous activities with the intention of creating national states.... Nor did they ordinarily foresee that national states would emerge from war making, extraction, and capital accumulation' (Tilly, 1985: 172).

15. What should be added here, however, is the reverse effect of a lost war on the condition of citizenship: Reinhard Bendix, discussing the military history of tsarist Russia from a sociological point of view, notes that 'for a government which prides itself on military prestige, defeat in war is arguably the worst possible basis for extending the rights of citizenship to the lower strata. Such extension was neither desirable nor even conceivable from the standpoint of the tsarist government' (1984: 99).

16. Pfetsch (2012) operationalizes citizenship by breaking it up into four dimensions—the legal, the psychological, the political, and the social and economic. While the aim here is to create smaller units feasible for scholarly analysis, there is also an element of misdirection here, since the categorization suggests a lesser degree of interlinkage than there actually is. This is especially true for the 'psychological' and the 'political' dimension, as will be shown later.

17. See also Dover (1974) for a detailed discussion on the role of cultural and popular imagery in the making of the citizen.

18. In fact, Forsdyke (2012) shows that citizens and slaves often worked side by side as farmers in the fields, or as rowers in the fleets. This can be understood when seen in the light of Stoic philosophy, which regarded slavery as contrary to nature, and thus held that there were no valid justifications for the institution as such. This view was later to some extent shared by the Romans (see Wilkinson, 1975: 69).

19. It will be shown below how a related argument can be made about the use of street and mime theatre in contemporary India.

20. Interestingly, Aristotle in Book V of his *Politics* writes on the coastal city-state of Megara and the conflict between the rich and the poor: "[...] the democracy at Megara was overturned; there the demagogues drove out many of the notables in order that they might be able to confiscate their property. At length the exiles, becoming numerous, returned, and, engaging and defeating the people, established the oligarchy" (Aristotle, *Politics*, V, 5).

In the same context he also mentions that Theagenes, tyrant of Megara, won the confidence of the masses by "professing their hatred for the wealthy". Aristotle notes that Theagenes "slaughtered the cattle of the wealthy, which he found by the river side" (Aristotle, *Politics*, V, 5), an action which is "incomprehensible without more background information than is available" (Encyclopedia Britannica), but which seems to have been linked to the successful establishment of his tyranny. Aristotle lived in the fourth century BC and refers to much earlier political events here. Not much is known about the life of Theagenes, but he is dated to the seventh century BC.

21. For Plato (as later for John Locke), economic security and private property are requirements for citizenship. Among the fictional dialogues in his *Republic*, we find the following one: "'Now, some intelligent man would say that, in addition to this education, they must be provided with houses and other property such as not to prevent them from being the best possible guardians and not to rouse them up to do harm to the other citizens." "And he'll speak the truth'" (Bloom 1991: 95).

22. Cultural artefacts are also an important body of source material for the ancient historian striving to reconstruct daily life and human relations. When no letters, diaries, autobiographies, or other records of private thoughts or conversations are available, only formal, public records, speeches, and drama are used as sources. Public speeches are valuable because they contain 'what is thought to be appropriate behaviour and attitudes to adopt in front of a representative body of citizens', but they concern the wealthy more than the poor. Tragedy, however, touches on social issues, and 'its overall conceptions of human value in an uncertain world reveal preoccupations characteristic of Athenian society' (Fisher, 1976: 4–5).

23. On the other hand, certain cultural practices excluded people from holding citizenship. Thus, while homosexuality was tolerated, and, if based

on affection, not seen as a deviation from the norm, the economic pursuit of homosexuality as a male prostitute was despised and led to the loss of citizens' rights (Fisher, 1976: 13–14). This illustrates the close link between social practice, social status, and citizenship. The relation between sexual preferences and exclusion, which obviously existed when citizenship was first conceptualized, has only recently received scholarly attention within the conceptual framework of 'sexual citizenship'. In this context, homosexual rights and their connection with citizenship have been theoretically considered, for example in the work of Evans (1993) and Richardson (2000).

24. Historians have noted that the text 'may well be purely theoretical', for we find that parts of the text differ from historical sources of the time (Auboyer, 2002: 38).

25. This is a case of what I in chapter two called 'micro-level flow'—the exchange of intangible ideas and views, and tangible objects.

26. Arrian, Lucius Flavius Arrianus (c. 86/89–after 146/160 CE), was a historian of the Roman period, and one of the main ancient chroniclers of the life of Alexander the Great. Among his works is *Indikā* which records the voyage of Nearchus, one of Alexander's officers, from India to the Persian Gulf after the conquest of the Indus valley. Besides this, the work describes the history, geography, and culture of the Indian subcontinent at the time.

27. However, as L.N. Rangarajan notes in his introduction to the Kauṭilyan state and society, these terms 'may refer to strangers to the locality rather than to true foreigners' (1987: 53).

28. While the *Arthaśāstra* specifically mentions male homosexuality as a punishable offence, the only references to female homosexuality are defloration or rape (Rangarajan, 1987: 67–8).

29. The German word *Bürger* stems from the Old High German *burga*, 'protection', from which the German *Burg*, meaning castle, is also derived. Cities were then fortified. *Staatsbürger* (citizen) is the modern extension of the idea of a *Bürger*, a medieval city dweller, to the entire national territory.

30. Under this statute, which was applied throughout the Holy Roman Empire, cities were not allowed to give refuge to the subjects of worldly or spiritual rulers.

31. These regulations include mainly rules of good conduct necessary in urban life, such as traffic rules, fire prevention, and hygiene (Kauṭilya, 1987: 369–76). They are thus related to concrete municipal issues rather than to notions of a socio-political community.

32. In his discussion on 'Castes as Subject-Citizenries', Inden draws on examples from Indian discursive texts on statecraft and polity, such as the Charters of Karnataka during the Rashtrakuta and Chola imperial formations in the eighth to thirteenth centuries (1992: 220).

33. The lack of a geopolitical entity called 'India' at the time that Inden is referring to poses a major challenge to his approach.

34. The *ius civile* was a body of common law applicable to all citizens of the Roman Empire.

35. For a detailed discussion of the development and the features of Roman citizenship, see Howarth (2006), and Sherwin-White (1973).

36. Detailed information on the strategies underlying this early use of media for nation-building purposes is provided by Luce (1968).

37. *Pax Romana* is to be understood as the absence of war and the non-interference of Rome in local politics if taxes were paid and uprisings suppressed. However, it also entailed the granting of Roman citizenship to conquered peoples.

38. The ever-growing extent of the Roman Empire and the multitude of the cultural influences it was exposed to are apparent in the fact that after having reached India by land, Emperor Marcus Aurelius in 166 sent a trade mission to China by sea (see Wilkinson, 1975).

39. While the literature often speaks of 'cultural exchange', maybe in a move to emphasize the aspect of agency in the process, the term 'flow' is favoured here for the reason that it does not suggest a quid pro quo business relationship where one commodity or idea is traded for another. As opposed to exchange, flow is asymmetrical and may be one-sided.

40. This is not to say that Roman authorities respected the cultures in their empire equally. Rather, they were 'confident in general that they had a mission to give laws (*dare iura*) to undisciplined lesser breeds, and that barbarians should be grateful to be under their rule in a culture based on urban life' (Wilkinson, 1975: 142). Also, in the provinces, local culture was often suppressed by the elites in favour of Greco-Roman ways of life (Wilkinson, 1975: 167). This indeed bears some similarity with the arguments of contemporary critics of cultural globalization and their deploring of the loss of indigenous culture due to strong influences of Western 'cultural imperialism'. Antiquity saw a precursor of this phenomenon in Rome.

41. See Hoy (1992) for a comprehensive study of Bakhtin's work on popular culture as social articulation.

42. This is different from the conceptualization of the state by Aristotle. Contrary to Rousseau, Aristotle regarded the state, which is nothing but 'a partnership of several villages', as 'natural' and believed that it emerged 'so that people could live, but its raison d'être now is that people can live the good life. All states therefore are natural, since the very first partnerships are natural' (Bambrough, 1963: 384).

43. The image of freedom as first and foremost 'freedom from chains' can later be found—if in a more concrete understanding—in the writings of

the liberal philosopher Isaiah Berlin (1909–1997). In *Four Essays on Liberty* (1969) he writes that 'the fundamental sense of freedom is freedom from chains, from imprisonment, from enslavement by others. The rest is extension of this sense, or else metaphor' (Berlin, 1969: lvi).

44. Strictly speaking, Aristotle does not refer to legislation here, but to the holding of office and the submission to other office holders, since he understood citizenship in terms of eligibility for office (Walzer, 1989: 214).

45. Thomas Hobbes and John Locke had earlier developed the idea of the social contract, thus moving away from the Aristotelian understanding of society as an organism.

46. Thoreau asks rhetorically, 'Must the citizen ever for a moment or in the least degree, resign his conscience to the legislator? Why has every man a conscience, then?' (1989: 86).

47. It was also via Gandhi and his Civil Disobedience Movement that the writings of the American Thoreau travelled back to their country of origin. Banned by Senator McCarthy's House Committee on Un-American Activities in 1951, the text was discovered by Martin Luther King, leader of the civil rights movement in the United States, through his interest in Gandhi's politics (Klumpjan and Klumpjan, 1986: 135).

48. The question of how to accommodate diversity in modern societies is also explored theoretically with the help of the concepts of 'differentiated citizenship' (Young, 1989) and 'multicultural citizenship' (Kymlicka, 1995).

49. Lukose (2009) and Chowdhury (2011) are more recent publications that approach the aspect of the relation between the economy and citizenship from a sociological and a culturalist perspective, respectively. While Anupama Roy (2010) provides a good overview of the legal side of citizenship in India, Agarwal (2000) discusses the underlying values associated with the citizen in the Constitution.

50. The arrangement of the Constituent Assembly was as follows: 292 members were elected through the provincial legislative assemblies. Ninety-three members represented the Indian princely states, and four members represented the chief commissioners' provinces. The total membership of the assembly thus was to be 389. However, as a result of the Partition under the Mountbatten Plan of 3 June 1947, a separate Constituent Assembly was set up for Pakistan, and representatives of some provinces ceased to be members of the assembly. As a result, the membership of the Indian Constituent Assembly was reduced to 299. Available at: http://parliamentofindia.nic.in/ls/debates/facts.htm (last accessed 26 January 2016).

51. For a thorough discussion on the work of the Constituent Assembly, see Granville Austin's landmark book *The Indian Constitution*, chapter one, where he refers to the body as 'India in Microcosm'. The term denotes the

representation of minority communities—ethnic, linguistic, religious, and social—in the assembly, 'usually by members of their own choosing' (Austin, 1966: 13).

52. The move to draw inspiration from the former colonizers was of course not appreciated by everyone. Mahavir Tyagi, a member of the Constituent Assembly, was 'very much disappointed [to] see nothing Gandhian in this Constitution', and K. Hanumanthaiya complained that while freedom fighters like himself had wanted 'the music of *Veena* or *Sitar*, what they had got instead was "the music of an English band"' (cited in Guha, 2007: 121). The problem with these demands, as Austin (1966) points out, is that it was never defined what 'Indian' in this context meant, which is why the proponents were on thin ice. 'To declare that the Constitution is un-Indian or anti-Indian', Austin writes, 'is to use the undefined—if not the undefinable—as a measuring stick' (1966: 326). The difference here is between the 'non-Indian', which the Constitution in large parts is, and the 'un-Indian', which it is not (Austin, 1966: 326).

53. A number of the (Western) observers of the foundational years of the Republic of India, among them Barrington Moore (1966), Selig Harrison (1960), and Karl Wittfogel (1962) were highly sceptical of the ability of the young republic to remain politically stable and democratic, and not dwindle and fall into either authoritarian structures or anarchy. This pessimism is in line with earlier statements on the country and its political future. Wittfogel quotes Karl Marx, who thought that Indians would not inherit the fruits of new social elements that the British bourgeoisie had brought to the country until the ruling classes were ousted by the industrial proletariat, or Indians themselves became strong enough to shake off the English yoke once and for all (cf. Marx, 1960: 224, cited in Wittfogel, 1962: 525). Wittfogel himself spoke of an 'institutional insecurity' that characterized the independent state, along with 'most non-communist nations of the Orient that under the influence of a semi- or crypto-communist ideology ... weakens its political independence' (1962: 551).

54. See also Mitra (2010b), who employs Bhabha's term of the 'third space' to refer to citizenship in India as building on both the state and the society, thus constituting the 'interface of the legal specification of individual citizenship in the Constitution, and the primordial concept of personhood germane to Indian society' (Mitra, 2010b: 46).

55. For a thorough discussion of the legal framework of citizenship in India, including an analysis of the Citizenship Act of 1955 and its amendments in 1986 and 2003, see Roy (2010).

56. Stefan Herbrechter, personal conversation, 10 July 2013.

57. I am indebted to Stefan Herbrechter for drawing my attention to this crucial point.

58. In §24 of his *Philosophical Commentaries* (1707/1708), Berkeley writes that 'nothing properly but persons i.e. conscious things do exist, all other things are not so much existences as manners of the existence of persons' (cited in Renaut, 2000: 91). Berkeley here draws on the earlier work of René Descartes (1596–1650) who argued that representation was a criterion of being: 'if something that appears to me can be thought of as real and existing, this is because of a certain quality of representation capable of being forged from it, characterized by clearness and distinctness' (Renaut, 2000: 92).

59. This is a classification by Janoski and Gran (2002: 18).

60. The prominent case relates to the Muslim woman Shah Bano, who was divorced by her husband according to Muslim personal law. She then demanded a monthly allowance, which she was not entitled to according to sharia law, but which she was eventually granted by the Supreme Court of India. In view of the fierce protests by Muslim communities that followed, notably the All India Muslim Personal Law Board (AIMPLB) that was set up in 1974 to monitor any changes that may be brought to the sharia, the Rajiv Gandhi administration overruled the Supreme Court's decision by bringing the Muslim Women (Protection of Rights on Divorce) Bill into parliament. This bill in effect strengthened the role of Muslim men at the cost of women. As observers note, the 'Muslim Women (Protection of Rights on Divorce) Bill ... was a step in the wrong direction as far as women's rights were concerned' (Anant, 2011: 99).

61. Kymlicka (1995) also differentiates between minority rights as 'external protections' and 'internal restrictions'. While the former secure equality between minority and majority groups in society and are therefore legitimate from a liberal point of view, the latter term is used to refer to the suppression of the autonomy of members of the minority group, and can therefore not be endorsed by a liberal (Joppke, 2002: 254). In this context, and the question of how to deal with illiberal minority cultures, feminist authors like Ayelet Shachar (1999) point to the fact that endorsing minority cultures may amount to the suppression of women and internal dissidents—an issue which, according to Joppke (2002: 254), has been convincingly rebutted by defenders of multicultural citizenship.

62. Set up by the Janata Party government under Moraji Desai in 1979, the task of the Mandal Commission, headed by the parliamentarian B.P. Mandal, was to write a report on the situation of the socially, economically, and educationally marginalized groups in India, particularly the Scheduled Castes and Other Backward Classes, as well as the Scheduled Tribes. The practice of

affirmative action, or positive discrimination, that was affirmed by the report of the commission resulted in an increase in quotas for the groups under consideration. This created unprecedented upward mobility, leading to a rise in access to government jobs (with 27 per cent of the vacancies in civil posts being reserved for the 'Socially and Educationally Backward Classes') and seats in public universities (GoI, 1980).

63. 'Aadhaar' is the Hindi term for 'cornerstone' or 'basic structure'.

64. Some of the ideas which have fed into the Unique Identification Scheme are outlined by the mastermind behind this plan, Nandan Nilekani, in his *Imagining India: Ideas for the New Century* (2008). Taking up a term used by Szreter (2007), Nilekani writes that 'Unique identification for each citizen also ensures a basic right—the right to an "acknowledged existence" in the country, without which much of the nation's poor can be nameless and ignored, and governments can draw veils over large-scale poverty and destitution' (2008: 368).

65. For a more detailed discussion on the concept of 'the individual' in Indian philosophy and polity, see Badrinath (2000).

66. In his *Tractatus Logico-Philosophicus* (1963 [1921]), Ludwig Wittgenstein (1889–1951) writes that 'whereof one cannot speak, thereof one must be silent'.

67. In his methodological writings, Max Weber defined *Verstehen* 'as a method of understanding the"subjective meaning" of social action. Hence, for Weber the understanding of subjective meaning or *Verstehen* is possible only insofar as such actions have meanings attached to them by the acting individuals' (Herva, 1988: 144–5).

68. In his *Passage to India* (1965a [1924]), Forster writes on the inability of two characters, Ronny Heaslop and Adela Quested, to identify a green bird, saying that 'nothing in India is identifiable; the mere asking of a question causes it to disappear or to merge in something else' (Forster, 1965a: 83–4). This is particularly bad for the (Western) observer, since classification is also an act of reassurance. Ronny and Adela 'would have liked to identify it, it would somehow have solaced their hearts' (Forster, 1965a: 83).

69. Discussing the rationale behind the formation of political parties and their objectives, the sociologist Max Weber notes that parties are a means towards the end of power for their leaders, and offer idealistic or material opportunities for their followers. In his posthumously published *Wirtschaft und Gesellschaft*, Weber defines parties as follows: 'the term "party" will be employed to designate associations, membership in which rests on formally free recruitment. The end to which its activity is devoted is to secure power within an organisation for its leaders in order to attain ideal or material advantages for its active members" (cited in Swedberg, 2005: 194) (Weber,

1964: 211). And in his 1919 essay 'Politics as a Vocation' [Politik als Beruf], Weber argues that party followers expect a personal reward from a victory, that is, offices or other benefits: The party following, above all the party official and party entrepreneur, naturally expect personal compensation from the victory of their leader—that is, offices or other advantages (Weber, 2009: 103). Inner-party dynamics serve the same objective: 'All party struggles are struggles for the patronage of office, as well as struggles for objective goals' (emphasis in original) (Weber, 2009: 87). The line of argument which Weber develops is that votes for a party lead to mandates, which means power and increasing benefits for party supporters (Weber, 2011: 50–1). Similarly, the political economist Anthony Downs assumes that party members 'act solely in order to attain the income, prestige, and power which come from being in office. [They] never seek office as a means of carrying out particular policies; their only goal is to reap the rewards of holding office per se. They treat policies purely as means to the attainment of their private ends, which they can reach only by being elected' (Downs, 1957: 28). While not completely excluding the possibility of politicians (and parties) acting for the 'best of society', like Weber, Downs centres his theory of parties around what he calls the 'self-interest axiom' (Downs, 1957: 28).

70. This is a take on Collier and Levitsky's 'Democracy with Adjectives' (1997).

71. Do note that with a shrinking welfare state in many Western countries, a renewed emphasis is put on social security as a citizen right.

4. CENSORSHIP IN INDIA

1. Jansen (1991) states that 'the established vocabularies of contemporary intellectual discourse ... indicate that the Western world solved "the problem of censorship" during the eighteenth century when the great heroes of the Enlightenment, Voltaire, Diderot, D'Alembert, Franklin, Jefferson, and Madison, took away the stamps of church and state censors. In short, they tell us that Liberal societies have abolished censorship' (Jansen, 1991: 3).

2. Plato, Socrates's disciple, narrates this incident in Symposium and the Death of Socrates (1997).

3. In the German original, Aulich (1988) refers to censorship as a 'transepochales Kulturphänomen'.

4. See also Lin (1936).

5. The King James Bible narrates the incident as follows: 'And it came to pass, that when Jehudi had read three or four leaves, he cut it with the penknife, and cast it into the fire that was on the hearth, until all the roll was consumed in the fire that was on the hearth' (Jeremiah, 36: 23).

6. In this vein, Jansen defines the marketplace, rather than the priest or feudal lord, as the ultimate arbiter of liberal power-knowledge in the modern liberal state (Jansen, 1991: 16).

7. The 'PG-13 certificate' indicates that parents are strongly cautioned—some material may be inappropriate for children under 13, as these films may contain moderately long horror moments, blood, and/or moderate action violence.

8. The main task of the provincial criminal investigation department was, in Nehru's words, to 'shadow politicians and all those who were suspected of anti-government sentiments' (1985: 378). As every action provokes reaction, the countermove of those surveyed was to 'check' the surveyors, document their moves and strategies so that the provincial governments would be able to preserve civil liberties. This, in turn, did not obstruct the work of the criminal investigators, but made them function and attend to their tasks 'with greater energy' (Nehru, 1946: 378).

9. The Quit India Resolution was passed by the All India Congress Committee on the evening of 8 August 1942.

10. Article 352(1) states: 'If the President is satisfied that a grave emergency exists whereby the security of India or of any part of the territory thereof is threatened, whether by war or external aggression or [armed rebellion], he may, by Proclamation, make a declaration to that effect [in respect of the whole of India or of such part of the territory thereof as may be specified in the Proclamation].'

11. Shivaji Sarkar, personal interview, New Delhi, 11 March 2011.

12. For a discussion of the issue of 'paid news', see Guha Thakurta (2009: 139–45).

13. For a discussion of self-censorship and its consequences for the freedom of speech and opinion, see, for example, Broder (1976).

14. Goethe (2006 [1833]) wrote in his *Maximen und Reflexionen*, 'Zensur und Preßfreiheit werden immerfort miteinander kämpfen. Zensur fordert und übt der Mächtige, Preßfreiheit verlangt der Mindere' (cited in Dittmar, 1987: 52). [Censorship and freedom of the press will always struggle with one another. Censorship is what the mighty claims and exercises, freedom of the press is what the inferior one demands.]

15. See, for example, Noorani (1995).

16. While its official name is 'University of Delhi', the academic institution is commonly referred to as 'Delhi University' (DU)—a convention which is also adhered to in this book.

17. The diacritical marks used here correspond to the ones in the text cited.

18. The *Rāmāyaṇa* is, along with the *Mahābhārata*, one of the two great canonical texts of Hinduism. It is the story of Lord Rāma, the son of

Daśaratha, king of Ayodhya, his queen Kausalyā, and Ram's bride Sītā. Sītā is later captured by the demon king Rāvaṇa and taken to his kingdom of Lanka. With the help of the god Hanumān, his army of monkeys, and Sugrīvā, an exiled prince who, like Rāma, has also suffered the loss of his wife and kingdom, Rāma is able to go to Lanka, ultimately kill Rāvaṇa, and, after a chastity trial by fire, bring Sītā back to Ayodhya. However, because of continuing rumours questioning his wife's chastity, Rāma banishes the now pregnant Sītā. She finds refuge with the sage Vālmīki, to whom the composition of the Rāmāyaṇa is traditionally attributed. Eventually, Sītā abandons the world to return to the bosom of the earth from where she came. Bereft by the loss of his wife, Rāma finally ascends to heaven with members of his retinue (cf. Richman, 1992: 6–7).

19. These include Balinese, Bengali, Cambodian, Chinese, Gujarati, Javanese, Kannada, Kashmiri, Khotanese, Laotian, Malaysian, Marathi, Oriya, Prakrit, Sanskrit, Santali, Sinhalese, Tamil, Telugu, Thai, Tibetan, and Vietnamese to mention only the Asian languages.

20. Ramanujan notes, for example, that Sanskrit alone contains 'some twenty-five or more tellings' belonging to various narrative genres (1999: 133).

21. *Rākṣasa* is a term denoting a demon in Hindu mythology.

22. Kumbhakarṇa is a demon, and the younger brother of Rāvaṇa. He is described as being of a monstrous size, but generally of good character, knowing that Rāvaṇa was wrong but still fighting by his side out of loyalty.

23. In order to illustrate this, Ramanujan, quoting Sen (1920), gives the example of the Bengali *Rāmāyaṇa*, where Rāma's wedding is very much a Bengali wedding, with Bengali customs and Bengali cuisine (Ramanujan, 1999: 157). Dineshchandra Sen begins his discussion of the widely diverse *Rāmāyaṇa* narratives with the observation that 'it will certainly be wrong to suppose that the Bengali *Rāmāyaṇas* are mere translations of the great epic of Vālmīki. On the other hand, we have, in these indigenous stories of Rama, unmistakable evidence of the existence of traditions and ballads that may be traced to a period even earlier than that of Vālmīki' (Sen, 1920: 1).

24. The ABVP, the All Indian Student Council, was founded in 1948 and formally registered in 1940. It is the student wing of the Hindu nationalist Rashtriya Swayamsevak Sangh (RSS).

25. Kampan (or Kambar) (c. 1180–1250) was a medieval Tamil poet and the author of the Tamil *Rāmāyaṇam Ramavatharam*, popularly known as *Kambaramayanam*, a Tamil *Rāmāyaṇa*.

26. This analysis does not take into account other related events that are being discussed in the media: in 2009, four Kanpur colleges banned denims, long earrings, sleeveless tops, and high-heeled shoes. Many Chennai colleges have a dress code. In October 2011, the vice-chancellor of Hyderabad

University talked of starting an anti-drug and alcohol drive with north-eastern students, which sparked a row over 'racial profiling'.

27. Group 4 'Discourse, Power, Knowledge' of the Research Center for Social and Cultural Studies Mainz organized the conference 'Discursive Crossings: Subversion and Affirmation of Power Relations', held at Johannes-Gutenberg University Mainz from 19 to 20 October 2012. I would like to thank them for inviting me to participate in the discussions that linked 'crossing' to power and discourse, making it available as a heuristic device for the social scientist.

28. The writings of the German poet August Heinrich Hoffmann von Fallersleben (1798–1874), the author of *Lied der Deutschen* (Song of the Germans) (1841) which later became the German national anthem, were subject to censorship because of their pan-German sentiment which was considered revolutionary in nature. In consequence, Fallersleben had to leave Prussia and go into exile.

29. In this context, Lelyveld notes that his '"aim is to amplify rather than replace the standard narrative of the life of Gandhi led on two subcontinents by dwelling on incidents and themes that have often been underplayed. It isn't to diminish a compelling figure now generally exalted as a spiritual pilgrim and secular saint. It's to take a fresh look, in an attempt to understand his life as he lived it. I'm more fascinated by the man himself, the long arc of his strenuous life, than by anything that can be distilled as doctrine."' (Lelyveld, 2011: xiii). He also states that Gandhi is a figure that does not let anyone off easily. There are 'various Gandhis' which 'tend to be fenced off from our surroundings and his times'. Beneath these layers, Lelyveld thus seeks to discover '"the original, with all his quirkiness, elusiveness, and genius of reinvention, his occasional cruelty and deep humanity"' (Lelyveld, 2011: xiv–xv).

30. Interestingly, Gandhi had developed his own version of the 'right relationship between men and women', by combining ideas of chastity which Leo Tolstoy had developed for married and unmarried people alike, outlined in his *Kreutzer Sonata* (1889), with Hindu notions of brahmacharya (Kakar, 1990: 95)—which may be seen as a point on 'flow'. This unique conceptual blend came to regulate not only the life of Gandhi, but of all those who lived with him in the ashram.

31. The telegram which Gandhi sent to his nephew Jaisukhlal was, as Lelyveld observes, 'oddly worded'. It read: 'If you and Manu sincerely anxious for her to be with me at your risk, you can bring her. [sic] (Lelyveld, 2011: 308).'

32. The text speaks of a 'nightly cuddle', by means of which Gandhi 'established his grandniece ... in his household and bed' (Lelyveld, 2011: 308).

33. Brahmacharya denotes one of the four stages of life in Hinduism. It is characterized by the study of the Vedas and strict celibacy, which is seen as a prerequisite for spiritual practice.

34. See here also Lelyveld's remark on Gandhi's funeral: the 'prophet of nonviolence ... transported to the cremation ground on an army weapons carrier pulled by two hundred uniformed troops, preceded by armored cars, mounted lancers, and a police regiment. Air force planes dipped their wings and showered rose petals on the mourners. Later a naval vessel would be used for the immersion in the Ganges' (Lelyveld, 2011: 346).

35. In Hindu belief, moksha is the liberation from *saṃsāra*, the cycle of life, death, and rebirth—the ultimate aim.

36. For an account of the fatwa on Salman Rushdie, and the global repercussions after the publication of *The Satanic Verses*, see, for example, Malik (2009).

5. THE INTERPLAY OF MASS AND NON-MASS MEDIA IN INDIA

1. For a comprehensive account of the history of the printing press in India, see Priolkar (1958).

2. Interestingly, early forms of printing can be traced back to China, where it was used for the same purposes for which the Christian missionaries employed it in India much later: block printing is believed to have been used to print portraits of the Buddha in an effort to propagate Buddhism in 650 CE (Priolkar, 1958: 1).

3. See Prabha Chand (1976) for details on Jawaharlal Nehru's role in journalism during the independence movement.

4. The Films Division was set up in 1948 as 'the official organ of the Government of India for the production and distribution of information films and newsreels, documentaries and other films' (Garga, 2007: 130) that aim to satisfy an informational need as well as to serve an educational and cultural purpose. The Films Division characterizes itself in the following words: 'The Films Division of India ... was established to articulate the energy of a newly independent nation. For more than six decades, the organization has relentlessly striven to maintain a record of the social, political and cultural imaginations and realities of the country on film. It has actively worked in encouraging and promoting a culture of film-making in India that respects individual vision and social commitment.' Available at: www.filmsdivision. org/about-us.html (last access: 30 January 2015).

5. With the colonial government having realized the propaganda potential of film, the INP in 1943 was described by Syed Sultan Ahmed, member for Information and Broadcasting of the Viceroy's Executive Council, as

having 'no direct propaganda bias', but as serving 'as a continual encouragement to our people by reflecting the war effort in their daily lives ... it will
encourage among us interest in international affairs and among foreigners a
more direct knowledge of India and how it lives' (Garga, 2007: 101).

6. Government of India, Ministry of Information and Broadcasting,
Emotional Integration, 1961, p. 5.

7. Article 51A of the Constitution of India, inserted under the 42nd
Amendment in 1976, w.e.f. 3 January 1977, reads as follows: 'It shall be the
duty of every citizen of India—(a) to abide by the Constitution and respect
its ideals and institutions, the National Flag and the National Anthem; (b) to
cherish and follow the noble ideals which inspired our national struggle for
freedom; (c) to uphold and protect the sovereignty, unity and integrity of India;
(d) to defend the country and render national service when called upon to do
so; (e) to promote harmony and the spirit of common brotherhood amongst
all the people of India transcending religious, linguistic and regional or sec-
tional diversities; to renounce practices derogatory to the dignity of women; (f)
to value and preserve the rich heritage of our composite culture; (g) to protect
and improve the natural environment including forests, lakes, rivers and wild
life, and to have compassion for living creatures; (h) to develop the scientific
temper, humanism and the spirit of inquiry and reform; (i) to safeguard
public property and to abjure violence; (j) to strive towards excellence in all
spheres of individual and collective activity so that the nation constantly rises
to higher levels of endeavour and achievement; (k) who is a parent or guard-
ian to provide opportunities for education to his child or, as the case may be,
ward between the age of six and fourteen years.' Note that subsection (k) was
inserted under the 86th Amendment in 2002. It is not yet in effect.

8. This view of cave paintings as being the precursor of comics is challenged on both a factual and an ideological basis by Ole Frahm, who sees
comics as a young medium with only a 'short history'. Claims that comics
do not necessarily have to be comic but are indeed a serious medium, and
all attempts to portray them as an 'anthropological constant since the cave
paintings', are not an expression of historical truth, but of the desire to justify
the analysis of comics beyond a fascination for the trivial, since researchers
believe that comics are currently underrated (Frahm, 2011: 145).

9. Aristophanes's comedy *Knights*, for example, satirizes the style of politics
in 424 by constructing a fantasy in which power passes from Kleon to a sausage-
seller. A slave who personifies the Athenian people ascertains that the sausage-
seller has the right qualification for political leadership (Dover, 1974: 35–6).

10. For further details on this, see also Whitman (1964: chapter two).

11. The American *Phantom*, which would later become a best-selling
comic in India before being overtaken by ACK, was one of the first costumed

superheroes. It first appeared as a newspaper comic strip in 1936 (Chandra, 2008: 1).

12. See, for example, Sreenivas (2010), Chandra (2008), and McLain (2007, 2009) for details on content and message in ACK.

13. Academia here shares the perception of non-academic opponents of comics: they are often regarded as the domain of children, the uneducated, or the illiterate. Hence their character is thought of as infantile, and they are seen as negligible and not relevant to serious study. This is a misconception which Scott McCloud counters in his *Understanding Comics* (1993), a book on comics which, as far as its content is concerned, follows academic conventions, with a coherent chapter structure including introduction and conclusion as well as footnotes and a bibliography, but takes the form of comic strips, thus uncompromisingly linking comic form and scholarly content. Another example of a merger of comic form and academic content is the *Introducing...* series, subtitled 'A Graphic Guide', which combines elements of the graphic novel with speech bubbles and short text passages that provide information on scholarly subjects, such as sociology and cultural studies. The books have been translated into different languages and cater to the visual need of the scholarly consumer (Sardar and van Loon, 1999; Osborne and van Loon, 2004).

14. In her writing, Kaur (2012) mentions Hawley (1995), McLain (2009), Nayar (2006), Pritchett (1995), Rao (2000), and Sircar (2000) as the works that have engaged with the ACK series, a list to which can be added Debroy (2011) on the dialogue between East and West and graphic novels as a 'truly Indian product', and Barth (2007) as an example of the thorough engagement with ACK in the form of a doctoral dissertation in the German academic context. This underlines the status of the series as a legitimate theme of philosophical-religious analysis, even outside the subject boundaries of Indology. Indian adventure comics, however, among which Kaur counts the *Parmanu* series, have received even less scholarly attention (Kaur, 2012: 332).

15. Government of India, Ministry of Information and Broadcasting, *Publicity Campaign in Support of Unity and Emotional Integration of the Country*, 1961.

16. In the town of Meerut in 1857, Indian sepoys of the East India Company's army mutinied, causing violent uprisings throughout the country. The mutiny was contained only with the fall of Gwalior on 20 June 1858. The fact that one of the reasons for this uprising was that soldiers were given powder cartridges greased with tallow derived from beef and lard from pork, which they had to bite to load their muskets, gives the event a distinct cultural dimension. For a detailed account centred on the 'greased cartridge', see Paul (2011).

17. Government of India, Ministry of Information and Broadcasting, *Proposal for Utilisation of the Entertainment Media at Present Adopted by the*

Song & Drama Division for a Publicity Campaign for Unity and Emotional Integration, 1961, p. 3.

18. Government of India, Ministry of Information and Broadcasting, *Proposal for Utilisation of the Entertainment Media at present adopted by the Song & Drama Division for a Publicity Campaign for Unity and Emotional Integration*, 1961, p. 3.

19. Government of India, Ministry of Information and Broadcasting, *Publicity Campaign in Support of Unity and Emotional Integration of the Country*, 1961.

20. In this context, it is noteworthy that in December 2011, the Indian cartoonist Aseem Trivedi was charged with sedition for drawing cartoons insulting national symbols (Trivedi depicted bloodthirsty wolves rather than lions on the Ashoka pillar, and replaced the chakra at the bottom with a skull and bones, the sign of danger), as well as the Constitution during Anna Hazare's anti-corruption movement in Mumbai. He was released from prison on 12 September 2012, and granted judicial custody until 24 September (*Times of India*, 12 September 2012). From this instance it becomes apparent that cartoons are seen as a political and potentially threatening medium which can upset order and incite violence. Other than that, the drastic move of the Indian government cannot be explained. Also, on the part of the cartoonist, his medium is seen as a weapon, which he uses in a 'battle'. After his release from prison, Trivedi stated that 'although I am free, the battle will continue. Wherever there is an infringement of legal rights, our fight will continue' (*Times of India*, 12 September 2012).

21. On 14 July 2012, the National Monitoring Committee, which reports to the Ministry of Human Resource Development, decided to set up a subcommittee on the Thorat report, which labeled many of the Thorat Committee recommendations inadequate and in effect left most of the cartoons unchanged. However, some, like a caricature by Keshav Shankar Pillai on Ambedkar and the making of the Constitution, and another one on the anti-Hindi agitations in the South 'could be dropped as a response to the larger public debate on them' (Chopra, 2012).

22. For a visual introduction to the project, see a video by the GC Network, available at: https://www.youtube.com/watch?v=kcTz7A6WUhU (last accessed 22 October 2015).

23. According to the 2011 census, the literacy rate in India was 74.04 per cent with sharp divisions between men and women and between different States. See the census report on Literacy in India. Available at http://www.census2011.co.in/literacy.php (last accessed 15 October 2013).

24. Interestingly, in comparison with the Western world, one observes a contrary perception of the educational value of comics here: while in the

West, comics are accused of advancing illiteracy (Frahm, 2011: 143), in India, a country actually afflicted with widespread illiteracy, they are employed in a development context to mitigate the problem of illiteracy.

25. Founded by William Drayton in 1980, the Ashoka Fellowship is awarded to social entrepreneurs worldwide for their innovations. The non-profit organization Ashoka: Innovators for the Public describes the programme as 'offering a platform for people dedicated to changing the world' through their 'entrepreneurial talent and new ideas to solve social problems'. Available at: http://india.ashoka.org/about (last accessed 20 October 2015).

26. See the homepage of the Department of Development Communication and Extension for further details. Available at: http://www.ladyirwin.edu.in/dce.aspx (last accessed 9 August 2013).

27. Under the rubric 'Departmental Activities', 'Grassroots Comics' or 'Comics for Development' are also mentioned, with a visual example of a wall poster comic. Available at: http://www.ladyirwin.edu.in/dce_departmental.aspx (last accessed 9 August 2013).

28. McLuhan's view is challenged by the contemporary media theorist Ole Frahm who argues that on reading comics, it is precisely not necessary or even desirable to create a unity, but to 'enjoy their heterogeneous signs, print and picture in their distinctiveness and materiality, which does not link up to a unity' (Frahm, 2011: 144).

29. Interview with Dr Aparna Khanna, Lady Irwin College, Department of Development Communication, on 21 November 2011.

30. *Humsafar* is Hindi for 'we walk together on a journey'. Here it means a 'supporter'. It is a Mumbai-based organization dedicated to promoting a 'holistic approach to the rights and health of sexual minorities and promoting rational attitudes to sexuality' (see www.humsafar.org). (last accessed 19 April 2016).

31. Available at: http://www.bbc.co.uk/news/world-south-asia-14024774 (last accessed 24 September 2013), and http://www.aljazeera.com/news/asia/2011/07/20117515437104974.html (last accessed 24 September 2013). For a scholarly critique of the Supreme Court decision, see Baxi (2014).

32. *Alag Chitra Katha* literally means 'a different comic book', or 'different picture stories', and is a take on 'Amar Chitra Katha'. The latter's trademark of a spiked circle which carries the series name in Latin script and which has a fixed place in the top left-hand corner of the cover, is parodied in *Alag Chitra Katha* by an encircled star displaying the title of the publication (in both Devanagari and Latin scripts) in the middle. The *Alag Chitra Katha* emblem is placed both in the top right-hand corner and the bottom left corner of the cover page. Sharad Sharma confirmed that he consciously chose the title,

trying to offer a counter-text to the aggrandized ACK (personal conversation, New Delhi, 26 September 2015).

33. MSM is the common abbreviation for the phrase 'men who have sex with men', a medical and social research designation.

34. Santacruz is a suburb of Mumbai.

35. Even though a full-fledged content analysis is not attempted here with regard to *Alag Chitra Katha*, specific words are highlighted in the translation, for example, if Latin script or the English language is used, or a word like *nirodh* is preferred over 'condom'. This is done on the understanding that 'content analyses that consider only content ... without taking into account the language used to convey that content and the implications of that language in the social context of its deployment, miss by design the media messages ... that are carried by the choice of language used' (Farmer, 2005: 101).

36. The *Bhagavad Gita* is one of the essential texts of Hinduism. A conversation between Lord Krishna and Arjuna in 700 verses, it forms part of the Hindu epic *Mahabharata* and is understood as a guide to wisdom, devotion, and selfless action.

37. For details, see the report 'Nagas Contribution Neglected by Centre' published in the *Nagaland Post* online edition on 24 October 2011 (www.naga-landpost.com). Available at http://www.nagalandpost.com/ChannelNews/State/StateNews.aspx?news=TkVXUzEwMDAwNzkyNA==-TNwFNgDl-HTY= (last accessed 24 February 2016).

38. The NESC&H does not define media bias as such. However, it is safe to assume that this term refers to the under-or misrepresentation of north-easterners in the urban mass media. An important point to make here is that in the case of residents of north-east India or of migrants from that region, the majority of reports published are on crime, in which the migrants either play a passive or an active role.

39. FIR stands for 'First Information Report'. This is a written document prepared by the police when they receive information about the commission of a cognizable offence. For details, see the information sheet prepared by the NGO 'Commonwealth Human Rights Initiative', available at: http://www.humanrightsinitiative.org/publications/police/fir.pdf (last accessed 11 October 2015).

40. In July 2012, sectarian violence broke out in Assam between Muslims (mostly from the migrant Bangladeshi population) and members of the Bodo tribe over land, jobs, and political power. More than seventy-five people were killed and more than 300,000 people sought shelter in displacement camps. Rage spilled over to other parts of the country, with two killed and dozens injured in Mumbai during a Muslim demonstration. After repeated physical attacks on individuals, the month of August then saw an unprecedented

exodus of north-easterners to their home States due to mass text messages that were circulated via mobile phones warning the people of further attacks, and urging them to leave the big cities. Even though the warnings, to which the government reacted with a two-week ban on bulk text messages, were baseless, Pakistan is suspected to have been behind the move. The events and the reactions to them revealed the deep divides cutting across the Indian citizenry.

41. On the political iconography of Bharat Mata, see Mitra and König (2012, 2013).

42. In reference to Arjun Appadurai, who speaks of 'scapes', the term 'bodyscape' is used by Sumathi Ramaswamy in her work on the Bharat Mata iconography in India. What Appadurai refers to as 'scapes' are 'dynamic landscapes', which he defines as 'deeply perspectival constructs, inflected by the historical, linguistic, and political situatedness of different sorts of actors' (Appadurai, 1997, cited in Brosius, 2005: 17). Ramaswamy's 'bodyscapes' are personalized maps and a replacement of maps by icons and human bodies in the shape of the allegory. The visual practice of the 'bodyscape' which has been followed since the 1920s has facilitated the representation of Bharat Mata as a 'goddess of territory and polity' (Ramaswamy, 2001).

43. Incidentally, Kishalay Bhattacharjee set up the NGO Reachout Foundation in New Delhi in 2014. It is aimed at overcoming stereotypes which people from the north-east and Kashmir face. The website is available at: http://reachoutfoundation.org.in (last accessed 21 October 2015). One of the initiatives of the foundation is the website www.ourstories.org.in (last accessed 21 October 2015), which understands itself as a 'social experiment' with the credo that 'every story needs to be told'. This initiative tries to overcome the 'single story' by disseminating multiple narratives, with the ultimate aim of national integration. 'Social media', it is argued, 'has a tremendous potential for political and cultural communication, persuasion and thus integration.'

44. Interview with Aparna Khanna, Lady Irwin College, Department of Development Communication, 21 November 2011.

45. The creation of a *facebook* account and a *YouTube* channel for the organization, mentioned above, adds yet another dimension to the (self-) characterization of GC as a 'social media platform'.

46. In her work on 'interactive fiction', the label under which she subsumes this particular kind of web-comic, Janet Murray further expands on 'procedural authorship', which to her means 'writing the rules for the actor's involvement, that is, the conditions under which things will happen in response to the participant's actions.... The procedural author creates not just a set of scenes but a world of narrative possibilities' (Murray, 2000: 152, cited in Reichert, 2011: 134).

47. Marvel is a US publisher of comic books, founded in 1939 under the name Timely Publications.

48. The webpage of the GC initiative lists its main Indian and other country branches worldwide, united under the title 'World Comics'. For further details, see www.worldcomicsindia.com (last accessed 2 August 2013).

49. Video clips produced by the World Comics Network show how the medium has been employed in schools and rural communities. The material is accessible at: https://www.youtube.com/watch?v=s-gFrba4qhw (last access: 04 March 2016). The video 'Comics Activists without Borders' by Sharad Sharma documents a GC workshop for women in Bagh, a locality in the Pakistani part of Kashmir in 2009. Available at: http://www.youtube.com/watch?v=-N2ZLsrP8So (last access: 31 July 2013).

50. A clip showing the modes of display of Grassroots Comics in the north-eastern State of Assam can be accessed at: http://www.youtube.com/watch?v=cS9fWWq9uWI (last access: 31 July 2013).

51. 'GC in Conflict Regions' is the title of a documentary on the work and perception of the medium by local students in Kashmir and Manipur. Available at: http://www.youtube.com/watch?v=OIMNocQzcpg (last accessed 31 July 2013).

52. The YouTube channel of GC, containing animated comic strips and documentaries, is available at: http://www.youtube.com/user/trucktoon/videos (last accessed 31 July 2013).

53. For detailed information see the 2011 census results, available at: http://censusindia.gov.in/2011-prov-results/paper2/data_files/Mizoram/6-literacy-14-20.pdf (last accessed 1 February 2016).

54. The figure also stems from the 2011 census. Available at: http://censusindia.gov.in/2011-prov-results/paper2/data_files/kerala/10-litTR-31.pdf (last accessed 1 February 2016).

55. The term 'second-class citizen' is also used in the documentary *Dariya ki Kasam*, in which the organizers of the comics workshop introduce their concept to participants.

56. In line with the afore-mentioned phenomenon of inter-mediality, an online blog titled *Aapni Dikri Ro Hak* (Give your daughter her rights) was created during the 'Rights for Our Daughters' campaign. It provides textual and visual material as well as a video entitled *Dariya ki Kasam* (Swear by the river), which shows the comics workshop as well as the motorbike rally, and thus gives a multi-sided and very vivid description of how grassroots comics can be used in a campaign. The video blog is available at: www.halfworld.blogspot.com (last accessed 2 August 2013).

57. Benedict Anderson (1990) understands the nation as an 'imagined community of strangers', in the constitution of which newspapers play a

crucial role. Homi Bhabha (1993) conceptualizes the nation as something that only comes into existence by and through narration. Marshall McLuhan (1970: 171) pre-empts both by arguing that print 'links individuals with others in an impressive concentration of power'. He sees the awakening of nationalism as directly related to the invention of the printing press, and claims that nationalism is dependent on the speed of the flow of information (McLuhan, 1964: 175).

58. 'Middle-class children enrolled in English-medium schools' might not be seen as representative of India, but this is not the major point here. The intention of Anant Pai and the makers of ACK is to produce an elitist narrative of an imagined India—past and future—which is handed down to the political and economic elites of tomorrow, namely those educated at English-medium schools.

59. 'Authenticity', a value-laden, problematic term, is understood here by Pai as his comics imagining India as it ought to be rather than as it is. Contrast this with the description of Grassroots Comics as an 'authentic medium' in the interview with Dr Aparna Khanna above.

60. The domination of a particular socio-religious group is, however, not an exclusive feature of the ACK, but is also very present in Indian journalism, where a majority of journalists and reports are still Brahmins. Robin Jeffrey describes the consequences of this phenomenon in his plainly titled '[Not] Being There: Dalits and India's Newspapers' (2010), arguing that the underrepresentation of Dalits as responsible actors in the Indian (mainstream) media leads to an exclusion of news on Dalits.

61. Zulfikar Ali Bhutto centred his Pakistan People's Party in the late 1960s on the slogan *roti, kapra, aur makan*. Indira Gandhi equally promoted it in India in the 1970s, and Bhutto's daughter Benazir revived it in 2007.

62. This term has been borrowed from Butsch (2008). The variation 'audience-citizens' is used by Harindranath (2009), where it also forms part of the media-centric analytical framework of 'cultural citizenship', as described in Chapter three. In my understanding, 'citizen-audience' is a useful concept to emphasize and investigate the strong interrelations between media consumption (as audience) and the development of citizen consciousness.

63. The observation cited earlier that more girls were enrolled in schools in Rajasthan after the GC campaign on the 'girl child issue' points in that direction.

64. Personal interview, 24 July 2013.

65. Personal interview, 24 July 2013.

66. The name 'Alag Chitra Katha' is actually an intended take on the well-known ACK. See footnote 33.

67. Personal communication, 28 August 2013.

CONCLUSION: COUNTER-FLOW AND TRANSCULTURALITY

1. The song 'Mile Sur Mera Tumhara' is a case in point. Developed in the late 1980s and promoted by Doordarshan and the MIB, and still popular today, the song is a building block in the project of 'emotional integration'. Sung by people from different walks of life, including various celebrities, in different Indian languages, it advocates national cohesion and gives a pop culture face to the abstract concept of 'unity in diversity'.

2. Hinduunity.org is a Hindu nationalist website which has been banned by the government of India. For details see the report on 'Internet Censorship in India' by Ketan Tanna (2004).

3. Following an approach applied in earlier survey research by Mitra and Singh (1999, 2009) and Mitra (2012b), and drawing on infrastructural support from a specialised institution, such as the Centre for the Study of Developing Societies (CSDS) in New Delhi, a representative survey would aim at interviewing about eight hundred respondents representing all sections of society. In order to ensure a representative character, the sample should include male and female respondents across ethnicity, language, religion, caste, as well as class, determined by the level of education and income. To form a national sample, at least eighty interviewees should be selected in ten urban centres across the country. In all such interviews, in addition to the survey questions, standard questions are asked to determine the background of the interviewee as precisely as possible. I would like to thank Prof. Sanjay Kumar, Director of the Centre for the Study of Developing Societies (CSDS), for his valuable support with outlining this opinion survey.

4. In his 1994 volume *Sage Philosophy*, the Kenyan philosopher Henry Odera Oruka (1944–1995) explores the question of why philosophy that has emerged in Sub-Saharan Africa has nearly always been disregarded or sidelined in the global debate. Seeing the reason for this in the oral rather than scriptural dissemination of philosophical knowledge in Africa, Oruka employed an anthropological method of going to different villages and interviewing people who were regarded as sages by the villagers. To him, philosophers were those who have critically examined their thoughts on traditional philosophical topics like 'God' or 'freedom' and were able to give a rational explanation for them. While Oruka's approach documents the necessity of the methodological contribution of anthropology in the discovery of knowledge in non-Western contexts, as indicated in Marriott's concept of 'ethnosociology', it also reveals the unavoidable 'observer's paradox' and difficulties of measurement, in this case the dominance of Western categories in the quest for indigenous knowledge. The categories in terms

of which Oruka chose to investigate the philosophical content of African thought might not correspond to indigenous African categories, thus causing a bias in the research.

5. This definition, like the following one, can be found in the online edition of the *OED* at www.oed.com.

6. In a 1973 issue of the American weekly newspaper *New York Observer*, we find the line 'Sailing ships are gone but the sea shanty is still sung: the function is altered but the song remains: the stuff is transcultural' (*New York Observer*, 28 October 1973).

7. The *OED* is considered here as the principal reference work of the English language, with the help of which linguistic developments, which also reflect socio-political changes, can be traced and documented. It also helps to see a reality beyond the canvas of political science. While a reference work like the *Concise Oxford Dictionary of Politics* (McLean and McMillan, 2009) lists the lemma 'critical theory', it mentions neither 'culture' nor 'interdisciplinarity'.

8. Consider here what Rosaldo (1994b) notes on the relationship between cultural studies and anthropology. Paraphrasing the public discourse, he satirizes the attitude as follows: 'Cultural studies does nothing that anthropology hasn't already done long ago. These literary critics would do well to read Franz Boas or to take an introductory anthropology course.' Rosaldo agrees that 'culture in the anthropological sense ... is neither high or low; it is all-pervasive' (Rosaldo, 1994b: 526).

9. In one of the many different ways it can be conceived, 'translingualism' has also been employed as an analytical category in the context of this work. Translation of words in context is a first step in translating and making intelligible concepts and world views. *Geisteswissenschaft* and Amar Chitra Katha are not only labels, but carriers of social meaning which only become meaningful in the process of linguistic interaction. Keeping to the example of trans-lingualism, one may also observe that as outlined above, the prefix 'trans-' designates a superior status, which has to be preceded by the 'inter-'. This work has made some attempts at 'inter-lingualism', bringing together different languages both in the more immediate sense, and in seeking broader understanding across disciplines which also have their own vocabulary and are often unintelligible to one another. 'Trans-disciplinary' would designate elevation to the overriding level of a third language in which disciplines can efficiently communicate.

10. This term has been borrowed from psychology, where 'compartmentalization' refers to a form of addressing cognitive dissonances by separating or 'compartmentalizing' conflicting social identities and dealing with each one of them in a context-specific way. For details see Crisp (2010) and Singer 1972.

APPENDIX II *EK ALAG CHITRA KATHA* (2009): TEXT TRANSLATION

1. The author would like to thank Manika Premsingh for the translations from Hindi.

2. Key: LHS: left-hand side of the four-panel comic; RHS: right-hand side of the four-panel comic.

3. Rhyming with 'mood'.

4. Literally 'brother'. It is used in Hindi as a term of endearment.

5. *Nirodh* is the common Hindi term for 'condom'. The term is eponymous with the company which first produced condoms in India.

6. Used in English.

7. Sexually Transmitted Disease (STD); literally translates as 'hidden disease'.

8. The Hindi term *pehchan* that is used in the original, literally means 'recognition' or 'identity'.

9. Authors' names are mentioned as in the original.

10. There is likely to be a typo in the name here.

11. There is likely to be a typo in the name here.

12. It is not a speech bubble; that is a drawing confusion.

13. The correct word may be 'masturbate'.

14. The term 'HIV/AIDS' is used in English, but transcribed in Devanagari script.

15. The word used for 'penis' is *ling*, also meaning 'gender', as in 'Is ka ling kja hai? (What is his/her gender?).

16. Based on the Hindi terms *samaj* (society), and *ki soch* (thinking), the title literally translates as 'The Thinking of the Society'.

17. 'ILU' is the acronym for 'I love you.' It is a commonly used expression which became famous after the Bollywood song 'ILU, ILU' from the 1991 film *Saudagar*. In the comic, the acronym is written in Latin script.

18. Expression for 'I love you too.' In the comic, it is written in Latin script.

19. The word used in the original is *samlengrik*, literally 'same-gender'; cf. the comic *Permission*.

20. This is the translation of a popular Hindi phrase.

21. The Hindi original reads '*Han, han, homo*'. The word 'homo' is transcribed in the Devanagari script.

22. Santosh Bhoiyar is the artist. *Josh* means 'enthusiasm', and *kalyan* means 'welfare'. This appears to be an organization that is part of the Humsafar Trust.

23. The English word 'partner' is used, only transcribed in Devanagari.

24. The English word 'condom' is used, only transcribed in Devanagari.

25. The English abbreviation 'HIV' is used in Latin script.

26. The title can also be translated as 'problem' or 'confusion'. The Hindi word used is *uljhan*.

27. The English word 'hi' is used, but transcribed in Devanagari.

28. 'Habit' is the literal translation, but in this case, the meaning goes more in the direction of 'behaviour'.

BIBLIOGRAPHY

ARCHIVAL SOURCES

Government of India, External Affairs Department, Middle East Branch, 1946, *Proposal to Maintain a Steady Flow of News from Persia in the Indian Press Following the Abolition of Censorship in Persia*, File no.: 10 (32)-ME.

Government of India, Foreign and Political Department, 1914, Secret (W) Proceedings, October 1914, nos. 1–29, *Arrangements Connected with Censorship in British India during the Present Crisis*, File no.: 1/29/1914.

Government of India, Home Department, Education-Deposit, 1898, Proceedings, June 1898, nos. 33–38 Part A, *Proposed Introduction into Indian Schools of Sir William Lee-Warner's Work Entitled 'The Citizen of India'*, File no.: Progs. nos. 33–38, June 1898, Part A.

Government of India, Home Department, Education-Deposit, Proceedings, February 1903, no. 8, *Views of Local Governments as to the Suitability of Sir W. Lee-Warner's 'The Citizen of India' as a Text-book for Indian Schools*, File no.: Progs. nos. 8, February 1903, Deposit.

Government of India, Ministry of Information and Broadcasting, Film (C) Section, 1961, *Censorship Arrangements Obtaining in Foreign Countries—Collection of Information*, File no. 19/29/61-FC.

Government of India, Ministry of Information and Broadcasting, 1961a, *Publicity Campaign in Support of Unity and Emotional Integration of India—Role of All India Radio*, File no.: 8 (6)/61-B (P).

Government of India, Ministry of Information and Broadcasting, 1961b, *Emotional Integration*.

Government of India, Ministry of Information and Broadcasting, 1961c, *Publicity Campaign in Support of Unity and Emotional Integration of the Country*.

Government of India, Ministry of Information and Broadcasting, 1961d, *Proposal for Utilisation of the Entertainment Media at Present Adopted by the Song & Drama Division for a Publicity Campaign for Unity and Emotional Integration*.

Government of India, Ministry of Information and Broadcasting, Film Censor Branch, 1970, *A Resume of the Report—Chapter-wise as well as Subject-wise*, File no.: 19/7/70-FC.

SECONDARY SOURCES

Abdelhalim, Julten. 2016. *Indian Muslims and Citizenship: Spaces for Jihād in Everyday Life* (London: Routledge).

Agarwal, U.C. 2000. 'Citizenship Values and the Constitution', in Subhash C. Kashyap, D.D. Khanna, and Gert W. Kueck (eds.), *Reviewing the Constitution?* (New Delhi: Shipra), pp. 154–80.

Alam, Javeed. 2012. 'Democracy and Its Impact on Citizenship', in *Who Wants Democracy?* (New Delhi: Orient Blackswan), pp. 74–86.

Allan, George. 1972. 'Croce and Whitehead on Concrescence', *Process Studies*, 2(2), 95–111.

Almond, Gabriel. 1996. 'Political Science: The History of the Discipline', in Robert E. Goodin and Hans-Dieter Klingemann (eds.), *A New Handbook of Political Science* (Oxford: Oxford University Press), pp. 50–96.

Amadae, S.M., and Bruce Bueno de Mesquita. 1999. 'The Rochester School: The Origins of Positive Political Theory', *Annual Review of Political Science*, 2, 269–95.

Anant, Arpita. 2011. 'Group Identities and Rights: A Case for Theory beyond the Nation-State', in Mangesh Kulkarni (ed.), *Interdisciplinary Perspectives in Political Theory* (New Delhi: Sage), pp. 87–116.

Anderson, Benedict. 1990 [1983]. *Imagined Communities: Reflections on the Origin and Spread of Nationalism* (London: Verso).

Anderson, Malcolm. 1996. *Frontiers: Territory and State Formation in the Modern World* (Oxford: Polity).

Andrews, William G. (ed.). 1982. *International Handbook of Political Science* (Westport: Greenwood Press).

Appadurai, Arjun. 1997. *Modernity at Large: Cultural Dimensions of Globalization* (New Delhi: Oxford University Press).

———. 2000. 'Grassroots Globalization and the Research Imagination', *Public Culture*, 12(1), 1–19.

Aristotle. *Politics*, accessible at: http://classics.mit.edu/Aristotle/politics.5. five.html (last access: 25 February 2016).

Ashcroft, Bill, Gareth Griffiths, and Helen Tiffin. 1989. *The Empire Writes Back: Theory and Practice in Post-Colonial Literatures* (London: Routledge).

Asif, A.U. (ed.). 1998. *Media and Muslims in India since Independence* (New Delhi: Institute of Objective Studies).

Assmann, Jan, and Aleida Assmann (eds.), 1987. *Kanon und Zensur: Archäologie der literarischen Kommunikation II* (München: Fink).

Atal, Yogesh. 1977. 'Communication and Nation-Building in India', in M.N. Srinivas, S. Seshaiah, and V.S. Parthasarathy (eds.), *Dimensions of Social Change in India* (Bombay: Allied Publishers), pp. 442–73.

Auboyer, Jeannine. 2002. *Daily Life in Ancient India: From 200 BC to 700 AD* (London: Phoenix Press).

Aulich, Reinhard. 1988. 'Elemente einer funktionalen Differenzierung der literarischen Zensur: Überlegungen zu Form und Wirklichkeit von Zensur als einer intentional adäquaten Reaktion gegenüber literarischer Kommunikation', in Herbert G. Göpfert and Erdmann Weyrauch (eds) *'Unmoralisch an sich...': Zensur im 18. und 19. Jahrhundert* (Wiesbaden: Harrasowitz), pp. 177–230.

Austin, Granville. 1966. *The Indian Constitution: Cornerstone of a Nation* (Oxford: Oxford University Press).

Badrinath, Chaturvedi. 2000. 'The Place of the "Individual" in Indian Thought and Polity', in Imtiaz Ahmad, Partha S. Ghosh, and Helmut Reifeld (eds.), *Pluralism and Equality: Values in Indian Society and Politics* (New Delhi: Sage), pp. 33–47.

Bambrough, Renford. 1963. *The Philosophy of Aristotle* (Toronto: Mentor Books).

Barry, Ann Marie Seward. 1997. *Visual Intelligence: Perception, Image, and Manipulation in Visual Communication* (Albany: State University of New York Press).

Barth, Norbert Victor. 2007. 'India Book House und die Comic-Serie Amar Chitra Katha (1970–2002): Eine kulturwissenschaftliche Medienanalyse'. PhD thesis, Faculty of Philosophy, Julius-Maximilians-Universität Würzburg. Available at: http://opus.bibliothek.uni-wuerzburg.de/voll-texte/2008/2789/pdf/indiabookhouse.pdf (last access: 24 July 2013).

Bates, Robert H., Avner Greif, Margaret Levi, Jean-Laurent Rosenthal, and Barry R. Weingast. 1998. *Analytic Narratives* (Princeton: Princeton University Press).

Baudrillard, Jean. 1995. *The Gulf War Did Not Take Place* (Sydney: Power Publications).

Baxi, Upendra. 2014. 'Naz 2: A Critique', *Economic and Political Weekly*, 49(6), 12–14.

Bendix, Reinhard. 1964. *Nation-Building and Citizenship: Studies on Our Changing Social Order* (New York: Wiley).

———. 1984. 'The Citizenship of the Lower Classes', in id. *Force, Fate and Freedom: On Historical Sociology* (Berkeley and Los Angeles: University of California Press), pp. 91–107.

Bentham, Jeremy. 1996 [1789]. *An Introduction to the Principles of Morals and Legislation* (edited by J.H. Burns and H.L.A. Hart) (Oxford: Clarendon Press).

Berkeley, George. 1944 [1707/1708]. *Philosophical Commentaries* (edited by A.A. Luce) (London: Thomas Nelson and Sons).

Berlin, Isaiah. 1969. *Four Essays on Liberty* (Oxford: Oxford University Press).

Bery, Renuka. 2003. 'Participatory Video that Empowers', in Shirley A. White (ed.), *Participatory Video: Images that Transform and Empower* (New Delhi: Sage), pp. 102–21.

Bhabha, Homi K. 1993. *Nation and Narration* (London: Routledge).

——— (ed.). 1994. *The Location of Culture* (London: Routledge).

Bhargava, Rajeev, and Helmut Reifeld (eds). 2005. *Civil Society, Public Sphere and Citizenship: Dialogues and Perceptions* (New Delhi: Sage).

Bhattacharjee, Kishalay. 2013. *Che in Paona Bazaar: Tales of Exile and Belonging from India's North-East* (New Delhi: Macmillan).

Bhowmik, Someswar. 2003. 'From Coercion to Power Relations: Film Censorship in Post-colonial India', *Economic and Political Weekly*, 38(30), 3148–52.

———. 2009. *Cinema and Censorship: The Politics of Control in India* (New Delhi: Orient Blackswan).

Blanchetti-Revelli, Lanfranco. 2003. 'Moro, Muslim, or Filipino? Cultural Citizenship as Practice and Process', in Renato Rosaldo (ed.), *Cultural Citizenship in Island Southeast Asia: Nation and Belonging in the Hinterlands* (Berkeley: University of California Press), pp. 44–75.

Bloom, Harold, and Lionel Trilling (eds). 1973. *Romantic Poetry and Prose: The Oxford Anthology of English Literature* (New York: Oxford University Press).

Boyce, Charles. 1996. *Dictionary of Shakespeare* (Ware: Wordsworth).

Boyd, Robert and Peter J. Richerson. 1985. *Culture and the Evolutionary Process* (Chicago: The University of Chicago Press).

Boyd-Barrett, Oliver, and Daya K. Thussu. 1992. *Contra-Flow in Global News: International and Regional News Exchange Mechanisms* (London: Libbey).

Bradbury, Ray. 1991 [1953]. *Fahrenheit 451* (New York: Ballantine).

Brass, Paul R. 2000. 'Foucault Steals Political Science', *Annual Review of Political Science*, 3, 305–30.

Broder, Henryk M. (ed.). 1976. *Die Schere im Kopf: Über Zensur und Selbstzensur* (Köln: Bund-Verlag).

Brooks, Max. 2006. *World War Z: An Oral History of the Zombie War* (New York: Crown).

Brosius, Christiane. 2005. *Empowering Visions: The Politics of Representation in Hindu Nationalism* (London: Anthem Press).

Buchstein, Hubertus. 2003. 'Jürgen Habermas', in Peter Massing and Gotthart Breit (eds.), *Demokratie Theorien: Von der Antike bis zur Gegenwart* (Bonn: Bundeszentrale für Politische Bildung), pp. 253–60.

Burke, Peter. 2009. 'Varieties of Terminology', in *Cultural Hybridity* (Cambridge: Polity Press), pp. 34–65.

Burnham, Peter, Karin Gilland Lutz, Wyn Grant, and Zig Layton-Henry. 2008. *Research Methods in Politics* (Basingstoke: Palgrave Macmillan).

Butler, Judith. 2006 [1997]. *Haß spricht: Zur Politik des Performativen* (Frankfurt am Main: Suhrkamp).

Butsch, Richard. 2008. *The Citizen-Audience: Crowds, Publics, and Individuals* (New York: Routledge).

Carr, Edward H. 1961. *What Is History? The George Macaulay Trevelyan Lectures Delivered in the University of Cambridge January–March 1961* (London: Macmillan).

Chand, Prabha. 1976. *Jawaharlal Nehru as a Journalist: A Project Study* (New Delhi: Indian Institute of Mass Communication).

Chandra, Nandini. 2008. *The Classic Popular: Amar Chitra Katha, 1967–2007* (New Delhi: Yoda Press).

Chaney, David. 2002. 'Cosmopolitan Art and Cultural Citizenship', *Theory, Culture, and Society* 19(1–2), 157–74.

Chatterjee, Partha. 1993. *The Nation and Its Fragments: Colonial and Postcolonial Histories* (Princeton: Princeton University Press).

Childe, Vere Gordon. 1966. *Man Makes Himself* (London: Collins).

Chopra, Ritika. 2012. 'Cartoon Row: NCERT junks Thorat's Panel Suggestions', *India Today*, 12 July, available at: http://indiatoday.intoday.in/story/cartoon-row-ncert-junks-thorat-panels-suggestions/1/208274.html (last access: 24 February 2016).

Chowdhury, Kanishka. 2011. *The New India: Citizenship, Subjectivity and Economic Liberalization* (Basingstoke: Macmillan).

Cicero, Marcus Tullius. 1964. *Der Staat [De Re Publica]* (edited by Rainer Beer) (Reinbeck: Rowohlt).

Claus, Peter. 2013. 'Es fehlt der rechte Biss', *Die Rheinpfalz*, 145, 26 June.

Cohen, Stephen P. 1969. 'The Indian Military and Social Change', *IDSA Journal*, 2(1), 12–29.

———. 2002. *The Indian Army: Its Contribution to the Development of a Nation* (New Delhi: Oxford University Press).

Collier, David, and James Mahon. 1993. 'Conceptual "Stretching" Revisited: Adapting Categories in Comparative Analysis', *American Political Science Review* 97, 845–55.

Collier, David, and Steven Levitsky. 1997. 'Democracy with Adjectives: Conceptual Innovation in Comparative Research', *World Politics*, 49, 430–51.

Comte, Auguste. 1865 [1844]. *A General View of Positivism* (London: Traubner and Co.).

Cottam, Martha L., Beth Dietz-Uhler, Elena M. Mastors, and Thomas Preston. 2004. *Introduction to Political Psychology* (Mahwah: Erlbaum).

Craig, Robert T. 1993. 'Why Are There So Many Communication Theories?', *Journal of Communication*, 43(3), 26–33.

Crisp, Richard J. 2010. *The Psychology of Social and Cultural Diversity* (Malden: Wiley-Blackwell).

Croce, Benedetto. 1941. *History as the Story of Liberty* (London: George Allen & Unwin).

Datta, Nonica. 2011. 'Fixing Histories', *Tribune* (Chandigarh), 15 November.

Day, Aidan. 1996. *Romanticism* (London: Routledge).

De, Amalendu. 1989. 'Role of Bengali Muslim Press in the Growth of Muslim Public Opinion in Bengal (1884–1914)', in Nisith Ranjan Ray (ed.), *Growth of Public Opinion in India: 19th and Early 20th Centuries (1800–1914)* (Calcutta: Naya Prokash), pp. 149–63.

Dean, Jodi. 2000. 'Introduction: The Interface of Political Theory and Cultural Studies', in Jodi Dean (ed.), *Cultural Studies and Political Theory* (Ithaca and London: Cornell University Press), 1–19.

Debroy, Dipavali. 2011. 'The Graphic Novel in India: East Transforms West', *Bookbird: A Journal of International Children's Literature*, 49(4), 32–9.

Diamond, Larry. 2002. 'Thinking about Hybrid Regimes', *Journal of Democracy*, 13(2), 21–35.

Dittmar, Peter. 1987. *Lob der Zensur* (Köln: Kölner Universitäts Verlag).

Doniger, Wendy. 2009. *The Hindus: An Alternative History* (New York: Penguin).

Donnan, Hastings, and Thomas M. Wilson. 1999. *Borders: Frontiers of Identity, Nation and State* (Oxford: Berg).

Dover, Kenneth J. 1974. *Greek Popular Morality in the Time of Plato and Aristotle* (Oxford: Blackwell).

Downs, Anthony. 1957. *An Economic Theory of Democracy* (New York: Harper).

Drabble, Margaret (ed.). 1985. *The Oxford Companion to English Literature* (Oxford: Oxford University Press).

During, Simon. 1999. 'Introduction', in Simon During (ed.), *The Cultural Studies Reader* (London and New York: Routledge), pp. 1–28.

Easton, David. 1959. 'Political Anthropology', in Bernard J. Siegel (ed.), *Biennial Review of Anthropology*, pp. 210–62.

Eisenkolb, Yvonne. 2007. *Medien* (Köln: DuMont).

Eisenmann, Charles. 1950. 'On the Matter and Methods of the Political Sciences', in UNESCO, *Contemporary Political Science: A Survey of Methods, Research and Teaching* (Paris: UNESCO), pp. 91–131.

Eisner, Will. 1992. *Comics and Sequential Art* (Princeton,WI: Kitchen Sink Press).

Elster, Jon. 1993. *Political Psychology* (Cambridge: Cambridge University Press).

Encyclopedia Britannica. 'Theagenes of Megara', accessible at: http://www.britannica.com/biography/Theagenes-of-Megara (last access: 25 February 2016).

Evans, David Trevor. 1993. *Sexual Citizenship: The Material Construction of Sexualities* (London: Routledge).

Fanon, Frantz. 2001 [1961]. *The Wretched of the Earth* [*Les Damnés de la Terre*] (London: Penguin).

Farmer, Victoria L. 2005. 'Mass Media: Images, Mobilization, and Communalism', in David Ludden (ed.), *Making India Hindu: Religion, Community, and the Politics of Democracy in India* (New Delhi: Oxford University Press), pp. 98–115.

Farouqui, Ather (ed.). 2009. *Muslims and Media Images: News versus Views* (New Delhi: Oxford University Press).

Fisher, Michael H. 2004. *Counterflows to Colonialism: Indian Travellers and Settlers in Britain, 1600–1857* (New Delhi: Permanent Black).

Fisher, Nicholas R.E. (ed.). 1976. *Social Values in Classical Athens* (London: Dent).

Forsdyke, Sara. 2012. *Slaves Tell Tales: And Other Episodes in the Politics of Popular Culture in Ancient Greece* (Princeton: Princeton University Press).

Forster, Edward M. 1965a [1924]. *A Passage to India* (Harmondsworth: Penguin).

———. 1965b [1940]. 'Does Culture Matter?', in *Two Cheers for Democracy* (Harmondsworth: Penguin), pp. 108–14.

———. 1965c [1942]. 'The Duty of Society to the Artist', in *Two Cheers for Democracy* (Harmondsworth: Penguin), pp. 103–07.

Foucault, Michel. 1979. *Discipline and Punish: The Birth of the Prison* (New York: Vintage Books).

———. 1994 [1981]. *The History of Sexuality*, vol. I (Harmondsworth: Penguin). Partly reprinted in John Storey (ed.), *Cultural Theory and Popular Culture: A Reader* (New York: Harvester Wheatsheaf), pp. 163–9.

Fox, Jonathan. 2005. 'Unpacking "Transnational Citizenship"', *Annual Review of Political Science*, 8, 171–201.

Frahm, Ole. 2011. 'Weird Signs', in Barbara Eder, Elisabeth Klar, and Ramón Reichert (eds.), *Theorien des Comics: Ein Reader* (Bielefeld: transcript), pp. 143–59.

Fraser, Nancy. 1990. 'Rethinking the Public Sphere: A Contribution to the Critique of Actually Existing Democracy', *Social Text*, 25/26: 56-80.

Fraser, Nancy, and Linda Gordon. 1994. 'Civil Citizenship against Social Citizenship? On the Ideology of Contract-versus-Charity', in Bart van Steenbergen (ed.), *The Condition of Citizenship* (London: Sage), pp. 90–107.

Frost, Frank J. 2005. 'Aspects of Early Athenian Citizenship', in id. *Politics and the Athenians: Essays on Athenian History and Historiography* (Toronto: Edgar Kent), pp. 27–40.

Gandhi, Mohandas Karamchand. 2010 [1927–9]. *The Story of My Experiments with Truth: An Autobiography* (New Delhi: Om Books).

Gaonkar, Dilip Parameshwar (ed.). 2001. *Alternative Modernities* (Durham: Duke University Press).

Garga, Bhagwan Das. 2007. *From Raj to Swaraj: The Non-fiction Film in India* (New Delhi: Penguin).

Gautam, P.K. 2008. *Composition and Regimental System of the Indian Army: Continuity and Change* (New Delhi: Shipra).

Gay, Peter. 1973. *The Enlightenment: An Interpretation* (2 vols) (London: Wildwood House).

Geertz, Clifford. 1980. 'Blurred Genres: The Reconfiguration of Social Thought', *American Scholar*, 49(2), 165–79.

———. 1983. *Local Knowledge: Further Essays in Interpretive Anthropology* (New York: Basic Books).

Goethe, Johann Wolfgang von. 2001 [1774]. *Die Leiden des jungen Werther* [*The Sorrows of Young Werther*] (Frankfurt am Main: Insel).

———. 2006 [1833]. *Maximen und Reflexionen* [Maxims and Reflections] (München: C.H. Beck).

Gohain, Manash Pratim. 2011. 'Questioning authority seen as blasphemous' (interview with Mushirul Hasan), *Sunday Times of India* (New Delhi), 30 October.

Government of India (GoI). 1949. *Report of the Ministry of Information and Broadcasting, 1948–1949* (New Delhi: Ministry of Information and Broadcasting).

———. 1950. *Report of the Ministry of Information and Broadcasting, 1949–1950* (New Delhi: Ministry of Information and Broadcasting).

———. 1961b. *Proposal for National Unity and Integration* (New Delhi: Ministry of Information and Broadcasting, Directorate of Field Publicity).

————. 1980. *Reservations for Backward Classes: Mandal Commission Report of the Backward Classes Commission* (New Delhi: Akalank).

Gray, Thomas. 1973 [1751]. 'Elegy Written in a Country Churchyard', in Frank Kermode and John Hollander (eds.), *The Oxford Anthology of English Literature*, vol. I (New York: Oxford University Press), pp. 2207–11.

Grover, Anand. 2013. 'Why Supreme Court's Verdict on Section 377 Is Wrong', *Economic Times*, 15 December. Available at: http://articles.economictimes. indiatimes.com/2013-12-15/news/45191798_1_lgbt-community-delhi-high-court-supreme-court (last access: 17 December 2013).

Guha, Ramachandra. 2007. *India after Gandhi: The History of the World's Largest Democracy* (New York: Harper Collins).

Guha Thakurta, Paranjoy. 2009. *Media Ethics: Truth, Fairness and Objectivity* (New Delhi: Oxford University Press).

Gunnell, John G. 2002. 'Handbooks and History: Is It Still the *American Science of Politics?*', *International Political Science Review*, 23(4), 339–54.

Habermas, Jürgen. 1987 [1981]. *The Theory of Communicative Action* (2 vols) (Boston: Beacon Press).

————. 1989 [1962]. *The Structural Transformation of the Public Sphere: An Inquiry into a Category of Bourgeois Society* (Cambridge: MIT Press).

————. 1992a. *Faktizität und Geltung: Beiträge zur Diskurstheorie des Rechts und des demokratischen Rechtsstaates* [Between Facts and Norms: Contributions to a Discourse Theory of Law and Democracy] (Frankfurt am Main: Suhrkamp).

————. 1992b. 'Citizenship and National Identity: Some Reflections on the Future of Europe', *Praxis International: A Philosophical Journal*, 12(1), April, 1–19.

————. 1996. 'Inklusion—Einbeziehen oder Einschließen? Zum Verhältnis von Nation, Rechtsstaat und Demokratie', in *Die Einbeziehung des Anderen: Studien zur Politischen Theorie* [The inclusion of the Other: Studies in Political Theory] (Frankfurt am Main: Suhrkamp), pp. 154–84.

Harindranath, Ramaswami. 2009. 'Making Connections: Media Audiences and Cultural Citizenship', in, id. *Audience-Citizens: The Media, Public Knowledge and Interpretive Practice* (New Delhi: Sage), pp. 227–48.

Harrison, Selig S. 1960. *India: The Most Dangerous Decades* (Madras: Princeton University Press).

Hasan, Daisy. 2004. '"Out of the Box": Televisual Representations of North East India', in Monica Narula, Shuddhabrata Sengupta, Ravi Sundaram, Ravi S. Vasudevan, Awadhendra B. Sharan, Jeebesh Bagchi, and Geert Lovink (eds.), *Sarai Reader 04: Crisis/Media* (New Delhi: CSDS, Sarai Programme), pp. 126–9.

Hawley, John Stratton. 1995. 'The Saints Subdued: Domestic Virtue and National Integration in Amar Chitra Katha', in Lawrence A. Babb and Susan S. Wadley (eds.), *Media and the Transformation of Religion in South Asia* (Philadelphia: University of Pennsylvania Press), pp. 107–36.

Hay, Colin. 2002. *Political Analysis: A Critical Introduction* (Basingstoke: Palgrave Macmillan).

Hearn, Kirsten. 1988. 'Exclusion Is Censorship', in Gail Chester and Julienne Dickey (eds.), *Feminism and Censorship: The Current Debate* (Dorset: Prism Press).

Heckmann, Carsten. 2001. 'Wir wollen Eure Hirne Melken', *Spiegel Online—Netzwelt*. Available at: http://www.spiegel.de/netzwelt/web/web-comics-wir-wollen-eure-hirne-melken-a-126623.html (last access: 8 August 2013).

Hegewald, Julia A.B., and Subrata K. Mitra (eds.). 2012. *Re-Use: The Art and Politics of Integration and Anxiety* (New Delhi: Sage).

Heine, Heinrich. 2007. [1844]. *Germany. A Winter Tale: Deutschland. Ein Wintermärchen* (New York: Mondial).

Hempel, Carl Gustav. 1966. *Philosophy of Natural Science* (Englewood Cliffs: Prentice-Hall).

Hermes, Joke. 2000. 'Of Irritation, Texts and Men: Feminist Audience Studies and Cultural Citizenship', *International Journal of Cultural Studies*, 3(3), 351–67.

Hertz, Rosanna, and Jonathan B. Imber. 1995. 'Introduction', in id. (eds.), *Studying Elites Using Qualitative Methods* (Thousand Oaks: Sage), pp. vii–xi.

Herva, Soma. 1988. 'The Genesis of Max Weber's *Verstehende Soziologie*', *Acta Sociologica*, 31 (2), 143–56.

Hignett, Charles. 1952. *A History of the Athenian Constitution to the End of the Fifth Century B.C.* (Oxford: Clarendon Press).

Hobbes, Thomas. 1996 [1651]. *Leviathan* (edited with an introduction and notes by J.C.A. Gaskin) (Oxford: Oxford University Press).

Hocart, Arthur M. 1970. *Kings and Councillors: An Essay in the Comparative Anatomy of Human Society* (Chicago: The University of Chicago Press).

Hof, Karina. 2006. 'Something You Can Actually Pick Up: Scrapbooking as a Form and Forum of Cultural Citizenship', *European Journal of Cultural Studies*, 9(3), 363–84.

Horowitz, Irving Louis (ed.). 1964. *The New Sociology: Essays in Social Science and Social Theory in Honor of C. Wright Mills* (New York: Oxford University Press).

Howarth, Randall S. 2006. *The Origins of Roman Citizenship* (Lewiston: Mellen).

Hoy, Mikita. 1992. 'Bakhtin and Popular Culture', *New Literary History*, 23(3), 765–82.

Humsafar Trust (ed.). 2009. *Ek Alag Chitra Katha—A Community Comic Book on Issues of MSM and Transgender* (Mumbai: Humsafar Trust).

Hunter, Albert. 1995. 'Local Knowledge and Local Power: Notes on the Ethnography of Local Community Elites', in Rosanna Hertz and Jonathan B. Imber (eds.), *Studying Elites Using Qualitative Methods* (Thousand Oaks: Sage), pp. 151–70.

Hunter, James D. 1991. *Culture Wars: The Struggle to Define America* (New York: Basic Books).

Inden, Ronald. 1992. *Imagining India* (Oxford: Blackwell).

Isin, Engin F., and Bryan S. Turner. 2002. 'Introduction', in Engin F. Isin and Bryan S. Turner (eds.), *Handbook of Citizenship Studies* (London: Sage), pp. 1–10.

Jamatia, Hamari. 2011. 'North-East Men Too, Find Capital Unsafe', *Indian Express*, 8 March.

Jandora, John W. 2008. *States without Citizens: Understanding the Islamic Crisis* (Westport: Praeger).

Janoski, Thomas, and Brian Gran. 2002. 'Political Citizenship: Foundations of Rights', in Engin F. Isin and Bryan S. Turner (eds.), *Handbook of Citizenship Studies* (London: Sage), pp. 13–52.

Jansen, Sue Curry. 1991. *Censorship: The Knot that Binds Power and Knowledge* (Oxford: Oxford University Press).

Jayal, Niraja Gopal. 2013. *Citizenship and Its Discontents: An Indian History* (Cambridge: Harvard University Press).

Jeffrey, Robin. 2010. '[Not] Being There: Dalits and India's Newspapers', in *Media and Modernity: Communications, Women and the State in India* (Ranikhet: Permanent Black), pp. 200–15.

Jones, Bryan D. 1999. 'Bounded Rationality', *Annual Review of Political Science*, 2, 297–321.

Joppke, Christian. 2002. 'Multicultural Citizenship', in Engin F. Isin and Bryan S. Turner (eds.), *Handbook of Citizenship Studies* (London: Sage), pp. 245–58.

Joshi, P.C. 1989. *Culture, Communication and Social Change* (New Delhi: Vikas).

Kakar, Sudhir. 1990. *Intimate Relations: Exploring Indian Sexuality* (New Delhi: Penguin).

Karl, Terry Lynn. 1995. 'The Hybrid Regimes of Central America', *Journal of Democracy*, 6(3), 72–86.

Karolides, Nicholas J., Margaret Bald, and Dawn B. Sova. 2005. *120 Banned Books: Censorship Histories of World Literature* (New York: Checkmark).

Katz, Elihu. 1963. 'The Diffusion of New Ideas and Practices: Reflections on Research', in *Forum Lectures Mass Communication Series* (Washington: Voice of America), 1–12.

Kaur, Raminder. 2010. 'Atomic Comics, Parabolic Mimesis and the Graphic Fictions of Science', Paper presented at the Centre for the Study of Developing Societies, New Delhi, December.

———. 2012. 'Atomic Comics: Parabolic Mimesis and the Graphic Fictions of Science', *International Journal of Cultural Studies*, 15(4), 329–47.

Kauṭilya. 1987. *The Arthashastra* (edited by L.N. Rangarajan) (New Delhi: Penguin).

Kidwai, Sabina. 2003. *Images of Muslim Women: A Study on the Representation of Muslim Women in the Media, 1985–2001* (New Delhi: WISCOMP).

Klaus, Elisabeth, and Margreth Lünenborg. 2004. 'Cultural Citizenship: Ein Kommunikations-Wissenschaftliches Konzept zur Bestimmung Kultureller Teilhabe in der Mediengesellschaft', *Medien und Kommunikation*, 52(2), 193–213.

Kleinkauf, Horst, Hans von Döhren, and Lothar Jaenicke (eds). 1988. *The Roots of Modern Biochemistry: Fritz Lipmann's Squiggle and Its Consequences* (Berlin: de Gruyter).

Klumpjan, Hans Dieter, and Helmut Klumpjan. 1986. *Henry D. Thoreau* (Reinbeck: Rowohlt).

Knutson, Jeanne N. (ed.). 1973. *Handbook of Political Psychology* (San Francisco: Jossey-Bass).

Krause, Sharon. 2000. 'The Spirit of Separate Powers in Montesquieu', *Review of Politics*, 62(2), 231–65.

Kunzle, David. 1973. *History of the Comic Strip*, vol. I: *The Early Comic Strip: Narrative Strips and Picture Stories in the European Broadsheet from c. 1450 to 1825* (Berkeley: University of California Press).

Kymlicka, Will. 1995. *Multicultural Citizenship: A Liberal Theory of Minority Rights* (Oxford: Oxford University Press).

Kymlicka, Will, and Wayne Norman. 1994. 'Return of the Citizen: A Survey of Recent Work on Citizenship Theory', *Ethics*, 104(2), 352–81.

LaPiere, Richard T. 1965. *Social Change* (New York: McGraw-Hill Book Company).

Lasswell, Harold D. 1950. *Politics: Who Gets What, When, How* (New York: Smith).

Lee, Felix. 2013. 'China schnippelt sich James Bond zurecht: Ärger über die zensierten Varianten von *Skyfall* und *Cloud Atlas*', *Die Rheinpfalz*, 21, 25 January.

Lelyveld, David. 1990. 'Transmitters and Culture: The Colonial Roots of Indian Broadcasting', *South Asia Research*, 10(1), 41–52.

———. 1994. 'Upon the Subdominant: Administering Music on All India Radio', *Social Text*, 39, 111–27.

Lelyveld, Joseph. 2011. *Great Soul: Mahatma Gandhi and His Struggle with India* (New York: Alfred A. Knopf).

Lerner, Daniel. 1958. *The Passing of Traditional Society: Modernizing the Middle East* (Glencoe: Free Press).

Lin, Yutang. 1936. *A History of the Press and Public Opinion in China* (Chicago: The University of Chicago Press).

Loraux, Nicole. 1993. *The Children of Athena: Athenian Ideas about Citizenship and the Division between the Sexes* (Princeton: Princeton University Press).

Luce, Torry J. 1968. 'Political Propaganda on Roman Republican Coins: Circa 92–82 B.C.', *American Journal of Archaeology*, 72(1), 25–39.

Lukose, Ritty A. 2009. *Liberalization's Children: Gender, Youth, and Consumer Citizenship in Globalizing India* (Durham: Duke University Press).

Lumby, E.W.R. 1954. *The Transfer of Power in India, 1945–7* (London: George Allen & Unwin).

Mahapatra, Dhananjay. 2012. '60-Year Old Cartoon and a Lesson in Intolerance', *Times of India*, 14 May. Available at: http://timesofindia. indiatimes.com/india/60-yr-old-cartoon-and-a-lesson-in-intolerance/articleshow/13128501.cms (last access: 16 April 2013).

Malik, Kenan. 2009. *From Fatwa to Jihad: The Rushdie Affair and Its Legacy* (London: Atlantic Books).

Mankekar, Purnima. 1999. *Screening Culture, Viewing Politics: An Ethnography of Television, Womanhood, and Nation in Postcolonial India* (Durham and London: Duke University Press).

Manville, Philip B. 1990. *The Origins of Citizenship in Ancient Athens* (Princeton: Princeton University Press).

Manyozo, Linje. 2012. *Media, Communication, and Development: Three Approaches* (New Delhi: Sage).

Marriott, McKim. 1961. 'Changing Channels of Cultural Transmission in Indian Civilization', in L.P. Vidyarthi (ed.), *Aspects of Religion in Indian Society* (Meerut: Kedar Nath Ram Nath), pp. 13–25.

———. 1990. 'Constructing an Indian Ethnosociology', in id. (ed.), *India through Hindu Categories* (New Delhi: Sage), pp. 1–39.

Marshall, Thomas Humphrey. 1965 [1949]. 'Citizenship and Social Class', reprinted in id. *Class, Citizenship, and Social Development* (New York: Anchor), 71–134.

Marso, Lori J. 1998. 'The Stories of Citizens: Rousseau, Montesquieu, and de Stael Challenge Enlightenment Reason', *Polity*, 30(3), 435–63.

Marx, Karl. 1960 [1853]. Article in the *New York Daily Tribune*, 8 August, reprinted in Karl Marx and Friedrich Engels, *Werke*, vol. IX (March 1853–December 1853) (Berlin: Dietz).

Mayer, Franz. 1995. *Einblick in das Studium der Politologie: Studenten vermitteln Inhalte ihres Fachs* (München: OPS Verlagsgesellschaft).

Mayhew, Henry. 2008 [1861–2]. *London Labour and the London Poor* (Ware: Wordsworth Editions).

Mazzarella, William, and Raminder Kaur. 2009. 'Between Sedition and Seduction: Thinking Censorship in South Asia', in Raminder Kaur and William Mazzarella (eds.), *Censorship in South Asia: Cultural Regulation from Sedition to Seduction* (Bloomington: Indiana University Press), pp. 1–28.

McCloud, Scott. 1993. *Understanding Comics: The Invisible Art* (New York: Harper Collins).

McDermott, Rose. 2009. 'The Case for Increasing Dialogue between Political Science and Neuroscience', *Political Research Quarterly*, 62(3), 571–83.

McDonald, Terrence J. 1996a. 'Introduction', in Terrence J. McDonald (ed.) *The Historic Turn in the Human Sciences* (Ann Arbor: University of Michigan Press), pp. 1–16.

———— (ed.). 1996b. *The Historic Turn in the Human Sciences* (Ann Arbor: University of Michigan Press).

McDuie-Ra, Duncan. 2013. 'Beyond the "Exclusionary City": North-East Migrants in Neo-liberal Delhi', *Urban Studies*, 50(8), 1625–40.

McLain, Karline. 2007. 'Who Shot the Mahatma? Representing Gandhian Politics in Indian Comics', *South Asia Research*, 27(1), 57–77.

————. 2009. *India's Immortal Comic Books: Gods, Kings, and Other Heroes* (Bloomington: Indiana University Press).

McLean, Ian, and Alistair McMillan (eds). 2009. *The Concise Oxford Dictionary of Politics* (Oxford: Oxford University Press).

McLuhan, Marshall. 1970. [1964]. *Die Magischen Kanäle* [*Understanding Media: The Extensions of Man*] (Frankfurt am Main: Fischer).

Mecklai, Noorel. 2010. 'Myth—the National Form: *Mission Istanbul* and Muslim Representation in Hindi Popular Cinema', in Shakuntala Banaji (ed.), *South Asian Media Cultures: Audiences, Representations, Contexts* (London: Anthem Press), pp. 145–62.

Merton, Robert K. 1957. *Social Theory and Social Structure* (New York: Free Press of Glencoe).

Mill, John Stuart. 1975 [1859]. *On Liberty*, in id. *Three Essays* (edited by Richard Wollheim) (Oxford: Oxford University Press), pp. 5–141.

Miller, David. 1992. 'Deliberative Democracy and Social Choice', *Political Studies*, 40, 54–67.

Miller, Toby. 2002. 'Cultural Citizenship', in Engin F. Isin and Bryan S. Turner (eds.) *Handbook of Citizenship Studies* (London: Sage), pp. 232–44.

Miller, Toby. 2007. *Cultural Citizenship: Cosmopolitanism, Consumerism, and Television in a Neoliberal Age* (Philadelphia: Temple University Press).

Mistry, Rohinton. 1991. *Such a Long Journey* (London: Faber and Faber).

Mitra, Smita. 2011. 'Strokes of Subversion', *Outlook*, 12 September.

Mitra, Subrata K. 1991. 'Room to Manoeuvre in the Middle: Local Elites, Political Action, and the State in India', *World Politics*, 43(3), 390–413.

———. 1999a. 'Introduction', in Subrata K. Mitra (ed.), *Culture and Rationality: The Politics of Social Change in Post-Colonial India* (New Delhi: Sage), pp. 15–38.

———. 1999b. 'Flawed Paradigms: Some Western Models of Indian Politics', in Subrata K. Mitra (ed.), *Culture and Rationality: The Politics of Social Change in Post-colonial India* (New Delhi: Sage), pp. 39–63.

———. 2008a. 'Level Playing Fields: The Post-Colonial State, Democracy, Courts and Citizenship in India, *German Law Journal*, 9(3), 343–66.

———. 2008b. 'When Area Meets Theory: Dominance, Dissent, and Democracy in India', *International Political Science Review*, 29(5), 557–78.

———. 2010a. 'Citizenship as Conceptual Flow: A Moveable Feast?' (Review essay), *Contemporary South Asia*, 18(2), June, pp. 215–24.

———. 2010b. 'Citizenship in India: Some Preliminary Results of a National Survey', *Economic and Political Weekly*, 45(9), 46–53.

———. 2011a. 'Turning Aliens into Citizens: Significance of the Indian Case', *Welt Trends: Zeitschrift für Internationale Politik*, 77, March–April, 52–9.

———. 2011b. 'From Comparative Politics to Cultural Flow: The *Hybrid* State, and Resilience of the Political System in India', in Phillip Stockhammer (ed.), *Conceptualizing Cultural Hybridization: A Transdisciplinary Approach* (Heidelberg: Springer), pp.107–32.

———. 2012a. 'Citizenship in India: Evolution, Involution and Rational Construction', in Subrata K. Mitra (ed.), *Citizenship and the Flow of Ideas in the Era of Globalization: Structure, Agency, and Power* (New Delhi: Samskriti), pp. 155–88.

——— (ed.). 2012b. *Citizenship and the Flow of Ideas in the Era of Globalization: Structure, Agency, Power* (New Delhi: Samskriti).

———. 2012c. 'Sub-National Movements, Cultural Flow, the Modern State, and the Malleability of Political Space: From Rational Choice to Transcultural Perspective and Back Again', *Transcultural Studies*, 2, 8–47.

———. 2013. 'How Exceptional Is India's Democracy? Path Dependency, Political Capital, and Context in South Asia', *India Review*, 12(4), 227–44.

Mitra, Subrata K., and Lion König. 2012. 'Icons, Nations and Re-use: Marianne, France and Bharat Mata, India', in Julia A.B. Hegewald and Subrata K. Mitra (eds.), *Re-use: The Art and Politics of Integration and Anxiety* (New Delhi: Sage), pp. 288–313.

———. 2013. 'Icon-ising National Identity: France and India in Comparative Perspective', *National Identities*, 15(4), 357–77.

Mitra, Subrata K., and Vir B. Singh. 1999. *Democracy and Social Change in India: A Cross-Sectional Analysis of the National Electorate* (New Delhi: Sage).

———. 2009. *When Rebels Become Stakeholders: Democracy, Agency and Social Change in India* (New Delhi: Sage).

Moore, Barrington. 1966. *Social Origins of Dictatorship and Democracy: Lord and Peasant in the Making of the Modern World* (Boston: Beacon Press).

Mukherji, D.P. 1947. *Modern Indian Culture: A Sociological Study* (Bombay: Kitabs).

Müller, Beate. 2003. 'Über Zensur: Wort, Öffentlichkeit und Macht: Eine Einführung', in Beate Müller (ed.) *Zensur im modernen deutschen Kulturraum* (Tübingen: Niemeyer), pp. 1–30.

Murdock, Graham. 1999. 'Rights and Representations: Public Discourse and Cultural Citizenship', in Jostein Gripsrud (ed.), *Television and Common Knowledge* (London: Routledge), pp. 7–17.

Murray, Janet H. 2000. *Hamlet on the Holodeck: The Future of Narrative in Cyberspace* (Cambridge: MIT Press).

Nayar, Pramod K. 2006. *Reading Culture: Theory, Praxis, Politics* (New Delhi: Sage).

Nehru, Jawaharlal. 1985 [1946]. *The Discovery of India* (New Delhi: Oxford University Press).

Nilekani, Nandan. 2008. *Imagining India: Ideas for the New Century* (London: Allen Lane).

Noorani, A.G. 1995. 'Informal Censorship', *Economic and Political Weekly*, 30(40), 2472.

North, Douglass C. 1990. *Institutions, Institutional Change and Economic Performance* (Cambridge: Cambridge University Press).

Nussbaum, Martha. 1990. 'Our Pasts, Ourselves', *New Republic*, 9 April, 27–34.

O'Neill, Onora. 1990. 'Practices of Toleration', in Judith Lichtenberg (ed.), *Democracy and the Mass Media: A Collection of Essays* (Cambridge: Cambridge University Press), pp. 155–85.

Ong, Aihwa. 1996. 'Cultural Citizenship as Subject-Making: Immigrants Negotiate Racial and Cultural Boundaries in the United States', *Current Anthropology* 37 (5), 737–62.

———. 1999. *Flexible Citizenship: The Cultural Logics of Transnationality* (Durham: Duke University Press).

Oruka, Henry Odera (ed.). 1994. *Sage Philosophy: Indigenous Thinkers and Modern Debate on African Philosophy*, Philosophy of History and Culture vol. 4 (Leiden: Brill).

Osborne, Richard, and Borin van Loon. 2004. *Introducing Sociology* (Cambridge: Icon Books).

Otto, Ulla. 1968. *Die literarische Zensur als Problem der Soziologie der Politik* (Stuttgart: Enke).

Ousby, Ian (ed.). 1994. *The Wordsworth Companion to Literature in English* (Ware: Wordsworth).

Packalen, Leif, and Sharad Sharma. 2007. *Grassroots Comics: A Development Communication Tool* (Helsinki: Ministry of Foreign Affairs Finland).

Packalen, Leif. 'Grassroots Comics: Clips from India'. Available at: http://www.youtube.com/watch?v=s-gFrba4qhw (last access: 2 August 2013).

Paman, Nake. 2011. 'On the Fringes of Your Memory', *Outlook*, 51(22), 6 June.

Parsons, Talcott. 1951. *The Social System* (New York: Free Press).

———. 1969. *Politics and Social Structure* (New York: Free Press).

Patalong, Frank. 1999. 'Gedruckte Comics haben keine Zukunft', in *Spiegel Online—Netzwelt*. Available at: http://www.spiegel.de/netzwelt/web/superhelden-im-netz-gedruckte-comics-haben-keine-zukunft-a-56691.html (last access: 8 August 2013).

Pateman, Carole. 1970. 'Rousseau, John Stuart Mill and G.D.H. Cole: A Participatory Theory of Democracy', in id. *Participation and Democratic Theory* (Cambridge: Cambridge University Press), 444–57.

Paul, E. Jaiwant. 2011. *The Greased Cartridge: The Heroes and Villains of 1857–58* (New Delhi: Roli Books).

Pavarala, Vinod, and Kanchan K. Malik. 2007. *Other Voices: The Struggle for Community Radio in India* (New Delhi: Sage).

Pfetsch, Frank R. 2003. *Theoretiker der Politik: Von Platon bis Habermas* (Paderborn: Wilhelm Fink).

———. 2012. 'European Citizenship: A Concept of Interrelatedness and Conditionality', in Subrata K. Mitra (ed.), *Citizenship and the Flow of Ideas in the Era of Globalization: Structure, Agency, and Power* (New Delhi: Samskriti), 111–36.

Pfleiderer, Beatrix, and Lothar Lutze (eds). 1985. *The Hindi Film: Agent and Re-Agent of Cultural Change* (New Delhi: Manohar).

Plachta, Bodo. 2006. *Zensur* (Stuttgart: Reclam).

Plato. 1991. *The Republic of Plato* (translated with notes and an interpretive essay by Allan Bloom) (New York: Basic Books).

———. 1997. *Symposium and the Death of Socrates* (translated by Tom Griffith, with an introduction by Jane O'Grady) (Hertfordshire: Wordsworth Editions).

Pollock, Sheldon. 1993. 'Rāmāyaṇa and Political Imagination in India', *Journal of Asian Studies*, 52(2), 261–97.

Popper, Karl R. 1959. *The Logic of Scientific Discovery* (London: Hutchinson).

Priolkar, Anant Kakba. 1958. *The Printing Press in India: Its Beginnings and Early Development* (Bombay: Marathi Samshodhana Mandala).

Pritchett, Frances W. 1995. 'The World of *Amar Chitra Katha*', in Lawrence A. Babb and Susan S. Wadley (eds.), *Media and the Transformation of Religion in South Asia* (Philadelphia: University of Pennsylvania Press), pp. 76–106.

Pritzlaff, Tanja. 2006. 'Ethnographische Politikforschung', in Joachim Behnke, Thomas Gschwend, Delia Schindler, and Kai-Uwe Schnapp (eds.), *Methoden der Politikwissenschaft: Neuere Qualitative und Quantitative Analyseverfahren* (Baden-Baden: Nomos), 125–32.

Radhakrishnan, Rajagopalan. 2003. *Theory in an Uneven World* (Malden: Blackwell).

Rahman, Tariq. 2003. *Language and Politics in Pakistan* (Karachi: Oxford University Press).

Ramanujan, A.K. 1990. 'Is There an Indian Way of Thinking? An Informal Essay', in McKim Marriott (ed.), *India through Hindu Categories* (New Delhi: Sage), pp. 41–58.

———. 1999. 'Three Hundred Rāmāyaṇas: Five Examples and Three Thoughts on Translation', in Vinaj Dharwadker (ed.), *The Collected Essays of A.K. Ramanujan* (Oxford: Oxford University Press).

Ramaswamy, Sumathi. 2001. 'Maps and Mother Goddesses in Modern India', *Imago Mundi*, 53, 97–114.

Rangarajan, L.N. 1987. 'The Kautilyan State and Society', in L.N. Rangarajan (ed.), *The Arthashastra* (New Delhi: Penguin), pp. 42–98.

Rao, Sandhya. 2000. '*Amar Chitra Katha* Comics: A Quick Fix Culture Course for Kids', *Bookbird: A Journal of International Children's Literature*, 38(4), pp. 33–5.

Rao, V.K.R.V. 1977. 'Some Thoughts on Social Change in India', in M.N. Srinivas, S. Seshaiah, and V.S. Parthasarathy (eds.), *Dimensions of Social Change in India* (Bombay: Allied Publishers), pp. 21–33.

Reichert, Ramón. 2011. 'Die Medienästhetik der Webcomics', in Barbara Eder, Elisabeth Klar, and Ramón Reichert (eds.), *Theorien des Comics: Ein Reader* (Bielefeld: transcript), pp. 121–41.

Renaut, Alain. 2000. *The Era of the Individual: A Contribution to a History of Subjectivity* (New Delhi: Motilal Banarsidass).

Richardson, Diane. 2000. 'Constructing Sexual Citizenship: Theorizing Sexual Rights', *Critical Social Policy*, 20(1), 105–35.

Richman, Paula (ed.). 1992. *Many Rāmāyaṇas: The Diversity of a Narrative Tradition in South Asia* (New Delhi: Oxford University Press).

Riker, William H. 1963. *The Theory of Political Coalitions* (New York: Yale University Press).

Riker, William H., and Peter C. Ordeshook. 1973. *An Introduction to Positive Political Theory* (Englewood Cliffs: Prentice Hall).

Roether, Diemut. 2008. 'Zensur', in Lutz Hachmeister (ed.), *Grundlagen der Medienpolitik: Ein Handbuch* (München: DVA), pp. 418–23.

Roll, Evelyn. 2010. 'Würdelose Unterwerfung', in *Sueddeutsche Zeitung*, 17 May. Available at: http://www.sueddeutsche.de/kultur/kino-wuerdelose-unterwerfung-1.146165 (last access: 17 April 2013).

Rosaldo, Renato. 1994a. 'Cultural Citizenship and Educational Democracy', Toward Ethnographies of the Future, *Cultural Anthropology*, 9(3), 402–11.

———. 1994b. 'Whose Cultural Studies?', *American Anthropologist*, New Series, 96(3), 524–29.

Rose, Dan. 1990. *Living the Ethnographic Life* (Newsbury Park: Sage).

Rousseau, Jean-Jacques. 1973 [1762]. *The Social Contract and Discourses* (London: Dent).

———. 1989 [1762]. *Émile oder Von der Erziehung [Émile ou de l'éducation]* (Zürich: Ex Libris).

Roy, Anupama. 2010. *Mapping Citizenship in India* (New Delhi: Oxford University Press).

Roy, Srirupa. 2007. *Beyond Belief: India and the Politics of Postcolonial Nationalism* (Durham: Duke University Press).

Rudolph, Lloyd I. 1992. 'The Media and Cultural Politics', *Economic and Political Weekly* 27 (28), 1489–1491+1493–1496.

Rudolph, Lloyd I., and Susanne Hoeber Rudolph. 1987. *In Pursuit of Lakshmi: The Political Economy of the Indian State* (New Delhi: Orient Longman).

Rushdie, Salman. 1998 [1988]. *The Satanic Verses* (London: Vintage).

Ryan, Bryce, and Neal Gross. 1943. 'The Diffusion of Hybrid Seed Corn in Two Iowa Communities', *Rural Sociology*, 8, 15–24.

Said, Edward W. 1978. *Orientalism* (London: Routledge and Kegan Paul).

———. 1994. *Culture and Imperialism* (New York: Vintage Books).

Sarai. 2007. *Sensor-Census-Censor: An International Colloquium on Information, Society, History and Politics: A Report* (New Delhi: Centre for the Study of Developing Societies).

Sardar, Ziauddin, and Borin van Loon. 1999. *Introducing Cultural Studies: A Graphic Guide* (Cambridge: Icon).

Saurma-Jeltsch, Liselotte, and Anja Eisenbeiß (eds.). 2010. *The Power of Things and the Flow of Cultural Transformations: Art and Culture between Europe and Asia* (Berlin: Deutscher Kunstverlag).

Sawhney, Rashmi. 2010. 'Through the Lens of a "Branded Criminal": The Politics of Marginal Cinema in India', in Shakuntala Banaji (ed.), *South*

Asian Media Cultures: Audiences, Representations, Contexts (London: Anthem Press), pp. 201–20.

Sayer, Andrew. 1992. *Method in Social Science: A Realist Approach* (London: Routledge).

Schama, Simon. 1989. *Citizens: A Chronicle of the French Revolution* (London: Viking).

Schnapp, Kai-Uwe, Delia Schindler, Thomas Gschwend, and Joachim Behnke. 2006. 'Qualitative und Quantitative Zugänge: Eine Integrative Perspektive', in Joachim Behnke, Thomas Gschwend, Delia Schindler, and Kai-Uwe Schnapp (eds.), *Methoden der Politikwissenschaft: Neuere Qualitative und Quantitative Analyseverfahren* (Baden-Baden: Nomos), pp. 11–26.

Schweidler, Walter. 2004. *Der Gute Staat: Politische Ethik von Platon bis zur Gegenwart* (Stuttgart: Reclam).

Sears, David O., Leonie Huddy, and Robert Jervis (eds). 2003. *Oxford Handbook of Political Psychology* (Oxford: Oxford University Press).

Sen, Dineshchandra. 1920. *The Bengali Rāmāyaṇas* (Calcutta: University of Calcutta).

Sha, Richard C. 1990. 'Gray's Political Elegy: Poetry as the Burial of History', *Philological Quarterly*, 69(3), 337–57.

Shachar, Ayelet. 1999. 'The Paradox of Multicultural Vulnerability', in Christian Joppke and Steven Lukes (eds.), *Multicultural Questions* (Oxford: Oxford University Press), 87–111.

Sharma, Kalpana. 2003. 'Censorship: Unofficial Might', *The Hindu*, 7 December. Available at: http://www.hindu.com/mag/2003/12/07/stories/2003120700020100.htm (last access: 16 April 2013).

Sharma, Sharad. 2009. 'Sexuality in Black and White', in Humsafar Trust (ed.), *Ek Alag Chitra Katha: A Community Comic Book on Issues of MSM and Transgender* (Mumbai: Humsafar Trust), 6.

———— (ed.). 2010. *Comics for All: World Comics India Bulletin*, no. 7 (New Delhi: World Comics Network).

————. 2011. *Grassroots Comics: A Tool for Democracy* (New Delhi: Sharad Sharma).

Sherwin-White, A.N. 1973. *The Roman Citizenship* (Oxford: Oxford University Press).

Sheth, D.L., and Gurpreet Mahajan (eds.). 1999. *Minority Identities and the Nation-State* (New Delhi: Oxford University Press).

Shklar, Judith N. 1969. *Men and Citizens: A Study of Rousseau's Social Theory* (Cambridge: Cambridge University Press).

Shome, Parthasarathi, Carlos J. Moreno, and Kavita Rao. 1996. 'Quantitative and Qualitative Methods to Social Science Enquiry: Econometric

Methods and Interdisciplinarity', *Economic and Political Weekly*, 31(30), PE87–PE92.

Sikand, Yoginder (ed.). 2010. *Indian Mass Media: Prejudices against Dalits and Muslims* (Gurgaon: Hope India).

Singer, Milton B. 1972. *When a Great Tradition Modernizes: An Anthropological Approach to Indian Civilization* (New York: Praeger).

Sinha, Arvind. 2006. 'Growing Need of an Alternative Media: A Critique of the Mainstream Media', in Uday Sahay (ed.), *Making News: Handbook of the Media in Contemporary India* (New Delhi: Oxford University Press), pp. 118–30.

Sinha, Basanti. 1994. *Press and National Movement in India (1911 to 1947)* (New Delhi: Manak).

Sircar, Sanjay. 2000. 'Amar Chitra Katha: Western Forms, Indian Contents', *Bookbird: A Journal of International Children's Literature*, 38(4), 35–6.

Skocpol, Theda, and Margaret Somers. 1980. 'The Uses of Comparative History in Macrosocial Inquiry', *Comparative Studies in Society and History*, 22(2), 174–97.

Smith, Nicholas H. 2002. *Charles Taylor: Meaning, Morals and Modernity* (Cambridge: Polity Press).

Spivak, Gayatri Chakravorty. 1988. 'Can the Subaltern Speak?', in Cary Nelson and Lawrence Grossberg (eds.), *Marxism and the Interpretation of Culture* (Urbana: University of Illinois Press), pp. 271–313.

Sreenivas, Deepa. 2010. *Sculpting a Middle Class: History, Masculinity and the Amar Chitra Katha in India* (New Delhi: Routledge).

Staub, Hans O. 1980. 'The Tyranny of Minorities', The End of Consensus?, *Daedalus*, 109(3), 159–68.

Stepan, Alfred. 2008. 'Comparative Theory and Political Practice: Do We Need a "State-Nation" Model as Well as a "Nation-State" Model?', *Government and Opposition*, 43(1), 1–25.

Stepan, Alfred, Juan J. Linz, and Yogendra Yadav. 2011. *Crafting State-Nations: India and Other Multinational Democracies* (Baltimore: Johns Hopkins University Press).

Stevenson, Nick. 1999. *The Transformation of the Media: Globalization, Morality and Ethics* (London: Longman).

——— (ed.). 2001. *Culture and Citizenship* (London: Sage).

Steward, Julian H. 1963. *Theory of Culture Change: The Methodology of Multilinear Evolution* (Urbana: University of Illinois Press).

Subramanyam, K. 1989. 'Press and the Vandemataram Movement in Andhra', in Nisith Ranjan Ray (ed.), *Growth of Public Opinion in India: 19th and Early 20th Centuries (1800–1914)* (Calcutta: Naya Prokash), pp. 264–74.

Swedberg, Richard. 2005. *The Max Weber Dictionary: Key Words and Central Concepts* (Stanford: Stanford University Press).

Szreter, Simon. 2007. 'The Right of Registration: Development, Identity Registration, and Social Security—A Historical Perspective', *World Development*, 35 (1), 67–86.

Tanna, Ketan. 2004. 'Internet Censorship in India: Is It Necessary and Does It Work?', Sarai-CSDS, New Delhi.

Thakur, Ramesh. 1993. 'Ayodhya and the Politics of India's Secularism: A Double-Standards Discourse', *Asian Survey*, 33(7), 645–64.

Thapar, Romila. 2002. *Early India: From the Origins to AD 1300* (Berkeley and Los Angeles: University of California Press).

Thoreau, Henry David. 1989 [1849]. 'Civil Disobedience', in *Walden and Other Writings* (edited and with an introduction by Joseph Wood Krutch) (New York: Bantam Books), pp. 85–104.

Thussu, Daya K. (ed.). 2008. *Media on the Move: Global Flow and Contra-Flow* (London: Routledge).

Tilly, Charles. 1985. 'War Making and State Making as Organized Crime', in Peter B. Evans, Dietrich Rueschemeyer, and Theda Skocpol (eds.), *Bringing the State Back In* (Cambridge: Cambridge University Press), pp. 169–91.

Times of India (ToI). 2012. 'Cartoonist Aseem Trivedi Released from Jail', *Times of India*, 12 September. Available at: http://timesofindia.indiatimes.com/india/Cartoonist-Aseem-Trivedi-released-from-jail/articleshow/16364582.cms (last access: 16 April 2013).

Turner, Bryan S. 1994. 'Postmodern Culture/Modern Citizens', in Bart van Steenbergen (ed.), *The Condition of Citizenship* (London: Sage), pp. 153–68.

———. 2001. 'Outline of a General Theory of Cultural Citizenship', in Nick Stevenson (ed.), *Culture and Citizenship* (London: Sage), pp. 11–32.

Ultee, Wout C., Ronald Batenburg, and Harry B.G. Ganzeboom. 1993. 'Cultural Inequalities in Cross-National Perspective: A Secondary Analysis of Survey Data for the 1980s', in Ann Rigney and Douwe Fokkema (eds.), *Cultural Participation: Trends since the Middle Ages* (Amsterdam: John Benjamins), pp. 173–92.

Vaikuntham, Y. 1989. 'The Role of the Press in the Andhra Movement (1910–1914)', in Nisith Ranjan Ray (ed.), *Growth of Public Opinion in India: 19th and Early 20th Centuries (1800–1914)* (Calcutta: Naya Prokash), pp. 251–63.

van Gunsteren, Herman. 1988. 'Admission to Citizenship', *Ethics*, 98(3), 721–30.

Victorian Studies. 1963. 'Notes Towards the Definition of "Interdisciplinary"', *Victorian Studies*, 6(3), 203–6.

Vijetha S.N. 2011. 'History Department Demands Re-introduction of Ramanujan's Essay on Ramayana', 25 October. Available at: http://www. thehindu.com/news/national/history-dept-demands-reintroduction-of-ramanujans-essay-on-ramayana/article2568546.ece (last access: 4 December 2012).

Vincent, Joan. 2002. 'Introduction', in Joan Vincent (ed.) *The Anthropology of Politics: A Reader in Ethnography, Theory and Critique* (Malden: Blackwell), pp. 1–13.

Waldo, Dwight. 1975. 'Political Science: Tradition, Discipline, Profession, Science, Enterprise', in Fred I. Greenstein and Nelson W. Polsby (eds.), *Handbook of Political Science* (Reading: Addison-Wesley), pp. 1–130.

Walzer, Michael. 1989. 'Citizenship', in Terence Ball, James Farr, and Russell L. Hanson (eds.), *Political Innovation and Conceptual Change* (Cambridge: Cambridge University Press), pp. 211–19.

Weber, Max. 1964. *Wirtschaft und Gesellschaft: Grundriss der Verstehenden Soziologie*, vol. I (Köln: Kiepenheuer & Witsch).

———. 1991 [1948]. 'The Chinese Literati', in Hans H. Gerth and C. Wright Mills (eds.), *From Max Weber: Essays in Sociology* (London: Routledge), pp. 416–44.

———. 2011 [1919]. *Politik als Beruf* (Köln: Anaconda).

———. 2009. [1919]. 'Politics as a Vocation', in: *From Max Weber: Essays in Sociology* (translated, edited, with an introduction by H.H. Gerth and C. Wright Mills) (London: Routledge), pp. 77–128.

Welsch, Wolfgang. 1999. 'Transculturality—the Puzzling Form of Cultures Today', in Mike Featherstone and Scott Lash (eds.), *Spaces of Culture: City, Nation, World* (London: Sage), pp. 194–213.

Werner, Michael, and Bénédicte Zimmermann. 2006. 'Beyond Comparison: Histoire Croisée and the Challenge of Reflexivity', *History and Theory*, 45(1), pp. 30–50.

Whitman, Cedrick H. 1964. *Aristophanes and the Comic Hero* (Cambridge: Harvard University Press).

Wierzbicka, Anna. 1992. *Semantics, Culture and Cognition: Universal Human Concepts in Cultural-Specific Configurations* (New York: Oxford University Press).

Wilkinson, Lancelot P. 1975. *The Roman Experience* (London: Elek).

Williams, Raymond. 1983 [1979]. *Keywords: A Vocabulary of Culture and Society* (London: Flamingo).

———. 1989 [1958]. 'Culture Is Ordinary', in *Resources of Hope: Culture, Democracy, Socialism* (edited by Robin Gable) (London: Verso), pp. 3–18.

Wittfogel, Karl A. 1962. *Die Orientalische Despotie: Eine Vergleichende Untersuchung Totaler Macht* (Köln: Kiepenheuer & Witsch).

Wittgenstein, Ludwig. 1963 [1921]. *Tractatus Logico-Philosophicus* (Frankfurt am Main: Suhrkamp).

Witzel, Michael. 2003. *Das Alte Indien* (München: C.H. Beck).

Young, Iris Marion. 1989. 'Polity and Group Difference: A Critique of the Ideal of Universal Citizenship', *Ethics*, 99(2), 250–74.

N.N. 2012. 'Govt Humours MPs, May Ban All Cartoons in School Textbooks', *Times of India*, 15 May. Available at: http://timesofindia.indiatimes.com/india/Govt-humours-MPs-may-ban-all-cartoons-in-school-textbooks/articleshow/13141661.cms (last access: 16 April 2013).

N.N. *The Role of Chitra Katha in School Education.* 1978. (Bombay: India Book House Education Trust).

INDEX

147, 184, 197, 214, 222–4, 258,
267, 271, 276, 278, 285
deliberative democracy 147–8
hybrid democracy 48, 267
liberal democracy 47, 60, 143
participatory democracy 12, 120,
139–40
Desai, Moraji 283
diffusionism 65, 269
discrimination 204, 207–10, 219
discrimination protection 140
positive discrimination 12, 284
documentary films 184, 243
dominance 47, 72–3, 183, 236, 238,
262, 298
Doniger, Wendy 164
Doordarshan 25, 27–8, 158, 167–8,
225, 232, 298

Early Modern Age 96, 110–13, 118, 154
Emergency Rule (1975–1977) 158
emotional integration 184–6, 189,
195, 243, 272, 290–2, 298
empiricism 9, 135, 221
empowerment 13, 32, 72
disempowerment 165
England 19–20, 92, 103, 124, 182
Enlightenment 10, 12, 14, 18, 20, 22,
67, 262, 285
equality before the law 128
ethnic alienation 206–7
ethnic minorities 198, 260
ethnic rights 69
ethnic stigmatization 203
ethnicity 2, 10, 13–4, 57, 71, 95, 101,
115, 117, 125–6, 131–2, 141–2, 145,
198, 207, 210, 221, 241, 270, 282,
298,
European Union (EU) 145–6

Fabian socialism 122

Facebook 212, 215, 295
federalism 131, 231, 262
linguistic federalism 14
Films Division (FD) 26, 29–30, 180,
183–4, 186, 189, 243, 289
First World War 77
flow 58–9, 66, 75, 79–80, 84, 91–2
micro-level flow 79–80, 82, 279
macro-level flow 79–80, 82–3
institutional flow 86
inter-area vs. intra-area flow 79
conceptual flow 67, 70
Conditional vs. unconditional
flow 82
counter-flow 91, 235
policy flow 84
vertical vs. horizontal flow 75–6,
79
folk culture 185
Forster, E.M. 16–7, 144, 232–34, 284
Foucault, Michel 5, 49, 114, 151–2
free speech 10, 22, 123, 223, 258
free-speech theory 154
freedom of expression 12, 81, 163–4,
175, 230–1
French Revolution 113, 118–20, 262,
269, 276
functionalism 56, 78

Gandhi, Indira 27, 158, 222, 297
Gandhi, Kasturba 169–70
Gandhi, Mohandas Karamchand 87,
122, 127–8, 168–75, 182, 196, 245,
274, 281–2, 288–9
Gandhi, Rajiv 127–8, 283
gay community 221, 226, 246
gender 13, 107–8, 255, 270, 300
transgender 204–5
generalization (in the social
sciences) 6, 9, 41, 49, 52–3, 55–6,
85, 103, 150, 155, 237, 265

ABOUT THE AUTHOR

Lion König is a Research Fellow at St. Antony's College, University of Oxford, United Kingdom. His fellowship, to pursue postdoctoral research on nation-building in South Asia, has been awarded by the German Research Council (DFG).

Prior to joining the University of Oxford, he was Adjunct Faculty at the Centre for Culture, Media and Governance, Jamia Millia Islamia, and Visiting Lecturer at the Centre for the Study of Law and Governance, Jawaharlal Nehru University, both at New Delhi. Lion König is Associate Researcher at the South Asia Institute, Department of Political Science, and at the Cluster of Excellence 'Asia and Europe in a Global Context', both at Heidelberg University, Germany. He studied political science and English literature and linguistics at the University of Edinburgh and at Heidelberg University, where he completed his doctoral work on the concept of 'cultural citizenship' in India in 2013.

Lion König has held research fellowships at the Institute for Defence Studies and Analyses (IDSA) in 2011, as well as at the Institute of Social Sciences (ISS), and at the Centre for Social Sciences and Humanities (CSH), in New Delhi in 2014. He is the co-editor of *Politics of the 'Other' in India and China: Western Concepts in Non-Western Contexts* (London: Routledge, 2016), *Globalisation and Governance in and Governance in India: New Challenges to Society and Institutions* (London: Routledge: 2016), *Politics in South Asia: Culture, Rationality and Conceptual Flow* (Heidelberg: Springer, 2015), and *The Politics of Citizenship, Identity, and the State in South Asia* (New Delhi: Samskriti, 2012).

His areas of interest include political theory, interdisciplinary and area studies, as well as nation-building, identity, cultural politics and political iconography in the Indian- and the larger South Asian context.